Teaching Study Skills and Supporting Learning

Palgrave Study Guides

www.palgravestudyguides.com

Teaching Study Skills and Supporting Learning

STELLA COTTRELL

palgrave

First published 2001 by
PALGRAVE
Houndmills, Basingstoke, Hampshire RG21 6XS and
175 Fifth Avenue, New York, N.Y. 10010
Companies and representatives throughout the world

PALGRAVE is the new global academic imprint of
St. Martin's Press LLC Scholarly and Reference Division and
Palgrave Publishers Ltd (formerly Macmillan Press Ltd).

ISBN 0–333–92124–0

This book is printed on paper suitable for recycling and
made from fully managed and sustained forest sources.

A catalogue record for this book is available
from the British Library.

10 9 8 7 6 5 4 3 2 1
10 09 08 07 06 05 04 03 02 01

Printed and bound in Great Britain by
Antony Rowe Ltd, Chippenham, Wilts

Resource sheet sections in Part II may be photocopied by purchasers
and lecturers for use in individual, group and class work only but
may not be reproduced in any publication without permission.

Contents

Contents

Contents

Preface

This book has arisen out of work undertaken with students over 20 years across a range of educational establishments. Despite the range in student age-groups, differences in educational background and variation in the type of institution, certain common themes have emerged. One such theme is the fragility of many students, whether high achievers or not, and the desperation of students to hide their doubt in their own abilities from lecturers. It is much easier, publicly, to blame lack of success on financial concerns, on the need to work or on having dependants than to admit to fear of failing, of not being good enough, of believing oneself 'too stupid' to succeed at higher education level. In order to meet the need for study skills support at the University of East London in the early 1990s, I produced a booklet of materials known as *Skills for Success*. One notable aspect of feedback on this was that students said it changed their views about academic study as an activity where you were either 'born to succeed' or 'doomed to fall'. All too often, they had been told to 'do better' but had not known how to do so nor believed it possible. The realisation that there were methods and attitudes that might improve study outcomes meant that struggling students could see some point in directing their energies at their academic work.

A second theme which emerges from in-depth work with several hundreds of students is that although method is important, there is not a single way of approaching study that will work for all. For that reason, alternative approaches are built into many activities in this book and in the student activities in *The Study Skills Handbook* (Cottrell, 1999). Moreover, strategy is not sufficient to achieve academic success. Self-belief is equally important. It has been extraordinary to note how much improvement students can make from even extremely limited input. It is not necessarily the particular method

used that is important so much as that students believe there are ways of improving and that if one strategy doesn't work for them, another might. Students have commented on how important it was to them that somebody, and especially lecturers, believed in them and took the trouble to tell them how to improve in ways that made sense. They also comment on how valuable it is to know that some difficulty with academic study is to be expected and that this is not a sign of failure or stupidity.

Skills for Success became the basis of *The Study Skills Handbook* published by Macmillan (now Palgrave). The *Handbook* was very carefully designed so as to be easy to use, and to address areas such as memory, critical thinking and skills transferability which have often been neglected in other study skills books. The *Handbook* also raises more complex issues about the nature of intelligence, academic study and personal approaches to learning in order to foster, in students, a more reflective approach to learning. The book has proved very popular amongst students, and a number of universities are now using it as their main study skills text.

Widening participation has placed study skills much higher on the agenda within higher education. Increasingly, lecturers are coming to realise the importance of embedding study skills within the curriculum and of teaching in ways that develop students' academic performance. Responsibility for study skills may be given to lecturers who have not been trained to teach at all, much less to teach higher level subjects to students who have struggled previously at more basic levels. There is very little training in skills development available for lecturers; there are few texts aimed at either lecturers or specialists on the teaching of study skills.

Skills for Success was originally accompanied by *Tutor Notes* to guide lecturers on how to make the most of study skills materials with students and generally create conditions that might improve student learning. This book originally began as an extension of the *Tutor Notes*, as support material for lecturers who chose to use *The Study Skills Handbook*. Since then, it has expanded into a book in its own right. Whilst the *Handbook* is the natural complement to this book, *Teaching Study Skills and Supporting Learning*, this text has been designed so that lecturers can make use of its ideas and activities without using *The Study Skills Handbook* if they so wish.

Just as there are many ways to study, there is not one single way to teach study skills. This book does not aim to legislate on how study skills should be taught. Rather, it aims to assist busy lecturers to understand some of the issues, to put together programmes that incorporate study skills development, and to integrate a broader support for academic development into their general teaching. Although the book makes many suggestions, often drawn from a very wide range of contexts and inputs by others, it is hoped that these will be only the starting place for improved ideas by practitioners, a stimulus to reflection, and a basis from which lecturers can develop more supportive teaching strategies compatible with their own intakes.

Thanks are due to staff at both the University of East London and Birmingham University for piloting materials and approaches suggested in this book with their students and for the activities they contributed.

I would like to convey particular thanks to those who have made individual named contributions to the book, both Claire Dorer at Birmingham University for her piece on working with mature students, and Victor, a student at the University of East London, for his piece on using an engine analogy to develop academic writing. Heartfelt thanks is offered to the many unnamed students whose individual struggles have been the inspiration and backbone of this book. In addition, special thanks are due to the following staff at the University of East London: Hazel Cross, who was a rich source of ideas in the early stages of this book; Tony Wailey for ideas emanating from his work

on accrediting prior learning such as the use of the 'personal statement', and Robert Simpson for permission to adapt materials he used with staff on the Social Work Diploma and Cultural Studies Courses; Jonathon Leader and Sally Gotti for critiquing chapters when these were still in their early drafts; staff and students from Fashion and Design with Marketing for allowing me to adapt materials on student self-assessment, and Valerie Goodworth for her enthusiasm and insights on using Honey and Mumford's learning styles.

I would like to acknowledge the wide range and extremely valuable input I have received from staff and students in educational establishments where I have either taught, led training, undertaken the role of external examiner, or acted as a consultant. These include, especially, the colleagues and very special students to be found at the Universities of Luton and East London, but also those at the Universities of Strathclyde, Central Lancashire, North London, Paisley, Brighton, Kent at Canterbury, the London School of Economics, Somerville College, Oxford, Glasgow School of Art, the Robert Gordon University, Oxford Brookes, Anglia Polytechnic University, Napier University, the Surrey Institute of Art, Roehampton Institute, the Workers' Education Association (Oxford), Brixton College (Start-up), Hackney Community College, Waltham Forest College and Peers School, Oxford.

I would like to express my appreciation to staff at Palgrave who have assisted in getting this book off the ground: Margaret Bartley who encouraged me to undertake the project in the first place; Suzannah Tipple who took over the production of the book; Houri Alavi, the Senior Editor; Valery Rose, the copy-editor; Sanphy Thomas, Felicity Noble and all those who worked so hard behind the scenes to produce the final text. A special mention and warm thanks are owed to Kate Williams from Oxford Brookes University for her sound sense and very valuable contributions to both *The Study Skills Handbook* and this text; I consider myself very lucky that she read and advised on early drafts for both and, even more so, for the extreme generosity and kindness with which she made suggestions for improvements.

Finally, I thank my partner for being a tower of strength, for suffering my endless redrafting when we could have been out doing more exciting things, and for keeping me supplied with the mint Aeros essential to my learning style.

Stella Cottrell
University of Luton

Acknowledgements

Acknowledgements and thanks for permission to reproduce or adapt materials for this text go to Ralph Thomas and staff at Birmingham University (Selly Oak Campus) for the use of their induction activities; Claire Dorer at Birmingham University for her piece on working with mature students; Valerie Goodworth, Dawn Branigan and staff and students from the Fashion and Design with Marketing programme at the University of East London for allowing me to adapt materials on student self-assessment and their induction exercise; Robert Simpson and Tony Wailey for permission to adapt materials used by staff on the Social Work Diploma and Cultural Studies Courses at the University of East London, including the idea of using Position Papers; the Southern England Education Consortium and the Higher Education Credit Initiative, Wales, for the SEEC/HECIW level descriptors in Appendix 2; TMP Worldwide Research for *Soft Skills: Employers' Desirability and Actual Incidence* (1998); 'Victor' from the University of East London, for his expertise metaphor.

Learning Style Inventory (LSI), by R. Dunn and K. Dunn, referred to in the text is available from Price Systems, Box 3067, Lawrence, KS 66044, USA.

List of Abbreviations

AP(E)L	Accreditation of Prior (Experience and) Learning
BTEC	Business and Technical Education Council
CPAS	centrally provided additional support
CPD	continuous professional development
CVCP	Committee of Vice-Chancellors and Principals
FE	further education
HE	higher education
HECIW	Higher Education Credit Initiative, Wales
HEI	higher education institutions
ILT	Institute for Learning and Teaching
LSQ	learning style questionnaire
MBTI	Myers–Briggs type indicator
NLP	neuro-linguistic programming
NVQ	National Vocational Qualification
PDP	personal development planning
PPAD	personal, professional and academic development
PPD	personal and professional development
QAA	Quality Assurance Agency
QCA	Qualifications and Curriculum Authority
SALS	specific and additional local support
SASSA	study aids and study strategies assessment
SEDA	Staff and Educational Development Association
SEEC	Southern England Education Consortium
SIT	support integrated into teaching
SpLDs	Specific learning difficulties
UEL	University of East London
VSI	video supplemental instruction

Introduction

The overall aim of this book is to assist staff in higher education to deliver study skills and learning support. It does so by focusing on the needs of the student from several perspectives. It looks at the importance of addressing the over-arching learning environment, whether at the level of the institution, the course, or individual teaching sessions. It offers suggestions for enhancing support structures and for creating opportunities for improving student performance at each of these levels. It is argued that support for learning cannot be centred solely in dedicated modules or specialist services, important though these are, but that all lecturers have a role to play in helping students to improve their own learning and performance. The book aims to provide support both for skills specialists and for those who consider themselves to be primarily 'subject' lecturers.

The book makes practical suggestions for action. In doing so, its aim is not to be prescriptive. As Birnbaum (1989) has illustrated, this rarely works in universities. Rather, the book suggests measures which can be adapted locally to suit the particular needs of different cohorts of students. At the same time, by being very specific about the details of activities, procedures and processes, it aims to make it easier for staff to grasp the nature of the student difficulties quickly and to offer practical support with the minimum of duplicated effort.

The book is in two parts. Part I focuses on the overall context in which skills development can best flourish. It argues for a developmental approach, where skills are not regarded as discrete or generic entities formed in the abstract, but are, rather, part of an overall set of outcomes which can be achieved when embedded in interactive and supportive learning environments. Although the book offers materials for use in skills modules, the emphasis is on skills being grounded in the concrete reality of the course. Skills training works best when its relevance to assessment and to academic and professional success is made explicit and when it is well-anchored and contextualised within the subject specialism.

Throughout the book, it is argued that in the area of study skills, a fine line can be drawn between what should be a 'skill' on the part of the student, and what is the responsibility of the institution in orientating students and meeting them at their current level of knowledge, experience and performance. Chapter 2 identifies ways that students learn, and looks at the challenges facing learners in today's universities. Chapter 3 offers suggestions on ways that institutions can support all aspects of the student experience so that students have a greater chance of settling into higher education, staying there, and being successful in their studies. In particular, Chapter 4 looks at induction as a strategically important time for orientating students to the demands of higher education, setting ground rules, recognising mutual responsibilities and settling students into good study habits. It is also a key time for identifying students most at risk and targeting specific support.

Supportive learning environments mean that skills are required not only of students but of lecturers and all who come into contact with students. Lecturers need to be able to model and reinforce the skills they wish their students to demonstrate; skills sessions are not sufficient in order to develop skills to a high level. Skills need nurturing over time – and only lecturers will have sufficient access to students, as well as the necessary prestige, to complete the process of skills development over the whole time that the student is at the institution. To support the lecturer in developing these skills, this book offers dedicated chapters (see Chapters 5–7) aimed at the teaching lecturer. In addition, a section at the beginning of each study skill session in Part II offers background to lecturers on how some student difficulties may arise, along with suggestions of ways that lecturers could alleviate these. Chapter 7 is aimed at staff who have particular responsibility for developing skills units. In addition, some lecturers with pastoral responsibilities may find Chapter 8, on supporting individual students, to be of help. Chapter 9 offers an opportunity for teaching staff to reflect upon their own practice as well as their training needs in relation to skills teaching.

Part II offers a range of activities designed to help students to develop study skills, including those that will help students to improve their own performance in the longer term. These activities are organised into study skills areas commonly recognised by practitioners, such as organisational skills, revision and exam strategies, and writing. There are also sections on memory, foundation thinking skills, critical and analytical thinking and orientation to learning. The introduction to Part II offers some guidance on ways of making use of the activities suggested within the varied circumstances of different universities.

Material in the book is divided into that which can best be offered through:

- being incorporated into everyday teaching and learning (Part I and the opening sections of each of the sessions in Part II);
- study skills sessions (Part II);
- one-to-one support (Part I, Chapter 8).

However, these are very general categories and there are links made between all three aspects of skills teaching.

Developing study skills not only helps students to improve their learning and performance, it can also enrich their experience of university life. When students have a greater understanding of the learning process and of themselves as learners, they can gain the confidence to take control over their learning. With this confidence can come an increase in students' overall enjoyment of their study programme.

Part I

Learning in Context

 # Skills into the curriculum

The changing agenda

Since the early 1990s, there has been a dramatic change in the approach to skills development within higher education. Indeed, skills development is now high on the agenda for universities, colleges, schools, government and employers. Within the wider skills agenda, specific attention is beginning to focus on personal development planning and the main key skill associated with it, namely 'improving own learning and performance'. While personal planning and improving learning are not reducible to study skills, a reflective and developmental approach to study skills, such as is advocated by this book, is of central importance both to improving learning and, through that key skill, to creating a basis for other skills required of graduates.

The skills revolution has meant that there is an accompanying change in philosophy with respect to study skills. A decade ago, study skills was primarily conceptualised within a deficit model of the student: skills training meant 'remedial support'. Emphasis, now, is on how to map, deliver, teach and assess skills in terms of the general learning outcomes of a course. Concern focuses on issues such as how to raise the awareness of all students of the importance of skills development and how to present evidence, through progress files and transcripts, of the skills that students have acquired at univer-

sity. Skills are on the agenda, whether through 'Developing Learning' modules as at Nottingham (Hand *et al.*, 2000), integrated into the curriculum as at Luton, Kent and Portsmouth, or through local projects such as the 'Writing Workshops in Scottish History' at the University of Edinburgh or 'Group Skills Projects in Geography' at St Andrews (Hounsell *et al.*, 1996). In turn, this raises questions about where universities and colleges will find the expertise to meet the requirements of the new skills agenda. At present very few courses or materials exist to train and support lecturers in taking forward the new agenda.

The pressure for developing students' skills comes from many quarters: from government, from employers, from the inherent demands of widening participation, from teaching staff taking a more reflective look at what universities do and what they want graduates to achieve, and from a growing recognition that the information revolution is changing what is needed from both students and lecturers. University funding is likely to become tied, at least in part, to the ways institutions can indicate how the skills agenda, and especially aspects related to employment, are being met.

Traditionally, the main objection to addressing skills through the curriculum was that there would not be enough time to cover subject content. However, there is a growing acknowledgement that, given the enormous growth in research and academic publications, it is a vain hope to expect courses, much less students, to cover more than a fraction of possible course material and for students to understand what they have learnt. Indeed, there is research to suggest that 'excessive amounts of material in the curriculum' (Ramsden, 1992) or 'a heavy workload' (Gibbs, 1992) push students into adopting superficial or 'surface' approaches to learning. An HMI report (1989) linked over-dependence on information delivery (usually by formal lecture) with students adopting a rote-learning approach; it argued that students did not develop a range of skills appropriate to higher education nor approaches that led to understanding and application of what was learnt. In other words, 'coverage' did not ensure learning.

There is now an increased, and growing, recognition that it makes sense to ensure that students are trained in process (or study) skills which give them the foundation and the confidence to direct their own learning. This is partly a question of skills training and partly a question of developing a culture of on-going professional development: students need to leave university with a keen awareness that their education has not ended. It is more useful, long term, to train students to be self-managers of the learning process, able to direct themselves around the subject, recognising gaps and with the capability of updating their knowledge once they leave university rather than overloading courses with material. Using a variety of teaching and assessment methods can increase student skills without necessarily detracting from subject coverage. There is much to be gained from moving away from what Freire (1974) called the 'banking concept' of education where education 'becomes an act of depositing, in which the students are the depositories and the teacher is the depositor'. Instead, as lecturers, we can assist our students to learn effectively, creatively and reflectively – in effect, to teach themselves. All students can benefit from addressing how they learn, not least because learning is a lifelong activity, irrespec-

tive of whether it takes place on or off campus. Hence the importance given by Dearing (1997) to 'learning to learn' as a key skill for all students.

The benefits of a skills curriculum

Increasing skills through the curriculum brings benefits for everyone. Students gain because they have a better idea of what is required of them and how to deliver it. The overall student experience is improved through the relief of some of the unnecessary stress which occurs when students are not sure how to improve performance. By the time they leave university, students will have a greater sense of the wider learning they have achieved at university, over and above subject content. They should have a greater sense of what it is to be competent, skilled, and able to transfer knowledge and experiences from one context to another; they should be more self-aware and confident about taking their place in the professional world.

The experience of the teaching staff can also be improved. When their students are trained to be more responsible for their learning, capable of applying problem-solving strategies to learning contexts, of using each other as resources, then there should be a reduction in their dependence on the lecturer as the source of all help. Moreover, lecturers can take pleasure in seeing a greater number of their students succeeding with better grades. Learning environments which promote skills and personal development tend to be more invigorating and enjoyable than traditional podium-led teaching contexts. Such environments can take the pressure off the lecturers to be sole 'deliverer', giving a more active role to students; this also offers lecturers a more rounded sense of their students. Employers benefit from receiving graduates who are more aware of what they have to offer to employers and who are able to apply academic skills to a wider range of contexts. Higher education institutions gain because, if students are trained to succeed, retention rates are improved, with the financial gains this brings.

Developing independent, self-reliant learners

The emphasis within current pedagogical thought is on increasing students' active participation within the learning process in order to foster independence and autonomy. This is partly a response to demands from employers for greater self-reliance from new employees. The former Employment Department funded six projects in 1994–6 to explore how autonomy could be developed within higher education, arguing that individual autonomy was a requirement of successful survival in modern society (McNair, 1996.) It is also a necessary development if students are to succeed in HE with reduced staff to student ratios.

However, students are not always ready, at entrance, to take on autonomous roles. Little (1991) suggests that students, far from being naturally independent, need to be trained in a 'capacity for detachment, critical reflection, decision-making and independent action'. Moreover, students from different ethnic backgrounds may have different expectations of formal teaching structures and become demotivated if these are removed precipitously (Press, 1996). From her experiences of developing autonomy in language learners, Hurd (1999) cautions a need for 'careful preparation of learners and teachers before any degree of autonomous learning can be successfully implemented'. Perry's research with American students (1970) revealed how long it can take even for 'elite' students to develop from 'absolutist', 'authority-seeking' attitudes towards more relativist and then 'personally committed' positions. Students need to be guided towards autonomy as part of their skills development (Cottrell, 2000).

Fazey (1996) suggests that student autonomy cannot be discussed without reference to skills development. Conversely, guiding students towards autonomy can help them to identify their skills requirements. She identifies four sets of skills needed in this regard: academic skills, personal management skills and self-awareness, which bring us back to the kind of skills agenda recommended by Dearing. In addition, she adds 'metacognitive' skills. She cites work by McCombs and Marzano (1990) who argue that students need training to recognise the link between themselves, 'the "I" component of the self', in order to realise a sense of personal control over learning activities. For this, opportunities are needed within the curriculum and through academic guidance for reflection, planning and self-evaluation.

The challenge of widening participation

'Widening participation' does not simply bring *more* students into HE but, rather, attracts *different* types of students. Lifelong learning initiatives attract students of more varied ages and from work-based settings. Governmental emphasis on increasing the number of school-leavers in HE means that students whose learning styles and current level of performance would previously have been a barrier to entering HE, are now finding the doors of HE opened to them. Many of these are students who will not succeed if conventional ways of delivering and assessing the HE curriculum are continued unchanged. Universities are slowly realising that it is not simply enough to open the doors: what goes on behind the doors has to change to accommodate new types of student intake.

Changing part changes the whole. Lewin (1952), for example, argued that when change is introduced into part of a social system, the effects on the whole system need to be considered in order for that change to become successfully established. One effect of the change in student intake is that work which was previously considered remedial and supplementary is now entering the mainstream as an essential part of the curriculum, of benefit in its own right. The notion of 'learning support' has broadened to encompass learning development in its widest sense. Wolfendale (1996), for example, argues:

> Learning Support recognises that students have differential learning needs, study at different rates and paces, and manifest a myriad of learning styles. Such an ideology does not

have to compromise traditional conceptions of subject or discipline learning. Rather, it promotes and enhances the idea of striving to achieve excellence.

Although the success of students without traditional qualifications shows that such students can succeed in HE, and indeed enhance the overall university experience for other students, other students struggle and even fail unnecessarily. There are many and complex reasons for student non-completion, but amongst these is the evident mismatch between the skills, habits and attributes which universities have traditionally required at entrance, still regarded as desirable, and actual student performance levels at entry. Many students are inadequately prepared for university life and study. In other cases, departmental views of what teaching or learning might be are too narrowly conceived: the do not take into account the very different strengths of students who may not have succeeded academically in the past.

Universities set demands which students, especially those from 'widening participation' backgrounds, can find very difficult to meet without initial assistance. If universities wish to retain their students and improve their achievement, then they need to adapt to the performance levels of students at the point of entry, rather than to a notional view of what a new student 'ought to' be able to do. Either the curriculum has to change in order to orientate and train students so they can succeed, or a foundation or gateway course is needed to provide that orientation. This book argues that, whichever route is taken, skills development needs to be subject-specific; this necessarily requires the involvement and support of subject specialists. Chapter 2 argues that skills training needs to be embedded within, and delivered as part of, the curriculum, integrated with other course material. In this way, students can see its concrete relevance to their studies. It also increases the likelihood of those who most need skills training being able to access it: they are often those with the least disposable time for attending additional support. Moreover, fieldwork on

employability skills (CVCP, 1998) has shown that skills programmes are most successful where training is embedded within the academic subject curriculum rather than through discrete modules.

The development of skills curricula impacts upon teaching, assessment, course design and, indeed, almost every aspect of the student experience. It increases pressure for change. In the past, university teaching could sometimes be characterised by a 'sink or swim' stance, assuming that those who did not succeed somehow did not deserve to do so. Universities were able to rely on highly motivated, hand-picked students, skilled in the art of university learning even before they arrived at university. Those students were likely to succeed irrespective of the strengths or failings of the teaching they received. There was little incentive, much less training, for effective teaching

One of the benefits of widening participation is that it encourages, if not forces, universities to become more reflective about what they do and why. Where academic staff could send struggling students 'away' for support from specialist units, the trend now is towards all lecturers being taught to teach, and to teach in such a way that students who would have struggled are much less likely to need 'additional' help. In 1991, The Committee of Vice-Chancellors and Principals (CVCP), in a bid to elevate university teaching, issued a Green Paper proposing criteria to identify quality in teaching. Since then, many universities have developed SEDA-accredited postgraduate certificates in teaching learning in higher education, whilst the establishment of the Institute for Learning and Teaching (ILT) has gone some way to raise the importance of professional development for academics. Courses for academic staff on 'embedding skills' are already being made available and, although such training is still embryonic, this trend is likely to increase. Changes in the student body go hand in hand with the need for different kinds of teaching and with an increased emphasis on skills development – including study skills.

Employability versus academic skills?

One of the main incentives for bringing skills into the curriculum is the growing emphasis on graduate employability. The issue of employability has been creeping up the HE agenda since the late 1980s. The Enterprise in Higher Education initiative (1987–92) was intended to encourage the development of student-centred learning from a skills perspective and to bridge the gap between the world of work and that of higher education. In particular, it aimed to address employers' criticisms that graduates were ill-equipped for employment. A range of initiatives have developed from that project, including piloting Records of Achievement (Fenwick *et al.*, 1992), self-directed learning (Hammond and Collins, 1991) and the development of skills materials including early versions of materials that formed the basis of *The Study Skills Handbook* (Cottrell, 1999), and the staff training materials from which this book has developed. In 1996, a report from the Committee of Vice-Chancellors and Principals endorsed the employability agenda when it stated that 'it is one of higher education's purposes to prepare students well for working life'.

Employability skills are sometimes seen as being in conflict with the aims and objectives of a university. However, the differences between skills required for academic study and those desired by employers are often overstated. TMP Worldwide Research (1998) identified skills desired by employers. The three most desired skills were oral communication, team working and listening. The second cluster of skills employers required included written communication, problem solving, relationship development, the ability to adapt communication style, time management and the ability to share knowledge with others. These are all skills which are of benefit from an academic perspective as well as that of employment. The actual incidence of such skills, as perceived by employers, fell far below the levels required, despite the employability initiatives described above. Even skills in written and oral communication, which headed the incidence list, were thought hard to find in graduates.

A CVCP Report, *Skills Development in Higher Education* (1998), brings home the relation between skills required for both academic and employment purposes. The first of four skills categories identified by the Report was 'traditional intellectual skills', including items such as critical evaluation of evidence, problem solving, the ability to argue logically and to challenge assumptions. Its second category refers to 'key' skills such as communication, application of number, working with others, use of technology, and improving one's own performance, equally valid in employment and academic contexts. The same could be said of the third category which covered 'personal attributes' such as self-reliance, adaptability, creativity and 'nous'. A final category was 'knowledge about how institutions work'. Although this final category is clearly more employment-orientated than is usual on some university courses, it is still possible to integrate this within the main curriculum. Moreover, it is important to bear in mind that improved employment opportunities feature very highly in surveys of students' reasons for pursuing higher education (Glasner, 2000).

Of these four categories listed in the CVCP 1998 Short Report, the first three would be as useful to students for their studies as for employment. There are good pedagogical reasons for encouraging students to learn through co-operation with others, to develop self-management skills, to develop problem-solving strategies and information management skills. Employers value such skills, as well as those such as critical thinking, analysis of data, and written and oral communication skills. Both lecturers and employers have an interest in students being able to be self-reliant, able to manage projects, write well, meet deadlines and use information technology (IT). In other words, the skills and attributes students acquire in academic study are often transferable to the workplace, provided that there is supportive intervention to help students to articulate their learning in the language of alternative contexts, such as for higher academic study or employment.

It is worth noting that the employability skills listed by the TMP and CVCP reports include many skills that require personal interaction with others. This is one area where 'residential' universities have an advantage over e-universities. Courses which deliver information primarily through passive and receptive means (large lectures, note-making, essays and exams) may face increasing competition from e-universities who are likely to package informational courses more effectively and conveniently. It is, therefore, in the interests of residential universities to make the most of the benefits of working with others as a value-added component on their courses. Learning through interaction over time is much harder to deliver through virtual courses, even through an energetic electronic debating forum.

Key skills are now being offered as courses at some universities and have already been built into a number of university courses. For example, the Graduate Skills Programme at the University of Luton was elaborated with local employers (Collop *et al.*, 1998) and is offered as a post-exit work-based learning programme. In addition, all Luton students are now offered a range of academic and employability skills, based on SEEC/HECIW descriptors amd integrated into the curriculum. In other words, universities can address academic skills and a significant part of the employability agenda simultaneously. Similar moves have been taken at Portsmouth (Glasner, 2000), and universities all over Britain are engaged in mapping courses against the SEEC descriptors, QCA key skills and similar frameworks, as well as against QAA benchmark skills. Imaginative curriculum design can also incorporate careers research and career planning as assessed project work or discrete modules within most programmes of study. A focus on skills development can operate to the benefit of both academic standards and student employability.

Personal, professional and academic development

Through studying for a degree, students develop not only academically, but also increase their chances of moving into a professional career and to develop, or mature, personal qualities and attributes. However, students are not always aware of what they have achieved beyond the content of their subject disciplines; they may not be able to articulate their broader learning in terms of skills and personal qualities, especially when competing with other graduates for work.

To help address this, the Quality Assurance Agency for Higher Education (2000) recommends that personal development planning (PDP) be built into provision for students over the next few years. It is expected that the progress file will pay particular attention to employability skills. The minimum expectations are that:

- institutional promotional materials should indicate how skills and attitudes that underlie Personal Development Planning are promoted;
- at the start of an HE programme, students will be introduced to the opportunities for PDP within their programme;
- students will be provided with opportunities for PDP at each stage of their programme;
- the rationale for PDP at different stages of a programme will be explained for the benefit of students.

It is useful to introduce this concept of personal development to students early in their time at university, especially if a more integrated approach to skills development is used. It can help students to make more sense of interactive teaching techniques and to value tasks such as oral presentation, which can be very daunting initially. It also places skills development within an adult, and therefore more acceptable, context. Success in personal development planning for most students is likely to be heavily dependent on their abilities in the key skills of improving their own learning and performance.

What do we mean by 'skills'?

'To be skilled is to be able to perform a learned activity well and at will' (Cottrell, 1999). Skill is associated with performance, with a way of using knowledge and experience in action. Argyris and Schon (1974), for example, describe skills as 'dimensions of the ability to behave effectively in situations of action'. Levels of ability are implicit within the idea of a skill: a skill can be more or less accomplished. There is also an element of control: a skilled performance does not arise by chance, by mere fluke, but through an act of will, by an application of previous knowledge and experience. As a result, there can be a reasonable expectation that a roughly equivalent performance could be repeated. Skills are sensitive to practice and strategy, and improve when there is time for rehearsal: skills refer to 'a quality of performance which is developed through practice, training or experience' (Starkes and Allard, 1993). However, in order to fine-tune a skill, personal qualities are also required, including motivation, commitment, awareness of what is required, perseverance and the ability to manage set-backs.

The boundaries of 'skill' merge with those of personal attributes. They also merge with those of knowledge: skill cannot be divorced from experience and context. This is especially the case with academic or 'study' skills. In some ways, 'skills' is a misnomer, an easy point of reference rather than an accurate description. Study skills development cannot be divorced from other aspects of a student's learning experience, including the subject discipline's knowledge base. Sometimes, a false antimony is erected between 'knowledge' and 'skills', arising from fears that skills development will undermine the 'knowledge' requirements. However, as Bruner (1966) argued, 'Knowing is a process, not a product.' Knowledge is not an end-product, a discrete set of information that passes from one head or text into another. Rather, it is intrinsically linked to processing of information, to 'making sense', developing understanding at increasingly sophisticated levels, bringing attention to certain kinds of information dependent on the requirements of the context, panning out and homing in at appropriate levels of detail. To be knowledgeable within a subject discipline goes hand in hand with skills such as recognition of relevance, critical ability, application of data to specific problems, making decisions, and being able to communicate what is known to other people. In other words, study skills development is not an alternative to the knowledge base but a way of enhancing learning potential so that the knowledge is more accessible and better understood.

Terminology

The literature on skills uses a plethora of different terminology which can be confusing: core skills, transferable skills, key skills, study skills, learning skills, employability skills, lifelong learning skills, process skills and many others. There is no shortage of skills taxonomies. However, it is easy to be diverted by what are usually minor differences between lists. Some sub-skills are relevant to several different skills. For example, time management can be seen as a relevant component of problem solving, personal management, or even as a group skill. Taxonomies may opt to cite these sub-skills in different places. A list of graduate skills and qualities collated from a number of recent lists, is given below (Appendix 1). Despite this, the overall range of skills cited from one list to another shows a great deal of similarity, as will be shown below.

Study skills

There is a growing awareness that students' performance, even in higher education, can be improved through training in relevant academic skills. These are generally referred to as 'study skills'. Hurley (1994) describes study skills as 'key skills for all areas of education, including advanced study'. He argues that students benefit when these skills are taught explicitly. In other words, study skills need to be developed at each academic level: it should not be assumed that the skills a student brings from school, or even from the first year of university, are sufficient to carry them through their degree. Skills such as personal management, task management, research and information management, working with others and critical thinking need to be fine-tuned and extended as students move from one level to another.

'Transferable' skills

Ball (1986) argued that employers needed not only academic skills but what he called 'transferable' skills. The term 'transferable skills' is generally used to refer to skills which are regarded as transferable either from one course to another, or between academic study and the world of work. Bridges (1993) refers to transferable skills as 'meta-skills' which enable people 'to select, adapt, adjust and apply' skills to different contexts and even cognitive domains. Skills usually cited in this category are those such as working with others, written communication, use of IT, and problem solving. There is some convergence evident in what were formerly referred to as 'transferable skills' and the more current terminology of 'key skills'.

It is manifestly evident that some skills which appear to be readily transferable from one context to another do not transfer as easily as might be expected. In practice, any skill is potentially 'transferable', and no skill is automatically transferable. For a skill to be transferable, there is usually a need for:

- at least three practice attempts in order to develop a more abstract schema of the activity, building upon concrete and situated experience; *and*
- the tutor or trainer to make explicit the way in which the skill might be applicable to more than one context.

Transferability is very much dependent on training in recognising cross-application. A good training in problem solving could develop the meta-skills that would enable students to develop such recognition more independently. Chapter 8 suggests that 'transferability' may depend less on apparent surface similarity in the skills (writing letters, writing essays, writing

business reports) than on the individual's perception of the task. For some individuals, apparently disparate skills (such as dressmaking and writing) may share an underlying problem-structure which allows for competence to be transferred more easily to a new context.

Core skills

Hurley (1994) uses 'core skills' to refer to cross-curricular skills such as language and numeracy, IT and personal effectiveness. It might be argued that there are subject-specific requirements, even in HE, in terms of numeracy, IT and language. If students need additional English, they are unlikely to have time to learn the whole English language but time devoted to key language patterns and phrasing used within the subject area could be of great assistance. This book does not focus on core skills.

Key skills

Hurley argues that key skills are 'relative to the level and programme of study, and are the essential learning skills and competences required for successful completion of study at that level'. Key skills include communication, number and study skills, but could be any skill needed for the programme, such as pattern cutting, use of specialist equipment, or higher level interpretative skills. The Qualifications and Curriculum Authority (QCA) identifies key skills as those 'needed to succeed in work, education and everyday life' (QCA, 2000). Six key skills were identified by the QCA in the 1980s in consultation with representatives from higher education and employers. These are:

   *Communication
   *Application of number
   *Information technology
   Working with others
   Improving own learning and performance
   Problem solving

Those skills marked with an asterisk are compulsory for all students on courses offering a General National Vocational Qualification, (GNVQ). These key skills, along with working with others and improving one's performance, are required for modern apprenticeships and national traineeships. They enter into higher education curricula via Foundation Degrees, whose prospectus states that programmes should offer 'assessed or accredited key skills', covering 'communication, team working, problem solving, application of number, use of information technology and improving own learning and performance' (HEFCE, 2000). Some universities such, as Portsmouth, have adopted the QCA's six key skills categories for all students, not just those on Foundation Degrees. Whether these six key skills are sufficient key skills for HE graduate courses is open to question. The SEEC descriptors suggest some alternative skills which might be considered as 'key' to HE, such as 'creativity' and 'analysis'. It might also be argued that research and investigative skills, rather than being incorporated under problem solving, might require more individual focus and are, for HE, key skills in their own right. It could also be argued that, in the current climate of vocational education, 'preparation for the workplace' (or similar) could be regarded as a key skill in its own right. This could include such elements as career planning, knowledge of the labour market, understanding of how organisations work, and appropriate behaviours in the work place.

QAA Benchmark Skills

The Quality Assurance Agency (QAA) offers benchmarks for skills in different academic disciplines. Although a different selection of skills is identified for each subject discipline, and the vocabulary used to describe the skills varies slightly in each case, an underlying set of six skills emerges, which are generally in line with the 'key skills' identified above. In essence, the skills expected are those which require students to be able to manage themselves, their interactions with others, and their responsibility for the task in hand, as well as being able to communicate, use IT and manage information. Although the lists can be expanded to include many more headings, these six areas cover most of the skills required. What is meant by each

skill is likely to vary somewhat according to the subject discipline or professional area. The skills and sub-skills extrapolated from across the first 29 sets of draft benchmarks are roughly as follows:

(1) **Improving own learning and performance (Self)**
    Taking responsibility for one's own learning and performance; reflecting on practice; learning to learn; applying learning to new contexts; applying learning theory; reflective professional practice; self-management and self-reliance.

(2) **Working with others (Others)**
    Interactive group skills; project work; listening skills; working with the public or different client groups; constructive criticism; teamwork; working with colleagues and managing work placements; negotiation, consultation, interviewing, observing; committee skills; the ethics of interaction and intervention; managing emotion; assertiveness; being aware of the effect of one's own behaviour upon a group.

(3) **Problem solving and task management (Task)**
    Time and space management; working to deadlines; organisational skills; investigative skills; research; recognising problem structures; applying knowledge and skills to new areas; trying out models; applying theory to real contexts.

(4) **Communication**
    Writing in a range of styles for different audiences and purposes; oral presentation skills; listening skills; team presentation; using IT to aid presentation; communicating to a range of audiences using different media.

(5) **Using IT**
    Basic applications (word-processing, spreadsheets, databases, graphics, email); using the internet; using course software; using statistics packages; using specialist IT for specific purposes.

(6) **Information management/investigative skills**

Being able to collect, manage, select and interpret data of various kinds including statistics and qualitative data; understanding the conventions of research; evaluating the quality of data; presenting data to others; the 'application of number'; using IT to enhance research skills and store information.

SEEC/HECIW Level Descriptors

The South England Education Consortium (SEEC) and the Higher Education Credit Initiative, Wales (HECIW) initiated a UK-wide collaboration in developing a standardised framework for defining levels and standards of modular units (see Appendix 2). The six headings described above under QAA benchmarking would apply primarily to the SEEC/HECIW category of 'Key transferable skills'. Most of the CVCP's second category of skills would also fit under the SEEC/HECIW 'Key transferable skills' heading. The framework is useful for course staff in mapping out learning outcomes and developmental skills so that students can chart their performance. Some institutions now require the learning outcomes of all courses to be written in terms of these SEEC/HECIW descriptors. To facilitate the work of courses that already use SEEC/HECIW descriptors, I have used SEEC/HECIW descriptors, mostly pitched at level 1, for each of the sessions and activities suggested in Part II (below).

Study skills within the skills agenda

It is important that essential study skills are included within newer skills agendas such as 'employability' and personal and professional development initiatives. The QAA benchmark skills and the SEEC/HECIW descriptors, discussed above, although very useful in advancing the skills agenda, do not necessarily address skills from the perspective of the student. For example, on courses where there is formal timed assessment (examinations), memory skills are

paramount for students, as are strategies for managing the revision and exam process itself. These barely feature in the QAA benchmarks or SEEC/HECIW descriptors. Students referred for study support often require training in the basic study skills, upon which higher academic skills can then be more fruitfully developed: investigative skills including course-specific reading strategies, thinking skills, task management and organisational skills. If students lack these skills, it is much more difficult for lecturers to teach them subjects at HE levels 2 and 3.

The skills identified and addressed through this book go a considerable way towards providing a solid basis upon which university courses can develop the skills agenda, both in terms of academic skills and 'employability' skills. The book does not cover all areas of the skills agenda. Numeracy, language, IT, careers planning and 'world of work' aspects of employability are specialisms in their own right. In terms of the skills agendas described above, this book addresses:

(1) developing traditional intellectual skills (thinking skills; critical analytical thinking; memory; training towards assessment);
(2) managing one's own learning and performance (Self);
(3) working with others (Others);
(4) problem solving and organisational skills (Task management);
(5) communication skills (written and oral).

Institutional advantages of a 'skills curriculum'

Benefits to the university

A 'skills curriculum' in this context is one which looks at its own skills requirements alongside the skills needs of its students and seeks to integrate skills development as seamlessly as possible within the overall course provision. This creates a supportive environment which adds to the quality of the students' experience. Indeed, QAA quality assurance procedures have, until recently, employed 'Support and Guidance' as a separate category for checking universities' quality assurance mechanisms. The quality of support within a learning environment impacts upon other QAA quality categories, such as 'Progression and Achievement' and 'Teaching and Learning'. Although Support and Guidance is sometimes regarded as extrinsic to the course, as services offered by the Careers Advisory Service, Disability Co-ordinators, Student Services or other specialist departments, auditors are becoming increasingly aware of learning support as intrinsic to course delivery. The recent QAA Code of Practice on Disability (QAAHE, 1999), for example, which includes students with specific learning difficulties, argues that responsibility for support lies with all areas of the university, and should be integrated into teaching and curriculum design.

QAA auditors are becoming more skilled at identifying what support courses or departments offer to students, and how this dovetails with more specialist support. With the current emphasis on 'employability', for example, auditors are interested in how courses develop students' skills, rather than merely what the Careers Advisory Service offers in terms of advice. Similarly, the QAA Code of Practice on Disability states that provision for disability is seen as intrinsic to all delivery. Ideally, the support needs of students with disabilities should be met in ways that do not require students having to declare a disability or claim support on 'special' grounds or as a 'concession': the environment should be supportive of all of its students (Silver *et al.*, 1998). Chapters 3 to 5, below, look at the ways that institutions can structure support so that study skills are acquired in more seamless, integrated ways.

A supportive and professional learning environment can help to retain students. Yorke (1999) found that the culture of the course can have a decisive influence on whether students are retained. This culture can be imparted to the student from very early on, from pre-induction literature, from the induction process itself, and by comments made by lecturers on assignments or in class. Assessment processes can be a factor in student loss. Traditionally, a minority of British school pupils have succeeded in the formal assessment proceedures required at GCSE and at 'A' level. If students received low grades for school exams, they enter HE without the skills needed to pass exams well; it follows that they need training in order to make sense of what assessment processes require of them. Those who support students on an individual basis find that students, including those with traditional qualifications, may have little idea of what is expected, and are perfectly capable of succeeding once they have had training, practice and a boost to their confidence. Supportive environments can contribute to student retention, which, in turn, has a critical impact upon university finances, staff retention and projects which the university may wish to pursue.

Advantages of a skills curriculum to lecturers

There is no doubt that widening participation places heavier demands upon lecturers. There are many reasons for this, one of which is that many students have not yet learnt to manage their own learning and to be confident in their own decision making. Another is that students have weak internal schema of what HE is about, and sometimes little idea of what they are expected to do. For example, school and college students may be used to teachers telling them to open their books on a certain page and to turn to a particular paragraph. It is not unusual for students to then enter HE still expecting 'someone' to tell them when to read. This is often given as an explanation when students are asked why they did not read course handbooks or essential information: they are merely used to others telling them when and what to read.

A lecturer at Birmingham University described how she had prepared materials which she handed out at a pre-course introductory day, outlining how students should prepare for the course. At the end of the session, over half the new entrants left without it. Lecturers describe the increased 'nannying' that is required of them. It can seem as if students are incapable of organising themselves and must accost staff for information which is quite clearly laid out in course handbooks. Student inability to meet deadlines means that lecturers have to sit through long explanations and life histories as students barter for mitigating circumstances or extra time. Panic about deadlines or exams can also bring students running to the lecturer's door, asking for additional help.

Students often lack basic study skills so that they are ill-prepared for learning the more specialised skills required of them as they move through different levels. This impedes understanding, slows down mental processing of new material, and complicates the teaching of more complex material. Excessive, and often unnecessary, questioning during class-time can mean lecturers cannot cover the material they had set for a session. Teaching staff benefit from the introduction of skills such as self-management, written communication, assessment training, basic critical thinking skills and foundation research skills into the curriculum. If many students lack the requisite skills, it is better that training is built into their programme, rather than each student chasing lecturers for additional support. Lecturers also have their part to play in modelling, rehearsing and reinforcing the skills and behaviours they wish to see in their students. Skills training along with supportive teaching strategies can mean that lecturers are under less pressure from students. It also means that students are better prepared when they enter higher years or levels, to build towards more specialised skills required by the discipline.

The importance of lecturers to study skills development

The lecturer's attitude to, and comments about, study skills are key in this

Lecturers have a central role to play in developing students' skills. Students take study skills much more seriously when their lecturers indicate that they also consider them important.

Moreover, students who need additional learning support are often terrified that their lecturers will think they are not already perfect students. It is very common for students to believe that if their lecturers knew they were struggling, they would allocate lower marks. Whether this is the case or not, it is a commonly held belief. Students can feel that they must appear to have no problems at all, and that a brave front will, in itself, bring them higher marks. Lecturers can reassure students that this is not the case, and can also frame skills development and learning support in a positive way, bringing out the general importance for all learners of identifying and addressing areas for improvement. This is in line with the approach identified by Wolfendale above (1996) where learning development is part of a more general encouragement for 'striving after excellence'.

Lecturers make study skills real and pertinent

Many students need lecturers to provide a bridge between the material presented in a study skills guide (or a generic or introductory study skills unit) and the tasks they must undertake on a day-by-day basis for their chosen subjects. As has been shown with other types of problem solving, students cannot necessarily see the connection between the information in a book and the particular task before them, or even between similar types of task, unless somebody helps them to make the connection (Butterworth, 1992; Reed *et al.*, 1985.) Simply handing study skills materials out at the beginning of the year does not necessarily do the trick of helping students to learn how to learn.

Although study skills units and drop-ins help many students, it is important to bear in mind that the time a student spends on a study skills unit or at drop-in sessions is a very small percentage of their time on the course. As with any other learning, the student may forget what they learnt on the unit soon after they leave it, unless that information is reinforced by others. Lecturers are ideally placed to make study skills materials relevant to the particular subject, through the way they teach, in the way they mark and give feedback, in modelling good practice, in the language they use, and the attitudes they reveal.

Teaching strategies create opportunities for skills development

It is the lecturer who provides opportunities for discussion, interactive learning, problem solving, student participation and other strategies that enable a wide range of skills to develop. Conservative teaching styles may mean that students leave with a very narrow set of skills and very little idea of how to apply them across a range of contexts.

Willcoxson (1988) found that lecturers' method and style is influenced by whether they see learning as 'the transmission of knowledge' or 'the facilitation of learning'. Students may also enter HE with the notion that teaching is something that is 'done to them' rather than something which requires their active participation. Students need to feel confident that lecturers can guide them to learn rather than simply feed them with facts and answers. Research by Gibbs and others (1992) suggests that students take strategic approaches to learning, depending on how the course is structured and assessed. They are unlikely to see the value of independent and interactive approaches to learning if the teaching and assessment does not also reinforce a student-centred approach.

Final comments

University departments and subject areas will need to identify their own particular ways of facing the various challenges of widening participation, inclusiveness, employability and student achievement. This book argues the case for a different kind of supportive learning environments than has been traditional in higher education. It emphasises that support is not simply a question of 'bolt-on' additional help by experts from outside the main subject discipline, but is an ethos which needs to permeate an institution, from the level of policy, strategy and curriculum design through to that of individual staff responses to students. The rise of interest in skills, both academic and professional, is a useful vehicle for increasing the competence of all students and for reducing the need for remedial support. In an era of widening participation, where there are concerns for student retention and employability and where there is a growing emphasis on improved teacher training, a focus on skills development is one way of meeting several important aspects of the higher education agenda.

Understanding the learner

In attempting to enhance the student learning experience and improve performance, guidance can be drawn from theories of learning, from adult students' own accounts of their learning and from the experiences of lecturers. This chapter opens with an exploration of learning theories that throw light upon adult learning, such as constructivism, embedded learning and equilibration theory. Particular emphasis is given to ways that learning and performance may be either 'inhibited' (thus preventing students from achieving their potential) or 'motivated' (so as to take students to the 'take-off' stage of engaged, independent learning). Students' attitudes and approaches to higher education study can be key factors in successful learning and may act as either inhibitors or motivators. This chapter offers a theoretical and contextual background to the strategies suggested later in the book, with an emphasis on the implications for successful teaching and learning in an era of widening participation.

Theories of learning

Learning is a natural process. Our brains are set up to learn. Billions of neurons develop networks to help us to encode information for memory, to transmit information from one part of the brain to another, and to form associations between new and known material. There are also innumerable ways to learn: by listening, by watching others, through imitation, by daydreaming, by taking small steps or through an inspired leap, by practice, by thinking through the relationship between two different problems, and so on. We have extraordinary internal resources. In other words, learning could be, perhaps should be, easy: our most intense learning is achieved in the first few years, long before we have any formal education. For very young children, learning is easy and generally fun, and yet adults can find 'learning' to be both difficult and threatening. Nonetheless, even struggling learners can find that they are able to improve performance when the conditions of learning are changed in some way, by altering aspects such as the learning environment, the wording of the task, the strategy selected, or attitude towards the task.

Most of the best researched theories of learning are based on studies of children. Nonetheless, these are also instructive in understanding the learning of adults, not only because these theories have shaped the development of adults studying in universities today but also because, as is manifest when observing students, adults often regress to childlike states when they enter a taught session. It is, therefore, reasonable for us to ask what happens to inhibit the open, receptive and easy learning of young children so that we and our students, as adults, can find it difficult to learn? Why is it that sometimes we cannot take in new information or feel that it is impossible for us to learn new ways? Much of the research that contributed to the formulation of theories of learning focused on learning difficulty. The teaching and learning strategies which derived from such research have generally had a wider relevance and applicability, and can help us in supporting adult students. This chapter looks at some of the main theories of learning, their relevance to adult learners and some of the approaches that adult students bring to their studies which can lead to underperformance, withdrawal or failure. This chapter and those that follow identify teaching and learning strategies that can be adopted to retain students, improve performance and enhance the overall learning experience. In particular, this chapter draws out how theory can inform delivery of study skills and learning support so that there is a greater chance of a successful outcome.

Constructivism: internal schema

Of the different models of learning, the most influential has been constructivism. The underlying premise of constructivism is that when we encounter new situations we build upon pre-existing internal models, known as schema or schemata. Bartlett (1932) described a schema as 'an active organisation of past reactions, or past experiences, which must always be supposed to be operating in any well-adapted organismic response'. Piaget (1952), who further developed schema theory, argued that we acquire knowledge by 'acting upon the world': we seek out new experiences actively, and our brains either assimilate new experience into our own existing schemas or else we must alter our internal models to accommodate the new information. As we go through the day, all of our experiences continuously reinforce or alter what we already know, strengthening or undermining our mental schema. Constructivism argues that learning is an active process of constructing new models of reality – or reinforcing old learning.

Fry *et al.*, (1999) use this idea to support the notion of active learning approaches, linking schema development to an ideal of learning as 'transformative experience': 'Unless schemata are amended, learning will not occur. Learning (whether in cognitive, affective, interpersonal or psychomotor domains) involves a process of individual transformation.'

It might be expected that if we were exposed to new experiences which challenged our previous internal models, the schema would automatically change to accommodate the challenge. If this were always so, teaching would be very easy. Unfortunately, that is not the case. There isn't a predetermined link between experiences, which we might assume would challenge our internal models, and transformative learning. In other words, 'experience', of itself, is not necessarily transformative. A learning experience, such as reading a book, listening to a lecture, undertaking a new activity or attending a staff development session, does not necessarily lead to learning taking place. It may simply be an act of 'exposure' rather than an inner transformative event at any level. Moreover, as Bartlett showed (1932), we are more likely to adapt (or 'transform') new information until it fits our pre-existing viewpoints than we are to change our previous opinions to fit new data. Dahlgren (1984) argues that students' hold over new learning is often confused whilst changes in their conceptual models are 'relatively rare, fragile and context-dependent occurrences'. This chapter will explore some of the reasons for inhibited learning in adult students as well as looking at what can lead to motivated, engaged learning.

Learning contexts: external environments

In the 1970s and 1980s, theories of learning were very much influenced by a resurgent interest in Vygotsky. Vygotsky (1962) argued that what we regard as internal cognitive processes, such as memory, voluntary attention and language are determined by the culture in which we develop. Social interactions, and the overarching culture in which these take place, influence us in what we consider worthy of attention, how we create value systems, and how we value ourselves within those systems. If, for example, neat handwriting and spelling are strongly valued by teachers, a person with a good capacity for generating ideas but who writes illegibly and with bad spelling may be regarded as 'not very bright'. The person may internalise this model. This may be true even when it contradicts feedback they receive from others: the view of a particular lecturer or a poor exam grade can outweigh the impact of positive input received from elsewhere. Interpersonal behaviours and socially situated beliefs become intrapersonal cognitive processes.

The 'handwriting' example given above typifies the experience of many adults who return to higher education. They carry an internal model which has been socially formed by existing norms of what is clever and what is not, and which often underestimates their range of abilities, especially in those areas which are difficult to assess through formal testing, such as interpersonal skills, creativity, inventiveness, self-reliance and entrepreneurship. It is important that, as educators, we recognise the previous factors that have influenced students' beliefs about themselves as learners. At the very least, we must take care not to reproduce interactions which reinforce unhelpful and inhibitory ways of learning. In many cases, we will achieve more from our students if we address, head on, how they perceive themselves as learners, and invite them to consider whether this assists or inhibits their current learning (Cottrell, 1999). Indeed, it is often underlying beliefs about ability and performance rather than particular skills or actual performance which are most influential on a student's future progress.

Where Piaget argued that we do naturally develop from lower to higher states of learning development (Miller, 1989), Vygotsky (1988) argued that development to higher states of learning is far from automatic. He laid emphasis on the need for a teacher or mentor to structure activity and to support learning from one stage to the next. He described a 'Zone of Proximal Development' – a potential for a 'next stage' of learning which could only be achieved through support. In particular, he argued that the development of abstract modes of thought required specific instruction (Butterworth and Harris, 1994). Research tends to support the view that most adults do not naturally reach the stage of formal abstract thinking. King (1985) has shown that most adults fail on the highest stages of Piaget's tasks, the 'formal operation stage' of abstract or hypothetical thought, even though Piaget believed this would be attained by early adolescence. Nonetheless, King argues, adults incapable of Piaget's tasks in abstract reasoning are nonetheless capable of higher level inferential and analytical thinking in their life contexts and situated specialisms, whether this be in car mechanics or discussing animal tracking – in other words, when they are working from a knowledge base recognisable to them.

Bruner (1975) used the term 'scaffolding' to refer to ways that childhood learning is supported by adults who build on existing competence in order to accomplish next-stage tasks. The adult, being more experienced, can organise activity to structure the learning experience. This allows learners to move beyond their current levels of performance. Although Bruner used this idea in relation to very young children, it has been applied to classroom teaching (Edwards and Mercer, 1987) and is a useful concept to apply to adult learning. Research on problem solving has highlighted the key role the teacher has in leading students to apply learning acquired in one context to another. Research into mathematical problem solving, for example, suggests that for skills to be transferred, the student has to be *helped* to identify common features of the old and new problems or situations, looking especially for similarities in the underlying structure of the two problems. In other words, the teacher has to make very explicit the link between previous and new learning or else the student may not realise that two problems or exercises are connected. In addition, the new learning needs to be pitched at a similar level of complexity to that already covered (Reed *et al.*, 1985).

Often, when teaching has not honoured these basic principles, a pupil or student will feel lost and withdraw, thinking the fault lies with their intelligence, rather than in the way the problem was presented. Teachers can help students to identify and clarify what they already know, and use this knowledge as the basis for the next step in their learning. Whenever we speak about 'transferable skills', for example, we need to be aware of the need for a teacher or mentor to scaffold the process of recognising, applying and articulating in one context the skills acquired or required in another. Perry (1970) has shown how students, especially in the first year, are generally absolutist in their thinking, looking for right answers and the proper ways of doing things. They want to know how they can 'deliver' what lecturers want. There are different ways that this could be viewed. For example, when students ask 'how can I get a first?', this could be regarded as a retrograde step – a desire to be 'led by the hand' or spoon-fed (Miller, 1998). On the other hand, it could be construed as a willingness to learn, motivation to achieve, reflection on current levels of performance, evidence of some critical self-awareness and openness to the scaffolding process.

Learning as transformation towards autonomy

Boud (1989) outlined four traditions of adult education: 'training and efficiency', 'androgogical', 'humanistic' and 'critical', each with a different view of the learner and what the learner needs. Usher *et al.* (1997) identified, nonetheless, a common thread in these disparate approaches: each, they suggest, regards adults as having a 'natural potential' for autonomy that could be released if certain barriers were simply removed. For the 'training' approach, sometimes known as 'technicist', autonomy is acquired by gaining control over the learning process, albeit within predefined, externally prescribed, knowledge and skills areas. The androgogical approach (Knowles, 1978), argues that learners need to have their own experiences validated and used as the basis of their learning –

although the constructed nature of the interpretations made of that experience is perhaps underexplored in this approach. For the humanistic school, the learner needs to be emancipated from oppressive learning conditions (Rogers, 1967, 1983): teachers should become facilitators to enable students to regain their autonomy. Learners, it is conceded, to become autonomous, 'may need the context of a highly supportive and respectful environment' to help them recognise and explore individual needs. Critical pedagogy puts less emphasis on individual learners and looks for the emancipation at a social level (Brah and Hoy, 1989).

From a postmodernist perspective, there is not an essential 'autonomous student' waiting to get out; instead, the learner is perceived as a constructed, changing entity, 'caught up in' relations, texts, narratives. Usher *et al.* (1997), drawing on Shotter (1989, 1993) and Flax (1993), argue that there is not an originary or 'authentic self' to be emancipated: the 'self' itself is constructed and impermanent. It is always situated within social and cultural contexts, an educational and training history, ideological contexts and so forth. Education may change the 'self', may transform the learner, but not simply through the removal of barriers: an active construction or reconstruction of the learner would form part of that process.

The particular experiences of individual students are likely to result in their needing different combinations of response drawn from each of the learning approaches described above: different levels of training, learning which builds from experience, and supportive learning environments. In addition, students can benefit from gaining an understanding of how contexts, processes, and narratives have shaped their 'learning selves'. For example, those who hold their own learning in poor esteem can benefit from addressing the origin of their attitudes towards, and definitions of, 'intelligence' and how they came to be appraised as intelligent or not within the context of their previous educational culture.

Embedded learning and meaningful tasks

People can fail to perform well on tasks that are given to them because the tasks do not make sense to them (Donaldson, 1987). When a task is meaningful in terms of previous experience, people are able to undertake the kind of reasoning that they are not able to manage when tasks are presented in more abstract ways. Donaldson noted, for example, that adults can have difficulties with tasks that require very close reading or accurate interpretation of specific words, especially on abstract tasks that do not make sense in terms of everyday experience. She found that even adults tend to read globally, taking in information in a general sense and they may not consider using a close, word-by-word reading strategy unless trained to do so. This has a bearing on the behaviours of undergraduates in relation to course reading and assessment, where success may be dependent on close analytical reading and interpretation. Students who do not read analytically may need guidance in how to do so and with a rationale that makes the task meaningful. It is especially pertinent for interpreting exam questions where there isn't a wider context to inform those who use a global rather than an analytical reading style.

When students fail, it is often assumed that this is because they are not 'bright' enough. In many circumstances, this may be because the student has not yet been exposed to sufficient concrete experience of higher education in order to develop abstract schema of what it is to be a student at this level. They may not have sufficient experience of required conventions. This is especially true of mature students who return to education from work or through access courses, or who are first generation in HE. In addition, students can lack adequate acquaintance with the specialised language needed to make sense, at speed, of what is said (in lectures, for example) or to interpret assessment tasks. Assessment tasks such as essays or exams may have no real-life correlate for the student and, as the task appears to be meaningless, the student may find it difficult to work out what is required. In parallel with Donaldson's research with children, Prosser and Millar (1989) found that physics students' ability to explain Newtonian mechanics varied greatly depending on whether the task involved an example of a moving car or a moving ice puck.

It is now argued that individual 'cognition is typically situated in a social and physical context and is rarely, if ever, decontextualised' (Butterworth, 1992). A tradition of regarding academic knowledge and skills as being of a different order of thinking and ability has not helped to encourage learners and teachers to look for similarities in the underlying expertise structure of both academic and everyday learning. In what may appear to be a paradox, the more abstract a task is, the more it is likely to be a product of a very particular culture (Richardson, 1991; Johnson-Laird, 1985). The example of the disparity between Brazilian street children's ability for 'street' maths compared to their difficulties with maths in classroom contexts is well known. George and Glasgow (1988) argue that this is true of many other areas of knowledge that learners encounter, including botany, physics, medicine, psychology and biology. Adult learners, in particular, bring a store of knowledge and skills that they may not be able to apply in a new learning context without support and may therefore undervalue and underuse pre-existing skills and knowledge. Even skills such as time management and problem solving may be accessible to adults in the context of home or work but they may not recognise these as applicable to the HE context.

From concrete to abstract skills

Our ability to think in abstract ways about something may depend on having already had real-life experience of problems of a similar nature. Butterworth (1992), describes how abstract notions such as 'generosity' are actually concrete social realities. The real-life, concrete experience allows us to develop a mental model, which later provides the basis for abstract thinking. If we have gaps in concrete experience – for example, with manipulating numbers – we are likely to find it harder to move on to more abstract examples until we fill those gaps. Butterworth argues that when we are presented with a familiar problem in an unfamiliar context, we may be unable to recognise that the two are the same. This can make us look like complete beginners when this is not the case. We may need somebody to point out the similarity between what we already know and the new learning – and then we can do it.

What this research suggests is that if we want students to develop abstract reasoning skills, they need to begin from concrete experience that makes sense in the world they already inhabit. Donaldson (1978) writes: 'The paradoxical fact is that disembedded thinking, although by definition it calls for the ability to stand back from life, yields its greatest riches when it is conjoined with doing.' Hatano and Inagaki (1992) make a distinction between 'routine' knowledge which is tied to specific contexts, and 'conceptual knowledge' which is transferable to new situations. They found that experience of particular concrete situations could be used, through analogy, to develop conceptual knowledge applicable to new contexts. They found that those who merely observed others rather than having direct, practical experience were less able to develop to a conceptual level of thinking about the subject.

This is relevant to many aspects of HE teaching, and in particular to skills development. If abstract thinking is a (potentially) emergent property of concrete experience, then it is to be expected that students may find it very difficult to apply what is learnt through 'generic' skills training. Indeed, students generally are very discontented by study skills provision when this is taught in an abstract way, separate from other aspects of the curriculum. Content-free skills modules work counter to the natural propensity of students to build conceptual skills from experience. It is much easier for students to learn skills when the direct relevance of these to the curriculum and to assessment is made explicit, and when these are delivered using course materials and subject-specific examples.

Study skills can become 'conceptual' knowledge, transferable to new situations, when students are exposed to embedded training and experience over time. Even then, as was mentioned above, the skill may only become transferable, when its applicability to a new context is made explicit by someone familiar with both the original learning context and the situation to which the skill must be applied. In other words, lecturers cannot assume that students who have applied study skills well in one area of the curriculum will be able to apply them to different areas unless the link is made explicit.

Equilibration: managing confusion

Although Piaget's concepts of assimilation and accommodation are often referred to in explanations of learning, the key element in Piaget's model was the process of equilibration (1975), often omitted from accounts of his ideas. Piaget argued that equilibration occurs in three stages:

- equilibrium: a pre-existing state of satisfaction with our way of thinking;
- disequilibrium: a dissatisfied awareness of limitations in our existing ways of thinking;
- a more stable equilibrium: we move to a more sophisticated way of thinking that overcomes the limitations of our previous thinking.

Siegler (1991) gives the example of a child who thinks that only animals are living things. When she hears plants referred to as being alive, she becomes uncertain of what 'alive' means. This uncertainty, although temporarily uncomfortable, is a necessary stage in opening up to new ideas. Dissatisfaction begins an internal questioning which opens us up to exploring new options. For students to progress to more sophisticated ways of thinking, they need to be receptive to disequilibrium and to be able to manage or 'contain' short-term confusion. Otherwise, they may cling to the security of their former equilibrium.

Creating opportunities for disequilibrium

Although universities tend to place a premium on critical awareness and clear thinking, there is also a need to support students, constructively, to enter into and manage a process of disequilibrium. Courses may need to create opportunities which challenge students' world-view. Perry's research (1970) suggests that students need time and support to arrive at a position where they can live comfortably with uncertainty – where they can cope with disequilibrium. They may need to be supported through, and even taught to respect, interim states of confusion, the agony of indecision, the borderline states where answers really are unclear.

Moreover, although it is important to test our hypotheses with critical analysis, it is important to recognise that advances are often made by what Hurley (1994) calls 'eureka' methods. Hurley argues that, in reality, we often use conventional procedural methods 'as a means of post-rationalisation' after the event, whereas we may actually have gained our insights through unorthodox means. In order to encourage such 'eureka' moments, creative thinking needs to be fostered. Students need opportunities for different approaches to tackling tasks and encouragement to experiment with the unorthodox, whether this is 'disordered rambling', dialogues on themes, free associations, doodled sketches, games, imaginative wanderings or day-dreaming. As lecturers, we need to ensure that there are at least some gaps in the neat pavements of our subject disciplines, with their rigid methodologies, correct assignment structures and ordered paragraphs, for some seedlings of inventiveness and novelty to flourish.

Resistance to disequilibrium

By the time students enter higher education, they have often lost the open approach to learning which children manifest during their first years of school. There may be all kinds of reasons for this. However, many adults are able to articulate how their earlier learning experiences have served to inhibit progress in their current study context. Each time we enter a new learning context, we bring with us our previous learning experiences. It must be a rare student who enters HE without experiences that have undermined confidence and curiosity. To some extent, all learners bring a mixed bag of inhibitory responses to learning. These include anxiety about failure, fear of being humiliated in front of peers, beliefs that they cannot learn particular things, and a wide range of other emotional and attitudinal responses.

Students can bring a strong resistance to 'disequilibrium'. It is evident that some students do not want to move away from their current ways of thinking; that change itself is threatening. Others are emotionally weak at coping with disequilibrium and the confusion it causes. If they were led to believe that they were a poor student in the past, then they may interpret interim confusion as a sign of their incapacity to cope with university at all. Apparently 'strong' entrants may also have difficulties with disequilibrium. For example, students whose identity is tied to being the 'best' student at school can find it difficult to adapt to contexts where this identity may be severely challenged. Very able students can find the higher level of competition at university to be extremely threatening. If their identity already feels under challenge, it can be hard for the student to manage the additional disequilibrium of having core beliefs challenged. Some high-grade entrants cling to methods and beliefs that have brought them success in the past, and will not risk what seems to be a successful formula in order to try a riskier strategy, even though it might ultimately take them to even more sophisticated levels of operation.

Saven-Baden (2000) uses the term 'transitional learning' to refer to 'shifts' that occur when students' frames of references, or 'life world' are challenged by their learning, especially as the result of critical reflection. This learning is generally preceded by a disjunction, which, she writes, '[is] characterised by frustration and confusion, and a loss of sense of self'. For example, when students are asked to consider 'what constitutes relevant learning', and to reconceptualise the role of their lecturers as facilitators rather than as sources of knowledge, there can be a 'sense of fragmentation', with a sense that one's self and one's known world are falling apart. In the short term, students can respond by demanding 'right answers' and can find the process negative and undesirable whilst they are going through it. It can be a frightening time, for which students need support and reassurance. The objectives of the process need to be kept in mind, so that students can gain most from it. In the longer term, this can lead to a reconceptualising of the self and of the learning process which takes the students to new and deeper levels of understanding.

Inhibited and motivated learning

Despite our natural propensities for learning, most of us develop mental or cognitive frameworks or schema which inhibit our learning, generally because of our previous learning experiences. On the other hand, other experiences motivate us towards curiosity, openness and new learning. All those who enter higher education bring at least a modicum of self-belief and motivation. Each student arrives in higher education with a different pattern of inhibited and motivational responses. Dilts *et al.* (1990) identified six 'levels' at which transformational learning takes place: environment, behaviour, capability, belief, identity and higher purpose. This model has been adapted in Figure 2.1. Two

additional levels, 'object of learning' and 'emotion', have been added. Dilts offers a useful framework for exploring factors that can inhibit or promote learning and which can guide interventions with students.

(1) Environment (where? when? with whom?)

The overarching context in which learning takes place has a profound effect upon learning. This may be the wider social, cultural or ideological context or the immediate situation of the lecture or an intermediate environmental context such as the availability of peer support. For example, students may feel excluded or included by the language and content of the course. If their gender, ethnicity, age group or social class are not referred to, or are treated as problems (such as by references to 'the mob', 'the masses'), then students may feel excluded from the course. Students in any kind of minority group (including young white men if they are in a minority) can feel overexposed; they can feel all the more self-conscious about speaking, standing out, and especially about revealing difficulties. For others, sensitivity to light, heat or sound can make the environment a difficult place in which to learn. The ethos of the course (supportive or competitive) can be an issue for other students. If the student's difficulty is primarily environmental, this may be evident in the emphasis of their own speech: 'I can't learn *here*, *now*, with *them*, on this course, at this university, with that lecturer, from this book. . . .'

Lecturers can have an impact on their students' learning by the way that they manage the learning environment. What we do as lecturers, the type of assessments we set, the timing of assignments, the way we mark and offer feedback, the way we present information, the way we address students, the way we orientate students into their learning, the way we design our courses – all this and more can harness the natural propensity of our students to learn. Conversely, we can further entrench our students' previously acquired inhibitions. We can

Figure 2.1 Levels of inhibition and motivation (adapted from Dilts *et al.*, 1990).

even establish inhibition to learning in those who have always been successful before they reached us. Chapters 3–5 below look in more detail at how lecturers can create positive learning environments.

(2) The object of learning: content (what?)

Dilts's model does not look at the way that the object of learning might affect learning. Students may find the work load too heavy, the vocabulary alien or case studies at a variance with their personal experience or belief. The importance of framing tasks in meaningful ways, with appropriate pacing, structure, language and concrete examples for the particular learner is addressed above. Changing the wording of a task, rephrasing instructions, or finding relevant examples are ways that teachers can have an impact on learning at this level. Difficulties may be detected in comments such as 'I can't learn *that*', 'It doesn't make sense', 'What's it supposed to be about?', 'It's Greek to me', 'It's boring,' 'It's irrelevant.'

(3) Behaviour (what do we actually do?)

This refers to what we actually do. This might be at variance with what we believe we could do or what we would like to do. In a widening access context, this may refer both to the lack of previous study practice before entering HE as well as the amount of time students may have to devote to their studies. Students may not read or think enough around the subject, nor spend time talking through ideas with others. This may be a question of priorities (too many conflicting demands on their time) or of lack of induction into the HE culture (not realising that this is what students are expected to do.) Resistances to disequilibrium can feature strongly here. Lack of appropriate study habits and not awarding sufficient time to study are especially relevant to study skills related difficulties. The emphasis in speech would be on behaviours: 'I can't *learn* or *do* that'; '*Writing*

essays is too difficult', 'It takes me too long to *do* it.'

(4) Capability (how?)

If the difficulty is at the capability level, the student is likely to put the stress on verbs and phrases expressing ability: 'I'm *not able* to learn that', 'I *don't know how* to learn that.' Many students who enter HE from widening access backgrounds may have the potential to do well, but lack the current capability or skills to perform at their best. They have not had the opportunity to develop practised, consistent, automatic, habitual skills which they can perform at will. Lack of recent education or lack of previous educational success can mean that they are ill-equipped to know how to progress – they simply do not know the next step. Vague feedback which points out failings without guidance on how to improve their work may add to their frustration. In such cases, a training or 'technicist' approach can be ideal: scaffolded learning, strategies and tips for effectiveness and efficiency, knowledge of professional short-cuts, activities which build competence and opportunities to put feedback into practice. Furthermore, 'time' can be a significant ingredient: sufficient time to practice, experiment and develop habits and to build up appropriate mental schema that assist them as students.

(5) Emotion (how do I feel about it?)

Given a safe opportunity to express them, students may emphasise the emotions that seem to block or encourage their learning: 'I *feel like* I'll never learn this' 'This *irritates, annoys, angers, upsets, excites* me.' They may express the emotions through tears or other behaviours. The emotion may be related simply to difficulties with current study; however, there is very often a throwback to earlier learning which was distressing in some way. They might associate current learning with humiliation at the hands of a teacher, or the pain of seeing disappointment in their parents' faces for a bad school report, or even life experiences such as bereavement, abuse or bullying, which were linked chronologically and emotionally to key learning events. 'I didn't realise how much I associate writing with a physical feeling of pain – which started when my father left home', said one mature student when coming to terms with a lifetime of study problems. Another student commented: 'I was trying to work on Sunday afternoons and just couldn't concentrate. I then remembered trying to do my homework on Sundays as a child whilst my parents took my younger sisters out to the park. It had a very strong effect upon me – being left on my own in the house whilst they were out enjoying themselves. I felt they didn't care about me.' It is far from unusual for students to be able to link study blocks to early traumas of some kind; these may resurface without the students necessarily identifying the emotional link that blocks their learning. Over the years, initial difficulties may have become compounded by ongoing failure.

On the other hand, positive emotions can have a beneficial effect upon learning. Students with poor early educational experience often recount the story of how their learning was turned around. This often involves a teacher or lecturer taking the time to explain what was needed to improve marks, followed by a feeling of elation when marks began to pick up. A student recounted how a series of such interventions led him from being a 'fail' student to gaining a distinction and the award of 'best student' in a college of 7000 students. This was within the space of one academic year. Positive feelings about oneself, the learning context, the course and potential outcomes can produce very motivated students. Work with HE students who were most 'at risk' of failure has shown how very little may need to change in order to alter students' emotional response – and once positive emotions are engaged, performance can change dramatically.

(6) Beliefs and values (why?)

Our belief systems exercise a strong hold over our learning. We use our beliefs as a basis for

action. Beliefs about self-worth and individual potential are especially powerful: some students have a deeply held belief that they 'not supposed to be' at university or that they are not good enough. Beliefs about intelligence ('IQ'), and the causes of past under-performace can be particularly influential on continued under-performance in higher education. Also significant are preconceptions about the value of what is being studied. Students can feel that only some subjects are worth studying even if these are not their areas of strength or interest. Medical and legal subjects, for example, may be valued by the students' families whereas their personal interests and aptitudes may lie elsewhere. Attitudes and motivation have a very deep impact upon how a student orientates to study. Students whose difficulties lie on the belief level may reveal this through speech and behaviours: 'I'm not likely to star at this subject', 'This is a soft option: I need to focus my attention on the other modules', 'It's only a discussion group so I don't need to turn up'. There may also be a conflict between values and behaviours: 'Music is what is important to me, that's what I'd like to study, but I need a job at the end of this so, here I am, taking Business Studies.'

(7) Identity (who?)

Core beliefs and values are those which affect our identity, our sense of who we are. When they encounter difficulties, students may experience this at the identity level: they decide that they are 'the kind of person who can't learn'. They emphasise the 'I' in descriptions of their difficulties: '*I* can't learn it', or even 'People *like me* don't come to university.' The student may already identify with a particular professional outcome; they may see themselves as a social worker, doctor or artist or simply as a successful student. 'Study' can be perceived by people as an extension of their identity. A person may identify with being a good student because there was affirmation for being a good pupil at school – or their student identity may be that they are a 'lost cause' or 'mediocre' or 'the clown in the group' or 'the one who sits at the back'.

The 'learning self' has an identity which has been forged through previous learning experiences, through the interpretations made of those experiences by the individual and the people around them within given contexts. These interpretations are articulated through narratives which the person carries within them and acts out. Mature students referred for support almost always can cite someone who told them: 'You'll never amount to anything.' No matter how well such students perform, the former entrenched narrative can take precedence, drowning out stories of recent success so that an identity of failure can prevail despite successful performance. This can be true of high achievers just as much as weaker students.

Many students have not considered what it is to be a student, what their identity as a student might be. Students have varied views about whether they can 'create themselves' as a new person, as a successful student and professional, for example, or as a confident, self-reliant adult. Many act as if they believe their identity, and their lives and performance based upon that identity, are pre-determined. Challenging notions of fixed identity can lead to significant changes in people's approaches to their learning.

(8) Higher purpose

'Higher purpose' refers to overall direction and motivation, to what drives a person. In relation to study, this might be the good that the student hopes will stem from completing their degree: to help others, to be a role model for their children, to be more independent, to follow a profession that matters to them, or to improve their understanding. Usually, higher purpose will be associated with wanting good for others, with creativity and artistic endeavour or with a person's spirituality. If study is associated with higher purpose, the student is likely to be well motivated and to persevere through more difficult times.

Motivated learning: conceptualising success

The previous section looked at eight 'levels' or sites where students' learning may be either inhibited or promoted. Either one or several of these levels may be the main seat(s) of inhibition for any particular student. These same levels are also the sites where learning can be promoted and motivated. However, in order for students to achieve academically, they need to engage in the act of learning, and in order to engage they must have an attitude of relative willingness to partake (see Figure 2.2). Self-belief and engagement with learning are intrinsically linked: there is no point engaging with a task if there is no possibility of success. The more students believe they are capable of success, the more positive their attitude is likely to be, including their general willingness to engage with their own learning. Those lacking self-belief, who feel they are likely to fail, tend to be unwilling to take risks and to expose what they believe is their ignorance or lack of skill. This means that learning needs to be structured, presented and delivered in ways that ensure a reasonable chance of early success, and a belief in the possibility of success needs to be inculcated in students.

Recent emphasis in higher education has been on learning 'outcomes'. However, when working with struggling students, it is evident that a clear notion of outcomes is only part of the process. Indeed, even achievement of outcomes may not necessarily lead to continued academic success. Many students have never been successful at academic study: they arrive in higher education waiting to fail. Early good marks do not necessarily reassure them unless they are clear why the mark is high. Low marks do not usually spur them on to work harder: the student may reasonably interpret the marks to mean they will never be capable of success in an academic context, that 'widening participation' is not really for them.

The mark given or the outcome attained is less important than the way that meaning is attributed to it by the student. '65%' may be regarded as either a strong mark or as failure,

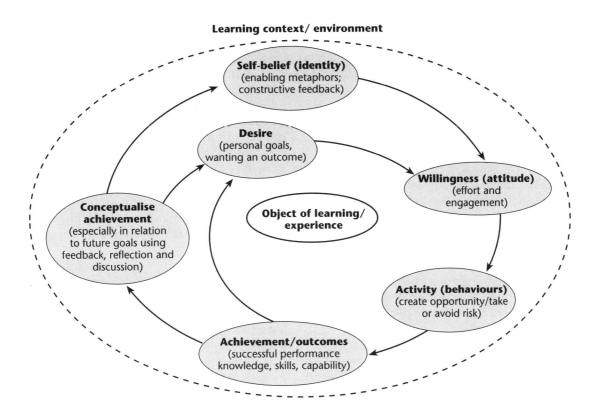

Figure 2.2   Student motivation cycle

not simply in relation to the marking scheme, but in terms of what the student feels they 'ought' to be receiving. Students may take high marks, for example, as indicators of success or as a series of 'flukes' which is not likely to continue. With appropriate feedback, and clear guidance on how to improve marks, students can interpret even relatively low marks as evidence that they are achieving milestones towards future success. For example, a mature student who received a mark 20% less than other students was reassured when it was pointed out to her that it was an achievement for her to pass the first assignment so well given her entrance route into the university, and that her marks were likely to catch up with her peers over time. Students can be very weak at articulating successful outcomes both to others and to themselves: their inner narratives or schema may not have changed to accommodate the notion of their own possible success. Indeed, in order to 'save face', students can deliberately sabotage their potential success by choosing to under-perform. Students report that it is preferable to fail having not tried at all, than to study hard and risk being 'no good' despite their best efforts. As a result, a primary motivating factor may be underdeveloped in students. This is a key area for lecturers to address. If students can conceptualise achievement and relate this to future goals they have a prime motivator towards future learning. Lecturers can also provide opportunities to address potential self-sabotage strategies.

'Take-off' stage to engaged learning

The 'take-off' stage is a notional stage where inhibitions to learning become outweighed or over-ridden by factors which promote learning so that the student becomes engaged with their learning, taking charge of it for themselves.

'Take-off' is a relative stage: it refers not to a level of objective performance but to the stage where a student can engage with the objectives of the course without support additional to that regarded as appropriate for the level of study. Typically, a new degree of self-reliance and insight into the purpose of learning is manifested by the student, accompanied by a changed relationship to the object of learning, so that there is a sense of the student having a degree of inner engagement with the object of study rather than it being 'externally imposed'. This is usually accompanied by a burst of energy, released when the inhibition they were tackling is overcome. This energy can be redirected into the main purpose of the course. For example, when students stop worrying about failing and look at how they might enjoy the course, the energy released from worrying can make studying easier.

For each student, 'take-off' will mean something slightly different. It comprises a mixture of desire, self-belief, clarity about objectives and the way to achieve these, trust in the learning process, preparedness for the level of study, focus, determination, and a willingness to engage with challenge. When these are not in place, greater motivation has to be provided by external incentives, such as charismatic teaching, financial motivation, or familial pressures. Past experiences of learning play a great part in determining how far a student may regard it as worthwhile to invest time or to take risks in self-exposure in order to continue on a course where they feel they are struggling.

Students from widening participation backgrounds often come with a long list of weaknesses and difficulties: cognitive, affective, behavioural and financial difficulties as well as gaps in their previous education. However, it is not always necessary to provide additional support on all of these levels for each student. Sometimes, when students address one or two areas of difficulty successfully, they become so energised that it is as if their other difficulties no longer existed. This is not necessarily because the problems have disappeared so much as that the students' attitudes to them, as inhibitions to

learning, have changed. For those receiving a great deal of support, even early signs of self-management may be regarded as 'take-off' once it is clear that the student has made a breakthrough in their understanding of what is expected of them, and has put their mind to grappling with the difficulties, even if they are not yet able to perform at the required level. In other words, 'take-off' is more a state of mind, related to a change in internal narrative, rather than a level of performance. However, in practice, this change of narrative to 'I can' and 'It is possible' generally translates into both changed behaviours and improved academic performance.

The 'state of mind' needed for the take-off stage is partly one of self-belief, and partly an understanding of, and trust in, the learning context. The learning context provides the framework for the kind of learning narratives the students will produce. It is to be expected that student narratives will reproduce the narratives of the institution or the department to some extent, if the student is to be successful. For example, if a course requires a superficial understanding of a subject, perhaps because it is an introductory course or subsidiary to the main course, the student needs to 'catch on' to the level of depth required. If they pitch their learning at a more intense level, they may have difficulties completing answers to the word limit required. If their approach is too superficial, they will lose marks for poor knowledge and understanding. 'Take-off' requires a student to become active in negotiating their own learning needs in relation to the stated objectives of the course. Generally, this tends to mean that the student has to be prepared to go into less depth than they would like on some areas that interest them and go into more depth than they would wish in other areas. For successful outcomes, their narrative of what is required needs to match that of their department.

'Surface' or 'deep' approaches

There is a growing body of research which demonstrates how students orientate their learning to match the requirements of their course, especially the 'hidden curriculum', manifested by what gets assessed, rather than the overt narrative of the course. In particular, students take a utilitarian attitude towards assessment and are likely to adapt their learning style to the demands of the mode of assessment (Snyder, 1971; Innes, 1996; Gibbs and Lucas, 1997; Gibbs, 1999.) If students are required, in effect, to regurgitate data for assessment, then they are generally more likely to adopt surface, short-term approaches to learning. Assessment which is designed to test understanding will promote 'deeper approaches' where students are more likely to retain what they have learnt for longer than the duration of an examination.

Assessment requirements can motivate students to adopt either more superficial or deeper approaches. 'Deep learning' occurs when students can digest and are nourished by their learning, are able to make sense of it, and extrapolate connections and applications to other contexts, rather than taking in and regurgitating what they are fed. Marton and Saljo (1984), who pioneered much of the early work on deep learning, emphasise: 'We are not arguing that the deep/holistic approach is always best: only that it is the best, indeed the only, way to *understand* learning materials.' Ramsden (1992) argues that, in 'deep learning', students find an inner connection to the task. They maintain the over-arching structure of the task, focusing on arguments and concepts, relating and linking new information to previously held knowledge and to other contexts in a holistic way, creating coherence and structure. 'Surface learning', on the other hand, is characterised by a desire only to meet the task requirements, by a feeling that the learning is externally 'imposed', by a 'focus on unrelated parts of the task', and by a lack of reflection and wider connection, so that the learning is not coherent, contextualised or meaningful.

Gibbs (1992) points to factors such as course design, opportunities for interacting with the material and each other, and a well-structured knowledge base, as key factors in determining students' approaches to learning. Chapters 3–5 below focus on ways of making the overall learning environment facilitative of improved student performance.

Student attitudes and approaches which inhibit learning

Vagueness about the object of learning

Students can hold very varied notions about what is the 'object' of their learning: its structures, logic, goals, purpose and significance may not be evident to them. They may not see the relevance of academic conventions either to the subject discipline or to life more generally. University can seem a very bizarre world; its languages can seem unnecessarily opaque, its accepted practices may appear arcane and learning can seem fraught with unnecessary hurdles. It is easy to make assumptions that the commonplaces of academic life, such as use of theory, essay writing, referencing, grades, and even assignments based on 'real life' simulations, make automatic sense to students. This is especially true for those who enter university from work, who may feel that experience has taught them that theory is 'unnecessary' to working life. For example, Utley (2000) cites research by Higgins which found that only 33 per cent of students understood their assessment criteria. Students often need acculturation to higher education, including rationales for its practices, clarifications of terms and explanations for the demands made upon them as students.

It can also be difficult for students to know what role they are supposed to play in the learning process: where their own ideas are supposed to come in, what it means to be 'autonomous' or 'independent', why common sense is not regarded as sufficient. They can wonder how they are 'supposed to' behave and think, how to 'be' or 'feel like' or 'act like a proper' student. In addition, they may not have a clear idea of what they really want from their studies whilst they are learning, as opposed to final outcomes such as a qualification and a better job. Some students deal with confusion by putting their noses to the grindstone and following sets of instructions. Others 'blank out' and wander their way through their university career in a confused daze. Some become depressed and demotivated whilst others focus on their marks and are sustained by their grades. Whether they are receiving high or low grades, many students are baffled by what it is they are supposed to be doing and why – 'what is the point of it all?' The following comments are indicative of this confusion.

Lauren
Why do we have to do theory, as social workers? I can understand why we have to know the law and have information about different social and racial groups, but isn't it a waste of time studying all these theories? Can you honestly tell me it's of any value to my professional life?

Barbara
I worked as a teacher's assistant for seven years. I teach Key Stage One. You see the results. You think you really know education. Then you do teacher training, and suddenly there's all this 'stuff'? What is it about? I can't see why I need it except I have to have this piece of paper to be recognised as a teacher.

John
What I wrote is basic common sense to me, but they say it has no worth unless I write a reference for it. What's the point of that? It's daft. It's like looking for a way to credit other people with your own ideas – I'd get nowhere in my business if I adopted that approach!

Jacob
I love studying here. It's what I wanted to do all my life. Especially research for our projects. I love looking things up and finding

out all this new information. I just don't see why I should have to write about it in 2000 words. I don't want to write to an essay title. I just want to write what I have to say. I don't want to write an exam: why can't they just mark what I have to say?

Aisling
I am finding study very difficult. I don't think I am stupid. Basically, I don't want to be here. I just want the diploma but I am finding it hard to get down to study.

Matthew
I can't see what it is I am supposed to be thinking as I learn. I don't mean that I don't understand the subject matter; its not that. I mean – about 'me', about how I am doing it. I don't know how I am supposed to be, what's supposed to be in my head as I read for example – what should I be saying to myself? Who am I when I'm studying? Does this make any sense?

When students lack an overview or 'meta-perception' of their subject, they lack a framework for assigning significance to what they learn. This makes it difficult to identify key points and select relevant information for assignments: all details may seem to be of equal status or relevance. As a result, students may either make notes about everything, or about nothing, or randomly, or begin at too detailed a level and so run out of time. It can also be hard for them to adopt a critical approach to the subject, except, perhaps, in identifying internal inconsistencies within a text or theory. In such cases, students are more likely to move from one topic to another without making links, or else make so many links that the most important ones are lost. Lecturers can help students by being aware of potential confusion, providing clear course overviews and making direct links between the subject material, its methodologies and everyday life.

Anxiety about 'not being good enough'

Anxiety about not being good enough is very common and is not necessarily linked to current performance. The notion of a genetically predetermined intellectual fate is often held by students, generally as a matter of private shame and worry which inhibits learning. Whatever their genetic predispositions, many students are underperforming for reasons which have nothing to do with potential, and relate more to self-belief, past experience, internal negative messages, anxiety and stress which make it difficult to focus and learn. When that cycle is broken, students' performance can improve.

Many students are already fragile when they enter further and higher education. Although students may be adults in chronological years, their egos can be very vulnerable and childlike in relation to the demands of university. They carry the scars of being belittled in front of classmates, of being told they were stupid, of receiving bad marks for work they thought was good, of being told they should try harder when they had given their all, of harsh criticism when they were eagerly awaiting praise. It is not simply that they lost confidence in their scholastic abilities, but that they lost confidence in their own judgement, in their ability to distinguish what needs to be preserved or changed in their study performance or habits. They lack navigational bearings in an ocean of comment, writing, effort, unfair criticism, unclear feedback, and non-specific advice. Almost everybody has experienced at least one horrific episode at school where a teacher has undermined their confidence, leaving them confused about whether they really are as good as they think or whether they are 'fundamentally stupid'.

Those who were regarded as 'remedial' at school, or who never excelled in an academic subject, can be especially nervous about coming to university. University was for other people. Widening access means that people who never envisioned themselves at university are now studying for degrees. Although they can do extremely well, they may feel they are foolhardy even to attempt a degree. Universities are 'for other people', richer people, cleverer people, people with better genetic make-up and social standing. It is important to challenge negative self-concept and beliefs in predetermined academic failure. In order to do this, an important first step is to investigate where such beliefs originated and their effect upon performance. There is little point in attempting to change bad study habits if the students believe they are doomed to fail anyway.

Students' fears of disclosing difficulties

When students are invited to express their anxieties about becoming a student, they often speak about their fear of other people realising that they experience difficulty. They fear:

- their lecturers holding a poor opinion of them;
- losing credibility with lecturers which will make it harder, in the long run, to achieve good marks, good work placements, good references when applying for jobs, or to be taken seriously for a higher degree;
- becoming upset and crying in front of the lecturer, which they consider humiliating and embarrassing;
- other people finding out that they needed help or that they became upset, in case they are teased, pitied, despised or discredited for it;
- other students rejecting them for project groups;
- appearing to be unwilling to help themselves, and so if they *really* need more help later, they will have worn out lecturers' good will;
- the possibility of becoming angry with the lecturer, because they feel the lecturer should have done something differently;
- being thrown off the course (even when this is an unlikely outcome).

It can be easy for lecturers to forget, when dealing with large numbers, working under pressure, faced with apparently wilful non-compliance and students' failure to read course documentation, that, from the students' perspective, lecturers appear to hold their lives, their hopes, their aspirations, their chances of work, of a home, and especially their self-esteem and vulnerability, in the palms of their hands. Students dare not challenge lecturers most of the time. They have too much at risk. They cannot take the chance that the lecturers will not find a way of 'paying them back' for a complaint, or even for being too much of a burden on their time. Given the vulnerabilities outlined above, and the pressures students place themselves under, it is not difficult for a lecturer to appear to be digging the knife into an open wound, or for a student to feel they should not be at university if a lecturer says something harsh. In other words, the language, behaviour and support of the lecturer can make a great difference to the students' sense of self and to their success on the course. Fear of disclosing difficulties is especially hard if students feel that lecturers do not value them. The President of Birkbeck Student Union, for example, questioned how much students were valued when universities gave the impression of waging 'a heroic battle to defend the besieged institutions against the students who wish to do them harm?' (Times Higher Educational Supplement, 21 January 2000, p. 17).

Anxious high achievers

Those who did well at school may have done so without understanding why they did well or what gained them high marks. Success is rarely explained. It is simply a grade or a comment such as 'very good'. This does not create a very solid basis for understanding what one is capable of achieving. This is true of students at even the most selective universities; these can be especially vulnerable to 'perfection anxiety' and to other people's perception of them. Some students fear that a great unveiling is going to occur which will expose to their lecturers, other students, and worst of all, to themselves, that they have been 'stupid all along'. Others feel they are expected to excel and hide difficulties in order to save face. Good marks do not automatically produce confident students. For those

who have done well in the past, failure to do as well as expected at university can be particularly hard to bear. This is also true of those who express themselves well orally or in practical subjects and who receive a great deal of admiration and passing compliments from other students. Written work may not come so easily to them, and it may be very hard to admit this.

It can be extremely important to some students to maintain a facade of being 'naturally bright', clever without working hard. In aristocratic vein, people may want to take pride in an apparent 'natural superiority' rather than in being seen to earn merit. In terms of success, 'inherited wealth' of intelligence has more status than being seen to soil your mind by hard work. This is a very demanding mental attitude, as such students often have to work secretly and place themselves under very great strain in order to appear not to be working too hard. Again, such students may have very low self-esteem, and are particularly unlikely to ask lecturers for help. Eating disorders, drug taking, alcohol abuse and self-harm are not unusual amongst those who are, or have been, high achievers.

It can be a challenge to universities which recruit high performing entrants to find ways of creating safe environments to address difficulty and also of introducing skills development in ways that raise prior high levels of performance. This is primarily a curriculum issue as high performers are unlikely to come forward for support or to identify with a need for skills development. One issue here is that high performers are usually accepted into traditional universities where the emphasis is on content (the knowledge base). As a result, students are often required to use the same strategies over and over but with different or larger chunks of information. They may enter university with a particular thinking style and a narrow range of writing styles and life skills, and leave without these being significantly developed or extended. Sometimes, the main skills that high-fliers achieve at university are merely those of producing longer essays, more quickly, in writing styles they will never use again.

Students do not know how to evaluate their own performance

Mary (postgraduate student)

It's so embarrassing. . . . I'm not sure even now that I know, really, whether I use paragraphs correctly or not. One tutor said I could 'improve my paragraphing'. Nobody else ever mentioned it so I don't know what to think, really. I didn't want to ask anybody at the time – being in line for a good degree, I mean I got a 2.1, made it, somehow, more difficult to say anything. I wondered . . . if I ask, will they start to look at me differently and think 'maybe, she's not as good as we thought. She actually doesn't know what she is doing, does she?' So I just left it.

Joachim

I can't believe I got this far and I actually don't know what I know. I think I am caught up in a fantasy world and at any minute the bubble is going to break. What am I, a school 'drop-out', doing on this course? And which should I believe – the good marks or the bad ones? Which are 'me'?

Waheed

Apparently I am going backwards. I got 72% for my early work. Since then, I have had one mark as low as 48%, the others are around 55%. I read through the different pieces of work and I can't see what is that different about them, why one received 72% and the others didn't. I kind of stare at the essays, as if the mystery will reveal itself to me . . . the mystery of what makes this mark or that mark attach to a piece of work. The marking criteria haven't really helped because I don't 'get them' – what they mean. I mean, I can see, roughly that there are some areas for improvement in all my work, of course, but I can't see what it is that I used to have that now I have lost. I need someone to say, 'Look, Waheed. Here, I gave you marks for X. X is the factor missing

from your later work'. It sounds crazy: what is factor X? But that's the mystery I need solved. . . . I am not sure I should carry on with the course if my marks are just going to go down. I don't want to fail.

The comments of these students reveal the internal dilemmas created when students do not understand how academic conventions operate, or where marking criteria and feedback are vague or unhelpful in their guidance. All of the above students had had a taste of success and yet this did not lead to them feeling confident or even knowledgeable about how to produce good work. Their lack of awareness about what constitutes success meant that they were left feeling uncertain about the level of their performance. They lacked tools to evaluate their own work and duplicate success.

Loss of motivation

It is very common for motivation to wane as a long course progresses. The eager enthusiasm that students had at the beginning can diminish when study becomes difficult and especially if life outside the course presents additional difficulties. Tutors can maintain higher motivation by making a space to discuss motivation, by timetabling some careers education, and more generally through teaching methods which make course content relevant to the lived realities of the students' experiences. It is difficult to maintain interest in abstract information when motivation is low. Concrete and relevant examples, case studies, and relating information to one's personal life, make abstraction meaningful, and can increase motivation.

When one becomes more expert in a subject, when the subject is both challenging but manageable, the intrinsic interest of that subject becomes more apparent. Motivation increases. Students can reach the take-off point, which, when reached, can sustain the effort that is required, so that the effort itself is not burdensome. It may even be welcomed. An adult grappling with crossword puzzles or exercise regimes is not forced to engage in these activities. They may never solve the puzzle or become an athlete, and yet they are drawn into the effort through an act of will or desire. They find pleasure of some kind in the activity. Many students, however, never get to the 'take-off point' at which a subject becomes enthralling, where learning becomes engaging, where they are drawn on to solve mysteries, to set themselves problems, to 'work out' purely for the sake of it.

Student testimony can describe, sadly, a contrary movement: further disenchantment, the loss of last hopes, profound disappointment with academia, flight from the pains of study, desperate boredom. Failing students are all too often 'broken' intellects: the heart has already been ripped out of their endeavours. In an effort to recoup something from the situation, the student may seek small Machiavellian successes or the least shame-faced exit they can achieve. School may have started the slow suffocation of their intellectual spirit; university can complete the job, crushing it completely. Lecturers have an important role to play in catching students before they enter spiral descent. Timely intervention and reassurance can help maintain and augment the level of motivation that brought a student to the course initially. Students need to be told about the difficulties that are inevitable in moving from 'novice' to 'expert' status and be assisted through the doldrums of that transition.

Information overload can also affect motivation. When students have to take in more information than they are ready for, they can't digest it. They can begin to lose appetite for the subject. The subject can then start to repel them. It is no longer an area of fascination, if ever it was, but a monster to be evaded, denied, repelled, killed off. Being unable to swallow what they are fed can feel very frightening. Learning falters. The subject becomes a matter of concern rather than of interest. From the place of fear, the student moves into 'survival strategies', into 'getting by', hoping that nobody notices their fear and their failure.

Information has to be fed in manageable, bite sizes or attention wanders and interest wanes. Tasks need to be progressive. Lecturers need to be aware of potential areas of overload. For example, if all course notes are handed out at the beginning of term or made available on web pages, it helps students if they are given guidance about when each section is to be read. This needs to be said verbally – the student needs to hear it. It also needs to be seen, such as in a preface to the set of notes. A shorter Guide may be needed to lead the students through the materials, with activities to prompt reflection and understanding. When information is given primarily by ear, many students will need visible points of reference, and reassuring reminders that are easy to access. Information overload is a particular danger on web-based courses. Searching for information on CD-ROM or the internet can present students with undifferentiated data which they do not know how to interpret, select from or evaluate.

Attachment to inefficient learning strategies

Students may be completely unaware of which learning styles would assist them most. They often try to reproduce the study methods that they were introduced to at school, even if these were not very successful for them. When they fail again, this can reinforce negative self-image and produce inertia or withdrawal. The methods of the school classroom may be necessary because of demands made on teachers, but are not necessarily the best way for individuals to learn when studying on their own at home. For example, some people learn better when they are moving around, talking out loud, working on three topics at once, getting up and down every ten minutes, alternating between writing and talking aloud, or when the house is silent at three in the morning, or when they can put their learning to music, or chat about it to a friend. Understandably, this insight may not have been developed at school.

Students can feel that they are not really studying unless they are sitting still, at a desk, in silence, for a single sitting of two hours, working alone, undertaking reading or writing. This can make it very difficult for some students to initiate study because there is an internal conflict between what they need to learn and the conditions they have set up for themselves, based on the ideal set in the classroom. In lectures or seminars, their needs may not be so apparent because somebody else, the lecturer, usually has responsibility for shepherding them into the work. When left to their own devices, they have to wait for a crisis or deadline before they can begin.

Some students referred for support study very long hours, often taking in little that they read, and are overwhelmed by boredom and frustration. They can be resistant to the idea of changing their study habits as their belief is that study is like medicine – if it doesn't hurt, it isn't working. The 'hurt' for study may be boredom itself. If there was some interest in the study, it might be too easy, and then they would not feel they were really working.

Students can also be overattached to themselves as a certain 'type' of learner. This can take a myriad of forms. For example, the student may have a habit of learning essays off by heart and rewriting them in the exam – or trying to adapt them in the exam. Although this freezes information into a particular structure, and means that information necessary for other answers had not been learnt, the strategy may have worked once at a crucial moment at school, and the student may be very reluctant to give it up. It offers security, even though it may have led to them failing several sets of exams since. There are students who have been told they are 'right-brain thinkers' and that they have no sense of order or structure. To accept that they use order and structure in many aspects of their lives very successfully can be a challenge to the identity to which they are attached. It can be counter-productive to challenge the identity directly; it is more helpful to bring out where they have demonstrated those skills successfully, using their achievements as the basis for exploring and extending the range of strategies acceptable to them.

Students can also be anxious about taking 'shortcuts', which they may regard as cheating; they expect punishment will inevitably follow in the form of lower marks. Typical examples are students who read all recommended books from cover to cover, taking extensive notes on each chapter, even though they can't see the relevance of what they are noting. The students are too anxious about total coverage to develop more important skills such as those of reflection, selection and relevance. They generate many more notes to read than is needed, which, in turn, generates more work as they then have more notes to reread and summarise. Students may revise in an amorphous, unfocused way, and know a great deal, but have to spend too much time in the exam room itself selecting essentials – and have underdeveloped skills at selecting at speed. They may run out of time because they write their first answers in too much detail, or they may not write enough because planning and selecting takes too long. These students can be helped by tutors who model effective shortcuts, and who give 'permission' for effective study through such modellling.

Widening participation

Changes in the composition of the student body highlight the need for more supportive learning environments. Characteristics of students drawn from a widening access profile generally include:

- a wide breadth of experience, especially of work, family life, caring, personal relationships, interpersonal skills, and personal management;
- linguistic diversity: English may be only one of a range of languages spoken and /or written;
- strong personal motivation such as career ambitions or a need to prove something to themselves or their families;
- strong commitment to the course of study if they are encouraged;
- willingness to endure struggle and hardship to achieve the qualification;
- greater awareness of the importance of skills development for employment;

- greater maturity in their approach to problem solving.

However, these students are often very unprepared for university. Such students are also characterised by:

- being more likely to have dependants, work and other commitments apart from study;
- gaps in education or long absence from education. This may mean the student never acquired certain study skills, has had only recent 'refreshing' of such skills on (typically) a nine-month Access course. Academic English and even general written English may be weak;
- little or no formal writing experience;
- lack of study habits, especially for independent study outside of contact time;
- poor reading habits. Students often report a very low total of books read over a lifetime;
- negative prior experience of education: often their experiences of education have been very undermining and the student may be very cautious about exposing themself to ridicule;
- little or no success at formal examination;
- unpreparedness for higher education; lack of background information about what a university is, its traditions, ethos and teaching methods; lack of awareness about the difference between school, college and university, and the demands that will be made of them as students;
- lack of confidence – a feeling that they are not entitled to be at university and of waiting to be judged and thrown off the course. They may have been told they would never be fit for a career or further education;
- a lack of awareness of how their current skills, experience and attributes may be applicable to higher education;
- more varied learning styles and preferences than traditional entrants.

Students drawn into universities through widening access are not simply poorer variants of the successful students who attended universities in the past. They are different kinds of learners. Often they did not succeed as well under the school system as traditional HE learners because the school system tends to promote a particular kind of learning – especially one focused on bodily stillness, the written word, recapitulation of given ideas in written formats, assessed through writing and under time-restricted conditions. Student intakes today are more likely to have higher proportions of students who learn best if they are offered alternative ways of studying: for example, where there are opportunities to be active, to generate ideas rather than merely analyse those of others, where they produce real objects or are located in real-world settings, and where they can demonstrate knowledge in ways other than by written examination.

Preparedness for HE: changes in entrance qualification

The range of acceptable qualifications for university entrance is now far wider than the traditional 'A' level route. This has an effect upon the preparedness of the student for the area they are to study. 'A' levels generally mirrored the education process which students would follow at university. History students, for example, were often dictated notes by teachers, wrote regular essays, learnt how to sit exams, sat exams, passed them and those who did best in this system went on to study in a similar fashion at university. Lab students did lab work, took notes and sat exams. Promising pupils were, in effect, groomed and trained for HE for several years before entry.

If the university course does not match the way that feeder courses teach and assess, then students are often in the dark about how to study. Today's undergraduates are drawn from a much wider range of feeder courses, including BTEC, Access Courses, and professional trainings. The teaching and assessment modes used on these courses do not necessarily dovetail neatly into those used at universities. Today's entrants may never have set an exam, and if they did, they may not have passed it very well. They may not have taken notes by hand whilst listening to a teacher deliver information. Some feeder courses, for example, present the bulk of work in workbooks, organised as activities, and which students tend to approach through paired or ad hoc group work. Learner Support units in some FE colleges proofread students' work and tell them how to make changes: it can come as a shock to new undergraduates to realise that this is not the function of support or learning development units in HE.

Other students enter without formal qualifications. Some come directly from work using routes which accredit their prior experience in terms of the skills and learning required for the area of study. They bring a range of personal attributes and skills which can be harnessed to enrich the teaching and learning experience. However, the requirements of the workplace are very different from those at university. University can seem incredibly bizarre, lacking in rationale and warmth, to those used to real-life problem-solving contexts and more intimate work settings. Even those who are very skilled professionally can struggle to adapt to the demands of HE, unless these demands are made explicit and appropriate training provided.

The demands and constraints on the time of today's students mean that they cannot afford to make up for deficits in resources or teaching in the way a student could in the past. Very small matters can assume much greater proportions for them. If they haven't been given a reference in writing, for example, they probably won't ever find the book. If they can't get hold of a book in a library when they come in, they are unlikely to have the time or even the bus fare to come back in to look again. Students expect to be given books that are in print and easy to access. They expect written summaries of hard-to-access information or to have key information networked. They expect staff to give them typed booklists in their hands so that they have the details accurately and so that lecture time can be used more productively than copying down from the board. They expect that if information is presented to them on overheads, it is left up long enough for them to copy at reasonable speed. Time is a great issue for widening participation students.

Inspiring students: the rewards of a widening participation

Although the change in the composition of the student body can make life more challenging for lecturers, it also means that professional development is more important and professional life enriched. Students' need for inspiration *by* their lecturers can be an inspiration *to* their lecturers – it draws out their skill as teachers and course designers. It is not very engaging or challenging, for lecturers to teach students who learn easily, who already know how to give what is required, and who know how to succeed on their own. To draw out students who are uncertain of their potential, assisting them to improve in performance, develop in confidence, and alter their life expectations, is one of the most rewarding aspects of teaching. This is brought out in the following lecturer testimony.

Lecturer testimony
Teaching mature students . . . it's hard to capture what makes it such a reward and such a challenge without sounding trite. What I admire most about the students I teach is their courage and tenacity. All of them have had the guts to give education another go, despite the fact that, for many of them, first time around was a bewildering, confidence-sapping experience. Leaving behind jobs, which if not secure are at least familiar (and I think that counts for more when looking at what makes people stay put) in the belief that there's more to life, takes real guts. It also means that they have to challenge lots of ideas about themselves and about who they are which is never easy.

In teaching mature students you start with such potential but also such terror! These people function in the outside world as workers, partners and parents and have a wealth of skills and experiences to bring into education. The trick is to convince them that they don't have to leave these skills at the door of the teaching room! I think it is hugely important not to de-skill students further by suggesting that academia is somehow alien and other than 'normal life' and that their life skills are of no value. I've found that life experience acts as the anchor for academic knowledge when teaching mature students. Perhaps with younger students knowledge of theory comes first and is applied to real life events as life experience grows.

With mature students I think the reverse is true. If you allow people to think and make sense of events within their frame of reference you can then introduce theory as if it were stone cladding on a house (but rather more attractive I hope)! In that way theory can become a part of them and their lives. In teaching, one of my greatest rewards is when I see students picking up ideas and running with them, weaving them into their experience in such a way that they live and breathe rather than exist in some abstract domain. To see people who have been told they are stupid repeatedly revel in the joy of thinking is wonderful and a large part of what makes the job worthwhile. To know that they will use these skills to make major life changes is even better. It's always particularly satisfying to see older women using education to re-write their life scripts – you feel like you've given them a large sledgehammer and let them loose on the world!

Wednesday was great. We had a visiting lecturer talk to the first years, who are in their second week of studies. At break time they were buzzing – all talking about ideas and experiences and many showing real surprise that they had found themselves to be thinking, feeling people! It's like seeing a spark ignite and I hope I never tire of seeing it. I think my job involves being elements of a tour guide, cheer leader and *agent provocateur* as much as it involves being a source of information and I believe if you focus only on the latter you are doing mature students a disservice. I think teachers have a lot of power to alienate students and that you have to do a lot of conscious thinking about the teaching process and how your teaching

is being received. I hasten to add that I don't always get it right! Yesterday I started teaching a course on methods and methodology and spectacularly failed to find the students' frame of reference in the early part of the session. I think it was salvaged in the end but I had forgotten that the concept of research seems particularly alien and frightening and that I had to find a way of grounding it somehow.

C. Dorer, lecturer (in social work), Birmingham University

Final comments

Widening participation, changes in student funding, a growth in the range of entrance routes into higher education, as well as greater reflection by universities about what kind of learning they wish to encourage, are ushering in changes in how learning, teaching and 'support' are envisaged. Perhaps the greatest transition is from a situation where learners had to 'sink or swim', adapt to the institution or take the consequences, to the current position where higher education is seeking to understand how its students learn and to assist them in the process. Widening participation means that different kinds of learners are entering higher education, who need different approaches to those which could be survived, and even enjoyed, by students in the past. These new learners in HE often lack the study skills to succeed. However, study skills training, in isolation from wider initiatives to support and structure learning in ways that suit today's university populations, are doomed to failure. This chapter has drawn on the testimonies of many hundreds of students as well as lecturers in order to demonstrate that many factors can inhibit or motivate students' learning. These impact upon how study skills can be addressed, and even what becomes defined as study skills: students referred to special units for study skills in the past often required as much attention to their attitudes and self-esteem as to academic skills. As skills development becomes incorporated into curricula, that aspect of support needs also be addressed in the way that teaching, assessment and feedback are structured.

This, in turn, creates needs from the lecturer's perspective. One lecturer, at a prestigious institution, commented that he was 'essentially a researcher' despite his teaching commitments, and was 'terrified' if called upon to deliver information except through reading a prepared paper. His teaching style would not be ideal for many students in today's universities. Demands are often made of university lecturers without addressing the lack of teacher training that has been widespread in higher education until recently. Recruited for strengths in research, many lecturers need to be trained, skilled in their own right, so that they can feel confident teaching people, learners, and not just a 'subject'.

Learning theory points to the importance of such factors as prior experience, structured guidance, personal relevance, and the importance of moving from the concrete to the abstract when developing the expertise of learners. This can help us to make sense of why students in higher education, and especially those from widening participation backgrounds, may have initial difficulties in adapting to higher education. It also offers us ways forward, such as through recognising the importance of assisting students to develop appropriate mental schema of the requirements of higher education or by scaffolding initial learning experiences. Students' own accounts of their difficulties also reveal unexpected ways in which either university procedures or their own mis-interpretations of these can hinder progress. Rather than seeing a 'deficit' in the student, we can identify a very wide range of ways that either past experience or the current learning context can impact upon performance and use this understanding to make positive interventions to assist the learning process.

Supportive learning environments

'At risk' students or 'at risk' environments?

Outside pressures, largely governmental, are increasingly forcing universities to change, in line with the social changes in which they are embedded. If universities are to maintain a measure of control, they must follow certain systematic strategies for systemic change.

Elton (1999)

Former approaches to learning support, primarily sending the student outside of the department for help, are not sufficient to meet the demands of the current intakes of students in many universities. The traditional notion is that support is remedial and exclusive to a few; the movement in HE is towards inclusive approaches, learning development and a more skills-sensitive curriculum as desirable for all students. The traditional model placed the deficit within the student; in today's teaching climate, it is important to identify not only 'at risk' students but also 'at risk' environments. To put this more positively, it is important to identify features of academic environments that make learning a more constructive experience with successful outcomes for the largest possible number of students. To highlight the difference from the student perspective, examples are given below of how two different support

models can impact upon students' learning and self-esteem.

The chapter offers an institution-wide model of support, with suggestions about how support can be built into structures, documentation and all aspects of the students' experience. It offers a way of moving towards student-focused environments and academic practice. This theme is further developed in the two following chapters, which focus on induction and teaching as key areas where support can be integrated to assist all students.

In trying to address the study needs of students, universities have tended to move towards establishing either specialist centres for study support outside of the department, or, increasingly, skills modules within the curriculum. Although both of these are important advances and often essential for students, if such support is divorced from teaching and from overall institutional attitudes and approaches, a remedial or deficit notion of support can persist that is ultimately self-defeating. At best, support may be accessed by only a small part of the student population which requires it. At worst, students may feel shamed and stressed so that low performance may be reinforced. In general, students may not grasp the relevance, significance and concrete application of skills support to new learning contexts.

Staff based in specialist centres or teaching

study skills modules are all too aware that the existence of study support centres, though essential for those with specialist needs and for those who require confidential or prolonged support, are tokenistic in terms of the overall need of the student body. Indeed, it is a strange notion that any student could be considered to be without learning development needs. Key questions in evaluating the effectiveness of these centres from a whole institution perspective are:

- How many students are estimated to be in need of additional support of some kind?
- How many students can such study centres cater for?
- What happens to the shortfall?

In many cases, especially where the institution has an emphasis on widening participation, it is all too evident that the bulk of students in need are not gaining access to support, and that if those who needed help came forward, the specialist centres would not be able to cope with the demand, given the resources available to them.

Remedial or deficit models

Learning support which is based upon remedial approaches, in employing 'experts' to provide the bulk of additional support, is extremely costly and of limited impact unless it is linked to a wider system of support at all levels of the institution. Even for those who do require additional specialist support, such as those with English language difficulties, or Specific Learning Difficulties (dyslexia), the effectiveness of the support available is highly dependent on how it relates to course delivery and systems. For example, the amount of support and individual attention a student can receive from additional support is unlikely to exceed an hour or two a week. Even if the funding were available for more, students rarely have time to attend. Weak students, who may spend much longer on coursework than others, have the least time to attend support based away from

their course and the greatest need for the highest possible integration of support into the course. It is easier to identify drawbacks in the remedial approach if one tracks the steps of a student through two types of support process.

Case outline of a remedial approach

The outline below is a composite schema that fits the descriptions given by support tutors across the higher education sector. Whilst this is not the only way in which support might work, the scenarios described will be familiar to many tutors and to student recipients of support.

Sonya

Like several other students in her department, Sonya is a mature student who has spent nine months on an Access course after many years' absence from formal education. Although she has made progress since starting her Access course, she has only had practice in writing two short pieces and a brief essay since leaving school where she had performed quite badly. Sonya's course recruits many students with weaknesses in English language; it sets an English test for its students during induction week and sends 15 students with the worst scores for support to an English language tutor who they 'buy in' and share with another course in the same building which sends five students. This is more support than is offered by many courses so the department feels they are being constructive.

Sonya writes as she speaks and her spelling is phonetic through lack of practice; she is one of those sent to English support. Although Sonya's English is not significantly worse than that of her friends – Jason, a mature student, and Louise, who speaks and writes partly in 'patwah' – their scores were not in the bottom 15 so they are not offered any support at all. Jason and Louise receive comments on the bottom of their essays such as 'grammar!' and 'please write in sentences!' which mystify them, as they believe they do this already. They even buy a grammar book, but don't know how to translate its information into practical application. Their marks remain low throughout their time at the university, as does their self-esteem. Junko has just arrived from Japan; she can't understand spoken English but her written English is adequate so nothing is done to assist her to understand what happens in class.

Sonya goes along with Kiran, Rahel, Nils and Elaine to English support. Kiran is a dyslexic student who has not previously been assessed as dyslexic, his difficulties having been wrongly attributed to 'second language problems'. The 20 sessions of grammar will make little impact upon his difficulties. Rahel has been four years in England and has a firm grip on grammar in several languages, but lacks practice in writing English. He catches up on his class peers very quickly and is bored in the support class. Nils is also frustrated as the support focuses on grammar he already knows but does not give him support in the particular aspects of language that led him to fail the test. Next to him sits Elaine, who is insulted that she has been sent to English support with students from overseas when she can speak English fluently. She needs support in structuring her ideas, guidance in the language styles used on her course and help in understanding the vocabulary. These are not covered in the support class.

The class covers basic aspects of English that many students get wrong, such as writing in sentences, parts of speech, and rules about using different past tenses. Some of this would be useful to those who were not in the bottom 15; for the 20 students who are there, the particular priorities of their learning support are not addressed. There is little contact between the department and the tutor they have bought in. No priorities have been identified for the outside expert: the course tutors do not even

know what would be of most use and they leave that to the 'expert'.

Sonya is a slow writer but a good listener. Although she misses out many technical terms as, not knowing them, she cannot catch them quickly enough, her notes are otherwise reasonable. She takes very brief notes, noting only key-points. Although she has a good strategy, she does not realise this and sees the rest of her peers writing pages of notes every session. She is so anxious that it makes her ill; she is very worried about what she is missing. To make up for this, she takes out all the reading books on her list, and spends most nights reading through them from cover to cover. Again, this contributes to making her ill.

When she comes to write an assignment, Sonya has no idea what is expected, despite the guidelines that are given. She cannot see an essay in her mind's eye or hear what it might sound like. She has never had contact with a good essay so has no schema of what to produce. In addition, she does not have any idea how long they take to write and leaves too little time to work on them. There isn't a supportive atmosphere on Sonya's course: students try to 'psych each other out'. Some boast that they complete assignments in a night and contribute to her false sense of what is involved. Sonya follows the guidance in the course handbook about references, but as she did not refer directly to all the texts she had read, her reference list is very short. After all her hard work, she receives a low mark, and the feedback advises her to read more widely and write more clearly. Sonya feels like giving up.

Exams loom. Sonya learns her essays off by heart and tries to write them out. She realises she cannot get down in an hour what she writes in a coursework essay. To get round this, she decides to miss out introductions and conclusions in her exam, and just lists lots of facts to prove she does know the course material. Again, when she receives low exam marks, she does not understand, as she feels she cannot possibly learn and reproduce more facts than she has already. No feedback is given to her about her exam performance other than the mark, and she has not got a copy of her exam essays to ask anybody else for guidance. Many students on Sonya's course have also done badly. The course tutors are worried about retention. They wonder if they are recruiting too many students with children and financial worries as so many are struggling.

A learning development model

A developmental model of learning enhancement argues that all students, indeed all people, have ongoing learning development needs: we can all improve our learning. If all students have study needs, it is more beneficial to adopt a developmental model of learning where additional support, skills modules or peer support are part of a multifaceted and integrated approach rather than its focus. Indeed, the diversity and range of student need is such that it is not sufficient to locate study support solely in any one mode of support. Learning enhancement needs to be built into the ethos and structures of the university, and especially into everyday teaching. As this may, at present, be contrary to students' understanding of learning and teaching, a culture of mutual responsibility for learning needs to be established even from the earliest point of contact with the student. A radical shift is required in thinking about what university teaching is about – and, from the students' perspective, what they think is 'learning'. An alternative model of what Sonya could have been offered as 'support' is suggested below.

Case outline of a learning development approach

Sonya's department realises that in each intake there are a number of students with

gaps in their education. They are also concerned about how to raise the standard of the study of all the students in the intake. A tutor from the course visits local schools and Access courses, to talk about the kinds of expectations they have of students. All students are interviewed, and information is given about a range of bridging courses run by the university during the summer to help orientate students to HE study. These courses are aimed especially at Access students and those coming directly from employment; they address English, writing and numeracy. There are also intensive English classes and orientation events provided for those, like Junko, arriving from overseas.

The bridging course gives Sonya more practice in writing and in reading texts at speed. This is extended by the Professional Skills module which the department offers as a first-year option. This uses course content to explore relevant skills in more detail. Overseas students have the option of continuing intensive English as a module, and home students an English Awareness module, accredited in similar ways to modern languages options. The English Awareness module is structured so that it suits students whether or not they are dyslexic, although some students, like Kiran, need additional language or dyslexia support. Sonya's course has been restructured so that all students are encouraged to take these two skills options. There is also an IT module. Sonya, Nils, Jason, Louise and Rahel have almost all their support needs met in this way. Although Elaine needs to spend one or two sessions with her tutor going over certain aspects of her work on an individual basis, she is less resentful about this as support is part of the ethos of the department. The tutor is also less resentful as fewer demands are being made on her time to support all the students in the department: her work has become more manageable.

Although this means that almost half of

the first-year curriculum is skills-orientated in some way, tutors find that students are better placed to progress with the rest of the course. The Professional Skills option Sonya has been guided to has been designed for a cluster of courses that follow similar teaching and assessment strategies. All students are required to take one module which has been designated as a 'Personal and Professional Development (PPD) Module'. In year one, those who are assessed in induction as needing a great deal of support, are advised to take additional support-related or PPD modules (usually from a menu of options such as Language in Context, Communication, Project Management, Learning to Learn, Academic Writing, Research Methods using IT), all of which have theoretical and discipline-specific content, so they are experienced as academic courses.

Sonya is taught to recognise the strengths of her study approaches and, through structured small-group group work and training in self-evaluation, reflection and problem solving, develops strategies through working with other students. She is also given a practice run for exams and feedback on her answer by both the tutor and her support group. Since the development of its varied PPD modules, the department runs a four-year option so that those with big gaps in their education can take their degree as a four-year course and follow an intensive PPD pathway through their course. At the end of the module, Sonya's seminar group is introduced to a 'mentor' from the year above, who will help it to continue mutual support work. The mentor, in turn, is trained and supported by tutors in the department, and given credit for the mentoring. The mentor is another resource for identifying students who may be struggling; mentors guide such students to the tutor with overall responsibility for learning support, so that the appropriate person can offer them additional support.

On Sonya's course, an expert has been bought in to teach the language modules. Given the short time students have to improve their English, departmental staff have liaised with the tutor to identify priorities for support. The expert has helped the tutors to identify language patterns, vocabulary and learning styles specific to the course and which it would help all students to recognise. Common mistakes are also identified. Lecturers use the course handbook to back up the language support work. For example, Sonya has been provided with a glossary of specialised vocabulary, and terms which students often confuse have been embedded into sentences so that it is clear how they should be used. Sonya's lecturers help by drawing attention to terms that often confuse students, repeating them so they are clearly heard, writing them on the board and reminding students that the word or phrase is in their course handbook. The language expert has also recommended that the students are given a list of a hundred words that are often mis-spelt, broken down into syllables, in order to encourage more accurate spelling. On the Language Awareness unit, Sonya is guided on how to devise her own spelling strategies and as she responds well to these, additional support is not required.

Sonya's department provides subject-specific materials to all the 'skills' tutors, so that all skills-related modules can be used to introduce course material, and are orientated to the needs of the students. For example, whenever Sonya is introduced to new writing styles, such as reports, case studies or new types of references, models are provided which she and her support group compare and mark and these are discussed as part of the session. The models are either annotated or the course tutor draws out the main features that gain or lose credit. At all times, every effort is made to ensure that Sonya and her peers have a mental schema and a rationale for what they are expected to produce. The marking criteria are clearly laid out and discussed.

Tutors provide assignment booklets which draw together the main theories and research, and guide students through the process of developing an assignment. All her tutors annotate their reading lists, so that it is clear exactly where in the book the essential information is, which texts are reasonable alternatives for key texts not available in the library, which reading is desirable rather than essential, and which is for the interested student wanting to pursue an aspect of the subject further.

At every stage, from induction to assessment, the way the course is delivered helps Sonya to orientate herself, to have practice and feedback before she hands work in for grading, so that she has a reasonable chance of success. This makes a great difference to the way she manages the course and her chances of being retained on it. In this way, costly individual support is reduced and reserved for those who really need it, whilst all students are supported in their learning.

Key features of the learning development model

The key features of this developmental approach to skills and learning enhancement are:

(1) All students can improve their learning. There is a positive and inclusive attitude of development for all students rather than a remedial notion of 'support' for a few.

(2) A holistic, on-going approach. 'Skills' are not regarded as discrete entities but are developed over time as part of a broader process of personal, academic and professional development. Students become increasingly responsible for their learning within an environment of constructive feedback and guidance.

(3) Student-focused delivery. Teaching contexts adapt to learner intakes, taking consideration of the demands which the institution places upon students.

(4) Dispersed responsibility. Learning development and skills enhancement are the responsibility of all teaching staff, although there will be different scales of involvement.

(1) All students can improve their learning

A developmental model benefits all students. An atmosphere which encourages all students to analyse and reflect upon their learning is key to improved learning and long-term skills development. These are essential to academic progress and employability. In such a context, it is easier for those in most need of support to accept it. A learning development model is forward-looking and positive rather than emphasising deficit and past failure. We do not reach a pinnacle of accomplishment in how we learn: there is always room to develop our learning further along different spectra. For example, even if we are skilled learners, we can make improvements in:

- **Attitude**
  Improving our confidence; clarifying motivation and purpose; motivating ourselves in difficult times; recognising how we frame study difficulties and being able to re-frame them where appropriate; increasing our level of responsibility for our own learning; managing stress and emotional states in relation to our learning; developing our ability to see opportunities for learning and to greet challenges as occasions for learning; willingness to go into areas where we might fail and to redefine what we mean by success or failure; coping with our own definitions of failure as well as our successes; knowing how to push beyond our perceived limitations.

- **Strategy**
  Improving speed and efficiency; selecting the best strategy for the task in hand; having a wider range of strategies to chose from; building practice through applying different strategies.

- **Flexibility**
  Being able to learn more easily in a wider

range of contexts; being able to learn with different kinds of people, including those with learning styles different to our own; being able to study alone, in pairs, in small groups, in teams; studying under pressure and without pressure, in non-ideal circumstances; changing task quickly if circumstances require.

• **Thinking skills**
   Improving our problem-solving ability; the aptness of what we select to read or use as examples; our ability to make what we know user-friendly to those who know less than we do about the subject; developing analogies and metaphors; being able to generate ideas; our ability to deduce and infer; in making links more easily and speedily between increasingly disparate subject matter; in our ability to recognise underlying common problem structures.

• **Awareness**
   Our ability to find meaning and to recognise significance; the depth and range of our understanding; our ability to sit with ignorance, paradox and confusion; our meta-awareness of ourselves as learners.

(2) Holistic developmental approach

In this model, 'skills' development is regarded as part of a broader process of personal, academic and professional development. Students have responsibilities for their learning within a supportive environment and are trained, where necessary, to develop personal and group responsibility.

A positive and supportive environment does not necessarily mean one that spoon-feeds students and certainly does not preclude challenges and problem solving. If institutions want students to feel safe about risk taking and admitting difficulties and ignorance, which are threatening activities for most people, then students need to feel there is a benefit and not a penalty attached to doing so. Reflection, problem solving, risk taking and professional development need to be built into the learning culture

and rewarded through assessment and grading. In turn, students need to be trained from the outset to take responsibility, including prior preparation for teaching sessions, rather than being reliant on tutors to frame their thinking in advance of their own reflection. It cannot be assumed that they will develop this sense of responsibility, and shift from a school-based sense of 'teachers are and should be in control', without guidance.

(3) Student-focused delivery: teaching contexts adapt to learner intakes

The model places less stress on 'at risk' students and places more on 'at risk' matches between student intake and course provision. Learning is facilitated when there is an adequate match between:

• the current learning position of the learner (experiences, knowledge, skills, abilities, practice, habits, emotions, patterns of responses, learning preferences and styles);

and

• elements of the learning context which are significant for that learner (institutional or course culture and ethos; course level; pace; teaching methods; teacher attitudes; assessment modes and timing; expectations of the student).

There does not need to be a perfect fit between course and student, but there does need to be a meeting and attunement of expectations and demands, and in such a way that students feel both emotionally contained and intellectually challenged, within parameters that they find 'safe enough'. In such a context the student will be able to take the risks that are needed to advance learning, such as asking questions which might make them look foolish but to which they need answers and, especially, taking the difficult step of exposing their ideas or coursework to the view of others. When students do not feel safe enough, they find it difficult to begin assignments, even more difficult to submit them and very difficult to admit that they have problems for which they need help.

If the course cannot be flexible in meeting the diverse learning needs of its students, then a percentage will reach their stress threshold and leave. Others will blame either themselves or the course for the mismatch and leave. As students respond very individually to different methods of teaching and bring very different learning styles, courses which want to keep students may need to be more flexible in the range of ways in which they present material and assess learning.

(4) Dispersed responsibility

The model advocates an ethos of learning enhancement in all aspects of teaching and learning with maximum integration of skills development into subject-specific teaching. If a discrete study skills unit is offered, this should be delivered within the subject, using course-specific materials and approaches, and the relevance of the skills to the subject made explicit. The 'skills' module, however designated, would be linked to the practices and requirements of the course or module, and its outcomes would be reinforced by the everyday teaching in the department. In other words, there would be liaison between those teaching the study skills module and those offering other forms of teaching for that subject area or discipline or programme. Lecturers would be modelling and giving opportunities to reinforce learning, and identifying areas that needed greater attention in the dedicated module or for additional taught sessions.

A tiered system of support which extends from the student through the department to specialist services and to the overarching institutional structures, policies and ethos can reduce the pressure on lecturers to meet all the needs of their learners on an individual basis. The demands made upon individual lecturers outside of teaching time by students who struggle with the system could be reduced. Support offered at one level alone is not usually sufficient for the more varied intakes of the widening access context. This is developed in more

detail in the next section. These features are familiar to many who work in the learning development field: see, for example, Hurley (1994).

Location of support: dispersed responsibility for skills and learning enhancement

(1) Over-arching ethos and culture

Ideally, the institutional and departmental culture should encourage and promote the professional and academic approaches which it wishes its students to develop. Structures, policy and everyday practice should reinforce the desired outcomes for student learning. For example, the degree structure should enable flexibility in the modes of assessment that can be offered and in the timing of assessment so that students new to the modes of assessment used on the course have time to develop expertise. Students should be inducted into, and helped to orientate towards, the culture of both higher education and of their course of study. The learning environment should offer both safety in admitting difficulties and a constructive attitude towards personal and group responsibility and problem solving. Staff training is needed to assist lecturers to be proficient in teaching, modelling and reinforcing the personal, academic and professional development of students, within the context of their own subject specialism.

Institutional responsibility

Institutions can set the tone of the students' experience by taking a positive learning approach. This does not mean that the institution needs to lay down exactly what students are required to study in each department. On the contrary, each subject area has its particular learning requirements, so an across-the-board solution, such as compulsory units, is not necessarily the best route to take. Indeed, skills development, devoid of context, can seem very irrelevant and dull. The more study and language skills are orientated to the particular subjects being studied, the more meaningful they are and the more they are likely to be of effect. Where students can select from an open menu of options, there are difficulties in developing relevant study skills, unless each unit is designed to maximise learning development and to meet the complex needs of students moving from one set of conventions to another. This is described in more detail, with respect to writing, in Chapter 6. None the less, although there must be flexibility so that departments can deliver skills in the way that best suits their subjects and their student intakes, it is important that this is supported and monitored at an institutional level.

Institutions need to ensure that there is some mechanism for guaranteeing that departments are addressing the learning needs of their students. For example, departments should be able to demonstrate how learning needs are identified, depending on the intake and the subject, and be able to offer a rationale for the support they offer on the basis of the needs identified. There are various ways that institutions could do this such as at validation and through subject reviews. Courses could also be required to demonstrate, at validation, how they meet SEEC descriptors, or a similar set of descriptors devised by the institution (see Appendix 2).

The structure and design of the degree programme is another area where institution-level planning impacts upon the support a student receives, and in what is permissible for departments to offer when designing support packages for very needy students. For example, the institution could require that each department designate a number of options as 'Skills' or 'Personal Professional Development' (PPD) modules, where a more in-depth approach to skills development is undertaken. Each first-year student could be required to take a minimum of one such module; a maximum number of how many such modules could be taken could be set by the institution. Universities could consider offering three- and four-year routes to a degree to enable weaker students to develop their skills, with a menu of PPD modules to build their

learning development as they moved through the university.

The change in emphasis from subject-centred teaching to include, especially in the first year, a skills and learning development emphasis, has implications for staffing, staff development, IT systems and funding. Some assistive technologies for students with disabilities, for example, can be networked, so as to increase ease of access. These technologies can sometimes be of use to a wide range of students without recognised disabilities. For example, software that enables dyslexic students to organise writing on-screen or proofread through hearing their work or spellings read aloud (using headsets) would also benefit a wide range of other students. To be most effective and economical, these technologies require updating, maintenance, training and advertising at a university-wide level.

With the rise of students with disabilities in HE, there is a need for a co-ordinated, institutional approach to assessment arrangements for an increasing number of students who cannot be assessed by conventional means, and whose learning is dependent on either IT or specific media.

(2) Curriculum

Wherever possible, personal, professional and academic development modules should be provided as part of the curriculum in order to contextualise skills and careers development at each level. Completely 'generic' skills modules are best avoided as, in effect, they require students to work from the 'abstract' towards the 'concrete', whereas concrete, embedded training is needed in order to help students abstract generic skills. These developmental modules could be kite-marked, perhaps as PPD modules. For example, all students could be required to take one 'PPD' module at each level. Such modules should refer to and incorporate the content, teaching styles, skills, assessment procedures and other features of the subject discipline or department. They need to use subject discipline materials and examples in order to make the skills relevant and concrete. Ideally, such units would be led by subject area staff with a 'skills' interest and training or skills specialists with an interest or training in the requirements of the subject area. Where courses opt for a fully integrated approach to skills development at any level, they could identify PPD module options which help students to draw together the skills and learning they have acquired over the year. These modules integrate and help students to articulate the skills developed across all the modules they have taken.

Whether discrete units or fully integrated approaches are adopted, the relevance of the skills to the subject should be made explicit and care must be taken to ensure that students receive adequate training in all the modes of assessment to which they will be exposed. The link between skills and learning development and the student's overall professional, academic or personal development should be made explicit. Wherever possible, units should be presented (and named) in such a way as to appeal to adult professionals and academics rather than designated as 'study skills' units. For example, they may be called 'Professional Skills for Lawyers', 'Continuous Professional Development', 'Skills for Psychologists', 'Research Methods and Reflective Practice', 'Project Planning and Reflective Practice', etc.

Given the variety of intakes that different departments or subject areas attract, and the particular requirements of specific subject disciplines, departments may find a different balance of elements of support appropriate. The important aspects here are that:

- there is a good rationale for what is selected;
- the support is properly monitored;
- it addresses each area of the students' experience.

Departments could provide modules designated as 'PPD' or 'skills' modules at different levels of study. These may be optional or compulsory, depending on the demands of the subject area. Departments need to ensure that staff teaching such modules are trained to identify students with learning needs, to support these students

as appropriate, and to be well informed about back-up support services.

Contextual awareness and employability skills

If skills are to be developed in relation to specific subject areas, it is important that students are able to reinterpret these skills in terms of applicability or 'transferability' to other contexts, and able to articulate these to employers. Universities which draw undergraduates from socially and economically disadvantaged groups need to make special provision to ensure that their students are assisted both in finding employment to manage the costs of the course, and in negotiating a labour market which may be very unfamiliar and bewildering to them. Students often have a very poor grasp on what careers they can aim for or where their particular degree may take them. Their ambitions may be pitched unrealistically low for their talents, or unrealistically high for the level of the qualification they are taking.

Careers education can be structured into the curriculum. For example, a module on research methods can use careers materials as the source material. Alternatively, students can look at work from a sociological, cultural, anthropological, or health perspective, depending on their subject discipline, or research how their course subject matter is applied in work contexts. Such modules can build in personal reflection so that students can relate their own experiences and career aspirations to the world of work.

Graduates often have the skills that employers are looking for; they do not necessarily realise this nor have the skills to articulate their learning in ways that would enhance their career prospects. As students they may have learnt to juggle many tasks, manage their time well, work independently on projects, deal with crises, work with others, undertake problem solving, use IT, work quickly with data and many other skills that employers value. However, they may feel they have learnt only to write essays, pass exams, and learn facts. Students benefit from having an opportunity to draw together their learning, to make sense of it in terms of their personal, professional and academic development, and to be trained to articulate their learning for future academic or employment routes.

(3) Support integrated into teaching (SIT)

Skills units in themselves are not sufficient to bring students to the desired level of personal, professional and academic competence they need to succeed both at university and as future professionals. The 'skills' or PPD modules, however designated, need to be linked to the practices and requirements of the course or module, and its outcomes reinforced through everyday teaching in the department. In other words, there should be liaison between those teaching designated 'skills' or 'development' modules and those offering other forms of teaching for that subject area or programme. Difficulties which students encounter are often as much an issue of a mismatch between course teaching methods and students' understanding of, and practice in delivering to, course requirements as of skills deficits. All lecturers can play a role in modelling, reinforcing and creating opportunities for their students to develop their skills.

The lecturer, often the person who refers 'at risk' students for help, in a developmental model has an important role in reducing the need for outside referral. However, it is very difficult for an individual lecturer, in *isolation*, to introduce teaching and learning styles which promote learning, especially in courses with very diverse intakes. Students can mistakenly assume that the lecturer who goes against the grain with good practice is a 'bad' or 'lazy' lecturer, or they may become confused about what they are expected to do, and lose confidence in the subject. Those used to sitting and taking notes at full speed, and reproducing these for assignments, can be greatly threatened if a single lecturer suggests that there may be better ways to study. A department-wide or institution-wide approach is needed in order to support individual lecturers. The role of teaching staff is so central to the on-going integration

of skills over time that this is addressed in more detail in Chapter 5.

(4) Specific additional local support (SALS)

For some courses there may be a need to offer workshops or other taught sessions within the department or subject area to meet the identified needs of particular cohorts. This may be for additional work on a particular study or professional skill, such as studio skills, subject-related numeracy or language skills, group revision sessions, workshops for re-sits, or areas of difficult content.

Support for specific groups

Departments should provide a mechanism for identifying 'at risk' students as early as possible in their contact with the university, either at Admission, Open Days or Induction (see Chapter 4). It is important to make appropriate provision for those identified as soon as possible after the identification exercise and or refer them to preparatory courses or additional support, as applicable. Special attention may need to be given to those requiring English language, numeracy and disability provision. Once again, English, numeracy or IT provision should be tailored to the specific needs of the subject discipline as far as is possible. In addition, departments now need to ensure that the needs of students with disabilities (including dyslexia) are being met. The QAA Code of Practice on Disability (1999) stipulates that disability provision should be integrated into all areas of the student's experience; more is required than simply referring the student to specialist support services.

Peer support

To facilitate the support process, departments should consider offering training, assistance and structures for peer-based support or 'peer mentoring'. Some universities pay students to do this, and prefer an anonymous system of attendance, which can work well. Attendance can be much higher when peer support is organised by the department. For example, a survey conducted at UEL found rates of attendance for peer support led from outside the departmental structure (using Supplemental Instruction), met with little enthusiasm from students, despite high-quality peer training, course support, keen student peers, and manifest need. Attendance was less than 2 per cent of students and those who did attend made inappropriate demands on the student leaders. An alternative scheme, in the psychology department at UEL, was led by a member of the departmental staff, who trained the student mentors. Each student mentor, drawn from level 2 (Year 2), was allocated to a pre-existing seminar group of six students. These groups began as small seminar groups for the Skills for Psychologists module; the mentor was allocated to the seminar group before it came to an end, in order to ensure continuity. Attendance on this mentoring scheme has been approximately 85 per cent. Staff gave clear guidance and training to students, via the earlier skills sessions, on how to make best use of peer support. This scheme was taken much more seriously by students, as it was more closely identified with their overall learning programme.

Electronic support

Discussion fora in virtual learning environments offer an extra form of using student peers to enhance each other's learning. Lecturers using WebCT software in the USA, for example, have found that students who held back from expressing their opinion on controversial subjects in class, were 'heated and voluminous' when using electronic discussion groups where they could remain anonymous (Hird, quoted in Renery, 2000). Anne Hird, Assistant Professor in Technical and Middle Level Education at Rhode Island College, found 'These "faceless discussions" were the ideal forum for students to grapple with difficult ideas without the "What will they think of me if I say this?" stigma holding them back.' A Program Director at another college found that quieter students were 'now very freely posting their observations and opinions'. (Renery, 2000). Electronic media can also be used to set up quizzes and other activities which can give students instant feedback on their performance.

(5) Personal contact

Students need to feel that at least one academic within the institution is aware of who they are and can offer them guidance. This continuity is especially important on modular schemes, distance learning courses and on courses with large entries. It is helpful to students if they are allocated a named key contact or personal tutor or academic tutor when they are accepted at the university, and who stays as their main adviser as they progress from year to year. Records should be kept of all meetings to allow progression in guidance and continuity if staff are replaced. Students should meet personal tutors during induction week, if not earlier.

(6) Centrally provided additional support (CPAS)

This refers to specialist, non-departmentally based, staff who offer support to those who want confidential or very particular support. This would include part of the support for students with disabilities such as dyslexia; those with extreme study anxiety; individual or small-group language support; those who have unusual study difficulties that course staff could not be expected to manage alone; those who have undergone a recent trauma or for whom study brings back former life trauma.

CPAS support may include:

(1) Disabilities (including dyslexia): diagnostic assessment; Study Aids and Study Strategies Assessment (SASSA); specialist support such as signers, scribes, dyslexia-support tutors and personal assistants; recommendations for specialist IT and training in its use; guidance to subject staff on student requirements; amended assessment conditions; support in using the Libraries and Learning Resource Centres; guidance on presenting disability to employers and on work placement.

(2) English language: for students whose academic English is below that of the rest of their year.

(3) International student support: orientation; English as a Foreign Language.

CPAS support needs to be:

(1) based on an early assessment of the needs of the cohort;
(2) offered in close liaison with teaching staff;
(3) tailored to the needs of the programme of study as far as is possible;
(4) supported by a good referral system from the departments to central services. Self-referral opportunities are also needed.

(7) Integration: 'closing the loop'

Liaison between all these elements is key to success. For example, lecturers need to identify areas of difficulty for their students and advise those leading dedicated modules or specialist support where to focus attention. In turn, those leading skills modules need to note patterns of difficulties which emerge and advise the relevant teaching staff.

Integration includes:

(1) liaison between the different tiers and clear routes from one to another where necessary;
(2) procedures to monitor the effectiveness of support;
(3) meetings between central services and course designers;
(4) screenings and other procedures to identify 'at risk' students;
(5) referral systems for additional support (CPAS or SALS);
(6) support offered in mutual collaboration between different providers and teaching staff;
(7) staff development.

The type and level of support should meet the requirements of the intake. Some intakes will require significant additional support for language and numeracy; others may not. The emphasis is on integrating support to the maximum extent possible in order to ensure relevance and ease of access. The range of support should be appropriate for the whole intake and accredited as part of the curriculum wherever possible.

Embedding support into systems and procedures

The section below tracks some of the stages a student is likely to pass through or experience during their time at university. Each stage represents an area where an 'at risk' undergraduate might be created. Suggestions are offered as to how that stage might be used to support the student's learning, primarily using supportive environment (learning development) approaches rather than remedial ones.

Admissions issues

Level of 'preparedness'

A key issue is finding an appropriate match between the entrant's readiness for a particular course and the level of preparedness required for that course. This means that courses need to be very clear about what they require and be able to convey this to applicants and to feeder courses.

Some of the difficulties students encounter on their degree course can be traced back to Admissions and earlier. Although some students without traditional qualifications fare as well as those with them, many people apply to university before they are ready for HE study. Sometimes, this is because they must apply to university through UCAS only a few weeks after they have begun preparatory courses, when it is not yet clear how they will fare over the year. Some of these students really need two years of preparation or more, but most available courses are of only 9–10 months length. This is not necessarily sufficient to make up for years of missed education.

Some students entering HE report that they were effectively absent from school, because of truancy or non-attention, from the age of 10 or 12. However bright they may be, the skills and knowledge gap is generally too great for them to make up in only a few months. Unfortunately, the students may hide this history prior to entry as they want to get through the degree process quickly for financial reasons: more than one year of preparation does not appeal. Once the student has been accepted, they expect the university to help them to make up the deficit: 'They accepted me. They are the professionals. Now it's their job to get me through.'

Moreover, Access courses, although they may take adults returning to study a long way in a very short time, do not necessarily prepare students for the learning environment they may encounter in HE. Students used to classes of 12–20 students can find it a great shock when they are merely one of 300 students in a lecture theatre. They may be used to asking questions whenever they do not understand, and this may not be possible in the larger teaching contexts of HE. They may have had access to a wide range of support tutors to help them put their assignments together. Although this meant they completed their assignments, they may not ever have completed an assignment without intense support. Students entering HE from college may expect a much higher level of individual support than HEs are used to providing.

Spell out requirements

It is not an easy matter to decide which students are ready for HE and which are not unless students are interviewed and the differences between FE and HE discussed. Admissions tutors need to be specific about how much independent learning the student is expected to do and how much support is available. They need to be aware that if they say 'we have study skills support', the student may interpret this to mean they are being promised limitless support and may be very angry or depressed later when this turns out to be very different from the intense, prolonged, personalised support they have received in school or college. Students from non-traditional HE backgrounds tend to make

severe underestimations of the reading, writing and time demands of HE and have little understanding of what is meant by 'independent study' or 'responsibility for your own learning'. Staff and course literature need to be clear and explicit about:

(1) how many hours, in total, the student needs to put aside each week for study;
(2) the demands of the course in terms of writing, reading, numeracy, time commitments, and independent study, field trips and placements which may require unusual hours;
(3) the kind of support available on-course – and what is *not* available;
(4) who is entitled to which specialist support and how to access this – and what is *not* available.

Pre-admission testing and support

It is useful to undertake some kind of baseline testing prior to Admission so as to identify 'at risk' students as early as possible. This is not simply a question of English or numeracy testing but of general orientation to the subject discipline. Some courses ask students to complete quizzes to see how much general knowledge they have about the area, or give them case studies to work on to see how well they think in the manner required by the course. Testing should be clearly linked to later on-course support. If possible, introduce the support tutors and talk through what you feel are the benefits of additional skills support. It is important to do this as otherwise students may resent the extra time they are asked to spend on skills development and do all they can to sabotage it.

Brief basic reading lists can help prospective students to develop the knowledge base for the subject. This should be limited to a few accessible texts. Ideally, refer students to chapters or sections of books rather than to whole books. If the books are too long, difficult or dull, they will be off-putting at this stage. To help prospective students to structure their reading and their developing knowledge base, it is helpful to offer exercises which they could mark themselves. Present the reading and exercises as optional work which you strongly encourage as it will make their life easier once the term begins, rather than giving them the impression that they should not come back if they have not done it. Make it clear how this advance preparation may be useful when the course starts.

In some cases, the student may need to be directed to bridging courses or to more in-depth preparatory courses. It may also be useful to offer introductory 'taster' days where the student is orientated to the learning required on the course and the nature of the subject matter. More and more courses are developing their own foundation year, or extended degree programme to prepare applicants for HE.

Course description

Applicants often misinterpret information about what courses entail. For example, they may expect technology, art, health, or computer courses to be completely practical or studio-based, and be very shocked to find that there are heavy reading and writing loads for some of these. Alternatively, they may underestimate the amount of practical work and make their choice either way on that basis. For some students, key factors in making a choice are:

(1) how far the course is practical or theoretical – many wrong course decisions are made because of misunderstandings here;
(2) the hours: especially if they have paid employment or child care to arrange;
(3) whether there are work placements or field trips – and the timing of these;
(4) what exactly is covered in terms of content;
(5) the teaching and learning methods used on course;
(6) how they will be assessed (especially whether there are exams).

A sense of belonging

After school and college, university can seem very unsettling. This is especially so on modular courses and subjects with large student entries where students can feel they are merely an anonymous face in the crowd. Mature students,

while managing their outside lives effectively, can find themselves completely daunted at entering large lecture halls where they feel everyone else is cleverer than they are; some students say they find even the refectories intimidating. Students with wider commitments may not spend much time on campus between taught sessions, and many mature students do not find the life of the bar and Student Union as appealing as do younger students.

With a much greater proportion of the student body working or responsible for dependants, there are far fewer opportunities for socialising than traditional students experienced. Indeed, for many students, their main contact with other students is in taught sessions. If these are primarily passive note-taking sessions, then students may not speak to anybody on campus. The first few weeks can seem particularly lonely, isolating and overwhelming, making it difficult to focus on learning. It is worth universities helping students to build a sense of belonging, even of loyalty, to the institution they have joined. Some ways that this could be approached are:

(1) Introduction or taster days: students meet each other and some staff before term begins. Provide activities where entrants can talk with each other. Encourage them to meet up and form networks before the course begins.
(2) Group identity. Build peer group identity, especially at induction and the start of the new academic year (names/photos; 'icebreakers'; sharing anxieties, experience and histories; constructive group behaviours; ground-rule setting, group tasks or projects; social activities, all build towards support groups). See Chapter 10.
(3) Course-long tutoring: offer students at least one tutor who will be a contact for them for the length of their course of studies. These are sometimes called personal, 'moral' or academic tutors. This offers continuity and gives students a sense that someone knows who they are and is watching out for them. Many students have commented that what has kept them going through difficult times

during their education was a sense that there was at least one teacher or lecturer who had faith in them and 'rooted' for them.

(4) Structured group activities: teaching strategies that require students to engage in brief discussions in pairs, small groups and teams help to build links with other students.

(5) Actively assist students to form support groups and e-mail networks.

(6) Emphasise what they are offered by the institution/course which is distinct from elsewhere.

Documentation

Induction guide

It is worth sending students well-produced induction guides in advance of the course, with key information about the course, HE in general and the institution. These may contain maps, the year calendar, an explanation of terminology, reading lists, activities, contact names and addresses as well as the induction programme and guidance on what to do during induction week. This can help clarify expectations, begin to orientate the student to the course culture, and can also serve as a marketing document.

The course handbook

The course handbook is they key document for orientating students to the course and HE. Students can be expected to make substantial use of it so it needs to be quite sturdy and to have clear contents pages and heading structures. An appealing course handbook helps students to value the course. It is such a key document that it is worth taking time to go through it carefully with students. Some students may assume that they do not need to read it until they are specifically told to, and may not discover for themselves that assignment outlines and deadlines are clearly laid out in it unless this is pointed out. Once students realise that the course handbook can be used as a support document, it can give them a great deal of reassurance. The handbook can be a useful tool for outlining mutual responsibilities and expectations. If a learning contract is used, this could be a photocopiable sheet provided through the handbook.

It is helpful if the course handbook details the names, rooms, extensions and e-mails of lecturers, as well as dates for exams, titles and deadlines for assignments, information about how to approach assignments, clear criteria about how the work will be marked, annotated examples of what is expected, annotated reading lists, a glossary of terms and, where necessary, some of the terms written into sentences so their use is clear. It is also an opportunity to offer guidance on how to manage the option or unit most effectively although some courses provide this as separate booklets for each unit or assignment. Make it clear which course staff should be contacted in case of difficulty and how to access this support

For each unit, option or subject, be explicit about :

(1) the content – the knowledge base that students have to cover;

(2) the learning outcomes and how these link to skills development and assessment;

(3) methods of delivery – teaching and learning strategies;

(4) what is expected of the student;

(5) how many essays, presentations, reports, practicals, will be required, etc.;

(6) when work has to be handed in;

(7) how deadlines operate;

(8) how learning outcomes are assessed and the marking criteria for assignments;

(9) procedures for what to do if a staff member is absent.

Induction and orientation

Induction can be key to many aspects of the student's experience, especially in the new contexts in which universities are operating. Chapter 4 focuses on this in more detail and looks in particular at how to orientate students to HE culture and identify students who may be considered to be 'at risk' for various reasons.

Curriculum

Bridging the gap

One of the main reasons why students may be considered to be 'at risk' is that there is a mismatch between the level of skill, knowledge and performance expected at the beginning of the course and the student's current level in these areas. There is a traditional notion of what undergraduates ought to be able to do at entry, and an increasingly large number of students who, for a variety of reasons, do not match the expected profile. It was mentioned above that courses need to be very clear about what they require and to be able to convey this to applicants and to feeder courses.

However, as many students are not going to meet the desired profile, what is then to be done? As universities take on students who do not meet the traditional profile, it is important that they address this difference. On the one hand, this means being able to draw out, in a positive way, the different skills, aptitudes and experiences of their intake and to train students to apply their experiences in an academic context. This may have implications for the curriculum. It also means, in many cases, providing opportunities for students to bridge the gap. This means that universities have to provide for students so as to bring them up to the required level. Increasingly, and especially since they began to pay towards their degrees, students expect courses to provide support for their learning. This has a cost and so needs to be included in institutional budgets and the overall cost of delivering a course. In some cases, what is needed is simply a set of extra taught sessions for a small number of students, focused either on the knowledge base of the course or on study skills. In other cases, it may mean providing additional classes in English or numeracy.

However, when a sizeable proportion of the expected cohort is likely to experience difficulty performing at the desired level, the requirement gap becomes a curriculum issue. When students struggle with their course work, it typically takes them longer to complete their work and they find it much more difficult to find the time to do anything else. Those with very busy sched-ules can experience study difficulties because of not having enough time to devote to it. Many students are both struggling and busy. It is difficult for such students to find time to address study difficulties or to 'catch up' on missed education in addition to taking a taught course. The amount of work some students need to do to develop to the appropriate level is too much to expect in addition to traditional degree work. In an era of widening access and multiple points of entry, it is becoming commonplace in the sector to find whole intakes who are unprepared for HE. Indeed, it might be argued that the gap between traditional levels of preparedness and current levels of applicants has created a widespread curriculum issue.

Changing curriculum emphasis

One way in which this is addressed is using the first year as a way of training all students in more reflective, skills-based practice. This would probably have been useful for traditional students in the past, as many were unaware of their underlying skills and of how these might be applicable in different contexts. Indeed, many traditional curricula merely reinforce the same skills over and over (especially reading at speed, note-taking, and essay writing) without looking at the broader range of skills that could be developed through a carefully constructed curriculum. For example, a history or politics student might have taken modules or subject specialisms, all of which required attendance at lectures, note-taking, and reading, building towards essays and exams. A more structured curriculum with an eye on skills development and employability might have required students to take a range of modules that included use of statistics packages, analysing numerical data, interviewing skills, oral presentation, group projects, writing historical information for different audiences, use of multi-media, and interdisciplinary approaches.

A skills-sensitive curriculum does not necessarily mean that the student has a poorer educational experience, as some now fear. On the contrary, it is more likely to mean that students leave university with a much wider range of ways of making information meaningful and a greater sense of their own capabilities. However, it may mean that the breadth of factual or specifically subject-based material cannot be covered in the same time. As the knowledge base for all subjects increases, choices have to be made about what will or will not be included in a three-year programme.

For example, some medical courses now require additional skills from trainee doctors, such as improved interpersonal skills. This may be delivered though role play and drama workshops. In addition, trainee doctors have to select options for clinical rotations, and if they take a rotation in a new area such as complementary medicine, something else has to go. This represents a culture shift: instead of courses, and especially professional bodies, stating that students have to cover a prescribed list of topics, the emphasis in the future will be on students being trained to access and make use of a wide range of information and techniques for a variety of settings. The only alternative is to increase the length of courses. There is a limit to how much students can learn and also develop themselves as learners and future professionals within the traditional time frame.

Course structures and arrangements

A certain number of key factors can make a great difference to students. In particular, students choose to attend traditional universities rather than take distance learning courses because they want direct contact with tutors. Personal contact with tutors is highly prized by students, so structures which permit at least some direct contact each term or semester are needed. This is especially important where students need guidance on making sensible unit choices, or where there is a need to monitor progress over time. Courses could consider:

(1) providing individual or small-group contact with tutors, such as with 'personal' tutors;
(2) allocating one tutor to follow the student throughout their degree course;
(3) offering curriculum-based support, as described above (skills modules or personal,

professional and academic development approach);
(4) offering additional support to meet specific needs – e.g. revision groups, English support, feedback on assignments, support sessions on topics that students find particularly difficult;
(5) offering training, assistance and structures for peer-based support;
(6) allocating a staff member with responsibility for identifying 'at risk' students for additional support or guidance;
(7) allocating a departmental or subject-based contact for students with disabilities.

Assessment

Examinations

If an institution had to choose only one place to focus on increasing support for its students, then the area of assessment would be a good place to start. Traditionally, universities selected applicants who were the best at timed, closed answer testing – that is, at exams. Those who did not do well at such assessments tended not to be regarded as suitable candidates for HE: they were often considered as not 'bright' enough. As entry to sixth form was also by timed examination ('O' level or GCSE), usually in writing, those who had difficulties with exams rarely proceeded to post-16 education. The majority of people have poor examination histories. With a push to widening participation, those with a history of moderate exam success or even past failure are being recruited into HE. Their entrance route is often by courses that do not set exams. Once in HE, they are suddenly expected, once more, to be able to pass exams, and this can lead to a feeling that they are being set up to fail.

The kinds of difficulties students have with exams are very wide-ranging. For some it is a question of confidence: their fear of failing again immobilises them even during revision. For others it is a question of stepping into the unknown: they may never have sat an exam. For some it is a return to an area of failure: their marks may always have been poor and they may not have any idea how to improve their performance. Even those who were successful in the past may not have had recent practice, or may feel pressurised to perform, or, if they are older students, worry that their memory or writing have deteriorated.

Poor or erroneous ideas of how to prepare for and sit exams abound: the worst of these is for students to insist on learning pre-written answers by rote and reproducing these in the exam, irrespective of the exact question. Some download essays from the internet and rote-learn these for the exam. Many students believe that they are incapable of writing in their own words without books to prompt them. Others have poor revision and memory strategies, or find it difficult to organise information at speed in order to write. Students entering from work tend to have much slower writing speeds. Those used to working on a computer worry that spelling and grammar will let them down in exams – and they may have atrophied handwriting ability. Emotional anxiety and downright terror mean that students may find it difficult to learn when revising and may not be able to recall information under exam conditions. Other students read 'globally' and find the context-free, word-by-word reading required for exam questions to be very difficult: they tend to guess at the questions from key words.

It is not inevitable that those who failed at exams in the past will do so again. However, some students will never achieve as well through timed examinations; others will simply avoid units that set exams. There are several ways that universities can help.

Alternatives to examinations

Alternatives to exams include coursework, dissertations, oral presentations, portfolio, practical or studio work, projects, demonstrations, creating a product for a market, practical work, work placement, residencies, case studies, producing a leaflet or booklet, producing information for different audiences including through video, film, or mixed media.

Training for assessment

Through teaching practices

Build towards exam assessment throughout the term, by making explicit reference to it. Give guidance on the types of questions that may come up associated with a series of lecturers you are delivering and spend some time in sessions going quickly though past exam questions. Ask students what kinds of questions they can think of that might come up in an exam. Make reference to what they may or may not need to know in exams, for example: 'In an exam, you would/would not need to refer to this/do this.' Set short recapitulation exercises on your previous teaching session or on the set reading by asking groups to brainstorm ideas around exam titles. Offer mnemonics or set mnemonic-forming as a group activity. Indicate where students tend to lose marks and make suggestions about how to keep potentially confusable information clear and distinct

Trial runs

For each mode of assessment the student needs to be given training in how to meet the set requirements. In order to learn how to solve new problems, we usually need at least three attempts, with feedback on each. If students who have failed exams in the past do not get this practice, then they can be expected to underperform. As timed assignments may be regarded as threatening, it is worth introducing students to the idea of timed tasks in stages. 'Pub quiz' approaches can accustom students to revising information for rapid recall. Short problem-papers, marked by peers, can be especially motivating, helping students to anchor learning throughout the year and familiarising them with 'test' conditions. Timed quizzes, three-minute summaries of the previous lecture, one-minute plans and such tasks can accustom students to thinking and writing at speed. Students need to be reassured that these are training exercises and that some may find them difficult. Encourage those who find them particularly difficult to talk this through with you: it may be a sign of panic or of a specific learning difficulty (or other disability) that needs to be addressed before the exams arrive.

Early trial runs may seem extremely threatening, and need to be presented to students carefully in terms of their being training exercises and not ways of evaluating students towards their final degree. Students should be encouraged to set up timed mock answers of questions for themselves at home. It is very important that several past papers or examples of papers are available so students can practise reading and selecting questions at speed. Students who are not used to handwriting at speed need to practise to build up speed otherwise they develop muscle fatigue in exams. Student assessment could be based partly on timed questions which they have prepared in advance.

Going through exam papers

Although generic study skills sessions on revision and exam techniques can be useful, they are very helpfully supplemented by revision sessions of subject-specific material. Course staff can offer sessions where they run through exam papers and say, in brief, what the examiner is looking for in each question. This is invaluable, as exam failure is often linked to uncertainty about how to interpret exam questions and misjudging the level of detail required. Annotated examples provide a useful way of focusing discussion on the differences between a course-work answer and an exam answer on the same subject: students worry about how they can convert 2000-word answers into answers they must produce in less than an hour. Their solution may be inappropriate: they may opt to save time by omitting introductions, conclusions and argument, in order to fit in as many facts as they can.

Timing

In many universities, students with poor exam records are expected to sit their first set of exams only weeks after entering HE. This does not provide adequate time for them to settle in, and for their tutors to train them in how to approach exams; for them to have trial runs, build up writing speed, build up their confidence, to begin to develop a sense of exams as a 'habit'; and to revise the material all before the first exam. Moreover, students may be learning, simultaneously, how to cope with other types of assessment such as essays. These essays would require different writing strategies from those required for exams. This puts students under a lot of pressure. One solution is to use the first year to train students in the different modes of assessment, in the ways suggested above, so that they are better prepared for exams by the end-of-year assessment. The key is in the training, not simply in deferring the exams for failure later in the year.

Exam conditions

Many students from widening access backgrounds find it difficult to complete exam answers in the time required. Traditionally, students are required to sit exams for three hours. Strong students will often argue that the reason they did well is that they can write quickly and so can take risks in writing extra information. Even if this is not the case, writing speed boosts the confidence of some students and makes others over-anxious. Given the great variety in writing speeds in mixed intakes, as well as the longer times that it takes some students to recall and organise information, it is worth considering being more flexible about the conditions under which exams are set.

Students could, for example, be told that they are expected to finish in around three hours, but be given the choice of staying in the exam room for longer, such as up to four and a half hours. This would allow some students the chance of a brief break between questions. In order to discourage very long answers from strong students, a maximum word limit could be set, although with widening particpation entrants, short answers are more typical. If the idea is for students to show what they know, and we know that time constraints pressurise students, why not allow them longer to complete their answers if they choose? Where courses have good IT facilities, students could also be offered the option of completing their exams on computers, especially when this is their main method of writing outside of the exam room. This would have the added advantage of reducing the number of students requiring special conditions on the grounds of disability, as an increasing number could then be accommodated by the usual exam conditions.

Changes in the nature of what is examined
Although students often panic about not having sufficient time in an exam, many leave early as they are not able to recall what they know under examination conditions. Essay-based testing is particularly unhelpful to mature students, whilst multiple choice questions carry their own limitations in testing understanding of complex issues. There is room for more inventiveness in the use made of exam time. Some courses in architecture and engineering, for example, set problem-based practical exams, where students have the whole day to address a complex, unseen but familiar problem, calling upon all that they have learnt and with access to their notes and books. This reduces the premium on regurgitation and rote-learning. If they have not studied steadily throughout the year and become familiar with their notes, this exercise is difficult. This kind of assessment can make 'more sense' to students as they can demonstrate what they have learnt more easily, especially if they are not strong writers. The scale of the problem set can ensure that sufficient breadth is covered by students so that they meet requirements of professional bodies.

Similar approaches could be taken by other subjects. Most vocational courses could set extended problems which tested for understanding rather than regurgitation. Even traditional courses such as history could offer documents for commentary and contextualisation rather than essay writing, or set hypothetical situations for students to argue in ways that show their awareness of historical issues and methodologies rather than more factual information.

Coursework
Students who wrote well at school were often those considered to be bright. How well you express yourself in writing is often taken as the hallmark of intelligence. Many of those now entering HE have poor writing histories. They may never have received good marks for written assignments. They may not have written so much as a letter between leaving school and starting on an Access or other preparatory

course. Alternatively, they may be accustomed to writing in very different styles from that required for the course: they may write technical articles, or documents where data but no explication or analysis is required. They may be story writers used to producing flowery narrative or local journalists used to writing in dramatic or factual ways. They may have a reputation for being a good writer that will be shattered once they receive comments for their first assignment. Support for writing and for exams is suggested in Chapters 6 and 8 and in Part II, Chapters 18–21 and 24. However, skills-based support is only one way in which students can be supported with assessment.

Again, students present with a myriad of reasons for why coursework may be problematic. A general lack of experience in academic writing may be at issue: lack of skills, knowledge, awareness, practice all play their part. For some students, the issue is a fear of new tasks: 'research' can sound frightening. If the task is framed differently, the student may realise that they do have the skills needed. Perfectionism of one kind or another also is common. Students tend to over-inflate task requirements, regarding them as things which only a genius could do; they may have only a poor sense of how to break assignments down into more manageable sub-tasks. They may be overwhelmed by the amount, especially if they do not have a sense of how much paper 2000 words actually covers.

Difficulties with time or timing feature largely. Poor time management is common, especially in planning for deadlines. In this respect, procrastination over starting is a major cause of problems. Students may have very poor strategies for beginning work and may sit for hours in front of blank paper or rewrite the first paragraph over and over. On modular courses, there may be an unmanageable 'bunching' of assignment deadlines: if time management skills are weak, this means that some of the assignments will be late. If a time penalty is allocated, this may be all that is needed to bring a struggling student down from a low mark to a fail. Some students know that lecturers give a good summary of what is required the week before an assignment is due in: they may rely on this and wait until the lecturer has delivered the summary before beginning work. If this is coupled with bunched deadlines, the student is likely to fail. Students can be assisted in managing coursework by a number of means, such as:

Clarification

(1) Check that students know what is meant by the assignment title and understand what is required.
(2) Suggest appropriate starting points.
(3) Go over the marking criteria.
(4) Encourage students to mark their own work using a marking criteria pro-forma (see pp. 239, 302, 321 below) so that their attention is drawn to the marking criteria.

Timing

Lecturers can help by setting short, straightforward assignments early in the term to build confidence. These can be used for diagnostic purposes and to ensure students get early feedback and guidance. Stagger assignment deadlines so that there is time for students to make full use of the feedback they are given on early assignments. Offer summaries of what is required at the point where the assignment is handed out, not the week before it is due in. Ideally, there should be liaison between tutors to avoid bunching deadlines where possible.

Offer some 'kick-starting' of assignments well in advance of deadlines, such as class discussion of major themes or book reviews of set reading. It can help to give a week-by-week time plan for early assignments and to remind students, in taught sessions or by e-mail, of where they should be in the process of completion. Encourage students to enter provisional 'deadlines' for different stages of an assignment into their diaries, so that they can see if they are roughly on target. Encourage them to see you or the appropriate member of staff at least 2 weeks before the deadline if they are panicking about completing it.

Clear criteria for assessment

Consider whether it is made explicit to students:

(1) how each unit or option or skill will be assessed;
(2) how each piece of work will be assessed;
(3) what are the marking criteria (clearly explained);
(4) how marking criteria link to learning outcomes;
(5) whether any peer or self-assessment will be included;
(6) what exactly is needed to achieve the highest grades.

Assignment booklets

Assignment booklets are useful ways of helping students to prepare for a particular piece of work. One advantage of having separate assignment booklets is that they can be updated more easily. Another advantage is that it allows more space for exploring issues, offering examples, and going into detail about requirements, without making the course handbook too unwieldy. It also helps students to locate assignment information more easily. Examples of what these might contain are given below.

Why use an assignment booklet?

(1) Students value the advice that lecturers give on how to approach an assignment, but may have poor skills at recording and remembering the advice after the taught session.
(2) It ensures that those who have to miss taught sessions are briefed clearly on the assignment.
(3) It is a useful tool for guiding students who are unsure of how to approach an assignment through its constituent stages.

Lecturers can use assignment booklets to:

Give an overview

(1) Offer an overview of the main topics and themes and bring out how these relate to each other.
(2) Summarise the main theories, approaches and schools of thought.
(3) Demonstrate ways that topics, themes and theories could be organised into tables or

charts which could help to clarify thinking and structure essay plans or revision.

Clarify methodology

(1) Offer a suggested time structure for approaching the assignment – this is especially useful for new students or for new types of assignment.
(2) Make suggestions for how long students need to spend on different sub-tasks of the assignment.
(3) Suggest ways of approaching the assignment: the order in which to read materials or undertake different steps in the process. This is especially useful for experimental work and case studies, but can be helpful for any written assignment.

Clarify marking criteria

(1) Identify the marking criteria.
(2) Relate the marking criteria to the learning outcomes for the course.
(3) Include an example of the marking sheet for students to complete and hand in.
(4) Offer annotated examples of 'good' and 'not so good' answers to similar questions, bringing out that good answers are not perfect, and making clear exactly where the weaker answers lost marks.

Student self-evaluation
Include a detachable form for students to evaluate their own work. Invite students to evaluate it according to:

(1) the marking criteria;
(2) learning outcomes;
(3) how they feel they could have improved the work or approached it differently.

Include one or two examples of what good self-evaluation would look like.

Reading lists
The assignment booklet can contain the reading list and guidance on other sources for the assignment. Break the reading lists down into:

(1) Essential reading – be explicit about sections or chapters that need to be read, and viable alternatives;

(2) desirable reading – with a brief description of what the text contains. Offer viable alternatives;
(3) wider reading for those who wish to go into more depth.

References

(1) Offer examples of how to reference any unusual sources for the subject.
(2) Refer the student to the departmental or subject area guidelines on referencing or to *The Study Skills Handbook*, pp. 122–5 (Cottrell, 1999).

Revision
Offer suggestions on how the assignment topic can be used as a basis for other revision topics.

The Open University has some good examples of booklets similar in some respects to the above, such as that by Stevens (1996) for social psychology, which offers a course overview, and the mini-booklets offered for assignments. Individual assignments may be presented in a separate booklet that guides the student step by step and provides resource materials for experimental work.

Tracking and monitoring

By the time students receive feedback and support for a module's work, they may have moved onto another module where different conventions apply. Moving between modules means it can be difficult to build progressively on support over the duration of the degree. Students may not gain a sense of their progress as their marks may remain stable over that time even though their performance relative to Level 1 work has improved. Encourage students to keep copies of feedback, along with ideas on their own goals, aspirations and learning style, in a portfolio which they bring to tutorial or specialist support. This facilitates progressive support built on previous guidance and in line with the student's own learning aims.

It can help to:

(1) train students in how to reflect on their own progress;
(2) train students in peer and self-evaluation;
(3) offer monitoring, evaluation and feedback prior to any formal assessment and grading;
(4) encourage students to keep a progress portfolio with a record of all feedback and advice they receive;
(5) provide a session at least once a term to go over feedback they have received from staff, to clarify their learning objectives, to monitor progress and draw out what they need to do to improve their performance.

Final comments

The chapter has outlined a number of ways that institutions, departments and individual approaches to teaching and learning can create a supportive learning environment. Although the model does not argue for the complete removal of additional support, it argues that much of what was traditionally addressed through additional support units could have been better addressed through different on-course strategies that would have obviated the need for referral. Indeed, widening participation means that what were often the needs of an isolated few have become mainstream and therefore need to be addressed through the curriculum. Widening participation has also meant that new types of need have been created, which tend to rise to the top of the priority list of hard-pressed support services. This is especially true of those with English language and disability requirements. These, too, have curriculum and whole-institution implications, but are more likely to be associated with demand for additional support, either locally within the departments or through specialist central services. The approaches outlined above mean that 'support' is more meaningful to students; it is incorporated into their general experience of the course, is concrete and relevant, and is easier to access for those who most need it. Moreover, the above framework argues for support in terms of a learning development model that can benefit all learners.

Skills framework checklist

Tracking skills development throughout the students' contact

Admissions

- Clarify the nature of the course and its demands
- Identify 'at risk' students where possible
- Offer introduction or 'taster' days
- Refer applicants to bridging or other preparatory courses where necessary
- Offer basic preparatory work such as guided reading and self-marking exercises

Induction

- Present skills development as an integral part of professional, academic and personal development
- Explain that the first year is regarded as a training and orientation year

Curriculum

- Deliver skills within the context of the subject curriculum and PPD
- Explain 'PPD' or that 'Skills' modules are identified or kite-marked
- Present skills positively in terms of personal, academic and professional development
- Ensure that courses specify learning outcomes and assessment criteria, such as through SEEC descriptors

Support integrated into teaching (SIT)

- Model desired skills and reinforce and integrate them through everyday teaching
- Offer some 'kick-starting' of assignments well in advance of deadlines
- Take care to ensure full access to the curriculum for all students
- Ensure staff refer, when teaching and marking, to study skills materials

Assessment mode and timing

- Offer alternatives to formal, essay-based examinations for at least part of the assessment
- Time formal assessment so students have time to practise and build the necessary skills
- Avoid bunching of assessment deadlines

Teaching to support assessment

- Build revision, mnemonics, and exam awareness into everyday teaching
- Give annotated examples of exam answers
- Set timed exercises, timed essays and mock exams to develop assessment skills

Feedback

- Time assessment deadlines so that there is room for students to make use of feedback
- Use clear marking criteria and offer readable feedback with respect to these

■ Link marking and feedback to learning outcomes
■ Use simple pro-forma for feedback which are easy to understand
■ Offer feedback both on content and on skills
■ Type any comments or write very clearly
■ Give clear guidance on how to improve marks for the next assignment

Monitoring and evaluation of progress

■ Monitor whether teaching and learning methods work for particular clusters of students
■ Monitor whether students are receiving consistent guidance from one unit to another
■ Encourage students to maintain a portfolio of learning aims, achievements and records of feedback
■ Train students in peer and self-evaluation
■ Train students in how to reflect on their own progress

Course structures and arrangements

■ Give support and training for peer-based support
■ Put in place key staff for identifying 'at risk' students and advising on support routes

Subject-specific additional local support (SALS)

■ Timely intervention – identify key times when students need support and timetable this
■ Identify difficult areas of the curriculum and timetable additional support

Centrally provided additional support (CPAS)

■ Identify 'at risk' students early
■ Identify groups who need additional support: language, numeracy, writing, IT, oral work
■ Ensure students are aware of disability and other specialist support as early as possible.
■ Maintain a referral system for those in need of specialist support

Employability

■ Introduce 'employability' early, to assist students to manage the cost of their education
■ Offer specific employability skills at each level
■ Assist students in mapping skills acquired through their learning as skills transferable to employment

Paper and electronic support for students

■ Recommend or give to all undergraduates key study skills materials
■ Explain that back-up materials for taught sessions are available on-line
■ Introduce a discussion forum for peer support (such as through Web CT)
■ Maintain on-line language and study skills materials and specialist software for disability

Induction, orientation and the identification of learning needs

When students get into difficulty with their study, it is often assumed to be a problem with academic skills. Whilst this may be part of the truth, there are generally other issues involved, especially those concerned with expectations of, and orientation to, HE. This is especially true as more first-generation students enter higher education. The first 4–6 weeks of the academic year can be very stressful and unsettling for students in any institution: homesickness, loneliness, acclimatisation to what can seem strange sets of customs, performance anxiety and self-doubt mean this can be a difficult time, and it is, indeed, a key period of student loss. A positive and appropriate induction experience can help to orientate students, build up their sense of belonging, and prevent some difficulties from developing later in the year. As such, induction can serve as a main plank in an institution's retention policy. Induction is such a key event in orientating students to HE that it is addressed here in detail. Activities to support this chapter can be found in Chapters 10–12.

Induction as a process

Higher education is seeing a move away from student inductions of the past where students queued up to enrol, joined the library, gathered for an afternoon of short speeches by university personnel and struggled through a cheese and wine event where they were supposed to get to know each other. Sometimes induction left students more confused and anxious than they were previously, lost in a sea of undigested information that lacked frames of reference to make it meaningful.

Instead, there is an increasing emphasis on induction as a settling-in period, where students acclimatise to what, for many, is a very alien environment, and on students being practically assisted with the transition to HE life. This is all the more necessary with the wider range of students entering HE. With the diversity of background, attitudes and skills that students now bring, induction is a time for identifying mismatches between previous experience and what is required on the course. Expectations, myths and attitudes need to be addressed if students are to be aware of what is required of them, and to succeed in the way that their tutors would usually wish. It is also a time to identify students who may be considered 'at risk' of failure or of leaving – even if the risk is only relative to that of the rest of the cohort.

Furthermore, it becomes apparent that the needs of today's students cannot always be met within an initial week or few days of induction. More and more, courses are coming to regard the first semester or even the first year as a longer process of induction and orientation, where students are not only acclimatised to the environment, but trained to succeed within it. It is becoming more generally appreciated that HE students need to be assisted to learn, and that even successful students of the past were not necessarily aware of why they did well or able to transfer their skills to new contexts. 'Learning to learn', professional development, skills training, information management, employability awareness, 'capability' and a range of other concepts are current and are being built into curricula, starting at induction. Indeed, the QAA recommends that students are introduced to personal development planning (PDP) from the earliest opportunity.

It will become clear that the activities recommended below are unlikely to fit into an initial induction week but may be incorporated into a longer induction process. When induction is extended into a longer process, students are better able to absorb information and late enrolees are able to catch up more easily.

Introducing induction to students

Advance guidance

Send the induction literature out well in advance of induction week, stressing that induction is an essential part of their first year of study. Cite the first day of induction as the first day of the academic year; students unfamiliar with HE can assume that induction is an optional extra, especially if documentation suggests that the first teaching week is the beginning of their year. These are invariably the students who prove demanding later in the year as they have missed out on key information or have not bonded with their peers. Let students know the dates of induction week early in the year so that they can make arrangements to be present.

If students have to select module choices during induction week, ensure that information about modules is clearly laid out, and with the key information that students will want to know. This covers not only the content but also:

- prerequisites for study;
- total time required for study, including independent study;
- the kinds of skills which are expected at entry or which will be developed on the course;
- the proportion of practical work compared to theory;
- the amount of reading and writing required, and the level of numeracy if relevant;
- which assessment modes are used: some students will only select modules which state that there is no exam and will defer choice until they have this information;
- any additional costs or conditions that the student needs to know about, such as fieldwork or late hours.

It is helpful if all key information delivered in induction week is presented both by ear and by eye and preferably through an activity so that students have a better chance of retaining it. Ideally, all information should be gathered together in an induction guide, so that it is easy to find. This is especially useful when students have to miss part of the induction process.

Features of the induction process

There are five main areas to be covered in induction:

(1) settling in;
(2) registration and enrolment;
(3) social orientation and group bonding;
(4) orientation to the institution;
(5) orientation to the course and academic study – this is the area where extended induction is most necessary.

(1) Settling in

This would cover welcoming students to the university, the course, basic information about key personnel, the campus, domestic arrangements and some introduction to each other. This period could also include guidance to students on how to manage the wealth of information they will receive during induction week.

(2) Registration and enrolment

There will be a number of processes which students will need to go though during the first week. These will include registration (matriculation), gaining a student number and a student card, joining the library, logging on to the university network and getting an e-mail address, arranging for student loans, and, in some cases, choosing electives or other modules. These processes and procedures can be very stressful for students so the easier the documentation is to follow and the better orchestrated events, the happier they will be. Good organisation of such events is invaluable: long waits in queues and misinformation can set easily up a bad atmosphere before the term has even started and it is often the classroom lecturer who then suffers.

Students do not necessarily realise that enrolment and unit or module registration are separate procedures or even that they must do more than turn up on the day in order to be enrolled. It may help to include a list of all the things that enrolment entitles the student to do – and the consequences of not enrolling.

Presentation

The stages in each process need to be clearly laid out in paper version so that students can follow them as they move about the campus without having to come back and ask for clarification. Use bold headings and colour-coded paper or text to ensure that key information stands out clearly. Go through the processes together or show them on video, leaving time to clarify points that are not clear. Spell out:

- where to go, how to get there and how long it takes to get there;
- when to be there and the time by which they should be able to leave;
- the order in which to approach the various processes (such as gaining a student number first);
- what to take with them for each event.

Timing

Ensure that there is a clear timetable for when students should attend for particular processes such as enrolment (matriculation, registration) so that they are not forced to queue unnecessarily. It can help to enlist the services of students from previous years to shepherd students to the appropriate place for the appropriate time.

(3) Social orientation and group bonding

This is to provide a welcoming environment which facilitates interaction between students and staff and gives students a sense of belonging to the course and the institution.

Introducing students to each other

Group bonding is useful for a number of reasons. In the first instance, it makes students less anxious as they feel they know who they are dealing with. They are more likely to be responsive and supportive class members as a result. It is particularly useful if bonding exercises give a place to addressing anxieties, so that worries are not festering away under the surface waiting to erupt at inconvenient moments later in the term. If students feel they belong to a group, they are often more committed to the course and even to particular completion dates – so they can finish with their friends. It is also essential for building up an atmosphere of trust if there is to be any interactive work, peer critiques or peer assessment. Finally, informal support networks built upon friendship groups are useful to students, but difficult to form if students are not given opportunities to get to know each other.

Bonding exercises are particularly important under the following conditions:

- where there are mature or non-traditional students;
- where student confidence is low;
- where the intake is very varied or where course numbers are large;
- where students have to work under pressurised conditions;
- where there is group, team or project work of any kind;
- where students are likely to come onto campus only for taught sessions because they

have other commitments, as bonding outside of contact sessions is then unlikely.

A useful format for bonding that works with most groups is outlined below in Chapter 10. Its main features are:

- establishing names and introducing ice breakers;
- addressing anxieties;
- turning anxieties into challenges;
- setting ground rules;
- setting up group activities or a project;
- arranging social events, parties, outings, picnic, etc.

Social events or outings work better when students have already bonded – otherwise they can be rather tense affairs. It is important to time social activities so that students with dependants are able to attend, and to be aware that certain religious groups, such as Muslims, are not supposed to attend functions where alcohol is present.

(4) Orientation to the institution

This covers both informational aspects (such as regulations, campus tours and meeting university personnel) and academic orientation. (What is university about? How does HE differ from school and FE? What is expected of students? What can students expect from HE?) Chapter 10 offers ideas on introducing this through activities rather than information delivery.

Assume that students are likely to be overwhelmed by the amount of information coming their way, and make access to the information as easy as possible. Anything which is said needs to be backed up in paper version and, probably, referred to again later. This may be collated into a booklet, such as an 'Essential Guide'. It is not enough merely to give out the Guide or an outline of an induction programme: students need to be clearly directed to what is important and to hear and see what they need to do.

Good maps are essential. However, the best way of getting to know the campus is to walk it, where this is possible. Students appreciate being taken to key places outside of the department in a guided tour, especially if quick routes are pointed out. Include all the places they may need, such as the departmental office, where to eat, Student Services, the Student Union, Library, sports facilities, where to go to arrange about loans and hardship fund, and other administrative services they may need if, for example, they have a disability or need to make special arrangements for exams.

It can be helpful to introduce some personnel from relevant central services, such as Student Services, Careers Advisory, and the Student Union, including welfare and finance advisers, so that students are aware that they exist and are approachable services. However, students do not tend to take in much of what is said at such events so it is important not to cover too much. Ensure students have back-up materials, perhaps included in a collated booklet. Emphasise how students can access services if they need them.

Orientation to libraries and learning resource centres

First visits
Many students, especially mature students and those with some disabilities, can be very anxious about using libraries; libraries can be associated with negative childhood experiences and bad behaviour in university libraries is commonplace – a symptom of student frustration and anxiety. It is useful to have set visiting times to introduce the library and to take students through the range of resources that libraries now contain. If there is a subject specialist librarian, it is useful if they are available to take students around and indicate the main sources for the subject. Encourage students to look up books from their reading list during their first visit if possible, so that they can experience the practical advantages of a return visit. Encourage them to play with the technology, to walk around the library and to find a spot that suits them.

Basic information
Offer students key information about how to make best use of the library. This might include:

- whether they need a student number and/ or identity card to join;
- how many items they can take out at once for use in the library;
- how many items they can take out on loan;
- how long it takes for books to come up from the stacks or from other sites;
- for how long they can keep books out of the library;
- what the fines system is;
- what help there is for students with disabilities or who have difficulties using the library;
- how to access library services by e-mail or phone;
- details of reserving books;
- how to make inter-library loans.

Follow-up activity
Library staff and course staff together can devise a search list for each subject as an exercise to be completed in the first week or so of the course. This should require students to search for a range of materials that they are likely to use on the course. It should include both paper and electronic materials, books and journals. It may also contain a selection of items such as maps, prints, newspapers, manuscripts, CD and tape material, depending on the course. This exercise can be assessed as part of an early assignment.

Identifying 'at risk' students

Students should be encouraged to state any difficulties they had in using the library and where they may need further help. It helps if there is a checklist to identify possible difficulties – otherwise students may be reluctant to identify them. This list should include such items as difficulties reading the CD-ROM screen, reading numbers on the spines of books, finding their way around the library, finding certain types of material, or following sequences of numbers when searching for books on the shelves. These are ways of identifying certain types of students who may be 'at risk' more generally. Staff should be alert, in particular, to students who may have undiagnosed dyslexic difficulties.

Introduction to information technology

It is useful for students to become acquainted

with the university's information technology as soon as possible so that they can, at the very least, use e-mail and gain access to information from electronic notice-boards and the internet. It is worth considering whether to split the group into those who consider themselves to be beginners and those with some expertise, as novices need to be taken through the basics much more slowly and will require longer sessions. Early sessions might include:

- terminology;
- using the university's desk-top;
- working your way round the computer and using the mouse;
- saving material on the computer and on diskette;
- what the course or subject area provides on web pages and how to download and print these;
- making references to material found on electronic networks;
- using e-mail: sending and receiving messages and attachments;
- linking to the library;
- finding information on the internet using search engines;
- what to buy if you are investing in your own computer.

Training for specific software and in word-processing and keyboarding skills may be offered as follow-ups. A basic IT skills checklist can be found in *The Guidance Toolkit* (Simpson and Wailey, 2000b).

(5) Orientation to the course and academic study

This includes orientation to the personnel and procedures of the course and to academic issues such as attendance and ground rules, course content, learning outcomes, assessment, teaching and learning, how personal and professional development will be addressed through the subject area, and so forth.

Introducing the departmental or course staff

It is helpful for students to meet all the staff

with whom they will have contact in their first term or semester, and be given a very *brief* overview of what they do. This may be best in stages: key staff at the beginning of the first day, and other staff once students have settled a little. Course or departmental administrators are especially important contacts for students. Ensure that students are given a list of names, titles, room numbers, telephone extensions, e-mail addresses, and clear guidance on who is the appropriate person to see about what and when. Draw attention to the person they need to contact:

- if they are having difficulties with course-work;
- if they have life issues which may be affecting their performance on course;
- if they have language or more general study difficulties;
- if they have a disability for which they need help;
- if they are absent (when there are attendance requirements);
- if they change address.

It is not unusual for students to go through a whole year of study confused about the difference between the names of units and the title of their overall course, and not knowing which staff they are supposed to contact for different kinds of issues.

The course handbook and procedures

Go through the course handbook with students, drawing attention to key information. Encourage them to go through it again in the following week. Explain any unusual vocabulary or abbreviations. Whilst going through the handbook, draw attention to the academic year, the timetable for taught sessions, assignment deadlines and exam dates. Give time for students to transfer these to their diaries. Be very clear about how work will be assessed and any training that is offered in developing appropriate skills for the modes of assessment used. Ensure that there is plenty of time for students to ask questions.

Course culture

Orientate students to the culture you want for the course. For example, make clear whether the atmosphere is one where difficulties are to be addressed in a supportive context, whether peer support and groups are to feature highly, whether individual or team competitiveness are expected, whether self-evaluation and reflection are valued, whether a problem-solving attitude is expected, and whether peer support mechanisms will be introduced. Clarify what students need to do to prepare for all taught sessions. You may require students to attend all sessions and to be there punctually, or the atmosphere may be one where students are expected to work independently and attend only when they feel it necessary. Whatever patterns of behaviour are expected need to be set in place and modelled by staff within induction week. A chaotic induction week or a supportive, interactive induction week set very particular tones which students use to orientate themselves to the course. Be explicit about such things as:

- the reading, writing, numeracy, IT, and time demands for the course or modules;
- whether students need to prepare for all taught sessions;
- how and when questions are to be asked in lectures, seminars and other taught sessions;
- what is supposed to happen in tutorials, seminars, practicals, etc.;
- what kind of study needs to be done independently and during vacations.

Tips from Year 2

Students will often take advice better from peers than from lecturers. Invite students from Year 2 to talk to the first-years about what they know now that they wished they had realised in Year 1. What tips do they have to offer to first-year students from their own experience?

Whet the appetite for the course

It may be a long time since some students decided to apply for your course; others may only have made their way to your course as a second or third choice. It is worth offering a brief introduction to the course to remind students why it was a good choice, and to inspire others who may not be sure that it is really the course for them. This is also a useful way of helping students to check whether they have selected the right course. Give a very brief overview of the course, bringing out what is distinct or unusual about it and why it is a good subject to study. Emphasise interesting debates or topical issues that will be addressed and indicate how the course may be useful to particular career choices.

Orientation to higher education

For a range of reasons, students enter university with a false set of impressions about what to expect. University life today can be very different from that recounted by parents and relatives. In an era of widening access, an increasing number of students are the first generation to enter HE and do not even have family myth upon which they can draw. It is not unusual for entrants to be unaware of the differences between a college, campus and a university, or the different role that a university is supposed to play. Students can import a model of support and guidance based on school or further education experiences, where numbers were smaller, study more structured, where fewer teaching staff were involved and where groups were small enough for everyone to know everybody else. Students can arrive at university with false expectations, and often with unrealistic notions of the amount of pastoral care and study support that will be available. They often expect a 'school' atmosphere, with staff who will take responsibility for their learning and attendance.

It can come as a great shock for students to find that they are expected to select options with what they would consider minimal guidance, to direct their own study outside of contact time, and to manage most of their study problems for themselves. Many students have little notion of how to make use of undirected study time. They may not realise that they will be expected to hunt down information for themselves through reading, the internet or

other means: they assume that it is the lecturer's job to feed them whatever information they need and may even be outraged at the amount of things they are expected to do for themselves. They may assume that lecturers are there to do all the work of making sense of complex materials for them. It is not unusual to find students in HE who have never read a book prior to entry and who are surprised that anyone should expect them to read.

Students may also have little idea of the difference between FE and HE levels of study. Students sometimes comment that they came to university 'in order to develop their writing' or 'to improve my grammar', as if that were their main goal. They have not grasped that this is not the prime function of a university. Others believe that they only need to turn up and that they then deserve a qualification to be handed to them at the end. They may feel that the sacrifices they are making in terms of time and money are sufficient to merit a degree. These issues ought to have been addressed prior to Admissions, but it is worth being clear about mutual expectations during induction, to reassure students about how they will be trained to develop required skills, and to formalise responsibilities into ground rules or learning contracts of some kind. See pp. 196–207 below for related activities.

Introducing personal, professional and academic development

It is important to discuss with students the way that their time at university can prepare them for a range of different progression routes, and to encourage them to actively reflect upon, evaluate and monitor their wider learning. At induction, students can be introduced to this way of thinking about their learning. Make it explicit how the course and the university more generally will assist them in this process of personal and professional development. Point out that students are not always aware of what they have achieved beyond the content of their subject disciplines, they may not be able to articulate their broader learning in terms of skills and personal qualities, especially when competing for work. Point out also the benefits of this approach to their academic study.

It is useful to introduce this concept of personal development to students early in their time at university, especially if a more integrated approach to skills development is used. It can help students to make more sense of interactive teaching techniques and to value tasks such as oral presentation which can, at first, seem very daunting. It also places study skills development within an adult and therefore more acceptable context and offers a starting place for exploring student responsibility for their own learning.

Advantages

Bring out the advantages of the personal, professional development approach:

(1) It will train students to study more effectively so that they make best use of the time available, and have a better chance of attaining a good grade.
(2) Learning should be more enjoyable and less stressful as it becomes more consciously skilled.
(3) Students will be more aware of how what they learn applies to wider contexts, such as to other academic courses and to the world of work, and will be better able to articulate their awareness to employers.
(4) It will give greater focus to their learning.
(5) Students will develop skills of self-evaluation and reflection which are useful in most life contexts.
(6) They will receive more than just a degree from their education.
(7) They will be better able to compete for jobs.

Clarify how personal, professional and academic development is delivered

Make clear whether this will be offered through:

- 'professional or academic skills' modules or integrated throughout their course (or both);
- opportunities for work placement;
- opportunities to receive credit for current employment;
- careers education;

- other routes;
- how their learning will be drawn together so that they can articulate it to others (such as through personal tutors, portfolios, progress files, transcripts, dedicated units, etc.).

Managing their own learning

One misunderstanding that creates difficulties for students is over how much time they are supposed to study. Students with little idea of what HE is about may imagine that they can take a full-time degree course on a part-time basis. This misconception can be reinforced when only a few hours are scheduled as directly taught sessions: independent study may be a new concept which the student finds difficult to grasp.

It is important to be explicit about how many hours students are expected to study each week, and useful to offer guidance and discussion on how to make best use of independent study time. It may help to give one or two outline plans of how a study week might break down into different activities for your subject area (such as 6 hours of taught sessions, 10 hours of reading and other research activity, 2 hours preparing for taught sessions, 5 hours of writing, 15 hours of studio work or whatever is appropriate.) Students who lack confidence in their studies tend to compare themselves with peers who claim to complete their work in 'a few hours' rather than against a realistic model of what is involved for the subject. It can help to know that the reason they may be struggling is because they are not studying the required number of hours.

It can also be useful to draw attention to the differences between teaching and learning in HE and in the students' previous institution, whether school or FE. Emphasise that students are expected to develop, over the first year, much more personal responsibility for their own learning. This includes becoming aware of difficulties they may be experiencing and taking appropriate action. 'Action' might be problem solving, using hand-outs, using support information on web pages, using university services or, if these are not sufficient, advising course staff of their difficulties. Managing their own learning includes reading the information given to them and using it as appropriate rather than being reminded what to do, and in developing a professional, self-reliant approach which they can take into the world of work.

Attendance and punctuality

These can be serious issues with widening participation intakes. Some intakes of students are severely 'at risk' if they do not attend the majority of sessions. It needs to be laid down very clearly what the policy is on attendance and punctuality, and for students to grasp, where relevant, how attendance affects potential success on the course. Some courses lay down a percentage attendance rate: where this is the case, it needs to be repeated that it is not simply a question of turning up for the minimum number of sessions, but of appreciating the importance of attendance to academic success. If students feel they are allowed to turn up late, leave early or attend on an irregular basis, they will tend to do so, especially those with many commitments outside of the university. There are very noticeable differences between courses in this respect, depending on the culture that is developed at induction or even during the admissions stage.

Preparing for taught sessions

It is rare for students to prepare for taught sessions, and yet much better use can be made of valuable and limited teaching time if lecturers use that time to clarify what students have not been able to make sense of alone, rather than taking them through the basics. Some students realise that they can only make sense of what they hear in lectures if they have looked at the material in advance: the lecture then brings the material together for them. Some students will not catch specialist vocabulary or complex ideas unless they have seen these in advance. It is difficult to persuade students to prepare in advance unless this is presented as the culture of the course or, for combined honours modular courses, the university as a whole.

Advance preparation by students also means that a wider range of activities can be set in taught time, and that sessions can be more varied, interesting and interactive. Suggest that students prepare for some induction activities; for example, ask them to go through a section of the handbook and prepare questions on it, or to prepare for a quiz. Get into the habit of setting 'one-minute summaries' at the beginning of taught sessions for students to scribble down what was done in the previous session, or to identify what the main issues are likely to be for the current session.

Managing difficulty

Ask students to consider what their response is likely to be when they hit more difficult times. It is worth pointing out that there are bound to be times when they feel that the course texts are impenetrable, they are going over and over what they read without it making sense, and struggling to sort information out in order to write their assignment. They may feel like running away, leaving, deferring, or their self-esteem may be affected. It can be helpful to students to realise that such difficulties are part of the learning process and not a sign that they are unfit to be on the course.

Point out to students that when there isn't a 'right answer' or when it is not clear what answers may be possible, learning can seem very complex and challenging. When we move from more basic ways of thinking to more sophisticated ones, there can be times when this feels like a painful process. Experiencing difficulty may be a good sign: it can indicate that thinking is being stretched beyond its previous limits. If students persevere, they are likely to come through with expanded ways of thinking or performing. Encourage students to take a problem-solving approach and to form support networks to help them through such times. (See also pp. 199, 204, 243 below.)

Introduction to academic thinking
'Strange ways of doing things'

It is far from obvious to students why higher education is organised the way it is, why different requirements are set for different modules, why writing genres vary so much, and why there is such an emphasis on theory and referencing. One way of addressing this is to offer an introduction to 'the scientific model' and discuss how this influences disciplines differently. A very simple way of mapping out the course or module's position is offered in Chapter 20: 'Polar opposites in academic approaches'.

The 'right answer'

Perry's research into students at Harvard and Ratcliffe colleges (1970) demonstrates that it can take some time, possibly years, for even advanced students to work from a position of desiring dogmatic answers, through relativist positions towards more self-orientated, personally responsible approaches. This issue needs to be addressed, as many aspects of HE study, and especially set assignments, do not have a simple 'right answer'. Those with shaky educational pasts or poor academic self-esteem are all the more likely to look for certainty from their current learning: they will want to 'get it right' this time round. It can be helpful to talk this through with students, possibly using Perry's stages of relativistic thinking.

Perry's stages of contextual relativistic reasoning

'Right answer' stages'

(1) Absolutist stage: The student sees the world in terms of polar opposites of right and wrong (like a spelling test) and wants an Authority to teach them.

(2) Bad Authority versus good Authority: uncertainty is unnecessarily created by bad authorities or created by the Authority to help them find the 'right' answer themselves.

(3) Temporary Uncertainty: 'the Authority hasn't found the right answer yet'. Students are unclear what standards the Authority is looking for when marking work.

Relativism stages

(4) Uncertainty is accepted: 'Everyone has a right to their own opinion', despite what Authority might think. For assignments it is important to find out what the Authority's opinions are.

(5) 'All knowledge and value are contextual and relative.' For assignments, students enquire: 'what is required of me in this context?'

Commitment stages

(6) Personal orientation: the student realises the necessity of making a commitment to certain viewpoints (out of a range of possibilities) with an understanding of, and tolerance for, other viewpoints.

(7) An initial commitment is made.

(8) The implications of commitment are experienced; the student explores issues of responsibility.

(9) The student 'realises commitment as an ongoing, unfolding activity' through which lifestyle and identity are expressed.

If these are discussed with students during their course, they are assisted in becoming more aware of their own thinking and in particular their responses to different teaching styles and assignment requirements. It is worth exploring with students which positions they adopt in relation to different topics, why they do so and how this affects their openness to learning new material. (See also pp. 205, 207 below.)

Offer students reading materials that discuss the nature of 'truth' or 'fact' or 'right' in your subject area. Is this a consistent viewpoint across the discipline? How does it differ from the idea of 'truth' in other academic disciplines?

Plagiarism: opinion, originality and using the work of others

Plagiarism is not an easy concept for students to grasp. For example, students benefit from working with others, but may not appreciate where mutual support must end and their individual approach begin. If they plan work out together and discuss references, their work may seem uncannily similar and yet be their own work. Some students come from backgrounds where they were encouraged and given credit for using the words of 'authorities' at length and without referencing. Some students think they only need to use references if they use the author's exact words, or, strange though it can seem, that it is permissible to quote at length without referencing as long as inverted commas are *not* used. Others assume that it all right to copy directly from books as long as they pick and choose from various sources: they think their work is 'original' because their assembly of sentences amounts to a new paragraph. Students often use such tactics because they lack confidence in their ability to express ideas in their own words.

Students can be baffled about what is meant by producing 'original' work. This is especially the case if they are told not to include their own 'opinion' in their work, and where they are expected to refer to the work of others. They may be anxious that they have not devised a completely new theory or point of view. On the other hand, when they read through journal articles, it can often seem to students as if the contribution even of professional academics is very small: academics seem to quote other people endlessly. The notion of 'originality' can be very confusing.

It needs to be made explicit to students, with examples or simulations of student writing from the subject area, how to balance references to others with personal input, and how to use the work of others to support an argument. Students may need to be reassured that their 'role' in the process of producing an assignment is likely to be in such areas as selecting, critically evaluating appropriate sources, weighing up different points of view, and being able to construct this into a line of reasoning. Their assignment will then read differently from anyone else's, and in that sense will be original, even if they are not expressing an entirely new viewpoint or piece of research. Draw students' attention to any materials they are given on referencing, making quotations and plagiarism.

Introduction to skills development

Why introduce skills awareness during induction?

It is vital to introduce the importance of learning as a process, and to clarify, at the beginning of the course, that learning development, including skills development, is an integral part of the student experience. This is especially important if study skills are not to be regarded as 'remedial'. All students can benefit from analysing their current study practices and skills, and considering ways of improving their performance. It is important to emphasise learning as a developmental process over which students have control, and for which they are expected to take responsibility. Some advantages of introducing study skills work during induction are:

- It saves lecturer time, as it reduces the need for additional help later.
- It enables struggling students to be identified more quickly before they start to fail – or leave altogether.
- Depending on how study skills are taught, it sets the flavour of what is expected from students in terms of a self-reliant, reflective and responsible attitude to learning.
- It encourages students to consider what they have to offer on the course, and how skills could be transferred from one area to another.
- It encourages students to realise that they do have some control over their learning, and can take action to improve their performance. This has an effect upon motivation and discourages defeatism in those who feel that they are not 'academic'.

This process is likely to take longer than the initial induction week. An extended induction, or study skills provision built into modules which run over one or more terms, is usually needed, depending on the match between the current skills of the intake and the demands of the course. Moreover, as Chapter 5 indicates, there is also a need for study skills to be continually reinforced by all academic staff through their general teaching. See Chapter 12, for activities related to addressing study skills and learning development.

Offer information about study skills

The way study skills are introduced in induction sets the tone for whether students regard these as part of their essential learning development and something for which they have to take responsibility, or whether study skills are regarded as 'remedial' or an embarrassment. When lecturers undermine the importance of study skills, as occasionally happens, students who need support are left particularly vulnerable. The course handbook could contain the following information, which lecturers should go over verbally as the students follow and ask questions.

- Draw attention to the importance of skills development from a professional and careers perspective. This will make skills development more palatable to adult learners and removes the taint of 'remedial' work which many find off-putting.
- Make explicit which skills students are expected to develop by the end of the study skills series or from the course more generally, such as 'being able to reference sources accurately and providing a list of references at the end of your work'.
- Make clear how study skills will be addressed by you and by the department or subject area so that students know how they will be taught: e.g., integrated into all modules; through module options; study skills sessions; in seminars, lectures or tutorials; through structured support groups; activities; drop-ins, etc.
- Make suggestions of study skills texts to use. (Refer to these during your teaching and in feedback on the students' work.)
- Indicate whether supplementary, subject-specific, study skills materials will be provided and how these will be used – for example, to prepare for each session or for discussion.
- Discuss whether and how study skills will be assessed – and the importance of self-evaluation as part of that assessment.

It is also important to make it clear which person or people from the subject area students should approach if they are having difficulties. Students find it useful to know:

- to what extent the first term or first year is seen as a foundation, 'training' or 'diagnostic' year;
- what kinds of trial runs or mocks are set – especially for first assignments and exams;
- ways that support for learning is built into teaching methods – such as how you model the skills required, how you use language, or how you build in self-evaluation work (see Chapter 5).

Using an Action Plan and portfolio

The section below offers some suggestions for identifying students who may be considered to be 'at risk'. Ideally, however, this process should go hand in hand with a whole intake approach to learning development as outlined above and linked to Chapter 12 on identifying study strengths and difficulties and developing skills. Once students have gone through this process they should be encouraged to draw up Action Plans for addressing their learning priorities. If possible, this should be done either individually or in small groups, in conjunction with the tutor allocated to support them through their course of study (such as a personal tutor), and updated at least once or twice a year. The materials should be kept in a portfolio which the student brings to meetings with their personal tutor and, where relevant, to support sessions.

Encourage students to keep in their portfolio:

(1) Self-evaluation and profile sheets, feedback from tutors on assignments, and their Action Plan. An example of a recent piece of work is useful when seeing support tutors.
(2) A profile of vocational, technical, academic and other skills they have developed.
(3) An updated summary of their education, including school, college, training courses and relevant short courses.

(4) Certificates of any qualifications (exams, copy of driver's licence).

(5) An updated list of all work experience, with the dates, addresses of employers, brief job description, main responsibilities, skills or qualities they demonstrated, and what they learned from doing that work which is of value to their current aspirations.

(6) A curriculum vitae (CV) – a careers adviser can help with this.

(7) Their goals and aspirations, such as what they want to achieve from the course, where they see themselves in seven years' time, who or what inspires and motivates them, and what they need to do to achieve their goals.

(8) A personal statement or Position paper: about 500–1000 words drawing all this information together. It should summarise progress, immediate priorities, and long-term goals and aspirations, linking past experiences to current learning aims.

Diagnostic work: identifying skills and needs

Why is diagnostic work needed?

As we have seen above, changes in the student body mean that it can no longer be taken for granted that students will arrive in HE with the requisite skills, attributes and attitudes for academic success. As students enter HE with such different base levels of expertise and experience, it is often necessary to assess where students are at the point of entry in order to provide appropriate support for them. Those who have failed in the system previously may have worries about being judged and found lacking. It is therefore important to include adult learners in the process of identifying their own needs. Moreover, skills work is best addressed by bringing out the areas where students already have expertise. In working with the most severely challenged students, it has been found extremely productive to use students' current areas of expertise as the basis for developing

transferable skills. Even though the expertise may seem to have little connection with academic work, it is often a more enabling and productive approach than trying to build from skills which are apparently more 'academic' but where the student lacks confidence and existing expertise. Some examples of this are detailed in Chapter 8.

The benefits of early diagnostic work are:

- It can be used to build a reflective, self-evaluating approach to study from the offset.
- It gives a message to students that skills, strategies and attributes are important to learning as well as 'facts', and emphasises the importance attributed to skills development.
- It encourages students to see that staff believe that their learning can be improved: many students have been told that they would never make it into HE and are aware that they are not strong yet academically, so this message is an important one to convey.
- 'At risk' students are identified as early as possible.
- Support for 'at risk' students can be put in place earlier in their academic career, so that it is of maximum effect. Emergency and last-minute solutions are called for less often.
- Teaching staff can identify weak cohorts so that teaching or additional support can be adapted to meet the needs of the intake.

Involving students in the diagnostic process

If students are invited into the diagnostic process, the benefits of which are made clear to them, they are more likely to take responsibility for their own progress than if they are simply 'tested'. This is partly because they will be developing the tools to evaluate their own performance, and it is particularly true for students who have been dismissed in the past as low achievers in tests. Building up profiles of strengths and areas for improvement, and monitoring progress, are ways of exploring where there are perceived difficulties. On the other hand, examples of the student's performance on tasks similar to those expected on course, help the tutor to identify students in real need and to check the accuracy of a student's self-evaluation.

The process of identifying needs through self-evaluation activities and writing personal statements can itself form part of the strategy for helping the students to improve their learning. One way for students to overcome difficulties is to recognise that they have omitted essential steps or sub-skills. Their difficulties may be alleviated when they realise that they can work on skills development in stages and with a method. Students are more likely to recognise their difficulties, keep them in perspective, and to take action to overcome them, when there is:

Personal involvement:
- they are involved in an on-going process of self-evaluation, with guidance;
- they feel they are valued and respected, and that it is 'safe' to admit difficulties;
- they can see the relevance to their professional or careers development.

Relevance to and status within the course:
- they feel their tutors value the underlying skills they are learning;
- they can see the direct relevance of the skills or competences they are developing to their chosen subjects or vocational route;
- when there is a link between the skills they are learning and the ways their work is assessed;
- when the different processes of evaluating difficulties, marking, offering feedback on assignments, and offering support are brought into close union.

A link to support:
- they can see that there is some point or purpose to self-evaluation and to acknowledging what may feel like embarrassing difficulties;
- when evaluation of need is clearly linked to appropriate support mechanisms.

Time
- they have the opportunity to learn underlying skills, in stages, and over time;

- when help is structured into the delivery of their programme as far as possible, so that their overall study workload is not unduly increased.

Attainment versus potential

Testing can give an indication of a student's current level of attainment. With intakes of mature students, current levels of attainment can be very inaccurate guides to potential or final degree grade. Some students with low scores may have very rusty skills which can be polished within a few weeks to a few months. Such students can do extremely well. Other students may never have developed writing, thinking and number skills and may need early referral to Access courses and even basic skills courses before embarking on a university degree.

Mature students, NVQ, Access and BTEC entrants
Students who have not sat formal examinations in recent years may underperform to a significant extent when given 'tests' to complete. Telling students the test is 'diagnostic' or that most people get through it, may not help very much to improve performance. The diagnostic procedure can indicate where students need support in developing test-taking strategies in preparation for exams.

Students with specific learning difficulties (dyslexia)
Dyslexic students are likely to underachieve and may not get through the test, even though they may be capable of achieving a very good degree. This is particularly true for mature students and black students who are less likely to have been advised previously that they might have a Specific Learning Difficulty (SpLD) and may never have received appropriate support for managing their difficulties. Some of these students will be eligible for specialist support through Disabled Students' Allowances.

Ecological validity

The diagnostic testing which is offered should be related as closely as possible to the types of task which will be required of the student on the course. For example, on some courses, the numeracy requirement will be basic or performed on a calculator, and the testing should reflect that in terms of level and equipment allowed. Other courses require more advanced mathematical operations and that too should be reflected in the task set. If students are required to write continuous prose for their course, then this should be the task set rather than, for example, testing only by computerised grammar exercises.

Wherever possible, the testing should be for 'embedded' skills, related to real life or a relevant academic task. Just as Brazilian street children may be capable of complex mathematical operations for trading purposes but incapable of performing much simpler school mathematical problems, so too, may students perform differently depending on the perceived relevance and contextualisation of the tests used. Students may be capable of writing in one context or with a particular stimulus but not another. They may be able to calculate answers for real-life problems, such as how many yards of canvas or wood they need to make frames for a series of oil paintings, but not recognise similar problems when written as abstract fractions or decimals.

Student relevance

As far as is possible, the diagnostic procedure should:

- be a process which helps the student to develop skills of reflection, responsibility, constructive self-criticism, and future planning;
- be used to identify the needs of different groups and individuals: English speakers of other languages (ESOL), English as a foreign language (EFL), English first-language speakers with poor academic English, and potentially dyslexic students, who would benefit from advice or strategic support;

- be clearly linked to support;
- not penalise those who participate.

Exercises to identify 'at risk' students in different circumstances

Different contexts place different students 'at risk'. For example, studio-based courses do not place dyslexic students at as much risk as those with heavier reading and writing loads. All of the following are useful ways of gleaning different types of information about students; which ones are relevant will depend upon the demands the teaching circumstances place upon students. A cross-comparison of several of the following exercises gives tutors a sense of which contexts place students at more risk than others.

- *Asking students to identify difficulties:* can be very useful although some students will try to hide difficulties. This needs to be used in conjunction with other evidence.

- *Library task:* identifies those with sequencing and/or reading difficulties, and those stressed by library environments.

- *Continuous prose test:* identifies a range of difficulties with written work as outlined below. Very simplistic answers may be disguised ways of avoiding making spelling or grammar errors and not necessarily an indicator of thinking potential. This would be identified if the students were also required to take a dictation where their spelling and grammar error rates were much higher than on the continuous prose test.

- *Dictation:* identifies spelling and technical writing difficulties as students cannot self-censor to avoid making errors. When cross-referenced to other writing, it can also identify those who experience severe difficulties in combining listening and writing tasks.

- *Use of English:* can be used to identify a range of written English skills, including proofreading ability. This could be computerised if used in conjunction with other writing tests.

- *Numeracy:* abstract or embedded problems may yield different results.

- *Subject quiz:* can identify students with poor foundation knowledge for the subject. This may impact upon reading speed and vocabulary, and their speed for processing course-specific information, especially in Year 1. If this is coupled with study skills difficulties, the student may find the course extremely difficult.

- *Answering questions based upon a reading passage:* can identify 'at risk' students, although it may not be clear what the underlying difficulty is. Short or poor answers may be due to weak comprehension, slow reading, difficulties with reading unseen text, or visual perceptual difficulties with text. Students may have undiagnosed dyslexia or Meares–Irlen syndrome which would lead to underachievement on this task depending on the test conditions. Where possible, the text should be given out a few days in advance of the written test.

- *Position paper: untimed free writing or word-processed writing:* gives a clearer indication of what students are capable of when they have time to rework a piece of writing over time.

Diagnostic procedures

There are many ways in which needs might be identified. Those suggested below are paper and pen exercises, which are easy to deliver. Computer assessment of skills difficulties is developing slowly but is not covered here because:

- it can create delays whilst students wait to acquire computer skills and computer access;
- it is hard to control for errors created by poor keyboarding, weak IT skills or sensitivity to screen glare and flicker;
- test–retest validity of available diagnostic tests have shown that they are not very dependable;
- computer exercises do not generally have eco-

logical validity for assessing students' performance on courses except where students will be assessed by computer.

However, this is a rapidly developing field and it is reasonable to expect that there will be advances in the next few years. Subject awareness, use of English, numeracy and IT skills could be tested by computer-based multiple-choice assessment.

Adaptations of the following diagnostic activities have been used on a range of courses. Students with SpLD (dyslexia) can ask for their disability to be taken into consideration. The exercises, when undertaken as part of a diagnostic process, are introduced with reassurances about the benefits of the exercise. Courses vary in which exercises they find appropriate for their students, for the kind of follow-up support on offer, and in the way they adapt them. The main methods covered below are:

(1) extended induction;
(2) timed continuous prose test;
(3) use of English;
(4) diagnostic dictation;
(5) course-specific skills evaluation;
(6) profiling of skills;
(7) Position Papers.

(1) Extended induction

For many students, the ideal diagnostic process would be a supportive extended induction period of several weeks and, for some intakes, the first semester or the first year are more appropriate time scales. The process can train them to identify their own learning characteristics, strengths and weaknesses in a more realistic way, based on an experience of study at a higher education level and with a positive approach based on improvement rather than remediation. It also offers greater opportunities for guidance, training and support.

The advantages of this procedure are:

From the tutor's perspective

- Tutors have a more rounded view of their students and where their strengths and difficulties lie, as well as the experiences and knowledge they bring to the course.

- It gives teaching staff an idea of how quickly or slowly the student is improving so that it is easier to predict their progress. Some students, for example, whose progress is slower, may have a greater chance of success following a part-time route.
- Tutors will know which study needs are common to the year and, consequently, what study assistance needs to be built into the programme or offered as additional workshops.
- The process itself gives tutors the opportunity to intervene in positive ways to improve their students' learning.
- Retention is likely to be improved, both through the more positive approach students take to learning development as a key element of their higher education, and through the early identification of those who need additional support.

From the student's perspective

- The process encourages students to consider that current performance is not fixed, and that they can monitor and develop skills over time.
- There is an opportunity to explore skills, experience, knowledge, as well as influences and inspiration on their lives, so that they are viewed as whole people rather than simply as someone with a problem.
- There are opportunities for formative assessment and to record progress, change and skills gained. This is more positive than there

simply being a record of students with difficulties. It is reassuring to students who worry that they will be branded and graded as a weak student if they seek help.

- The emphasis is on the development of the learning of all students, who have differing needs, rather than on identifying problem students.
- Students who have particular difficulties can be identified early in the programme and they can be given extra help at the earliest possible opportunity.
- If a student's needs are such that they are unable to continue with the course, they can be offered early guidance on preparation courses or career alternatives.

Chapters 10–12 offer suggestions on how this longer process can be used with students. Chapter 12, for example, draws together the work undertaken in Chapter 10 and 11 into an action plan and Position Paper, which can be further assessed and developed over the term, semester or year. Below is an example of how support work could be distributed over a year. It is adapted from work undertaken by Robert Simpson with the Social Work Diploma course at the University of East London. Support, linked to early identification of needs, begins during the Admissions process and continues throughout the time the student is at university. Personal reflection is a key element of this programme. There are many ways that this could be adapted and linked to dynamic Accreditation of Prior (and Experiential) Learning (AP(E)L) work (Simpson and Wailey, 1999, 2000a).

Example of extended reflective and diagnostic work

Admissions	Aptitude testing	Action taken
	• Course-related text sent to students to read in advance. • Open days: group discussion on the subject of the text • Written quiz to explore subject awareness. • Discussion and text used as the basis of diagnostic writing activity.	• Staff analyse written scripts and student descriptions of difficulties to identify those 'at risk' • Students with recent educational psychologist assessments of SpLDs (dyslexia) may be exempted.

	• Students are asked to comment on any difficulties they may have had with any aspect of the testing.	• Staff discuss difficulties with students where appropriate, especially where additional support or a preparatory course may be deemed a compulsory necessity.
Pre-term	• Preparatory materials sent out in advance of the week.	• Some students referred for bridging courses.
Induction	• Staff offer a framework for student self-assessment against academic and professional conventions. • Students undertake a range of activities, discussions, and self-evaluation questionnaires on a range of skills, attributes and subject-specific awareness. • Students are asked to make specific links between past experience and skills and current study and career needs. • Students are guided towards producing a diagnostic written interim position paper for week 2 (with examples offered) and submitting a self-assessment of their writing. • Students are given a dictation for examples of handwritten work.	• Go over academic conventions and marking criteria. • Further skills development work. • The dictation is likely to identify those with specific learning difficulties. • Staff identify those who need additional support and those to whom a dyslexia referral will be suggested.
Week 2 onwards	• Ongoing skills support (specific sessions and through general teaching). • Additional support for areas of weakness. • Monitor assessment marks. Meetings with tutor to discuss progress.	• Feedback given on interim position paper and the self-assessment. • Skills feedback given for coursework.
End of year	• Reflection sessions: using the theory covered, and experience gained, during the year to redraft the position paper	• Students hand in final version of position paper and self-assessment.

(2) Timed continuous prose test

The value of timed continuous prose as a diagnostic tool

Timed continuous prose tests can be used to establish a range of literacy and learning needs:

- use of English, such as spelling, vocabulary, grammar, punctuation and phrasing;
- ability to write continuous prose in English;
- how quickly or slowly a student writes;
- how confident students are about their writing;
- students who might have specific learning needs (dyslexia);
- students' capacity to organise their time and study.

Conditions for continuous prose test

(1) Offer half an hour for the writing to be completed. It should be written in conditions where it can be established that the student has not received outside assistance.
(2) It should be handwritten, in ink. Word-processed work conceals many useful indicators of 'at risk' students.
(3) The subject should be fairly simple for students beginning the course.
(4) Give five additional minutes to read the instructions – to ensure that students do read them.
(5) Give students five additional minutes at the end to say how hard they found the test – and describe any difficulties they encountered.
(6) Make sure all students hand in the instruction sheet, all notes and all copies of their answers. These should be stapled or clipped or tied together.

Suggested titles

(1) In your opinion, why do some children do better at school than others? If you wish, you may refer to your own experience, or the experiences of people you know.
(2) At the start of this degree course, what are your expectations and what are the skills and knowledge that you are bringing with

you that will help you? Is there anything that you need to improve about your study or your attitude to learning?
(3) What skills, knowledge and personal qualities are you bringing with you to this university? Is there anything that you need to improve about your study?
(4) What creative skills and personal attributes do you think you possess to make you a successful student on this course?
(5) Write about a book you have read or film you have seen recently.

Students may need extra help from tutors if:

- they found the test just a little difficult;
- the content of the writing was of a low standard;
- the student made a few, generally minor, technical errors – e.g., incorrect use of apostrophe, one or two spelling mistakes;
- the student showed a lack of confidence in her/his approach to the test;
- there were some minor difficulties in using English – e.g., strange use of idiom;
- any of the above do not seem to improve after help from the tutor.

A student may need extra support both from the subject area and additional specialist support if the following are found:

- the test is illegible or incomprehensible;
- the student printed the answer in immature handwriting;
- the student obviously misinterpreted the task;
- the student wrote significantly less than 300 words;
- the student asked for help in reading the questions or instructions;
- the student made either a lot of spelling mistakes or the spelling mistakes looked very odd – e.g., words lacked syllables or letters were in the wrong order;
- the student's use of English is weak – e.g., incorrect vocabulary, very basic sentence construction, or many errors in punctuation and grammar.

Marking the continuous prose test

The way you mark the test depends on the purposes to which you will put the results and on the nature of your intake.

For a strong cohort

You may wish to mark the test in detail and return it to the students so that they can see the areas they need to improve.

For needy cohorts

If you have little time and a needy cohort you may not have time to mark every script closely – and there may not be a need to do so. Group support may be more appropriate for more students than individually based support. A brief glance at the tests and skim-reading them is likely to be sufficient to pick out those who need limited additional guidance from you or group support, and those who need specialist support. Look especially for students with very short answers, bizarre spellings, very immature handwriting, illegibility, and obvious language difficulties.

Examples of student writing: identifying priorities for support

Examples of student scripts are offered below. All of these students felt they had difficulties, although not all could be considered priorities.

- How quickly could you identify priority cases?
- What indicators are there in these pieces of writing of the kinds of support some of these students might need?

Examples of free writing (continuous prose)

Laura

The content refers to her experience of difficulty. Laura was unable to evaluate her own performance. She needed some direct guidance on how to improve her work but was not in need of ongoing support.

> Until recently, i thought i was doing well, then i received my first piece of coursework back. I was very disappointed with my mark, and the remainder of the whole day went wrong. I couldn't concentrate, i could not even park the car (and I've always prided myself as being a brilliant parker.)
>
> I looked at the essay and comments made by the tutor and i realised that i was being picked up for punctuation, grammar and clumsy formation of argument points. These are the same points that i was picked up on my first year.

Jean

The content refers to ongoing difficulty since school. Jean thought she might need dyslexic support but the educational psychologist did not confirm this. Language support was needed.

I was persuaded to join the part time English Course after my results, the problem was I didn't know what I was doing wrong to keep on getting a 'D' grade. I retook my english for the forth time in the summer of 95 and this time get a 'C'. I went back in September to finish my A levels. My spelling lessons continued, she was very helpfull over the years and I feel that I improved dramatically from where I started. My biggest problem still is essays and exams and find it very frustrating because i can't write what I want to because I can't spell it.

Isobel

Isobel was unable to evaluate her own performance and under-estimated her writing abilities. Academic support was not needed although she did see a counsellor about her anxiety.

I am vaguely artistic. I find that if I have a prolonged period without any creative output (this could be as little as making a card for someone), I become frustrated and annoyed with myself. So I would assume that my creativity would count as a skill and/or strength.

I enjoy writing and this is a strength, the same is true of reading.

Jacob
A very bright student who scored at the 99 per cent percentile for the Ravens Progressive matrices. Jacob's marks varied between 4 per cent and 60 per cent. His writing varied enormously from one subject to another. He was identified as a previously undiagnosed dyslexic multilingual student. IT support and a very limited amount of support for dyslexia enabled him to achieve success.

Anne
Anne worried in case she was not good enough for HE and needed reassurance but was not in need of additional academic support.

Dimitri

The student's educational history combined with his writing errors suggests that additional support may be needed. Support focused on organisational issues and staying with a chosen course of action.

> I think it would be appropriate to mention here that early schooling really did not exist for me. I have tryed to reason out why on earth, in my adult life, I did not want to go to school.
>
> One over barring thought always emerges this is that my parents are Greek Cypriot. This could be because I am looking for someone else to blame instead of accepting I was, maybe still am, a difficult person.
>
> If I accept that my cultural formative years were guilded by my non-English speaking mother then it seems almost justifieable to rebel towards school.

(3) Use of English

Proof-reading exercise

The following 'use of English' exercise can be used in combination with other activities.

The following passage contains a number of errors

in use of English, such as in grammar, spelling, punctuation and vocabulary.

- *Underline the errors.*
- *Write your correction in the space under each line.*
- *Do NOT rewrite the passage in your own words.*

Planning for the Future

Early preparation for employment can have a major affect upon an individuals later working life and especially on there earning capacity One effect of this preparation are a greater awarness of the labour market. This includes a better understanding of the skills qualities and attrbutes require by employers as well as knowledge of the range of career open to gradautes of different disciplines. John cauldwell off the Great Britian Agency for Employers (GBAE), commenting last week on, student's readiness for work, said A degree is no longer a passport to success. We beleive that students leaving university need to be equipt for professional life.

In recognition of value of specific training for the world of work, some forward-looking universities is incorporating more work-related training into there courses. Goverment initiatives is supporting this change Universities' will be expected to provide personal development planning, work-related learning and similiar opportunity for courses that will orientated students to the work-place. Future employees should definately have a easier time settling into work.

Planning for the Future (corrected text)

Early preparation for employment can have a major effect(1) upon an individual's(2) later working life and especially on their(3) earning capacity.(4) One effect of this preparation is(5) a greater awareness(6) of the labour market. This includes a better understanding of the skills,(7) qualities and attributes(8) required(9) by employers as well as knowledge of the range of careers open to graduates(10) of different disciplines. John Cauldwell(11) of(12) the Great Britain(13) Agency for Employers (GBAE), commenting last week on(14) students'(15) readiness for work, said, "(16)A degree is no longer a passport to success. We believe(17) that students leaving university need to be equipped(18) for professional life."(19)

   In recognition of the(20) value of specific training for the world of work, some forward-looking universities are(21) incorporating more work-related training into their(22) courses. Government (23) initiatives are(24) supporting this change.(25) Universities will be expected to provide personal development planning, work-related learning and similar(26) opportunities(27) for courses that will orientate(28) students to the work-place. Future employees should definitely(29) have an(30) easier time settling(31) into work.

Type of error

(1) incorrect word: affect/effect confusion
(2) grammar: possessive singular
(3) grammar: possessive 'their' rather than the place 'there'
(4) punctuation: full stop needed at end of sentence
(5) grammar: 'One effect' is followed by a singular verb
(6) spelling: awareness
(7) comma needed after 'skills' as it is part of a list
(8) spelling: attributes
(9) grammar: required
(10) spelling: graduates
(11) capitals for proper name
(12) of/off confusion
(13) spelling: Britain
(14) no need for a comma
(15) plural possessive needed
(16) punctuation: comma and inverted commas to introduce direct speech
(17) spelling: believe
(18) spelling: equipped
(19) close inverted commas at the end of direct speech
(20) the word 'the' was omitted
(21) plural: 'are' rather than 'is'
(22) incorrect use of 'there' (place) instead of 'their' (possessive)

(23) spelling: government
(24) initiatives are plural (so use 'are' rather than 'is')
(25) full stop needed
(26) spelling: similar
(27) opportunities (plural) is needed
(28) confused tenses (future and past). -ed ending not needed for 'orientate'.
(29) spelling: definitely
(30) 'an' rather than 'a' in front of a vowel
(31) spelling: settling

Spellings
awareness
attributes
graduates
Britain
believe
equipped
government
similar
definitely
settling

(4) Diagnostic dictation

A dictation can be a useful additional tool for identifying students at risk. One limitation of the continuous prose test is that students can censor their writing so as to include only words they are sure of spelling. This can mean that the student may opt to deliver a reasonably spelt script which is written in rather a simplistic style and with little content. In other words, a potentially able student with poor spelling may come across as a not very bright student with good spelling. It is difficult to identify such students unless they are also requested to write a dictation where they cannot select the words they write. There can be very marked differences in dictated script, not only in terms of spelling, but also in terms of omitted words and handwriting.

Guidelines for the dictation exercise

Students are told that they will be asked to write down the passage which will be read aloud by the tutor or taped. They should try to write legibly, include punctuation and try to write every word they hear, leaving no gaps. Even if they do not know how to spell a word, they should still make an attempt, as the kind of error is as important as whether the word is right or wrong. If they make a mistake, they should correct it by writing the word above or next to the error; they should not cross out their first attempt in a way that prevents it from being read.

Those most at risk may find this a threatening exercise unless it is introduced in a way that makes it feel safe. Emphasise that it is being used in order to offer additional help and let the students know that if anybody finds this particularly stressful they can stop at any time, although it is more helpful in terms of the help that can be offered them if they have a go. Reassure them that even wild and imaginative guesses are fine.

The tutor reads out the text at a reasonable writing speed, repeating each phrase twice. Students are given two minutes to look over their work and make any corrections and check punctuation. Students are asked to make any corrections above their first answer rather than crossing this out, so that both attempts can be seen, and to underline any words they believe are incorrect but do not know how to correct. Their name should be on the dictation before they hand it in.

Marking the dictation

This exercise works best in conjunction with the continuous prose test. As with the continuous prose test, just a quick check-through should be sufficient to identify obvious 'at risk' students. A cross-comparison of the dictation with the free writing can be revealing: significant differences between the two can be a cause for concern. Look for evidence of difficulties in writing at speed, more than one omitted word, spaces where they could not attempt a response, substitute words which suggest the student 'misheard' the word (such as 'particular' for 'peculiar'), many crossings-out or reworking of the letters within a word to correct a mistake, bizarre mis-spellings, or a spelling error rate of around 4 per cent or more (depending on the nature of your intake), especially if these are not common errors. Look too, for poor or deteriorating handwriting.

> ### Dictation passage
> Late one night, I was woken suddenly by my friend who was staring silently out of the window. The moon was partially obscured by clouds after the torrential storms. A peculiar shape was approaching gradually. I had scarcely leapt from my bed when we heard a weird, whistling and whirring noise. We jumped back anxiously. I thought it was a flying saucer or some other unidentified flying object. My friend thought it was a helicopter. It had been whistling around our house in a precise circle, before it started floating gracefully across the flower beds. Unfortunately, it gathered up the garden gnomes and swallowed them inside. To our immense relief, it missed the prize geraniums and regained height. Immediately, we launched ourselves out of the window and ran helter-skelter across the fields, to alert the neighbours to the disturbing phenomenon that had occurred. Of course, nobody believed us.
>
> 150 words

Examples of dictated writing

Balvinder
Some guidance on spelling was offered but there wasn't a need for additional support.

> *Late one night I was woken suddenly by my friends, who was staring silently out of the window. The moon was partially obscured by clouds after the torrential storms. A peculiar shape was approaching gradually, I had scarcely leapt from my bed, when we heard a weird whistling and whirring noise. I thought it was a flying saucer, or some other unidentified flying object.*

Mehmet
The dictation reveals obvious errors of sequencing in spelling. Mehmet was referred for a dyslexia assessment but was not found to be dyslexic. He was offered language support.

> *late one night I was woken suddenly by my friend who was staring silently out of the window. the moon was partially obscured by clouds after the torrential storms. A peculiar shape was approaching gradually, I had scarcely leap from my bed when we heard a weird whistling and whirring noise.*

Diane
The dictation shows a high error rate for spelling, and words were omitted. Additional support was needed on a range of study and language skills because of serious gaps in her previous education.

> *Late one night, I was woken suddenly, by my friends, who was staring silently at of the window. The moon was partly obscured by clouds after the terenstial storms. A perculer shape was approaching graduley, I had scarcely lept from my bed, when we heard a wried whisten noise, I thought is was a flying saucer or some other UFO, My friend thought is was*

(5) Course-specific skills evaluation

Offer either a case study or a piece of text for students to read and answer questions. Ask students to identify any difficulties they had with the exercise.

Example of Social Work Case Study

As part of the application process, applicants to Birmingham University (Selly Oak campus) are sent issues of relevance to the course (in this case on anti-oppressive practice) to read in advance of a written test (which they take on campus). The passage they are sent provides background for both Part 1 and Part 2, below. The written test is used as part of a process to identify students' readiness to cope with the study requirements of the course and their awareness of, and sensitivity to, course issues. Similar types of exercises could be used with other students at either application or during induction.

Birmingham University (Selly Oak campus)

Part 1

Please answer **all** of the following questions. The questions require you to give concise answers in the time allowed (*75 mins*). It is better to try to answer all the questions than spend too long on a few.

(1)   Write a summary of the chapter in no more than 200 words.

(2)   Identify the 5 social divisions used in the chapter. Select two of them and briefly relate them to your work experience.

(3)   What is the PCS model? Take each of the three (P, C and S) and link them to yourself.

(4)   What is institutional oppression? Give an example from your work experience.

(5)   Language can have 'negative connotations'. From your work experience illustrate by identifying two words which have such negative connotations and the negative consequences they might have for clients/service users.

(6)   What are the differences between prejudice and discrimination?

(7)   'Race and gender issues can be contrasted with age and disability issues in at least two ways'. What might be wrong with this statement in year 2000?

Part 2

Choose **one** of the following situations. Identify as many **possible** areas of oppression and diversity as you can with some reasons for the areas identified. Link with any reading you have done. (*Time allowed 45 mins*)

Situation 1

Ellen Jones is 52, of mixed African/Welsh parentage and has epilepsy. She was placed in a large hospital when she was 12 and lived there until she was 45. She is now in a group home in a working-class white council estate in Coventry. Her closest friend in the group home is Mary Sutton who is 63, of Irish origin and who has mild learning disabilities with some associated mobility difficulties. When the two are out together, they get a mixed reception; some younger people make fun of them, others go out of their way to protect them.

Situation 2

Paul Cheung is 15, of mixed Chinese/Scottish parentage and has been causing his mother some concern because of his abusive behaviour to older people on the estate. He has a slight speech impediment about which a group of girls tease him. He hangs out with a group of 13-year-old boys who have similar interests in petty thieving from shops. He has been excluded from school twice for bullying younger boys and girls. His mother feels he needs firmer control from a male but his father left home 3 years ago to live with another man.

(6) Profiling of skills

What is meant by 'profiles' or 'profiling'?

- Profiles are snapshots of current performance. They are one tool which can be used in processes such as reflection, personal and professional development or identifying needs.
- Profiles are built up by making analyses of a student's strengths and weaknesses, or skills and difficulties. This can be done by students, by tutors, or a combination of both.
- The profile can be built up through evaluation, testing, reflection, observation or discussion.
- Profile sheets on various skills can be found in *The Study Skills Handbook* and in this book on pp. 232–3 and 286.

Using profile sheets with students

Profile sheets or questionnaires are a useful first stage in helping to pinpoint areas of difficulty, for discussing perceived needs, and for helping students to identify priorities for action. However, students need guidance on what to do once their difficulties have been identified, either from tutors or specialist support.

Lecturers can devise profile sheets for skills in their own subject area by breaking each major skill into sub-skills. Subject areas or programmes which offer structured feedback sheets for marked assignments can use such sheets to help students to build up a profile of their performance over a number of assignments. It can be helpful for the student to compare their own perception of their performance with their tutors'.

Profile sheets can be photocopied, and the exercise repeated at intervals, by students who are experiencing difficulties. This enables the student (and tutor) to monitor performance over time. Tutors can also put together profiles of whole groups, or target groups, in order to pinpoint the types of support which need to be built into the programme to assist a particular intake.

(7) Position Papers

Activities which help students to build towards writing a Position Paper (Wailey, 1996) are offered in Part II, along with resource materials. Students are led through stimulus material such as structured questions and questionnaires, and take part in discussion groups, guided reflection and support sessions to evaluate their skills, knowledge, experience and personal qualities. They analyse how their past education and experience has prepared them for their current study, and how current study and experience is useful to their career aspirations. A Position Paper makes links between past and present and helps students to identify current needs and requirements in relation to future goals.

Position Papers can include:

(1) Relevant prior learning and experience.
(2) Present knowledge and skills.
(3) Learning aims and objectives: what do I want to achieve?
(4) What needs to be done in order to advance study and career aims?

Position Papers can be used to serve several purposes. They are useful in pulling together ideas, self-evaluation and reflection from a range of induction activities. They can be used to assess English, writing skills, and students' general ability to develop ideas and write them down. They also offer a course profile of the skills a particular cohort finds difficult. This work can be developed over the whole length of a student's time at university. Early drafts, as interim papers, can be used for diagnostic purposes and to offer formative assessments.

A staged assessed process

It is best if this process is managed in stages, with feedback at different points in the process, as in the example of the extended reflective and diagnostic work outlined above.

- Set a requirement for a draft or interim Position Paper to be handed in early in the semester, on which students are offered feedback but not a grade.
- Set a requirement for students to hand in a final version at the end of the semester or the year, which includes an evaluation of how their studies and skills have improved over the year, and what their next set of priorities will be to develop their learning further. This may be assessed, with the marking criteria including credit for reflection, the level of critical analysis, the efficacy of their action

plan, and on how far the Position Paper itself demonstrates the application of what they have learnt.

Ideally, this type of work ought to be picked up at Levels 2 ands 3, and linked to careers education, so that students leave higher education with an updated position paper and curriculum vitae and a clear understanding of the link between personal, academic and professional development. Simpson and Wailey (1999, 2000a) have spearheaded extensive work at UEL in developing a reflective diagnostic process culminating in a written Position Paper. Three examples of Position Paper work are given below. See pp. 95–6 and pp. 235–6 for variations on layout and content for Position Papers.

Example 1: Interim Position Paper: Birmingham University (Selly Oak Campus)

Below is one way in which the guidelines outlined in this book and the Position Paper structure given on pp. 235–6 were piloted. Students are given the following hand-out along with the other materials.

Guidelines for the 'Position Paper'*

Assignment length 1250–1750 words (please indicate word count on front sheet)

Assignment due in: Monday, 9th October 2000

Preparation reading: *The Study Skills Handbook* by Stella Cottrell (1999), Chapters 1 and 2.

A position paper represents a picture of where you are now in terms of skills and learning needs for the Diploma in Social Work course. It is a chance for you to use some of the material generated in our induction sessions and to devise your own action plan for managing learning whilst on the course. You will be asked to evaluate and revise this position paper in the final week before Christmas.

Whilst this assignment will be marked, it *does not* form part of your formal assessment on the course. It is a chance for you to get a taste of what writing for the course will be like and to receive feedback on your writing. We are using it as an opportunity to see how you write. The aim of this is to help you identify your relative strengths and weaknesses and direct you to support as needed. This will help you when it comes to writing the assessed essays for the course.

In addition to writing the paper you are asked to fill out the enclosed 'self-evaluation form' and to hand this in with your paper. We want to know how you have found writing the paper and what difficulties, if any, you have identified during the process. This again helps you, and us, in structuring your learning on the course.

The summary below gives you an idea of what to include and how to organise information. You do not have to include each point and *should not* use headings in your final version. Ideally you should include references to texts, films, songs, etc. that have influenced you, in order to support your reasoning.

* These guidelines are adapted from Cottrell (2000), pp. 235–6, and are based on work undertaken at the University of East London.

Example 2: Interim Position Paper

This example is adapted from the social work course at the University of East London.

By the end of this session you will have practised some writing and will be ready to go away and write an interim Position Paper (to be handed in by September 30). Today's work is a continuation of the exercise you wrote at your admissions interview/initial induction week exercise and will be continued throughout Unit XYZ in year one. This work will also act as a framework to help guide and support you throughout your skills work. It will culminate in a final redrafted Position Paper at the close of semester B, year two. This process will help you to monitor your own academic and professional development, and assist you in presenting your skills and personal qualities when applying for jobs. The process will also be supported through academic guidance/tutorial sessions.

Interim Position Paper checklist:

(1) **Relevant prior learning**   **Where have I been?**

• Demonstrate prior learning, skills, knowledge and experience relevant to being . . . (a social worker, architect, nurse, teacher, accountant, engineer, designer, etc.).

(2) **Present knowledge and skills**   **Where am I now?**

• Categorise your present learning aims and objectives.
• What do you feel are your strengths and weaknesses in relation to starting a course of study in social work, architecture, product design, media and communications, etc.?
• Analyse, briefly, present knowledge and skills.

(3) **Learning aims and objectives**   **Where do I want to go next?**

• How do you think we can best work together in facilitating your career aims?

(4) **Proposed programme of study**

Resource implications   How will I get there?
                                 What will I need to help me?

Assessment scheme   How will I show I have reached goals?
                             (grades, portfolio, CV, skills profile, final Position Paper)

Example 3: Personal Statement Guidelines

This example adapted from the fashion with marketing course at the University of East London.

> (1) Make a self-evaluation of the qualifications, skills, knowledge and experience that you bring with you and which are relevant to your study.
>
> (2) Your aims and aspirations (where would you like to see yourself in 5 years' time? Be imaginative and bold.)
>
> (3) Your reasons for choosing this particular degree.
>
> (4) The skills required to achieve your ambition.
>
> (5) The skills and attributes you want to develop whilst at university.
>
> (6) Your major strengths.
>
> (7) What worries do you have?
>
> (8) How do you plan to overcome them (you may want to discuss this with teaching staff).

Linking identification of need to support

There is little point identifying study difficulties if there is no help on offer. This book offers ways of approaching some study difficulties. However, it will not meet the whole spectrum of student difficulty. Structured support sessions such as 'study skills' or intellectual skills or professional skills modules can help many students. It is best if this is supported by active personal tutoring on a group or individual basis. Some students need additional support from their tutors, or even specialist local support, such as language workshops for those with weak academic English. For example, students are often unaware of how to correct grammar and phrasing, or of how to avoid similar errors in future; they may require very specific guidance and support which course staff may not be trained or able to offer.

There are also many students who are uncertain about how to address ongoing study difficulties because of a range of emotional and personal reasons. Such students may need a great deal of encouragement and guidance. Some will need specialist support such as for specific learning difficulties (dyslexia, dyspraxia, etc.), individual academic English sessions, or counselling. Clarify for students the procedures for accessing such support.

Final comments

The key factor in assessing student needs is that the methods used leave the students with as much dignity as possible and do not have counter-productive effects upon their chances of a positive outcome to their studies. If diagnosis of need is linked to a wider process of induction, learning development and support, and if it is part of the curriculum for all students, then it loses much of the stigma that it can otherwise carry. Students are less likely to regard themselves as being 'problem students' who stand out in shameful ways and whom other people are trying to 'fix'. It reduces the chances of adults repeating the negative experiences which may have originally prompted them to leave school early. It also means that learning development is not merely an opportunity offered to struggling students, but can be built into the student experience so that even the strongest students are pushed beyond their initial capacities. Stronger students as well as others have the chance to leave higher education with a much deeper self-understanding of what they have achieved and how, and of themselves as future professionals.

5 Integrating study skills into teaching

For many years I taught in universities. Like most academics I assumed that the only qualification I needed was expertise in the discipline I taught. It did cross my mind that how to teach might be a discipline in its own right, but I never gave it much thought. I marked thousands of examination scripts without examining what the scripts could teach me about my capacity as teacher and examiner.

Ashby (1984)

The role of lecturers in promoting learning skills

Lecturers play an essential role in the development of students' study skills and general learning development – and this role is likely to increase in the future. This growing importance can be attributed to changes in the composition of the student body, the spread of computerised information and the increased emphasis on skills development, often linked to 'employability'. Additional skills development often enters universities purely as discrete provision, offered by a specialist centre or skills unit. It may become supplemented by modules which emphasise or specialise in study skills in a particular way. However, it is increasingly evident that, in addition to these two necessary forms of provision, learning development and skills

enhancement do not thrive if they are divorced from the students' overall teaching and learning experience. This necessitates the involvement of all lecturers.

Information versus process

As the 'content' of courses becomes more generally available through publishing and the internet, it becomes less significant that lecturers are bearers of content knowledge and more important that they are able to promote process skills such as information management, critical analysis and learning in interpersonal contexts. It has been a slow process in universities to move away from the medieval notion of academics as carriers of essential information to a realisation that information is not now a limited commodity and that the key issues for students today are less about gaining access to information as about knowing what to do with it once they have it: how to cope with the amount, to select, manipulate, make meaning, deal with multiple meaning, and how to present knowledge and understanding for assessment or for different audiences.

The link between study skill provision and teaching

As learning development takes root in universities, there is a growth in study skills or personal and professional development modules, and 'centres' to which students can be referred. Whilst these are useful developments, they can be a waste of expensive resources if they are offered in isolation from the everyday teaching the student receives. The lecturer plays a key role in making meaningful, and therefore valuable, what is offered through study skill work offered outside of the general subject context. Although this is often ignored, it is not difficult to see why this is the case.

The amount of time students spend with study or language specialists is very small compared to that spent with other teaching staff. It is very rarely likely to amount to more than a few hours of support, in total, for any individual. When students are offered study skills modules, with accompanying seminar and tutorial series, they have more time for reflection and are able to begin to apply what they are learning to other areas of their study. However, students often forget what they have covered unless their attention is called back to what they have learnt, and they may not see the relevance of what they covered in skills sessions until they receive unexpected low marks or hit a difficult patch on their course.

Research (Gick and Holyoak, 1980, 1983; Reed et al., 1985; Brown and Clements, 1989) has shown that for skills to be transferable, students need to have the link made explicit between the skill and the new area to which it will be applied. They also need guided practice in using the skill in the new area and preferably bridging analogies and multiple examples of how to do so. When students have learnt study skills in discrete units, they have not necessarily had any significant practice in applying the skill to a real context at all. The skill may seem quite abstract – like knowledge of how to dive given away from the swimming pool. It may also seem more complex than it is, because it lacks a concrete reference point. The more that skills sessions are linked to a particular course of study, the more the student is likely to feel confident in how to apply them.

The lecturer occupies a unique place in being able to model gently how skills are applied in the subject area, in demonstrating how they may need to be fine-tuned to meet the specific contexts of the course, and in creating opportunities to draw attention to the process of learning. It is through the lecturer's repetition and modelling that study skills are made meaningful in the context of particular course material and assignments. Without this repetition, the skills may soon be forgotten. Moreover, study skills sessions generally emphasise how students can attune themselves to the demands of HE, but attunement needs to be a two-way process. It is pointless teaching students to structure their notes by listening out for 'clues' in the lecturer's introduction if a lecturer does not give such clues – or even an introduction. Similarly, if a course gives out a complete set of lecture notes to students, the study skill required is not aural note-making skills but how to make use of printed material. Sometimes small adjustments to ensure basic good teaching practices can reduce a great deal of student anxiety and difficulty.

This chapter offers practical ways of building supportive strategies into teaching, firstly by looking at general teaching approaches which promote learning, and secondly at ways that practical study skills support can be integrated into teaching without too much effort. In this way, learning development can function as a joint enterprise, where the teaching strategies employed by the lecturer meet the students at their current level of performance and lead them to more autonomous ways of studying. This is an integrative and inclusive approach to learning development rather than a remedial one, and one which recognises that lecturers can build upon students' self-confidence, language development and chances of success through every aspect of their teaching.

General teaching approaches which promote learning

(1) Orientation and overview

Study skills difficulties towards the end of a course, such as failure to meet assessment deadlines or objectives, sometimes originate in an early failure, on the part of the student, to grasp essential information about what is required of them. It is hard to open up to learning without the security of a good orientation to the course, its expectations and its methods. Many learners benefit from being offered a brief overview of the material and objectives so that they can see in advance how the course fits together and what is required of them. Although this is usually catered for through course handbooks, it makes more sense to the student if it is also addressed in the first session or during induction.

Orientation at admission

Students enter HE with misconceptions about what is expected of them and then struggle to keep up with a range of external commitments. It is important to clarify course expectations in terms of reading, writing, numeracy and other skills, both at application, and when students are selecting options. In particular, applicants may hold very extreme underestimations of how much reading is involved. It is also helpful to specify the total study time requirements, including how many hours an average student would be expected to study a week and in holidays. It can help to identify how much additional time students would need to leave aside for study if they lack the knowledge or skills base for the course.

Students may also have a false sense of what the course involves, so it is essential to give details of the content, aims of the course and the main features of teaching and learning, especially if there is any possibility that students may have mistaken a more theoretical course for a practical one. This saves weaker students from losing essential teaching time early in the year when they realise they need to switch options.

Orientation to the space

Ensure that students are clear about where are the nearest facilities, including refreshments. This is especially important if the student is likely to be taking lectures in several different buildings or on different sites.

Orientation to time

Be clear whether you are likely to begin each session promptly. There may be good reasons for a slightly delayed start, such as when you know students have to walk over from another building between lectures and could not begin on time. If you say you will begin on time, then do, or else the early arrivers will become resentful at being kept waiting, and students can tend to arrive later and later, knowing you will wait. Be clear at the beginning how the session's time will be broken up on that day: such as half an hour for feedback on an assignment, an hour to go over the next topic, 15 minutes' break, three quarters of an hour for group discussions and half an hour for feedback from the groups. It is very important to keep clear boundaries on time as it builds up trust in what you say. It also helps anxious students to feel more secure.

Orientation to the course

Ideally this should include:

- an overview of the purpose of the course or module, and an indication of the relevance of the unit or module to the overall course or career pathway;
- aims and objectives of the course or module;
- the main themes that run through the course or module. Why have these been selected? How do they link up? Diagrams or charts linking key elements are especially useful?
- theoretical approaches which inform the course or module;
- an indication of why the course or module is relevant and interesting;
- teaching methods used on the course or module;
- what students can expect from you and from each session;
- intended learning outcomes and how students will know if they have achieved these.

Orientation to the teaching and learning environment

Introduce:

- teaching methods that will be used on the course;

- your expectations of the students as learners;
- essential reading for each session;
- assessment methods, dates and deadlines, what will happen if work is late, and marking criteria;
- ground rules: time-keeping, attendance, protocols for asking questions;
- who to see for help.

Orientation to each other

This will vary according to the type of work to be undertaken together and the size of the group, but it is generally useful if students are acquainted with people on their course, especially if they are likely to need to study support from each other. When students start new units, it is helpful if they at least have an opportunity of an activity for exchanging names, a few 'icebreakers' and some short activities in which they can interact with each other. (See the group-work activities below.)

General strategies

To develop as learners, students need their lecturers to:

- show they consider the development of study/learning skills to be important;
- relate general study skills to their specific subject area;
- make the 'hidden curriculum' explicit;
- structure the course so that there are opportunities to practise tasks which are assessed;
- design assignments and assessment methods which let students taste success;
- create an environment which promotes enthusiasm, mutual support and learning, and which is safe for self-exploration, experimentation – and making mistakes;
- develop self-evaluation skills – so that they are able to evaluate their own performance and progress.

Affective factors

Lecturers are often those who have enjoyed most success academically, and sometimes they can find it difficult to understand how low self-esteem can impact negatively upon performance. Students from widening participation backgrounds, even if they are able candidates, may have strong doubts about whether they are good enough and whether university is really a place for them. They can be very sensitive to criticism which does not clearly guide them towards higher marks. Students may have a very weak sense of themselves as thinking, creative, and problem-solving people. Lecturers teaching students from vocational backgrounds may note that students can quickly lose confidence again during vacations.

To achieve the most from their students, lecturers need to be aware that their students may have a very fragile sense of their own academic worth, and need to respond by creating opportunities for students to build confidence in their own ideas. A taste of success is extremely important. High anxiety about appearing stupid may encourage students to hide their difficulties from lecturers precisely at the point where some direct help is needed. In addition, students with multiple responsibilities can operate very close to their stress thresholds. This often leads to drop-out, health or mental health difficulties. It is important that lecturers create a feeling of safety about disclosing difficulty, within a context of peer support and mutual problem solving.

Lecturers can help their students to succeed through:

- building self-confidence and self-belief;
- helping students to stay in contact with initial motivation;
- encouraging them to consider how they view themselves as learners, as intelligent adults and as future professionals;
- checking which attitudes they bring to problem solving;
- encouraging them to look for enjoyment in the learning process;
- providing opportunities to address anxieties, stress management, self-concept and positive attitudes to problem solving.

(2) Structure: the 'magic 7' teaching session

Using a structured approach to sessions not only helps to orientate and settle students, it also models good organisational skills and gives students a structure they can use when they lead seminars. In addition, the model described below enables lecturers to monitor for learning so that they can adapt their teaching to match the areas of difficulty. The 'magic 7' teaching session outlined here can be adapted to suit most teaching situations.

The 'magic 7' teaching structure

(1) *Settle.*   Use an icebreaker activity or brief feeding-in period to bring the group together again. Refer to ground rules if necessary.

(2) *Orientate.*   Check for previous learning on the subject; link to the previous session if relevant. Ideally, this should be linked to work set as preparation for the session. For example:

- give students one or two minutes to jot down individually or to brainstorm in pairs or threes all they can remember from the last session – and map this out on the board from their comments;
- connect the learning to the objectives of the unit and to the students' individual learning goals;
- set questions to be answered or challenges to be addressed within the session.

(3) *Outcomes.*   Clarify what students will know or be able to do by the end of the session. This may simply mean going through the section of the course handbook where this is outlined.

(4) *Active learning.*   This is the main part of the session. Offer a series of activities and inputs which involve students in more than simply note taking.

(5) *Check for learning.*   Ask for questions about anything the students are still unsure about. Does anything need clarification? Set an activity, problem or puzzle where new knowledge can be applied. Set a one-minute learning task similar to the orientation exercise above.

(6) *Futures.*   Give an indication of how what has been learnt will be developed in the next session.

(7) *Anchor achievement.*   Ask students for a final comment about where they are now, such as the one most important thing they are taking away from the session.

(3) Awareness of learning styles

The more research that is undertaken into learning, the more it is realised that individual learning styles can have an important impact on learning outcomes. It is useful for lecturers to be aware of the range and subtle diversity of learning styles and preferences that can exist within the teaching room – and broaden teaching methods to include a wider range of students, even if it is not possible to suit all students all of the time. The traditional university student was, very generally, one who learnt best through auditory modes (listening), high personal responsibility and motivation, low activity (sitting still for long periods) or who had the capacity and insight to work out strategies to work around these requirements if they did not suit. Traditionally, those who did not learn in these ways did not do well at school and were unlikely to enter university. Today, they may be the students who struggle disproportionately under certain conditions and prosper under others. When working in a specialist unit, it is very common to see students begin to thrive as they realise they have a capacity to learn when the conditions for learning are changed.

The 21 variable matrix

The Dunn and Dunn Learning Style Model (1992, 1993) is perhaps the most comprehensive model and has been described as demonstrating the highest levels of consistent effectiveness (Dunn *et al.*, 1995; Given, 1996, 1998). It is especially helpful to teachers in identifying distracters to learning, and in considering approaches to teaching and classroom management; its guidance to students is rather thin and, in a way, feeds back to them what they have already identified for themselves.

The model identifies a matrix of 21 variables which affect learning. These are divided into five categories: environmental, emotional, sociological, physical and psychological. It was found, for example, that some people have a high need for external direction whilst others have a strong need for self-direction and self-exploration; some learn optimally only when they work alone, others learn best in pairs, small groups, teams, or as a whole class. Some learn only when 'doing' or using their hands; others only when they can 'see' the information rather than simply hearing it. 'Emotional' factors such as the degree of structure, flexibility, level of required responsibility, and motivation vary a great deal in their effect on individual study.

Most people operate within a high tolerance band for each variable: they can compensate when optimal conditions do not pertain. However, some people have a very reduced capacity for learning if particular variables are not in place and most of us are affected minimally when our preferences are not met. Lighting, temperature, the type and size of group, the method of delivery, a need to move around or even to nibble food when learning, can mean the difference between being able to focus, or having to leave the room in desperation, for some students.

Dunn and Dunn's model is useful as an assessment tool as it encompasses other learning style models within it. It has been used successfully with different cultural and age groups, although not really tested at an HE level. It is computerised to give both individual and whole-group profiles.

Sensory modality

There are different models and tools for assessing learning styles. Neuro-linguistic Programming (NLP) for example, argues that each of us has a preferred sensory mode (touch, sight, sound) for attuning us to, and making sense of, information. Visual learners respond best to images and visual representations, visualisations, reading, and language which incorporates 'seeing' words ('imagine', 'look at', 'looks like', 'picture this', 'notice'). Auditory learners respond to listening, to music, to word-based tasks, to going over things in their heads, talking things through and to words or sounds

which stimulate the auditory mode such as 'listen', 'hear', 'speaking of which'. Kinaesthetic learners prefer to incorporate movement – writing, walking around, doodling, so practical and activity-based learning often suits them best. They respond to language which includes 'doing' and 'feeling' words ('plot', 'map out', 'this may feel like').

An NLP practitioner would identify subtle variations in individuals' primary and secondary preferences for sense modality. In a teaching context, it may be sufficient to draw students' attention to the possibility of enhancing their learning using different modalities. The exercise on pp. 215–16 below can help students to identify their preferred modality. Lecturers can also ensure that they use a mix of activities and language patterns that appeal to visual, auditory and kinaesthetic learning styles. Cottrell (1999) also gives examples of how to use different sense modality preferences in a practical way to improve memory.

Learner types

In higher education, the Honey and Mumford learning style questionnaire (LSQ) is gaining in popularity as a reasonably easy-to-use alternative to MBTI (Myers–Briggs type indicator) based testing (Allison and Hayes, 1988; Lawrence, 1995). The LSQ identifies differences in the ways learners identify with the four distinct stages of Kolb's learning spiral (1984): experience (feeling), reflective observation (watching), abstract conceptualisation (thinking) and active experimentation (doing) – ideally each stage leading to the next stage in a continuous spiral.

Honey and Mumford classified four types of behaviours which indicate an overreliance on, or a preference for, different stages of the learning cycle. In brief, these are *Activists*, who prefer to learn from new experience but may need to learn how to stay with the subject to really work things through; *Reflectors*, who enjoy exploring different perspectives but may need to develop abilities in moving towards conclusions; *Theorists* who learn best by logical integration of their findings but balk at subjective learning and ambiguity; and *Pragmatists* who learn best through practice but may need to develop their reflectivity. Honey and Mumford (1994) recommend the use of learning journals ('logs') for reflection, self-monitoring and review for all students.

Unlike many learning style approaches, the Honey and Mumford approach offers practical guidance on how to develop abilities in weak areas as well as on how to work to individual strengths. Goodworth (1999), using the Honey and Mumford learning styles questionnaire to undertake a study of learning styles for different design-based courses, found that different courses attracted cohorts with alternative learning-style tendencies. The LSQ, like the Dunn and Dunn inventory, can be used to generate information for staff designing teaching activities, in helping lecturers to identify ways of offering guidance to students, and for students selecting partners for group work on the basis of complementary strengths. Goodworth found that students were very receptive to the idea that their learning was influenced both by teaching styles and their own learning responses, and that these were open to change.

Realistic adaptation

Whilst it is impossible for lecturers to meet all the learning needs of their students, variety in teaching styles and learning activities ensures that more students have some of their needs met some of the time. Lecturers can also be sensitive to what may appear to be idiosyncratic behaviour, such as eating in class, wearing lots of jumpers or wearing caps to block out light. If lecturers use multi-sensory techniques, use language and activities which appeal to different sense modalities, break teaching time up into different types of activities, vary delivery between tutor-led and student-centred activities, integrate activities to be undertaken alone, in pairs, small groups and teams, the learning environment will feel inclusive to a larger number of students.

(4) Precision about requirements

Students frequently say that they 'simply do not understand what the lecturers mean'. This is particularly true of essay titles, comments on returned work and long instructions which appear contradictory or vague to the student. For example, students find it hard to know what is meant by 'integrate analysis into your report'. They often do not know what 'analysis' is, do not know if they have ever seen an example of 'analysis' or even which parts of their writing may already be 'analytical'. Students may know the words used, such as 'discuss', but feel their interpretation of everyday words is different from the lecturer's. Lecturers often report that students do not do as they are asked.

Reasons why students do not understand what is required

(1) Many students have had no previous contact with higher education. Often they have not had the benefits of observing family members going through HE and have had no opportunities to become familiar with the conventions of academic life (such as what an essay is, or the importance of deadlines, or attendance, or working without constant supervision, or even what academic language looks or sounds like).

(2) Academic conventions in other countries can be different so students who have studied overseas, or who have family who did, may be trying to work to different sets of conventions than those required here. For example, writing out passages from books may elsewhere be seen as the sign of respect in a good student rather than regarded as plagiarism.

(3) Different academic areas have very particular conventions. Requirements for referencing, layout, academic writing styles and use of English vary a great deal from one subject to another, and even from tutor to tutor.

(4) Students are often told 'there is no right answer'. They can find it hard to develop an exploratory way of working unless they have some guidance. It can also be confusing to be given a low mark and feedback

which suggest their answer is 'wrong'. There appears to be a hidden agenda of 'right answers' about which they are not being told.

Most students want to succeed, and recognise that success depends to a large measure on 'giving lecturers what they want'. They often wish they knew what that was.

Lecturers can be more precise by:

- Explaining what is required, in everyday English. For example, if you want an essay to be 'discursive', you may need to explain exactly what that means, and discuss with reference to real examples, given to the students in hard copy.
- Discussing how marks are allocated, according to criteria. Be explicit and give examples of what is actually meant by the criteria you use. It can help to let students mark some sample essays using the criteria you use and discuss the exercise.
- Explaining conventions, such as the relative importance of the title to a piece of work. You may benefit from explaining which words actually are the title, and which words are explanatory text, as some students find it difficult to differentiate the two. Paraphrasing or discussing set titles may also help
- Giving more detail about what you want. How does the assignment relate to the course aims and objectives and, in general, to theory you have covered?
- Giving concrete examples – e.g., a copy of a reasonably good exam answer or essay. It is best if this annotated, so that good or weak points are made explicit.
- Giving concrete examples to support your feedback, e.g., if you want 'more detail', it is best to explain exactly what kind of detail is required. Show and discuss examples, brainstorm titles, discuss what is appropriate and inappropriate.
- Establishing a bank of annotated examples of different kinds of work required for each semester (essays, dissertations, projects, case studies, reports, seminar presentations).

- Drawing attention to, and discussing, the different types of writing required on course and how these differ from one another – and the logic behind those differences.
- Drawing attention to, and discussing, differences between the styles and conventions of writing for your module or part of the course compared to those required for other units the students may be taking.

(5) Repetition through concrete examples

For new areas of learning, we generally need to be anchored in concrete experience before we can move on to more open-ended or creative answers: we need multiple examples from which we can abstract generalities. Butterworth (1992) argues that we develop the potential for abstract reasoning out of familiarity with the concrete: it is easier for students to take in new information if it is anchored in concrete examples rather than as abstract information. Many students will remember better if their attention is drawn to the concrete, through written material or visual prompts, so that they are using their ears and eyes to the same purpose.

Most of us need to go over something three times in order to remember it – and more often if we are distracted or under stress. If you want to be certain students have grasped a point, or registered a particular instruction, repetition may be necessary. It follows that it helps students to see several concrete examples of each type of new assignment required of them (case study, essay, log notes, etc.). However, simply seeing an example will not help weaker students to draw out what is expected. It helps if examples are annotated to draw out strengths and weaknesses, and to indicate what loses or gains marks. Students can benefit from step-by-step guides to all new forms of assessment.

When you repeat things, you will tend to paraphrase what you said previously: this can be useful to those who may have difficulty in making sense of how the information was phrased the first time round.

Key areas for repetition

- Give an overview of the session at the beginning and a summary at the end.
- Give an overview and summary of any separate sections during the session.
- Repeat key points and draw attention to these through a hand-out.
- Repeat proper names when they are introduced for the first time in the session and write these up. Include these on the hand-out.
- Repeat specialist vocabulary when it is first introduced and write this up. Draw attention to this in a glossary, given either in a hand-out or listed in the course handbook.

(6) Using metaphor or analogy

Metaphor offers a valuable link between new and difficult material and concrete, 'graspable' experience. At the same time it bolsters confidence by validating prior experience as useful to current learning. This is especially important to 'mature' or anxious students, who gain from seeing that all knowledge and experience offers a foundation onto which more complex concepts can be grafted. It encourages them to value their own life experiences and to make the academic information seem accessible as part of a continuum rather than as discrete specialist knowledge for clever experts. L. V. Williams (1983) offers extended examples of how unexciting material can be made interesting (such as how a dry lesson on the dissection of clams came alive though through prior exploration of personal and animal fear) and how difficult material can be made accessible even to very small children through appropriate analogy.

Thinking metaphorically will liberate some students but others may find it difficult. It is important to higher education study as it teaches students to look for connections and applications, and to generate and test models. Difficulties in thinking metaphorically can impact on problem solving, applying knowledge to new contexts and even to basic 'compare and contrast' essays. Traditionally, students who were accepted into HE were those who, if tested, tended to do well on IQ tests which measured aptitude for discovering 'similarities' between discrete objects. Weak and struggling students, when tested, often perform poorly at this. It is therefore useful to encourage students to develop their thinking about how information overlaps, intersects or resonates through offering examples and practice.

Encourage students to develop metaphors of their own by asking them:

- 'What is similar about the way X and Y function?'
- 'What can you think of that operates like this in everyday life?'
- 'In what ways is this the same as X?'
- 'In what ways are the two things different?'
- 'How does it help or limit us to think of this being like X?'

Explore what kind of metaphors or analogies they can generate to describe their own lives or learning or approach to the course. What metaphors can they generate to describe your teaching? Do these match your own view of your teaching? Working with metaphor not only clarifies and reinforces learning but also develops important thinking skills.

(7) Multi-sensory approaches

Memory and learning are improved when several senses are involved. We are more likely to remember something if we can call upon our visual, auditory, motor and kinaesthetic memories – each assists the other. It will help your students if they hear, see and do something to register the information in their long-term memory. The following ideas are particularly useful in this respect.

Students listening to their own voices

Students are more likely to recall what they have learnt if they have heard the information spoken in their own voices. This can be encouraged through:

- discussion work in general;
- small group work, where more people have the opportunity to speak;

- student presentations and demonstration – very valuable as learning is clarified through the act of teaching another person;
- dividing the large group into smaller groups, each of which has responsibility to teach the rest of the group one aspect of the course (with the lecturer's support and guidance);
- encouraging students to record their own voices whilst they explore a subject aloud.

All of these are good strategies for examination revision.

'Playing' with the information

Anything which involves students in manipulating, rearranging, selecting, criticising, debating, teaching or organising information into diagrammatic form assists in developing understanding and recall of that information.

Writing

The act of writing things down assists the motor memory – which is why some people check spelling through writing the word down to see if it 'feels' right. This is unlikely to work if the information is not noted with focused attention. If too much writing is undertaken at one time, the information is unlikely to be transferred to the long-term memory. Tired writers note that they have written pages without any recollection of doing so.

Visual information

Pictures are easier to remember and faster to process than words. Using images as visual prompts either in lectures or in hand-outs will help students to locate and recall information. Images, including graphs, charts, pictures, cartoons, diagrams and videos, help us to make sense of what we hear, and to focus different senses on the same task. You can encourage students to visualise the information that you give them by asking them to run it as a film in their heads, or by suggesting that they imagine how course material would impact upon the lives of particular people that they know. You can also use a more visual vocabulary with concrete examples in your lectures, so that students' attention is drawn to their visual sense ('Can

you all see this?' and to internal visual representations of the material 'Can you picture this example?' 'Can anybody give me a real-life example of this?').

(8) Active learning methods

Learning is enhanced most through 'doing'. Some examples of ways that active learning can be incorporated into the course design are listed below.

Examples of active learning

Content
- Working from case studies
- Discussing the relevance of the material to one's own experience
- Looking for the relevance of the material to real-life situations
- Looking for the connections between related subject areas

Context
- Paired work, threes, small groups, teams, whole-group discussion
- Lab work, practicals, studio work
- Work experience
- Work-based learning

Focus
- Making or designing things
- Case work, client work
- Problem solving
- Experiments
- Devising quiz questions
- Setting exam questions or essay titles

Critical thinking and reflection
- Self-evaluation and assessment
- Setting criteria for assessing work
- Assessing other people's work (peer assessment)
- Justifying one's self-assessment

Gibbs (1992) cites the example of an Oxford lecturer who broke three-hour geography lectures into 16 sections, divided between activities and lecturer input. The longer the session, the more important it is to break it up in this way. As many students learn best through discussion or activity, this will meet the learning needs of a wider percentage of the intake. On a smaller scale, learning is more active when students, rather than merely reading or listening, also have to answer questions which they have set themselves or which they have been given in advance, or when they have to tick options, or give points or perform any other small activity which requires an increase in focus and interaction with the text or speaker.

The more that students are involved in the various stages of setting agendas for study, teaching other students, setting criteria, and assessing other people and themselves, the more actively they are engaged in their studies and the more likely they are to learn. The process is demystified and learning is made meaningful and more memorable.

(9) Motivation, interest and relevance

Little learning can take place without motivation – without 'wanting to learn'. Interest in one aspect of the syllabus may not always extend to having to write essays, or to covering other parts of the syllabus. If the subject is presented in ways which do not seem relevant to the students' own lives, histories, circumstances and aspirations, they may find it very difficult to focus their attention for long.

What lecturers can do to increase students' motivation

Focus on individual motivation
- Encourage students to focus, from time to time, on their own motivation either for taking the option, or in becoming a student.
- Build this into the reflective aspect of the course.
- Link their learning to their personal skills profiles or portfolios, or to the professional skills required for career pathways. Chapters 2–4 of *The Study Skills Handbook* (Cottrell, 1999) provide tools for such self-exploration.

Make subject matter relevant to the students' own lives
- Explore with the students the relevance of your course to personal life contexts.

- Include careers education within the curriculum.
- Information which always seems to be about alien circumstances or people with whom students do not identify can become a strain on their attention. Quite often the information will not make sense or may appear to contradict reality such as the students experience it. It can be exciting to explore that contradiction as part of a course, but if it is not acknowledged, many students will 'switch off'.

Increase interest in the subject
Some charismatic lecturers can do this through force of personality. This is a rare skill. Other ways of increasing interest are by:

- Using a variety of approaches, teaching styles, and ways of breaking up the time.
- Setting assignments and on-course tasks which require students to work out answers and solve problems for themselves.
- Building in opportunities for small 'successes'.
- Building in real-life learning (e.g., solving real-life cases, work experience).

Help students to feel good about their study
- Give praise where it is due. Students need to feel they can succeed.
- Help students to feel that they are getting somewhere with their work.
- Show students exactly what is required to excel.
- Give opportunities to do something creative or to deliver an end-product.
- Create opportunities for students to feel they are part of a good team or support network, for example, by developing good group dynamics early on.
- Help students to feel that study goals are worth the effort.

(10) Scaffolding and pacing

One of the difficulties faced by students in higher education is that the level of the first year, or even of a particular unit, does not begin at their current level of understanding, knowledge and skill. Students can feel that they are floating and adrift if they do not sense that the teaching supports them as they move from one step to another. Scaffolding is a concept Bruner (1975) applied to the development of children's learning, referring to the way an adult can support the construction of learning before the child achieves 'stand-alone competence'. Anxious adult learners, even competent learners, may be inhibited in their learning until appropriate scaffolding is put into place to help them step from their current position towards the desired learning goals.

With mixed ability intakes, this may mean that lecturers need to provide additional examples or problems to be worked through for those who have not grasped the learning the first time around. For students with weak knowledge bases, it is useful if lecturers can recommend some of the simplest foundation books in order to build up an overview of the subject and give students the moral support to do this. Additional study groups on complex material can also be invaluable, especially if these are tutor-led so that students can trust in the teaching. Additional student support groups, especially if supported by the staff and where training is given in working co-operatively, can help students to consolidate learning.

Some students need to be taken through information slowly, step by step. This is perhaps not as uncommon as may be expected. In VSI (video supplemental instruction) schemes in the USA, lectures are videoed so that mentors can lead the students through the same material a second time, discussing it and clarifying difficult areas:

> Lectures are stopped and started as needed allowing the facilitator to verify that students have comprehended one idea before moving onto the next. Students develop essential reading, learning and study skills while they master the content and earn top grades in core curriculum subjects.
>
> (Patterson, 1999)

This VSI model divorces 'delivery' through lectures from the real 'teaching for learning' which is left to paid students to undertake. If student facilitators can help students to achieve top grades in this way, how much more could a trained and skilled lecturer achieve if they used similar methods?

(11) Ensuring access to the curriculum

Students may have a very poor sense of how to manage reading lists and lack criteria for selecting wisely from options or in finding alternatives. First-year students may find set texts too difficult to begin work on a new subject, and need guidance on how to build towards more sophisticated texts after gaining an overview of the subject from more basic texts. Always offer a written overview of the lecture, with key points and references so that those who find it hard to follow by ear, or who are absent, still have access to the material. It is becoming increasingly common for such materials to be offered to students on departmental web pages. It is likely that students with disabilities, with family commitments and work commitments will miss at least some sessions; it is therefore sensible to cater for this.

It is essential that the teaching and design of first-year programmes matches the learning experiences and current performance levels of the intake. Lecturers can achieve a great deal through basic good teaching. This may include simple strategies such as structuring lectures with an introduction and conclusion, reiterating points, and drawing attention to the development of the lecture's line of reasoning. A guiding rule of thumb is whether the range of teaching methods employed through coursework, lecture, seminar and reading ensures full access to the curriculum for all students and that they are aware of this access.

Materials

- Easily readable font size on hand-outs (11/12 pt minimum in Times New Roman or 10/11 pt Ariel, or equivalent) and overheads (40 pt).
- Good clear photocopies of materials.
- Back-up notes and glossaries for all lectures, either in print or on web pages.

- Plenty of white space on hand-outs for students to add in their own comments.
- Headings, numbering and logical sequencing.

Lectures and seminars

- Break taught sessions into sections and build in activities, so that unreasonable listening demands are not placed upon students.
- Keep to a reasonable listening speed – which is slower than normal talking speed. Take pauses and breaks for students to assimilate each point.
- Repeat important points. Introduce points at the beginning, say when you are going on to a new point, summarise at the end.
- Be clear: avoid jargon and acronyms, especially with groups which include overseas students and those with language-related disabilities (deafness, dyslexia).
- Make the best use of time: use lecture time to clarify difficulties and to build on home preparation rather than reading from notes or delivering information *at* students.

Developing students' skills through teaching

(1) Reinforcement and modelling of study skills

Skills-based modules cannot be expected to do more than introduce students to skills. They cannot offer the full range of opportunity needed to make sense of and apply skills in a range of contexts and through practice over time. All lecturers need to be familiar with any study skills materials which students have received, and make explicit references to the appropriate sections when teaching or giving feedback on assignments.

It is important that classroom lecturers model skills through their teaching and create opportunities for students to put their skills into practice. For example, lecturers who use group work give their students a chance to explore their own ideas, problem-solve, and become used to discussing ideas with others. Students can be

asked to generate ideas through brainstorming or structured questioning. The way that lecturers develop an idea, using thinking tools such as mind maps and flow charts, can familiarise students with how to organise ideas and move from scattered note structures to logical linear sequence. Lecturers can draw attention to how they built up their line of argument for the lecture, their process of critical analysis, sorting information into categories and making selections of what to omit and include in order to keep to word or time limits. This makes the process of academic thinking explicit and students are more able to accept it as possible for themselves to think in an academic way.

(2) Conceptualising the subject

Start with visual representations

Images help students to conceptualise information more clearly and to retain it for longer. It makes an extraordinary difference to students' ability to absorb material if they can see the points written next to the appropriate parts of a concrete, real-life image or drawing. For example, if you are lecturing on 'migration', use a map or chart which illustrates the movement, rather than simply describing it. A drawing does not need to be 'good': a rough but recognisable outline can suffice. The image anchors the thought, grounds the information, stimulates the imagination, and helps focus attention for longer.

Give an overview

It is generally easier for most students to take in information and orientate to the subject if they have an overview of what will be covered.

Check what is already known

Orientate students to individual teaching sessions by checking quickly what is already known. This could be by:

- asking students to write for a minute on everything they know about the subject and writing up contributions from the group in pattern notes;
- putting headings of the main themes from

the previous session on the board, and asking what they can remember about each. Write this up under each heading;

- putting up headings of the main themes for the current session, and asking what they know already about each.

(3) Managing information

When books were extremely rare commodities, universities served an important role in transmitting, orally, information which was not otherwise available. Today, the problem facing students is not accessing information so much as managing the range and amount of information, of categorising, selecting, and applying it appropriately. Almost all students have to face the moment when they realise they cannot read, learn, and use all the information available on a subject, and that all data and theories are not of equal value. Lecturers can build into their lectures clues about how to manage information. This is far more important than 'delivering' information, when that information is available in books, on CD, or on the internet – or if it could be provided in notes and handouts.

Guidance in selecting key information

Struggling students can have extraordinary difficulties in deciding what is the most salient information to select – or even in allowing themselves to select information at all. Lecturers can help by:

- Demonstrating how they made their selections of materials, what they had to omit (because of shortage of time) and the criteria they used as the basis for selection.
- Setting activities where students have to make decisions about 'selection'. For example, 'Select the three most important out of five reasons why this outcome occurred' or 'If you could choose only one of these options, which one would you select and why?' Use class discussion to explore the rationale for the choices made. Lecturers need to be clear when there is or isn't a 'right answer'.

- Giving guidance in criteria for selecting the most relevant information. There are many short-cuts in reading and finding information and lecturers will be aware of these in relation to their own subject such as which parts of texts used for the subject require less attention, which publication dates are key for a certain topic, or which search engines on the internet are likely to be most productive for the subject).
- Giving guidance on how to 'read' different types of texts used in the subject. For example, for Law, where do students need to focus and read more slowly, and where can they skim-read, when reading wills, contracts, motions, briefs, letters, 'case cites' for the judge, reports for clients, legal columns in paper, etc.?

Hierarchies and links

The brain retains information better when it is organised into hierarchies and when it is linked to related material (Bower *et al.* 1969). Many students find it very difficult to see how course information links up and do not know how to organise similarities, connections and differences in a systematic way. They lack the mental schema for organising information in useful ways. Modes of learning based around note taking can exacerbate this difficulty, as students often produce files of more or less undifferentiated information, with little cross-referencing or linking. Lecturers can help by using a range of methods for organising information, firstly through demonstration of techniques, and secondly by building in exercises where students do this in pairs or small groups. For some intakes, it is very helpful if lecturers reinforce and elaborate upon the types of activities outlined in Chapter 15, using subject specific examples. This helps students to transfer the skills from one area to another, and to develop more complex mental schema of the operations involved.

Pattern notes

Pattern notes of various kinds, such as the 'mind maps' popularised by Tony Buzan, usually generate ideas by brainstorming key points around a central theme, placed in the centre of the note-making space. Each key point then becomes the focus of the next set of themes, which radiate from it. Patterns and images of all kinds can be built up, using images, colour and numbers to sequence movement around the pattern. Some students also find it easier to remember information from this kind of structure, as long as the map is well structured. However, students who find it difficult to categorise information will often become more muddled using mind maps, as they require a sense of hierarchical structuring in order to select the appropriate key themes from which other ideas should radiate. Weak students can end up with too many unconnected strands or with repeated information, and do not know how to convert the map into the linear sequence they need for writing. Such mapping needs to be used in conjunction with the other techniques outlined here.

Headings and bullet points
This helps to differentiate main points from sub-points, is useful for note making, and a good revision strategy for students to use. If you have used a brainstorming or mind map approach to explore an idea, it helps students to see how this information can be converted into linear sequences under headings.

Hierarchical ordering
When there are several sets of headings and points, demonstrate how two or more headings may come under a more general heading. This is a useful point at which to discuss categorising and organising information, and the more general notion of concept hierarchies. Further details about concept pyramids can be found in *The Study Skills Handbook* and in Chapter 15 below.

(4) Developing listening and note-taking skills

For new students who are likely to struggle with organising information, offer hand-outs which provide ready-made structures for some topics. For example, this might be a set of headings of topics to be covered in the lecture, with a set of numbered lines representing the points that the student must listen for in the lecture or look out for when reading. This encourages listening skills as well as modelling ways of laying out information.

Example: 3 functions of the X

(1) _____
(2) _____
(3) _____

If the lecture contains a significant amount of data and names, give this information out in advance as a hand-out so that students can focus on listening.

(5) Making sense of the subject

The amount of information available means that many students, and even some lecturers, take an 'amount'-centred approach to learning, rather than one which focuses on meaning, on making sense of what is learnt. Setting questions in advance of the lecture, with set reading, helps to focus the student's preparation. For some groups, using halfway materials or asking them to work out the material onto a matrix or chart provided, means that the student has practice in making sense of the material before the lecture. Lecture time can then be spent building from a knowledge base and used to address perceived difficulties, rather than in creating the knowledge base. Straightforward techniques can be used in the lecture such as:

• brainstorming what is already known about a topic – and drawing attention to gaps;
• asking students to develop matrices or charts if this was not part of their preparation;
• asking small groups to identify difficulties;
• asking small groups or pairs to problem-solve the difficulties themselves;
• working through the difficulties in class;
• introducing class discussion to bring out a range of perspectives;
• giving real life examples for groups to use to apply their understanding;

- setting problems or case studies to apply new knowledge.

(6) Developing group work skills

Advantages of group work

Macdonald (1997) offered four main reasons why he used group work with students at Sheffield Hallam University:

- Collaborative work in groups involves students in more active learning rather than passive receptivity.
- It enables wider choice which helps to increase motivation.
- He can set tasks which are too big for individual students to tackle alone.
- 'The excitement of finding out new things, playing with ideas, making connections with other ideas and beginning to make personal sense of the world' works best in groups.

There are many other reasons why groups offer benefits to both lecturers and students. Some of these include:

Biological
Group work allows opportunity for some physical movement. People are more able to shift around, talk, fidget, and take rests, following the natural needs of our bodies for movement, when working in groups than when sitting still and listening to lectures.

Social
Groups offer more chances for individual attention and more time to participate and sound out one's own ideas. Through whole-group and small-group work, other people in the large group become better known so that the large group is less threatening. It is easier to get to know others in small groups, and shy people are more likely to contribute. The small group offers opportunities for bonding and building up a sense of belonging.

Personal development
Small-group work provides an opportunity for developing a wider range of skills, such as team skills, listening, speaking, offering and receiving feedback, considering others' opinions, working

towards consensus, dealing with difference, conflict and emotions, problem solving, reasoning, defending a point of view, and critically evaluating the contributions of others.

Range
Working in groups gives students access to a wider range of perspectives, ideas, attitudes, and experiences than just that of the lecturer. It also allows for project work, where students can work on a larger scale than individually, developing a wider range of skills.

Advantages for lecturers
Group work allows lecturers to rest their voices and to engage in more varied sets of activities. It also allows them to develop a wider range of skills than that required simply to deliver information, and to work more creatively. Preparation time is more likely to be spent in considering how to stimulate engagement, interest and learning rather than in becoming word perfect about subject content.

Developing autonomy as learners
Group work is an ideal context for students to develop a sense of their own resources, so that they do not regard the lecturer as the sole source of answers. This is a useful starting point for developing mutual support networks.

Employability
Employers are keen to recruit graduates with the kinds of skills that are developed through team work and group work.

Principles of group work

Although groups offer benefits for learning, these do not necessarily come about automatically. Group skills may not manifest without assistance. As those who work regularly with groups know well, what works for one group will not necessarily work for another.. However, the following principles maximise chances of groups functioning as well as they can. Above all, the way that the group is initially set up and the degree to which it bonds, have a profound effect upon its later functioning.

Security
Groups can be frightening places. It is impor-

tant that lecturers create a sense of the whole group as a place where everyone can speak, where it is safe to make mistakes, and where contributions and efforts will be acknowledged. Students may also have concerns about confidentiality. Early consideration to developing a safe group atmosphere pays handsome dividends in terms of the quality and range of contributions offered later, and in chances of developing active mutual support networks.

Developing a sense of belonging
One of the main difficulties identified by students is a sense of 'not belonging'. It is difficult to establish the trust to risk making contributions if students do not even know each other's names. It pays to build in bonding activities, such as establishing everyone's names, creating a picture board of the whole class with their names, and using 'icebreakers' at the beginning of sessions.

Addressing concerns and difficulties
Students are likely to have anxieties about working in either the whole group or small groups, which will not go away simply because they are not talked about. Unless the group is one that is already likely to have advanced group skills, it is best if early anxieties are kept anonymous. This can be undertaken by everyone writing separate concerns anonymously on individual pieces of paper, which are drawn one by one from a hat, or by individuals pooling their concerns, which are fed back collectively to the whole group. Let the group know that this is what will happen, so that they feel safe to be open in their contributions. Typical contributions include:

- 'I may not fit in.'
- 'I can get hyper when I'm nervous and shout my mouth off.'
- 'If we all have to speak, I'll just clam up.'
- 'Maybe nobody will speak to me.'
- 'I don't want to have to deal with other people's racism on my own.'
- 'I will get here late and I hate everyone turning to look at me.'
- 'I'm scared everyone will think I'm stupid.'
- 'I don't want to be put on the spot to do something I don't want to do.'

- 'Everyone else is probably so clever and I'm not sure I'll be able to keep up.'

Turning anxieties and difficulties into opportunities
Once anxieties have been expressed, a useful early problem-solving task is to get either small groups or the whole group to share ideas on how these can be addressed. A SWOT (Strengths, Weaknesses, Opportunities and Threats) analysis focused on group-work can be useful in this respect (see p. 314 below).

Ground rules
On the basis of the above exercise, ask the group to formulate ground rules. The less involvement the tutor has in formulating the ground rules the more they are 'owned' by the group. Ground rules are useful for both the lecturer and students to refer to if a group begins to have difficulties.

(1) Ask for a volunteer to write up contributions.
(2) Brainstorm which issues should be included.
(3) Discuss how the group wishes to proceed when there is not consensus on what to include.
(4) Be clear that the group can return to ground rules later to amend them if necessary.
(5) Ensure that the ground rules are typed up and that everyone has a copy.

The lecturer may need to prompt consideration of certain issues if they have not been raised. For example:

punctuality
attendance
dominant members
mobile phones
interruptions
commitment
confidentiality
late-comers
children
respect/rudeness
leaving early
smoking
decision-making procedures
non-contributing members

issues arising from sensitivities
changing ground rules
issues arising from anxieties
how to enforce the ground rules

Sabotage and success
- Address, specifically, ways that everyone could sabotage the group. What could people do to ensure that the group failed and that everyone else was frustrated or miserable?
- Turn this on its head, and explore ways that everyone could make the group effective, fun and interesting.
- Ask people in pairs or small groups to consider their own fears about groups and to set themselves an objective for working better as a group member.
- If appropriate, build further suggestions into the ground rules.

Aims, objectives and advantages
Be clear about the purpose for working in groups. These may be specific for the course or simply general advantages inherent to group work. This is especially useful in allaying the fears of those who feel that group work is not really 'learning', and that real teaching is a question of 'chalk and talk'.

Set tasks commensurate with skills already attained
Ensure that students have built up group skills before setting them loose on a formally marked group assessment. Generally, it is useful to build towards speaking in a group, asking students to talk in pairs, then in small groups. Include an exercise where everybody has to go round and speak to each person in the group and to speak in the large group – if group size permits. The important thing is to ensure there are several opportunities to speak to, and work with, others, for brief or longer spells, so that students develop confidence. Ensure students gain experience of:

- contributing to groups, through work in pairs, threes, and small groups;
- addressing issues of constructive criticism;
- considering their own behaviour in groups;
- going through most of the steps outlined above.

(7) Checking for learning

Build in activities which emphasise that the material being covered is to be understood, rather than simply noted, filed and regurgitated. This approach models, for the student, methods of testing out their own learning. This relates to three elements of the 'Magic 7' teaching session outlined above. For example, lecturers can:

- Begin sessions by checking what has been learnt through advance preparation for the session, and where there are areas of difficulty or questions to be answered.
- At appropriate intervals, ask small groups to draw up a quick summary of the main points so far.
- Brainstorm, as a whole group, what the session has been about so far.
- Ask for questions, and throw these out to the group to be answered or set them as small-group tasks.
- Ask teams of students to write out a set of 'quiz' questions on the subject just covered or which is to be revised. These could be answered either through small-group work, or in team competition. It can help to give them a list of kernel questions to adapt in order to stimulate thinking, such as 'What is the difference between . . . ', 'What would happen if . . . ', 'What are the strengths and weaknesses of . . . ', 'What is a possible solution to . . . ' (King, 1990).
- Ask students to write everything they can think of as notes or pattern notes within a short set time (a few minutes).
- Ask each individual what is the most important point they are taking away from the session or what they found to be the most useful or interesting aspect of the session.
- Set a similar problem or situation to that already addressed and ask how what has been learnt applies to the new problem.

(8) Developing a culture of advance preparation

Lecturers can make the most of teaching time to cover subject material and to develop students as autonomous learners by developing a culture of advance preparation for lectures. This works best if it is adopted by whole departments. This reduces the need for lecturers to feel they must 'deliver' information which is usually available elsewhere, and allows them to move towards a more facilitative teaching style. As students become more familiar with web-based courses, and on-line information, their needs are likely to change from relying on lectures for information towards needing assistance in developing skills to manage their learning and information overload. Lecturers can aim to:

- build an early expectation that students read and prepare for taught sessions;
- use lecture time to build on students' advance preparation and to deal with problems and difficult areas they identify;
- vary activities to include a wider range of thinking and learning styles and develop key skills.

(9) Training students to cope with coursework assignments

Universities lose students who cannot manage the assessment process. Many students have no idea how to approach an assignment – and little experience upon which they can call. They need training and guidance in how to succeed.

Timing: help with deadlines

'At risk' students have particular difficulties with organising themselves to meet deadlines, and especially when the deadlines for several assignments fall at once. If penalties of reduced marks are given for missing deadliness, borderline students are likely to fail, without their difficulty having been addressed. Lecturers can help by:

- liaising with other tutors where possible in order to avoid 'bunching' deadlines – 'at risk' students cannot always organise their time to manage simultaneous hand-in dates;
- giving early guidance on what is expected rather than the week before the hand-in date: weaker students often wait for this summary before they begin work;

- giving guidance on how long students can expect to spend on different aspects of the assignment: e.g., reading: 20 hours; organising ideas: 5 hours; writing first draft: 12 hours; writing final draft: 7 hours (as appropriate);
- setting up automatic e-mails reminding students of deadlines.

Orientation to the assignment

Another key area of difficulty for students is in interpreting assignment titles. Assignment booklets can help with this (see Chapter 3). Lecturers can help by going over the title or question and checking that students understand what is required. For some intakes, it helps to suggest starting points and ways of breaking the assignment down into manageable chunks. Students create difficulties for themselves by trying to take on the whole assignment 'in one', as an amorphous activity, because they cannot conceive of it divided into separate tasks.

Generating ideas

When we are stressed or lack confidence, it can be hard to think clearly, which further undermines confidence. Students may also lack strategies for developing their thinking. In taught sessions, lecturers can help by modelling ways of generating ideas: rapid brainstorms, discussion, pattern notes or mind maps, fast writing, free association, structured questions, etc. They can create opportunities and activities for students to generate ideas at speed. (See Chapter 15.)

Organising ideas

Lecturers could also model ways of organising ideas into categories, lists, charts, flow diagrams, headings and bullet points. Students who struggle with organisational difficulties often find it easier to continue if they organise their essay plan as points under headings. Teaching staff could create opportunities and activities for students to organise information at speed.

Arguments/line of reasoning

Students may be baffled by what an 'argument' is. One student described an argument as 'a series of statements that contradict each other'. Another said it was 'a shouting match'. Some students are emotionally distanced from the idea of 'arguing' and using the terminology of 'a line of reasoning' may be easier for them to accept. Lecturers may need to explain what is meant by an 'argument' in academic writing and can help students to develop this by drawing attention to the line of reasoning in their lectures or material. If there is an opportunity, students can benefit from being given short texts and asked to identify the line of reasoning. Students should also be encouraged to write out their own line of reasoning as a 'skeleton' before they begin their essay, and to hand this in with early assignments.

Planning assignments

Again, students may have little notion of what a 'plan' is. Lecturers can offer examples of what a plan might look like. They could draw up a plan on the board, talking through decisions they make for their own writing. In class, groups could be asked to develop a plan of an assignment based around a title they have been given, using material from a discussion group or as a revision exercise. They could be asked to bring in a plan of an assignment to discuss with their peers. For early assignments, ask students to hand in a plan with their assignments and include this in the assessment criteria. Lecturers can use these plans to identify those whose planning skills are losing them marks and to offer guidance.

Local style

Draw students' attention to the characteristics and conventions of writing required for your subject area, and how these might differ from writing for other units (see Chapter 6).

Drafts

Many students run into difficulties through trying to write an assignment in one sitting rather than in several drafts.

- Encourage students to write in stages.
- Reassure them that the first draft does not need to be neat, well written or checked for spelling but is a launch-pad for later drafts.

- Encourage them to refer to the learning outcomes and marking criteria when writing and checking their drafts.
- Encourage them to read their work aloud, or, if they use assistive technologies, to use a screen reader to read their work aloud.

(10) Assessment: guidance, marking and feedback

Research suggests that the assessment process has the greatest single influence over the way that students orientate themselves to their learning. They will generally take a strategic approach to gaining good marks, even if this is in conflict with their learning aims or the stated objectives of the course. Elton (1995) argues that this quest for grades can lead to difficulties if the desired learning objectives of the course differ from those which are assessed. If work is graded, smart and experienced students will naturally search out strategic ways of maximising their grade. Those less familiar with higher education or who have less recent experience of education can be disadvantaged if they do not know how to 'play the game' to improve their marks.

Students are often desperate to make sense of requirements, to know what they can do to improve their work, to get it right. They also need to know what they are doing correctly or they may not realise what they are already achieving. The urge to gain good marks is not necessarily simply about pleasing tutors, as it may appear on the surface, but can be a strong motivator towards achievement – so long as good marks seem attainable. In addition, acknowledgement and praise not only boost morale, but also help the student to recognise what they do well.

Lecturers can use the process of marking and returning work to help students to improve their marks for future assignments. This can help students to be more aware and focused for assignments but less anxious. Anxiety inhibits the ability of many students to learn or to perform at their best. Moreover, constructive feedback from tutors models for students how to offer feedback to others. This is invaluable for interpersonal work, whether for building group atmosphere, for team projects, mutual support networks, or preparation for the world of work.

Marking criteria

These should be clear, precise and unambiguous. If there is likely to be any misunderstanding, offer examples of what is required. It helps to give a brief outline of the expected content and to clarify how the marking system relates to the learning outcomes for the course. For example, how would a student know if they have achieved the learning outcomes for the course or unit? Give guidance on what distinguishes answers at different grade levels, for example:

- What kinds of answers fail?
- What distinguishes an answer that gets 70 per cent, or a first, from others?
- What distinguishes a 2:1. from a 2:2 answer?
- How could students work out for themselves what kind of mark they are likely to receive for their work before they hand it in?

Lecturers can make the marking process fairer and more transparent by using marking criteria sheets such as those used in Part II, and described in Chapter 7 below.

Demystify the marking process

Students tend to have little idea of what lecturers are looking for; often the brightest students worry that if they are innovative they will use up their word allowance and lose marks for not including basic points. This can be very demotivating. It helps if lecturers talk through the marking criteria, clarify how these link to learning outcomes and show how to find the balance between meeting basic expectations and developing new ideas – all within a word limit.

Students report that they find it helpful if first-year tutors explain how they mark a piece of work; students often attribute magical mind-reading powers to lecturers. This needs dispelling. Give students the chance to mark at least one piece of work related to your subject, using your marking criteria, and discuss what they discovered by doing this for themselves.

Feedback format for coursework

Standardised marking sheets are easier for students to read. Link feedback to the learning outcomes of the course. Clarify how well the student has covered the expected content. What should the students have included that they did not? Did they get the weighting right? It is ideal if lecturers type out comments and attach these: students often cannot read their tutor's handwriting despite the efforts tutors make. Number comments which refer to numbers inserted on the student's script rather than writing on the script itself. When the assignment is still fresh in students' minds, it is useful to provide group feedback on assignments, drawing out ways to improve marks.

Constructive and selective feedback

Frame all feedback in terms of constructive advice on how to improve. Although a piece of work may seem dreadful, the student may be proud of it and be shocked to find it unacceptable: a cutting comment may encourage the student to feel that they do not belong on the course and to consider withdrawing. Too much feedback may overwhelm the student. Identify those changes which, if taken, would have the most impact upon marks. Guiding the student on the importance of a clear line of reasoning may be the most important starting place. Organising ideas and planning work, or undertaking a sufficiently broad range of reading and research may be other key aspects to emphasise.

Constructive feedback involves:

- some recognition of effort;
- indicating what the student has got right – and should continue to do in the future;
- indicating where the student has improved;
- indicating a small number of achievable goals for improvement, being explicit about what these are and how to achieve them, and giving feedback on progress;
- concrete examples of what is required.

It should:

- be formulated positively – as something

which can be done to improve performance, rather than what is wrong;

- take the person forward – it is not simply a vague directive to do something differently;
- be realistic – the suggestion can actually be put into practice by the recipient;
- be selective – it addresses priorities rather than every aspect of performance;
- be offered kindly – delivered in a voice and manner which make it easier to accept.

Poor feedback includes:

- Too much criticism (or writing too much on the student's own script). This cannot be absorbed in a useful way as it is off-putting.
- Generally negative feedback. Students tend to ignore this. The student can feel that their efforts are not recognised. They often throw it away.
- Comments which appear vague to students (such as 'No!', 'Unclear' or 'More detail needed'). The student believes their work to be clear already. They may not know what kind of details are required unless examples are given.
- Demoralising comments (such as 'this is non-sense/gobbledegook/rubbish!' or 'Please write in English!'). These can cause resentment and are usually counter-productive
- Illegible feedback. Students may not bother to decipher it unless they think it says something very positive about them.

Peer feedback

Students are more likely to understand the process, purpose and validity of criticism if they are involved in feedback processes themselves. Peer assessment offers a structure for students to do this. You can introduce this in stages, handing over more responsibility to students until they may be in a position to do some of the course assessment for you. Trials with peer assessment suggest that it works best when introduced from the first year (so it is regarded as part of the culture of higher education). Trials also suggest that, once they have become familiar with the process, students' assessments are consistent with those of teaching staff. This is

particularly the case when students have been involved in elaborating and setting criteria for assessment.

Include students in the marking

Offer students a self-assessment sheet to complete for each piece of work. Invite them to assess their work according to:

- marking criteria;
- learning outcomes;
- how they feel they could have improved the work or approached it differently.

This gives you an idea of how well the student can monitor their own performance, and whether they have an accurate sense of how to improve their marks. This could be used as the basis of your own feedback so that what you feed back to the student is more relevant to their own perceptions. Staff who have taken this approach say that it makes marking easier.

Final comments

As more lecturers receive training in how to teach, many of the above strategies are likely to become mainstreamed. For some lecturers, they will already be regarded as acceptable as common sense and the basis of their current practice. For others they will seem like common sense but not yet be integrated into their teaching practice. They are likely to be of most use to new lecturers, to postgraduate students given teaching responsibility at short notice, and to those moving to teaching or training in HE after excelling in a vocational area.

Material in other chapters may also be helpful to the classroom lecturer. Each of the skills sessions in Part II is preceded by a description of common difficulties that students face and suggestions of ways lecturers can help with those specific skills. Exercises used in the menu could also be used within a general lecture context, where needed, if study skills support is not provided for the course. The sessions provide examples of how to build a sense of a group so that students are more confident about contributing in class, asking when they do not understand, and using each other as a resource for learning. They also build in group skills and problem-solving techniques which, once established, can be used in most teaching settings.

Material in Chapters 3, 6 and 8 also relate to the work of classroom lecturers. Given that students are being asked, increasingly, to reflect upon their learning and evaluate their performance, it can be useful for lecturers to experience this for themselves, especially in relation to skills delivery. An opportunity to do this is provided in Chapter 9.

The strategies offered here help not only 'at risk' students, but also brighter students who dare not own up to their difficulties. Most of the suggestions made in this chapter are fairly simple for classroom lecturers to implement. They can assist lecturers in making better use of teaching time and can help to reduce unnecessary demands on lecturers for help. It is likely that their adoption will make life easier for both students and lecturers.

# Writing: the burning issue

Academic writing is a key area of concern for both students and lecturers. For lecturers, this tends to be a question of academic standards. Students' concerns focus on how to deliver what is expected, especially within the time allowed, as well as on their confusion about what exactly is required. Students' stories reveal a lack of prior practice and adequate guidance in the writing styles required for HE; it is not unusual to find students who have never undertaken any substantial piece of writing. Lack of acquaintance with academic traditions and conventions, lack of confidence and lack of motivation all play their part.

Moreover, all too often, weaknesses in academic writing are the result of poor thinking skills; work on basic thinking skills, critical analysis and organisation of ideas can pay dividends in terms of improved writing. This chapter offers a general background to developing writing skills and writing habits in students, primarily from curriculum and teaching perspectives. It focuses on two main areas. First, it looks at ways of inspiring and encouraging student writing. Secondly, it looks at ways of helping students to manage the plurality of writing which they will encounter in their studies and offers a conceptual model, the 'SPACE' model, for supporting student writing across the curriulum.

Inspiring writing

Opinion, formats and inspiration

What is there in an undergraduate assignment to really inspire a student to write? Lively engagement with the subject can easily become stifled during the process of meeting word limits, covering the basic material, answering a set question, and working around the known attitudes of the lecturer. Academic writing can feel like a strait-jacket. Walking the line between writing from opinion and building on previous research in the field is like walking a tightrope: it is easy for students to fall into either pure opinion or mere regurgitation. Students are often disappointed at the lack of opportunity for contributing something new through their writing. Frequent complaints include: 'It has all been said before' or 'It is all in the book anyway, so why do I have to write this?' Worsham and Olson (1991), speaking of postgraduates, wrote of the need to:

> help graduate students to become good thinkers so that they can produce first-rate work that is not just a simple recombination of other people's ideas, but that is the kind of combination that actually produces a significant intellectual intervention.

Creating opportunities for undergraduates to

write something that counts, something that is new, and which inspires them personally, is just as important as for postgraduates.

Undergraduates are often perplexed about how they are supposed to bring themselves into their own writing, how to be 'original' or even how they are supposed to avoid pseudo-plagiarism if they are not allowed to express their own opinions. Many universities emphasise that writing is not a place for your own 'opinions'. Where lecturers may mean they want only 'informed opinion' based upon some supporting research, students all too often interpret this as meaning that they must not include any ideas of their own nor a personal position. However, they are also aware that they must produce an 'argument', and are understandably confused about how they can produce an argument if they are not permitted an opinion.

Watching students working their way through this dilemma is like observing a novice with a Rubik's cube: they contort themselves and their writing to make the different aspects of the guidance fit. For example, they may judiciously arrange their selected quotations and paraphrases so as to create an order that hints at an argument without being explicit about the direction they are going, in case this is construed as subjectivity. Some are not aware of how passives and the 'third person' can be used to present a personal viewpoint: they are, therefore, left with the option only of quoting others as the spokespersons of their private opinions.

To return to the quotation by Worsham and Olson above, we need to ask how we can develop students as thinkers so that they also can make intellectual interventions – or at least feel they are part of the process, working towards making such a contribution, rather than acting out the role of student, like a rat on a wheel. This is likely to advance the process of writing at least as much as formulae about requisite conventions. How can we encourage students to think, to take risks, to hold onto their original inspiration in entering the discipline, to find their own niche for making a contribution? The sections below offer a range of ways of encouraging students to develop their writing,

to bring in the personal, and to use their inspiration.

Capturing the initial fire

Goertzel and Goertzel (1962), in a study of 400 modern eminent people, found that three in five, including several Nobel prize winners, 'had serious school problems' and rose to importance despite their formal education rather than because of it. Most followed their own inspiration rather than adhering to what they were taught. Many prominent figures and inventors, such as Edison, Faraday and Einstein, found it difficult to learn using conventional methods. In the past it was easier for people at all levels to make a living without a qualification in areas where today formal documentation is needed. Even painters, sculptors, sports trainers, counsellors and body workers are now being brought into the essay-writing net. The inspiration that brings students into many disciplines may be a long way removed from their experience within it. The challenge to universities and colleges is to harness that inspiration, rather than suffocating it by conventions which may not be entirely appropriate to the discipline.

In order to move towards inspired thinking and writing, students need to feel an inner inspiration. The path towards creative engagement with subject material may seem a forbidden one in many disciplines, where the methodology and writing conventions appear ancient, rigid and set in stone. If lecturers wish their students to be creative thinkers, they may need to create settings and exercises which encourage different ways of being with the object of study, to bring in an element of playfulness, mystery and suspense. Lecturers need to inspire the students with confidence in themselves, to be open to hearing students' opinions, and to be able to challenge them in ways that are thought-provoking rather than threatening. Students need opportunities to experience that there are many routes to the top of the mountain. Above all, assignment titles, assessment criteria and feedback need to be such that they encourage thought, creativity and risk-taking, showing that these are worth-while and will be rewarded, rather than simply set questions with set answers.

Creativity in the type of assignment set and the nature of the marking criteria are key to maintaining inspiration. Offering opportunities for students to develop an idea through varied media, devising their own project, researching a subject in their own vicinity or family, devising their own marking criteria, using presentations and video rather than script for assessment, are but a few possibilities.

Leaving gaps and opening up new paths

It is often said that charismatic lecturers inspire students. It is true that they can provide an external source of inspiration and may lead the student to greater appreciation of the subject matter or a vocational area. However, the interest of such lecturers may not be in the student nor in the student's own inspiration. Indeed, charismatic lecturers can leave students with the impression that they cannot compete or that a topic has been exhausted. Inspiration requires that there be some gaps, some openings or confusions where writers can make a contribution or impact of their own.

There are possibilities for such openings even in well-documented fields of study. For example, even where a theory seems well-established, its application to a particular area may never have been explored. Most theories will not have been applied to the specific circumstances of the students themselves – to their personal situations and those of their families, neighbourhood or ethnicity. Personal and local applications offer the student opportunities for original and meaningful writing in which they may even be the expert. Another possibility is to ask students to take turns to explore and write up, through short 'mini-projects', a particular aspect of the subject and to feed back this back for three minutes to the group. The writing they produce could be collated into a set of hand-outs for the group. It is more inspiring to enter onto a new path than

merely to cover the beaten track, yet students are rarely given opportunities to cover new ground.

Play

There is no shortage of literature on the significance of play to childhood learning. There is very little about the importance of play to adults, but there is no logical reason for assuming that play is not a vital form of advancing thought at any age. Indeed, there are many anecdotal examples of scientific ideas and inventions which came through non-logical, playful or relaxed states. It is easy to see why this is not an easy route for students, who are generally tense about the expectations put upon them to follow a sequence, understand within a time limit, produce writing to a time and word limit, and to expose themselves to judgement and failure. It can seem to be too great a risk to indulge in going for a walk, listening to music, playing with a crazy essay title that would never be set to see where it leads the thought process, or day-dreaming about a theme. The natural urge is to keep your foot safely on the mountain even when the rope is caught, rather than to swing out from the rock in order to free the rope. Permission and encouragement simply to 'play with ideas' may be needed.

Individual approach

Writing is a complex task. However, if students can find the metaphor that works for them, the majority of the task can fall into place. The possibilities are endless. K. Williams (1995) offers several delightful illustrations for visualising essays, each of which incorporates a beginning, a middle, and an end. One, for example, is of a swimming pool where the diving board is the title, entering the water is the introduction, swimming across the pool is the main body, and leaving the pool is the conclusion. Creme and Lea (1997) also offer visual metaphors for approaches that students take to their work: 'divers' who need to plunge in and write something before they can get to the point of writing a plan; 'patchwork writers' who build up their writing through building blocks of text written under headings; those who need to make grand plans before they can begin, and 'architects' who develop the structure before they approach the content.

Offering examples such as these to students helps them to see that there isn't a single approach to writing that works for everyone. Inviting them to provide a metaphor for their own style encourages them to think through what approach they do take now. It may not, of course, be the ideal one. For example, ask them to complete the generative thinking activity:

> 'Writing for me is like a . . . because . . . '
> 'Writing for me is like [verb]-ing . . . because . . . '

Ask them to expand the metaphor to find as many reasons as possible why writing is like the item they selected. Is this the metaphor they want to apply to their writing? Can they devise one that would suit them better?

An early assignment: a 'burning issue' for the student

For one of the students' first assignments, encourage them to identify a topic that is of 'burning concern' to them. Let them choose what format this will take, such as a letter to a newspaper, an article, a book review, a report, as long as continuous prose is included. This could be used as the basis for learning how to undertake literature searches in libraries or on the internet. The marking criteria could be based around:

(1) how appropriate the writing style is to the purpose;
(2) how well the overall piece of work is likely to achieve its end: for example, whether it argues its case persuasively;
(3) clarity of exposition;
(4) whether the student's real interest or concern shines through;
(5) how well they used the literature to support their ideas.

Early assignments: a 'burning issue' for the subject

(1) Set group research and individual writing on a current topic of debate in the area.
(2) Build the assignment around discussion groups, debates, poster displays, library search exercises (undertaken in pairs or small groups, for mutual support and encouragement).
(3) Aim to link the writing to the talking, researching and thinking processes.

The 'wild' hypothesis

Students often complain that written assignments for higher education are futile, since whatever they are asked to write is already written well in the texts they are given to read. This is extremely discouraging – and often boring. A trainee dyslexia tutor once designed a whole range of tactile tools for teaching maths. One supervisor complained, 'but none of her methods worked!' However, the student was given credit by her other supervisors because she had tested and appraised them herself: the next one she devises may work. The attitude of the first supervisor might well have discouraged her from trying out anything new again.

For one written assignment, encourage students to invent something new or to devise a theory or experiment for why something occurs. This should be related to the subject and in an area that particularly interests them. Emphasise that they should aim for originality rather than what is likely to be true: wild and bizarre hypotheses are acceptable. For example, 'The shape of a volcano is determined by its distance to the equator', or 'Computers appeal more to boys than girls because girls find binary oppositions tedious'. Direct students to research their wild hypothesis as for any other assignment. Emphasise that it is not important, for this exercise, if they ultimately have to prove themselves wrong. Students could write this up as an assignment and make an appraisal of their approach to the task and of their writing. This could be used as a basis for discussing how hypotheses and theories develop and become mainstream.

Writer's notebooks

Student artists tend to keep notebooks of ideas, but this practice is less common for other subjects. Encourage students to keep a pen and an ideas book with them at all times. Suggest they select a book that is small and can be carried around easily. A small filofax or a pad of 'post-its' may also suffice.

Encourage the students to:

- value their own ideas;
- catch their own ideas;
- use their ideas as a basis for writing;
- be prepared to stop and note their ideas wherever they are;
- not to worry if most of the ideas come to nothing: that's part of the creative process.

Reflective notebooks or diaries

Mature students, in particular, lack experience in generating words and developing ideas. Any additional writing is useful, and reflective journals on their learning and experiences can serve a dual purpose. Encourage students to:

- Develop the habit of writing down ideas for assignments. Encourage them to consider their ideas as part of the assignment rather than an assignment being simply about words on the page.
- Write some reflections about what they have read, whether they agree with what is written, and any ideas it inspired (without the book being present).
- Use writing as a tool for taking responsibility for their own learning. Encourage students to work through their difficulties by focusing on them and considering possible options. Include reflections about learning styles, their own inner process, their thoughts about the subject, their skills, their motivation, how the course relates to them and the real world.

To encourage reflection, give brief breaks during lectures specifically for students to jot down their reflections.

Holding onto the 'genie'

The world of the idea is subject to inner collapse. When there is a moment of insight, a neural network flashes into being, stimulating a stream of connections and infinite possibilities. The moment can seem electric: there is an electrochemical charge. An idea may seem so wonderful that the student thinks they could not possibly forget it – and yet a piece of bad news, a night's sleep, even a phone call can leech the original intensity that is needed if the idea is to be worked through. It fades away, leaving the words free-standing and empty. For whatever reason, a later return to an idea does not have the same charged effect upon the thinking system; the magic does not always return. Encourage students to return to the ideas in their notebooks as soon as possible and to elaborate upon their initial ideas in order to keep the inspiration alive.

Writing 'on the hoof'

One advantage of maintaining an ideas notebook is that students are less likely to become stuck in the pattern of 'having difficulty starting' an assignment. The starting point disappears: it comes into being gently, with each stage building naturally on an earlier one, from small beginnings. Many people learn best by moving around. Changing scenery, putting study aside whilst they take a walk, can shift a weighty block to a problem. Once the pressure is relieved, ideas may begin to flow – and so it's useful to have a notebook to hand to capture these ideas. Later, they can type the ideas from their notebook onto the computer. This gives them a starting place from which to elaborate ideas towards a plan and first draft.

Start where the energy is

Accomplished drivers start the car, turn on the radio, put on their safety belt and conduct a conversation with minimum attention as each of the skills have become automatised; trainee drivers to stop to think about each task separately. Writing also involves using sub-skills which can become automatised – such as developing an idea, organising it into paragraphs and correcting a typing error. Students often find writing difficult because they try to combine several stages of the writing process into one, when they have not yet automatised the sub-skills needed to do this. This is exhausting, and can kill off the initial spark of interest. They may need encouragement to divide the process into separate stages.

As students usually need to break the process into several stages, encourage them to begin where the energy is: whatever seems the most interesting or easiest place to start. They can fill in the rest later, and will feel more motivated to do so once they have something down on paper. Ideas have the most energy, so encourage students to write these down as quickly as they can. Their interest may be in elaborating one idea fully or it may be in getting the whole skeleton down: it does not matter for early drafts. Technical aspects of English such as proofreading and checking of spellings should be left to the end.

Thinking through writing

Typical advice to students struggling with writing is for them to first complete a plan and then to stick to it. When this works, it can be very effective, especially in terms of clarity, labour saving, and time. Some writing genres, such as lab reports, lend themselves more easily to this approach than do others, such as 'To what extent . . . ' essays. Starting with a plan does not work for everybody nor for every type of writing.

Early drafting helps the creative flow. Some people think better through their fingers. Some work best by pen, others by typing or word-processing, others by voice recognition systems. Writing is an excellent way of working towards conclusions. Many students benefit from just typing out what they know, what comes into their head, as a way of working towards their final plan. They find their thinking is enriched by treating writing as a drawn-out process, which they can engage with in stages, that they

can live with over time, rather than as a battle to be won in a single sitting. Students may need encouragement, and modelling by lecturers, to allow themselves to write, stop, read, mark, edit, chop up, rewrite, organise under subheadings, muse over, delete, add to, and sleep on their writing. Struggling with writing could be regarded as an engaging challenge, a mysterious puzzle. It can be a meeting place of ideas, information, form. All writing involves a degree of crafting. It can be approached as art, as a creative enterprise. Instead, students often hold an unrealistic model of a mythic 'good writer': someone who produces perfectly flowing writing in a single sitting. It can be a shock for students to realise that professional writers succeed precisely because they go over their work, spend time labouring at it, maintain ideas books, go to writing groups, have editors, and have feedback from expert readers before their final draft is submitted.

Writing is always 'in progress'

A lecturer once confessed in a workshop that for the first time he had allowed himself to regard his writing as a progress paper, as a temporary position. For years, he had struggled with writing because he felt that he had to have arrived at a final position on an issue before it could appear in print. He worried about his ideas being enshrined in print forever on a position he might no longer hold – and so never wrote. Eventually, it struck him that he was allowed to change his mind, and that a 'good enough' position has to be reached with any piece of writing.

Writing, by its very nature, cannot be perfect. It is always limited. Only so many words, so much space, so many digressions are possible at one time. A style that suits one reader will not suit another: a single piece of writing cannot meet all tastes without becoming repetitious and cumbersome. The content may be out of date before it is published; the ideological position may appear dated before long. Part of being a writer is to accept this and to live with it, to allow the mark to be made, and to accept any piece of writing as an interim position paper. This takes some of the pressure off any single piece of writing. Unless the myth of the perfect writer, the perfect piece, the finality of a piece of writing is challenged, then a mind-set of perfectionism can set in. When this happens, even able students may be unable to bring themselves to submit any writing at all. They lose connection with the immediate purpose of the writing, with its narrow focus and its acceptable limitations.

Pacing

Speed writing

Study books recommend varying reading speed according to purpose. This is also true of writing. The mythic writer in students' heads writes at an even pace – and fast.

- Encourage students to write as many words as they can that link to one word – such as 'red'.
- Encourage students to write as much as they can in three minutes on the subject of a recent lecture.
- Suggest they begin writing assignments by sitting for only two minutes and jotting down any ideas that come into their head, as in these previous two exercises.
- Be clear that it does not matter whether they write in a list, a pattern, prose or beautifully composed Bengali or English. The idea is to break the hold of the idea of writing as a sedate enterprise where the finished object emerges first time. It is also useful for students to experiment with speed writing by hand and by computer to see which suits them best. Over time, students will realise that a few minutes of energetic 'ideas generation' can be the source of pages of developed writing.
- Link the idea of speed writing to the importance of maintaining an ideas notebook. There may be days when, if the notebook is handy, they may wish to stop every few yards to capture an idea. If they try to hold onto the idea in their heads, it is likely to be forgotten.

Slow writing

Some students write extremely slowly. They may not need to write several drafts. A slow measured style may suit them best. If others write more quickly than they do, they may need reassurance that there is no 'right speed' at which to write.

Germination

Although it is important to 'catch the genie' to elaborate ideas, the converse is also true. Ideas caught and elaborated early on, or generated by the process, will not always come fully formed. Time is needed to let the seeds of early ideas germinate and grow. This is one reason why it is important for students to begin to think, read and discuss the assignment as early as possible.

Interventions in the drafting process

Drafting is a much underrated process. Particularly with non-traditional entrants, there is often a need for tutors to intervene earlier in the process than the final marking stage. A brief look at an assignment plan or opening paragraph may indicate whether a student is on track, or needs some assistance to prevent them from failing. This is especially the case if students have been asked to set their own titles.

Staged interventions

Staged interventions may be possible when there are several sessions of discussion around a single topic, or where work is focused on the idea of redrafting. Without these interventions the student may settle for an earlier draft, not realising that there is further to go with a piece of writing. In staged intervention, the lecturer encourages the student to settle on one idea, and then throws new perspectives into the equation, inviting the student to consider the impact of the new material upon their previous position. Does this new piece alter the overall picture or argument? Each aspect of the previous position may need to be re-evaluated in the light of the new. The likelihood is that this will throw up crags and boulders which seem impossible to scale – even temporary confusion as the student moves towards a new understanding.

Peer review of early drafts

If students have been introduced to action sets or mutual support groups, encourage them to bring a first draft to their group for peer feedback. Each person will need a photocopy. Peers write between five and seven things they particularly like about the draft or which are good and should be retained, and between three and five suggestions on the most important things the writer could do to improve the writing or their grade.

Tutor feedback on assignments

Students often find feedback very frustrating, despite the good intentions of their lecturers. They are less likely to read or make use of:

- detailed feedback written on the essay itself, which appears intrusive and can be demoralising;
- handwritten feedback – unless it is short, legible and very clear;
- feedback which does not make it clear exactly how to improve marks;
- feedback where there are more suggestions than the student can realistically take on board in the short term;
- comments the student considers insulting;
- comments on what else could have been included in the assignment, unless there is also guidance on what could have been cut in order to make room for this within the word limit.

Writing pluralities: writing across the curriculum

Managing bulk

At British universities, almost all assessment is through prose writing. Each student may be required to produce 16 to 18 – or more – written assignments a year, usually of 2000–3000 words. In some establishments there may be as many as 36 assignments, in addition to exams. Almost all exams require continuous prose: typically exams consist of three or four essays completed within three hours. Just getting through the amount required places great demands upon the student in terms of time management and self-confidence. In addition, many students find it difficult to switch from the thinking and reading required for one subject to that of another. The more modules a student takes, the more demanding this can be.

Writing through the fear

Writing, for many students, is not simply about placing hands upon the pen or fingers upon a keyboard, but about putting their head on the block. Writing assignments signify judgement, moments of 'truth', a possible betrayal of inner stupidity, a potential loss of tutor approval, maybe even 'final damnation' and exit from the course. It is difficult to overestimate the fear that writing represents for students and their consequent sensitivity to the feedback they receive. Missed deadlines are not always about non-completion, but about reluctance to hand in finished work for fear of exposure, criticism and judgement.

The writing labyrinth

The spectrum of writing varieties required by the curriculum becomes a spectre that haunts the student and adds to their anxieties. Negotiating course requirements can feel like being lost in a maze. Add to the fear the profound confusion which students experience in trying to determine what is required from them in order to achieve good marks. Any one subject may require several types of writing assignment. In the course of their studies, students may be required to write autobiography, abstracts, analysis, case studies, collaborative writing, course log books, creative writing, dissertations and long papers, essays, experiential writing, field reports, journalistic writing, laboratory reports, legal briefs, letters, projects, reflective journals, research proposals, reviews of articles, books, films or exhibitions, summaries, transcripts, translations and more.

If this were not demanding enough, what gains good marks for an essay or report in one discipline, or even writing in one branch of the discipline, is unlikely to meet the requirements of others. The idea of 'generic' study and writing skills adds to the haze. Lecturers, especially those who followed a single-discipline pathway when they were students, do not always realise that their criteria for a good essay are not universal. As they are unaware of the particularities of their own requirements, there may be nowhere that particular differences, and the rationale for these, are made explicit. The differing demands of writing across the curriculum are left unarticulated. As a result, students are left to navigate this ocean of difference with only a few stars to guide them. As there may be only one or two examples of each type of writing for each tutor for each module of study, the guidance, offered in feedback after the event, may be of no use to the student for future assignments.

Varieties of writing required for one course

Below is a small selection of the wide range of writing styles generated by a single honours course, psychology, at one university. All were written by the same student.

---

(1) Abstract for cognitive psychology report

Can differences in object recognition times be accounted for by differences in ease of articulating the object-label rather than by differences in object structure?
. . . The experimental hypotheses were that subjects would take less time to read words than name pictures, that subjects would take less time to name items from structurally distinct (SD) categories than from structurally similar categories, and that as a result of interactions (A × B) subjects would take longer times for SD objects only when presented as pictures. A related design was used . . . There was a significant main effect of factor A, stimulus format, $F(1,7) = 10,8m$ $p < 0.025$; subject differences were significant at $f(7,7,) = 5.09$, $p < 0.25$. Results for Factor B (stimulus structure) and for A × B interaction were not significant. Means errors for drawings were 0,6 (SS); 1 (SD).

(2) Introduction to social psychology report

Changing representations of women in women's magazines
The project investigates changes in media representation of women between 1956 and 1996. It is informed, primarily, by social representations theory. Both quantitative and qualitative content analyses were made of one edition each of SHE magazine for the years 1956 and 1996. 1996 samples were matched on a one-to-one basis with 1956 samples, according to manifest content and dominant function (article or advertisement). The focus was an exploration of 'trickle down effects' of post-modern ideas into social representations of women. Coding frames were constructed to analyse this in terms of multiplicity of roles, activities and choices. . . . The findings were consistent with previous research and post-modern ideas that by 1996 women were represented as constructors of their own 'selves' and destinies, compared to the narrower role-bound representations of 1956. . . .

(3) Field notes: social psychology project

Observation of a stranger
I had the sense that the man might be a young grandfather. The easy silence that reigned

between child and adult suggested that they were familiar with each other, as did the way the child leaned into the man and pointed things out to him. . . . The man's lack of attention to the child and his not initiating activities could be because he was not used to having sole care for children. This was also suggested by his not keeping a protective arm in front of the child whilst travelling, his lack of the typical 'parentese' used by adults with children, and by his leaving the child unattended whilst he arranged the pushchair.

(4) Conclusion to the social psychology project (*for example 3 above*)

The strengths and limitations of unstructured observational methods for studying social behaviour

Unstructured observation is a receptive and naturalistic method, offering a wealth of meaningful and ecologically valid findings, with minimal ethical problems. However, it has limitations such as the amount of data which is accumulated, the impossibility of close replication and issues of selectivity. There is also the danger that the observer might impose schema or assumptions without acknowledging these are present. Nonetheless, such subjectivity, if presented openly, might ultimately be a methodological advantage. . . .

Making the conventions explicit

Trimmer (1999) describes the difficulties undergraduates face when asked to produce a written assignment. Students, he argues, are confused by:

> a muddle of rules, models, strategies and theories. Occasionally, students can clear up this muddle by asking each new writing teacher, 'What do you want?' More often they remain confused by the clutter of conflicting assumptions and expectations embedded in each college composition assignment. No wonder graduates, when asked what they learned about writing in college, seem unable to make it all cohere. They smile and say, simply, 'A big zero'.

The most important lesson for students is that writing is shaped by conventions, rules, contexts, strategies, theories, and that these can be learnt. For their lecturers, the key issues are:

- being aware of what their own subject requires in terms of writing conventions and how these might differ from those of other disciplines;
- being aware of varying requirements for different assignments set within the subject areas – such as conventions for when to

change from one writing style to another;
- being able to communicate these conventions and varieties clearly to their students;
- being sensitive to the multiplicity of writing demands being made of their students, especially those on modular courses, and being understanding about students' confusion.

Supporting students' writing: the SPACE model

The SPACE model is one way of conceptualising what is needed to support students' writing on-course. SPACE stands for:

(1) Strategy
(2) Pace
(3) Analysis
(4) Context
(5) Engagement

(1) Strategy

Writing strategies include such aspects as how to get going on a piece of work, drafting, and editing, which are usually addressed in study skills sessions on writing. Lecturers can reinforce the message and strengthen these skills in students by modelling the process of how to apply the strategies to the specific course material. For example, lecturers can make explicit how they go about writing an introduction or conclusion to a piece of work, how they select what to include and leave out from their reading, or how they manage 'writer's block' themselves. For examples of how lecturers can help, see pp. 109, 250, 280, 287 and 294.

(2) Pace

Where intakes can be expected to have difficulties with writing, start with smaller writing tasks very early on. These may be the basis of diagnostic work, or for early feedback, but the main purpose is to 'break the ice' about writing. In particular, this can pick up students who have difficulties in handing in work, for whatever reason. Where possible, it is best to lead the student from more straightforward pieces of writing to advanced pieces over time, linked to where they are in their study skills sessions (if these are provided).

- Start small and build towards full assignments.
- Offer early diagnostic writing to identify those with 'deadline' difficulties.
- Set writing for formative assessment so that students receive early feedback and support.
- Make the writing tasks manageable.
- Look for development over time, and plan for improvements over a whole course of study.

(3) Analysis

Students entering HE at present often have very poor reading histories on which to base their understanding of formal writing. It is not unusual for students to report that they read only one book a year, and sometimes much less. It is not possible to make up for years of lost reading during the short period of an HE course. Textual analysis can help. Offer opportunities for students to look at, discuss and examine texts which contain the writing characteristics you expect for your course. In

order to grasp what is specific about the writing for the subject area, students will usually need to contrast course-appropriate writing with other types of writing and to have the differences made explicit. This activity lends itself to work at all levels of academic study, as students move from a basic understanding of what is required towards more sophisticated ways of writing.

Compare texts across disciplines

Textual analysis is a useful method both of assisting students to develop critical reading strategies and for making links between reading and writing. For example, comparing engineering texts with legal texts, social science or literary criticism enables students to gain a sense of what constitutes 'good writing' for an engineer, a lawyer or a sociologist. The object is not to say which is best, but to understand that each field develops styles of writing that seem appropriate to its needs and that 'good' writing is partly a matter of context and purpose.

Compare texts within the discipline

In order to develop the students' awareness of writing style, compare several pieces of writing for your own subject area. This is useful in demonstrating to students there is not a universal type of 'good writing' to which they must conform. Draw out questions such as:

- How successfully does the writing engage the reader?
- How clear is it?
- How is argument weakened?
- How far does it follow the criteria set for their own written assignments. What is different and similar about texts they read and the writing they are expected to produce?

Offer examples of short extracts from the discipline which exemplify good style. Read these aloud, drawing attention to the flow and the way the punctuation helps or hinders reading. Encourage students to read sections of good text aloud when they are at home in order to internalise the style of the subject.

Compare student texts

Offer students concrete examples, such as examples of past course essays, annotated to show what gained and lost marks, and what the student could have done to improve the assignment.

- Ideally, provide three examples of each type of writing your students are required to produce, e.g. three essays, three lab reports, three case studies, three exam answers.
- Bring out the essential features of each (organisation of material, layout of text and graphics, characteristics of the writing style, presence of the author).
- What makes each a good or bad example? Discuss this with reference to the marking criteria.
- Give students an opportunity to discuss and mark examples for themselves.

Self-assessment of writing

Invite students to write a short appraisal of their assignment, and if you use a feedback form, to complete one of these too. In the appraisal, encourage them to state:

- why the assignment developed the way it did;
- any difficulties they had in finding source materials;
- anything they feel could have been improved about the way they approached the assignment;
- what they think are the best or most interesting features of the assignment.

This gives them an opportunity to explain anything that might have been difficult about the assignment so that the tutor has a better sense of where teaching or resources need to be directed. It also develops self-awareness in students so they are less dependent on others to evaluate their own work, which is useful when they go into employment. To encourage response, allocate some of the marks for the assignment to the self-assessment. Give feedback and guidance to those who are over- or under-critical of their performance.

(4) Context

Textual analysis is best explored in tandem with an exploration of the context for which different varieties of writing (for the subject) are produced. 'Contextualisation' means placing the writing requirements within a framework and setting both for academic writing generally and for course requirements in a more specific sense. This includes being clear about the rationale for specific requirements. The aim is for the student to be clear what they have to produce and why this is so. There are five main areas to be clarified or 'mapped' for students:

- categories of writing;
- the academic and course context;
- required writing characteristics for the subject;
- marking criteria;
- audience.

Categories of writing

Be clear to students which of the following types of writing are required for your subject and encourage them to keep a record of the varieties of writing they are producing so that they gain a sense of achievement from their efforts. Be aware of the range of writing and different demands they may have from other lecturers.

- Abstracts
- Analyses (e.g., formal analysis of a single work of art; analysis of historical documents; policy analysis)
- Autobiography
- Case studies
- Collaborative writing
- Course log books
- Creative writing (poetry, imaginative free writing, screen-plays, stories, visualisations)
- Dissertations and long papers
- Essays
- Experiential writing
- Field reports
- Field and laboratory notes
- Ideas notebooks
- Journalistic writing
- Laboratory reports

- Letters to newspapers, editors and official bodies
- Personal writing (CVs, personal statements)
- Projects
- Reflective journals
- Research proposals, papers and reports
- Reviews (articles, books, films, exhibitions)
- Summaries
- Synthesising ideas
- Transcripts
- Translations

The academic and course context

This may usefully investigate the influence of the 'scientific model' or other models upon the type of research approach and writing requirements which are required. North–South pole mapping, (as described below) assists the student to reduce multiple demands to a more manageable framework and to see how the features of writing for your course relate to demands made of them elsewhere in the university. It is also important to draw out what is common to most academic writing.

The influence of the 'scientific' model on academic writing

With respect to the plurality of writing demands made of them, student writers need an anchoring point from which to take their bearings as writers. One way of doing this is to be explicit about the role played by the 'scientific model' in shaping academic research, and therefore academic writing, especially over this century. Academics of all disciplines are affected by the scientific model – even if only because their subject methodologies initially arose in reaction to it. If students are given some basic grounding in what science sets out to do and the rationale of its methods, then it is easier to see the underlying principles and logic of many other subject disciplines. Tutors can then draw out how their own subject varies from the traditional model and the reasons for this.

The scientific model is characterised by seven features: a desire for objectivity, the possibility of a testable hypothesis, replicable results, the potential to control for variables, the possibility of quantitative analysis, accurate description,

and some qualitative analysis in the discussion of results and evaluation of the experiment (Cottrell, 1999). Academic disciplines vary in how far they value the scientific model or aspects of it. The main variations are in different attitudes to subjectivity and to qualitative data. In subjects such as Counselling, Health Studies and Fine Art, a high value is placed upon subjectivity – that is, upon personal feelings, intuitions, experiences and emotions and the role of the researcher in evaluating evidence. In many subjects, students are required to combine both approaches: to analyse their <u>subjective responses</u> (their feelings, what they like or dislike, their interests or intuitions in a particular situation), *and* <u>objective criteria</u> such as the results of independent surveys, market prices or research based upon a number of case studies.

Polar opposites in academic approach

In order to assist students to come to terms with the diverse conventions used for different subject areas, lecturers could map out where their own subject lies for each of the different aspects of the scientific model. In the diagram given in Chapter 20 (see pp. 296, 299), the student is invited to use information about their course to plot out expectations along a series of spectra. This is one way of simplifying a complex area. The visual layout suits those with more visual learning styles and the activity suits more kinaesthetic learners. The model suggests a great variety of potential combinations which can be conceptualised in a very accessible way. It is also a useful tool for lecturers to use to clarify what they require from their students.

Assignments which combine experiential writing with more traditional academic writing can be particularly difficult, especially for early assignments. It is sometimes supposed that to write from experience will help the student to feel more at home in the subject, especially for students who return to study after a break. This can be the case, as long as both lecturers and students are aware that such assignments may call for simultaneous learning of writing requirements for both aspects of the 'polar divide'. In addition, both types of material (personal and academic) are associated with different types of writing style.

Differences between personal and other academic writing

Personal writing	Academic writing
emotional	logical
can be intuitive	uses reasoning
uses first person: 'I'	uses third person:
uses active voice:	'one', 'it'
'I find'	uses passives: 'It was
anecdotal	found that . . . '
database of one	uses evidence
person	wider database
subjective	objective
tangents may be	keeps to logical
important	sequence
more poetic, fluid	more clipped and
style	precise

Working with both styles can be difficult enough for advanced writers; it may be extremely stressful for new students unless there is clear guidance on what each style of writing looks like, on the specific features of each style, on how to move from one style to the other, and how to link personal experience to more academic material.

Bring out features common to most academic writing
Bring out the commonalties in academic approach, so that students feel there is something they can grasp onto within the swirl of different requirements. Most academic disciplines, for example, require students to incorporate:

- **Breadth: use source materials**
  Students are required to use material from reading, lecture notes and other sources to give reasons, evidence and examples (rather than only stating personal opinion), referencing these appropriately.

- **Perspective: compare and contrast**
  Most assignments require some element of comparing and contrasting, especially of theories, models or research findings. Students

generally need to weigh opinions against each other and to use clear criteria as the basis of their evaluations.

- **Depth: show awareness of complexities**
  Students need to demonstrate that answers are not always clear-cut, show they are aware of weaknesses in their own argument and strengths in opposing argument, and say why there are difficulties coming to a firm conclusion one way or another.

- **Direction: develop a line of reasoning**
  Students should organise and structure material and ideas along a thread or argument, which the reader can follow easily. This should be focused on specific questions implicit in the title.

- **Clarity**
  Generally students need to get to the point quickly, be clear, concise and precise, and offer examples to illustrate their argument.

Required writing characteristics for the subject
Offer a rationale for the writing characteristics required in your area. Link this to textual analysis. Be clear about requirements for style and ensure students have examples to work from. Students can spend far too much time and energy worrying about presentation. Again, as lecturers vary a great deal in what they prefer (two sides of the paper or one, diagrams to be included in the text or just put into an appendix, titles to be followed or students to invent their own, subheadings should or should not be used, etc.) it helps to clarify these for students in advance.

Marking criteria
Map out what is required for your subject in terms of marking criteria. It can help to use a standardised marking form (see pp. 239, 302, 321) which draws attention to what lecturers take into consideration. Ensure that students are clear about what receives a good mark, what a mediocre mark, and what tends to lose marks unnecessarily.

It is important to be clear about how, if at all, errors in spelling, grammar and punctuation will affect marking. Often these are not marked, or affect the mark by a small percentage, whereas students often feel these are the main reasons they received low marks, and therefore do not address more important aspects of writing such as clear thinking, planning, using research material and developing a good line of reasoning. This is particularly the case with mature students and those working in English as an additional language.

Audience

Encourage students to be aware that, by writing, they are 'writers' and as such have an audience, even if that is an audience of only the two lecturers who mark the work. Students can be encouraged to consider, when undertaking textual analysis, what they need as readers in order to make sense of what is written. Offer students a piece of writing that does not follow the desired writing conventions and discuss the difference this makes to them as readers. Guide them in extrapolating the value of the writing conventions to the reader. Ask students to use this to analyse their own writing in terms of its accessibility to an audience. Offer opportunities for students to write for different audiences, and to analyse the differences in writing styles and conventions used for those audiences. This is a useful way of connecting writing development to employability skills; students could be asked, for example, to produce materials for client groups they would encounter on work placement and evaluate their writing in terms of its desired purpose and target audience.

(5) Engagement

Engagement with the writing task is key to the whole writing process. If they are engaged with the writing required of them, students are better motivated to face difficulties along the way. The area of 'engagement' covers both addressing negative emotions surrounding writing, and promoting a more positive engagement with the writing task.

Inspiration

- Encourage students to find and discuss writing that inspires them – to write about their own 'burning issues'.
- Encourage students to make space to write 'just for themselves' in a way that suits them. Many students have only ever undertaken writing (beyond a postcard) because someone in authority has required this of them.
- Give students practice in generating ideas (see pp. 258–9).
- Reassure students that confusion is not necessarily a step backwards, but is often part of the creative process and may simply mean that they are opening up to a wider set of perspectives which have yet to be absorbed.
- Leave 'gaps' where students can make their own contribution to the subject area.
- Set writing projects that have a real-life purpose – such as creating materials for the public, employers, children or for publication.
- Encourage students to find personal metaphors for their writing.
- Create an opportunity for relating at least one piece of course writing to their own lives.
- Encourage students to note down what inspires them personally.
- Offer opportunities for risk taking and creativity.

Encouragement and empathy

- Find out from students where their difficulties and anxieties lie.
- Acknowledge the demands created through the plurality of writing genres required of students across their curricula.
- Train students in how to offer each other constructive support about writing (see p. 117).
- Offer at least one constructive comment on each piece of writing.
- Offer early, clear, legible and focused feedback on writing.
- Offer an opportunity for constructive feedback after an early draft for at least one piece of writing.

Final comments

Writing is an essential part of the student's experience at university, not least in terms of assessment and grading. Many people, including lecturers, can find it difficult to settle down to write, even if they understand the writing process or have a strong motivation to write. Those who are disengaged from, and ignorant of, the academic writing process are seriously disadvantaged. Increasing numbers of students are entering university who have underdeveloped writing skills, low self-esteem about their writing, lack of practice in writing and even a deep reluctance to write. Deficits in previous reading and writing histories cannot easily be compensated for simply through the provision of study skills sessions, important though these may be. A more comprehensive approach to writing is needed, especially in the first year, so that the student is led, though activity, intervention and feedback, to a position of understanding, confidence and engagement with the writing process.

SPACE CHECKLIST
Supporting student writing across the curriculum

Provide SPACE to develop writing within the curriculum.

Strategy

- **Provision**: ensure that students are offered strategies for approaching writing in different circumstances: coursework, exams, work placement, for different audiences and purposes.
- **Reinforcement**: build activities related to sub-stages of the writing process into teaching time (generating ideas, evaluating sources, sorting ideas, examining titles).
- **Modelling**: model strategies so students gain a sense of what is required.

Pace

- Offer early writing tasks to orientate the student – and for diagnostic purposes.
- Build towards more sophisticated writing assignments.

Analysis

- Provide three examples of each type of writing your students are required to produce, e.g. 3 essays, 3 lab reports, 3 case studies, 3 exam answers.
- Provide brief examples of good style from subject textbooks.
- Annotate these examples, bringing out the desirable characteristics of each.
- Offer opportunities to discuss text characteristics in groups.
- Draw out what is required for student writing as opposed to textbook writing.

Context

- Ensure clarity regarding the types of writing required.
- Contextualise writing: tasks, such as through North–South Pole mapping.
- Offer a rationale for the writing characteristics required in your area.
- Map out what is required for your subject in terms of marking criteria.
- Highlight contrasts between characteristics of writing required for your discipline and for other disciplines.

Engagement

Inspiration

■ Encourage students to find personal metaphors for their writing.

■ Create opportunities for relating at least one piece of course writing to their own lives.

■ Encourage self-reflection (exploring personal writing histories; keeping a journal about writing experiences on different modules; noting what inspires them personally).

■ Encourage students to write just for themselves (poems, letters, diaries, stories).

■ Offer opportunities for risk-taking, creativity or writing for the self.

Encouragement

■ Train peers in how to offer constructive mutual support for writing.

■ Offer at least one constructive comment on each piece of writing.

■ Offer early, clear, legible and focused feedback on writing.

■ Offer an opportunity for constructive feedback after an early draft of writing.

7 Study skills programmes

Objectives of study skills programmes

Those leading study skills sessions will wish to establish their own sets of objectives for their programme. Clear objectives are important as they indicate to students a particular approach to skills development, even a conceptualisation of what a skill is and how it might be 'achieved' or 'developed'. The objectives for the programme suggested in this book are:

- to train students in essential academic and other related learning skills within the context of their course of study, vocational pathway, or other meaningful structure;
- to locate study skills within a developmental model;
- to facilitate students' understanding of learning development as an evolving process rather than something which is accomplished within a single session or even a series of sessions;
- to train students to evaluate their own needs and achievements more capably;
- to enable students to become more self-managing and self-reliant, capable of taking responsibility for their own learning and addressing their own learning needs;
- to encourage students to appreciate proactive learning – rather than to see themselves as semi-passive recipients of information and feedback.

It may not be possible for those leading study skills programmes to operationalise objectives such as these. In such cases, programme leaders will need to develop objectives which contextualise study skills as far as they can and clarify longer-term benefits as well as short-term gains.

Developmental approach

Study skills is a quick and accessible term of reference but is not a term that accurately describes what is needed for successful study. It suggests discrete entities, 'skills' which can be learnt in a de-contextualised way, and independently of each other. This is not possible in practice. To teach study skills in that way almost inevitably undermines the project and subverts the possibility of 'skill' emerging.

In-depth work with several hundreds of students who lacked study skills suggests strongly that people become more 'skilled' as students through developing attributes, habits, attitudes, approaches, even beliefs, rather than solely by practising a strategy over and over. This is perhaps true of any skill. In order to maintain the required application needed to become skilled, to keep up the necessary practice, individuals need motivation, a perceived goal, a degree of self-confidence, a sense of having 'permission' to succeed, a belief that success is possible. They need moral strength and morale to keep going when progress is not obvious. They need openness to trying new methods.

Knowledge of what to do and how to do it, and repeated practice is important to the development of most skills. However, skilled practitioners rarely achieve success in isolation. A facilitative environment is usually required. To develop skills, practitioners require opportunities for practice, input from others, feedback, support, models to work to, structured programmes, a place where advanced practice can be discussed, debated and critiqued. To become really skilled at complex tasks, one has to be able to manage criticism, and, as a corollary of this, it helps if one can interact with others in meaningful ways. To be considered skilled, one needs to be able to do something well, and one would expect skilled practitioners to have an element of versatility: the ability to apply their skills in related fields and to use what they have learnt to address unforeseen problems. An element of problem-solving ability could be expected from those adept at complex skills.

Moreover, it is hard to develop skills independent of knowledge. There has to be a focus for one's skill. One can't become a skilled musician without music to practise and a tradition and context to make the skill meaningful. One can't become a skilled student without a subject to study. Study skills need to be developed in relation to a body of knowledge which makes sense of the 'skill', which allow the skill to be 'honed' and fine-tuned towards particular ends. Lecturers who underestimate the importance of study skills being taught within the subject discipline may lack an appreciation of the subtlety of their discipline and its distinctiveness in terms of conventions, attitudes and methodologies.

To become a skilled student, in other words, requires more than immersion in study skills. Students need to develop academically, personally and professionally in a broad-based way. The term 'study skills' does not suggest the range and depth of personal and academic development that can be an emergent property of study skills work. 'Study skills' as a concept begins to evaporate the closer one approaches. This is not to under-value the role of study skills. Expert engagement with concepts tends to lead one away from clear definitions: edges become blurred, concepts become 'fuzzy' (Rosch, 1975; Murphy and Wright, 1984). However, study skills cannot be just about 'study skills' if students are to become skilled as learners and as skilled future professionals. Study skills is an aspect of a 'process of becoming', and that process of becoming is reflexive in that it, in turn, is necessary to the development of skilled learning.

Unfortunately, despite its potential, the term 'study skills' does not speak to the adult in the student who is aiming towards professional life and rewards. Other terminology is often needed in order to appeal and motivate. However, the trend within many professions has been to embrace a process of 'becoming', of growing into, a more skilled practitioner, using the wider sense of 'skill' described above. There has been a movement towards 'reflective practitioner' models of training and practice (Schon, 1987; Mezirow, 1990; Jennings and Kennedy, 1996). In higher education, study skills can more usefully be embedded in the curriculum, as part of a wider, developmental approach, whether as Personal, Professional and Academic Development (PPAD), Personal Development Planning (PDP) or Continuous Professional Development (CPD).

Emphasising a developmental approach to learning confers several advantages. It reinforces, for students, the notion that excellence in academic and professional performance is achievable through activity and involvement, as part of a process of 'becoming'. This emphasis on the achievable, on manageable pathways towards success, can challenge defeatist and demotivating attitudes that may have been inculcated in students earlier in their education and from the wider environment, that their level of achievement is pre-ordained and their current performance an indicator of potential.

Such attitudes undermine students' beliefs that there is any point in applying themselves to study, as the outcomes appear to be predetermined. The developmental approach emphasises the learner's active engagement in the learning process and students' own responsibility for improving their learning; it can offer a basis and training for self-directedness. These have been identified as important considerations when working with adult learners (Knowles, 1978).

A developmental model offers a broader base for content, moving beyond an unrealistic emphasis on 'skills' divorced from the curriculum towards one of personal management, professional orientation, and contextualised problem solving. It facilitates the inclusion of learning development within the assessed curriculum, raising its status in students' eyes. It creates potential for coherent work over a longer time frame, so that study skills is not simply 'one-off' or 'bolt-on', with few links to the 'real' curriculum. It is also a trend which professional bodies ought to be welcoming within the curriculum, if not insisting upon, as one likely to lead to practitioners who have increased meta-awareness of what they are doing and why.

Academic content

When skills work is incorporated within the curriculum, there will be academic content related to the subject discipline. However, there is also potential for engaging students in wider pedagogical and epistemological debate related to skills work. In other words, there is a knowledge and understanding aspect to skills work, which, if developed, could enhance students' understanding of their curriculum. It is an opportunity to address with students fundamental questions about what higher education study is about, what is meant by 'theory' and why it is valued, why the discipline developed the methodologies that it has, and how these impact upon the ways that knowledge, understanding, 'fact' and 'truth' are perceived. Theory, methodologies and values implicit to the subject discipline impact upon how students can interpret what is meant by 'study skills'. It is easy to assume that there are shared understandings on questions of 'truth' or fact' or value when this is not the case.

Students can be encouraged to look at the role of educational practice, social and educational trends, ideology and belief systems in the process of learning, calling upon personal experience. This can encourage students to look at how their own beliefs, such as those concerned with inherited intelligence, or 'permission' for certain social groups to learn, might be inhibiting their own current performance. From here they could go on to explore the role and value of education, knowledge, the subject discipline, and universities to the development of discipline or vocational knowledges. Brookfield (1993) offers a useful and stimulating set of questions that could be adapted to encourage critical reflection in this area. Students can be asked, for example, to examine pedagogical texts in terms of empirical evidence, ideology, methodology, politics, from the perspective of their discipline, personal experience and vocational area. Brookfield suggests such questions as:

- What connections and discrepancies do you note between the descriptions of adult learning processes and adult educational practices contained in a piece of academic writing and your own experiences as an adult learner?
- Whose voices are heard in a piece of academic writing?
- To what extent does a piece of academic writing acknowledge and address ethical issues?
- To what extent does the piece of writing examined show a connectedness to practice?

Relevance

Timing

It is often hard for students to appreciate the relevance of study skills sessions before they have begun to encounter difficulties, especially if training is offered in isolation from the curriculum and not formally assessed. This sometimes leads to the question of whether study skills sessions should be left to later in the year or even the second year. However, the issue is less one of timing than of relevance. Students need approaches which make learning development personally meaningful. This may be in terms of their past experiences, or current motivation or future goals. Skills development must also appear to be of significance to the course itself and to their teachers. Significance will be made manifest by such factors as the time allocated within the curriculum, by references made to it, in passing, by lecturers, by the structures which support it (such as personal tutoring, progress files, mentor schemes) and its inclusion within the overall assessment of the degree.

Context

Study skills work needs to be appropriate to the students' level of study and to the particular subjects which the student is studying. Subject lecturers often underestimate how far different disciplines vary in what they require. This is made all the more confusing in that different subjects often use similar vocabulary to mean very different things. A 'report' or an 'essay' for different branches of the same subject, such as cognitive or social psychology, can vary enormously. What counts as 'discussion', 'evidence', a 'conclusion', or 'objectivity' for one subject, may be inappropriate for another. When study skills are taught as a discrete subject, divorced from the curriculum, then a large burden may be placed on the student to bridge the gap between the abstract or generic skill and its real-life application.

On modular schemes, students may receive only two or three pieces of coursework for a module, whereas students may need practice and feedback on several pieces of coursework in order to capture what is required and adapt skills to the context. At that stage, they may move on to another module where a very different set of conventions apply. This can feel to the student as if they can never deliver what is expected. They may blame the course or internalise the blame, becoming demotivated.

Wherever possible, study skills sessions should be linked to:

- the curriculum being studied;
- to any pre-sessional diagnostic work;
- to diagnostic and orientation work undertaken during induction;
- to specific additional local support (SALS);
- to specialist or additional support where relevant.

Anchored in personal experience

Students bring with them a very varied range of experiences which, on the surface, may not seem relevant to the immediate study context. However, the underlying skills needed to manage many aspects of study have parallels or roots in even the most mundane tasks. Skilled teachers are adept at making subtle parallels explicit. If students can anchor new learning in previous knowledge and experience, and find analogies in their current expertise with what is expected of them in HE, they have much greater confidence in taking on new learning tasks. In addition, the process of identifying what is transferable from one context to another involves, in itself, an investigation of underlying problem structures. This offers students both a grounding in problem-solving techniques, and a basis for approaching the notion of 'transferable skills' (as a problem in its own right) in other learning and employment contexts.

Elements of a study skills programme

From what has been argued above about the importance of contextualisation, it follows that the contents of study skills or personal development programmes will show necessary and desirable differences from one course of study to another. However, it is likely to be beneficial to incorporate certain key aspects, in addition to those covered in Chapter 10. These include:

(1) affective issues;
(2) reflection and evaluation;
(3) self-management and management of learning;
(4) interpersonal work;
(5) problem solving.

(1) Affective issues

These are often overlooked and yet are, perhaps, the most important aspect of orientating students towards their learning successfully. Typical issues that need to be addressed are:

- motivation and personal goal-setting;
- what inspires students in their life and learning;
- creating, adapting to, managing or surviving the course or institutional culture;
- self concept: belief in success;
- sharing anxieties and dealing with vulnerability;
- managing difficult times such as when study demands seem overwhelming.

(2) Reflection and evaluation

Students are required, increasingly, to take part in reflective and self-appraisal work. However, students usually need a structured approach to such work, especially in the early stages. Stimulus materials, discussion groups, self-evaluation questionnaires, question sheets, and paced exercises can lead students to a place where they are able to engage in less direct forms of reflection. Students need to be clear about the importance of criteria to evaluation, have practice in working to meet criteria and set their own criteria for self-evaluation, whether individually or in groups.

Student self-evaluation needs to be regarded as an *indication* of what is needed and as one part of the process of identifying appropriate support, rather than an accurate record of where support is required. Students most 'at risk' of failure or withdrawal are often vulnerable pre-

cisely because they do not have a good sense of what they need to do in order to improve performance. Peer and tutor input over the term, as well as feedback on coursework, offer useful additional perspectives to students to help them form more objective criteria for self-evaluation.

It is also important that students reflect on the process they are undergoing as they acquire new learning skills. Study skill tutors need to encourage reflection as part of advance preparation for sessions; they should set time aside during class to discuss this preparation and give time for students to make quick notes about their learning during taught sessions. The bulk of these reflections will be private, and confidentiality should be assured. However, it is useful for students to draw their reflections together at set times and to submit their current 'position' in writing.

(3) Self-management and management of learning

This involves creating opportunities for students to evaluate their own needs within a structured support programme and to adopt a problem-solving model such as that offered below. Students often arrive in a very dependent frame of mind and if this is not turned around early during their time at university, course staff are likely to become exhausted by the demands made upon them. Self-management, such as time-management skills, can be linked to course demands such as managing deadlines, and personal organisational skills to structuring an assignment or skills required on work placement.

(4) Interpersonal work

Appropriate training for interpersonal work tends to be overlooked, as if students were naturally able to relate to each other in skilled ways, able to offer and take criticism and work together productively. However, if students are trained to support each other and guided in how to be open with each other, there is an all-round gain. Students are in a better position to offer each other mutual support during the course, saving staff time. It pays to introduce and nurture 'action sets' or similar structures early on in order to encourage students to take their problems first to each other rather than to teaching staff. At the end of the study skills module, this can be the foundation for more productive peer support networks and for group and project work. Moreover, if students are trained to offer and receive constructive criticism, they can be more actively and meaningfully involved in the assessment process. Finally, as graduates, they leave with a range of key skills valued by employers.

(5) Problem solving

In traditional study skills sessions, lecturers often delivered information about how to study, sometimes in a lecture format where students took notes. A one-off session on study skills using a similar format is not unusual as part of induction programmes all over Britain. This can be a complete waste of time as it does not connect to the experiences of the student, and does not involve them in the process of identifying where their own strengths and difficulties lie nor how to use their strengths to address their difficulties. A problem-solving approach to learning skills encourages the student to see difficulty in terms of challenges for which there may be a range of solutions. It is more congruent with the overall aims of university courses which want to encourage analysis, reflection, hypothesis formation, application of perceived solutions, and evaluation of interventions.

If we wish to encourage thinking skills in HE, then it is useful to ask students to apply such thinking skills to their own learning. A problem solving approach encourages students to identify their needs within specific but variable contexts and to devise strategies to meet them. Problem-solving requires learners to look for underlying similarities and differences. It necessitates the identification of common underlying structures in the problem under consideration and previous experience. It encourages the application and adaptation of prior knowledge.

This gives students a meta-schema for adapting skills to new learning contexts, and a method for actively searching out ways of transferring expertise to different situations rather than assuming, in a new context, they either do or do not have the requisite skills. This is an especially useful and open-ended approach to learning development for modular structures and where separate areas of a degree programme set very different demands. In addition, it encourages students to see study problems as starting points for action, rather than as barriers to progression or proof of inadequacy. Many students need to have their attitude to study 'problems' challenged in this way.

Stages in reflective problem solving

(1) *Orientation: identify the 'next step'*
Identify in general terms what needs to be addressed. This is the basis for the more detailed analysis and decision making which follows.

(2) *Define the task*
The next stage is to identify objectives more precisely. This involves a process of:

- Clarifying the purpose. Why does this area of learning or skills need to be addressed now?
- What are the exact aims and objectives?
- What will be indicators of success in achieving aims and objectives?
- What approach will be taken (self-evaluation questionnaires, reflection, talking to others, using feedback from assignments, etc.)?

(3) *Clarify the current position*

- Identify areas of strengths and difficulties relevant to the context.
- Reflect on the relative significance of these.
- Identify priorities for attention.

(4) *Evaluate alternative solutions*

- What options are there for addressing difficulties? Which best suit the students' learning styles and preferred ways of working?
- Are there alternatives which might work better?
- How can strengths be used to address areas of weakness?

- What previous experience throws light upon, or offers solutions to, the current difficulties?
- What can inspire, guide, inform and support learning in this situation?
- What resources are available?

(5) *Decide on an action plan*

- Students discuss their proposed plan with other people, or their tutor where possible.
- Students decide upon a course of action for their priorities.
- Students set specific times and targets for action.
- Students identify how progress will be measured: how will it be clear that objectives have been met?

(6) *Action*

Students follow through on the action plan, monitoring their progress and adapting their action plan.

(7) *Evaluate action taken*

- Either alone, in discussion with others, or with guidance from a tutor, the student works out how effective their action has been so far.
- What worked and what has been achieved?
- What have students learnt that surprised them or was unexpected?
- What did not work so well? Why was this?
- Are there skills or other facets of learning which still need to be addressed?
- This may be written up as a position paper or interim position paper.
- This leads back to the first stage of the cycle: 'identifying the next step'.

Ideally, this process should be linked to induction work on identifying needs. Students should be assisted through to at least a revised action plan. The process can be written up as a Preliminary Position Paper which can be used as part of the early diagnostic process and, in its final version, for summative assessment.

Structured reflection for improving learning and performance

A more elaborate version of the above problem-solving approach is given at the end of this chapter in the form of a set of handouts addressed to students (see pp. 153–9 and 252). This model organises an approach to improving learning and performance around four key processes: orientation, strategy, action and evaluation, all encompassed within a reflective framework. Both reflection and a problem-solving strategy run through the four stages. This model includes the general structure for improving learning and performance required for the QCA key skill (level 4) but within an alternative framework that lends itself to study skills development and to personal development planning. It lays particular emphasis on an initial orientation to the learning process and encourages the student to plan forward at each stage.

The model suggests learning not as a cyclical process but as an upwards learning spiral. Students are invited to evaluate not only what they achieved in terms of their original learning outcomes but also what they have learned that was unexpected and which might take them to a different stage in their learning.

Continuity and progression

Ideally, personal, professional and academic development is a theme which is developed throughout the students' time at university, and not solely through a module set apart from the curriculum. It is unrealistic to expect that students will acquire the skills they need to develop their learning for three years of study through a single module set at the beginning of the first term or semester. None the less, this is what many universities currently do expect. Mechanisms need to be set in place which assist the student to integrate skills over time and in new contexts. Students need reflection time and supported practice in applying and accommodating skills and theory to new learning situations. In the early stages, they need reassurance that they can achieve. As they move through HE, they need more challenges, which raise their personal development and reflective practice to a higher level. Professional and employment skills may take a higher place in the curriculum after the first year, but there may still be a need to return to analytical and writing skills, oral presentation or teamwork skills from a more advanced perspective.

This might be achieved in a number of ways. One is through offering personal and professional development modules at each level of the programme. Another is by incorporating such modules at each level of the students' programme. In addition, elements of enhancing study skills can be incorporated into all aspects of the course. If there is a personal tutor system in operation, this could form the basis of a discursive enterprise where students elaborate their personal development with feedback and guidance. If students keep a portfolio or other developmental record, this can be used as a tool for ongoing objective guidance in how to advance their study skills. In particular, it can be important for encouraging students to continue to monitor their progress, recognising achievement in areas they may not have appreciated, and identifying new challenges. In addition, the content and nature of feedback on marked assignments can play a key role in keeping skills development on the agenda, especially if it is clear how learning development translates into marks. Personal professional development can also be raised with students in relation to their future continuous professional development as graduates and to the concept of lifelong learning.

Consistency

Particularly in their first year, students need to feel that the advice they are receiving about how to improve their learning is generally consistent from one tutor or module to another. This is something which may need to be addressed specifically, especially if students are on combined or multiple honours programmes. Personal and academic development can be used to address differences in the ways that subjects value specific skills or attitudes over others. Students can be assisted in coming to some understanding about why such differences arise, and in resolving or holding inner conflicts about 'fitting' in to varied demands.

Structuring study skills sessions

It is important to set a culture of advance preparation for teaching sessions, and this is just as true of study skills sessions as for other subjects. For example, it is not the best use of teaching time to set long self-evaluation questionnaires to complete during taught sessions. Similarly, many people find it difficult to read texts 'on the spot' or when other people are around. Wherever possible, unless it defeats the purpose of the exercise, reading should be set in advance of the session. The shorter the time available, the more important it is that maximum time is set aside for dealing with questions about areas of difficulty and mutual problem solving.

All sessions

Ideally, the structure needs to allow for:

Training in personal responsibility for learning

- Developing an appreciation of the benefits of advance preparation.
- Discussion or practical use of the reading, activities or stimulus material undertaken as advance preparation.
- Reflection on the consequences of decisions and actions taken in relation to their learning.

Modelling structured approaches

- A clear format (see the 'magic 7' structure on p. 101).
- An agenda: to model time management.
- A closing activity for students to draw together what they have learnt.

Identifying and addressing difficulties

- Opportunities for mutual problem-solving in

a structured and supported way, such as through action sets.

- Room to ask questions and clarify outstanding difficulties.

Flexibility of approach

- A variety of individual, paired, group and whole-group work to develop a wide range of interpersonal skills.
- A variety of activities so that students get a feel for their learning preferences.

Early sessions

In the early sessions, additional work may need to be undertaken on:

- The rationale for PPAD, CPD or study skills work.
- Managing anxiety (especially in relation to revealing difficulties in front of strangers).
- Interpersonal work (structured group work, giving and receiving feedback and listening skills).
- Personal motivation, goal setting, confidence and self-esteem.

Materials

There is a vast market of published study skills materials which can be drawn upon to save time in producing new materials. The sessions in Part II were originally designed to offer structured support to those using *The Study Skills Handbook* (Cottrell, 1999). However, the sessions can be used just as well with other materials if tutors prefer. Some ideas on using or creating alternative materials are offered below.

Self-evaluation questionnaires

Self-evaluation questionnaires are useful starting points from which to begin deeper analysis and discussion, rather than ends in themselves. Students usually need support and an alternative, more objective, perspective on their progress in order to evaluate the accuracy of

their own self-evaluations and the kind of criteria they use to make decisions about their strengths and weaknesses. In general, avoid long, detailed questionnaires as students tend to lose their focus. Begin with a more general questionnaire and follow it up with more specific ones as needed. Break longer questionnaires into shorter ones, focused on a single theme, such as 'Interpersonal skills for health professionals' or 'Reading skills for lawyers'. Where possible, complete work on one questionnaire before starting the next. Ask students to complete the same questionnaire later in the year and compare their answers. Check whether they can account for any differences in their responses.

Exercises and activities

Ground the first stages of the activity in prior experience. Begin from what the students already know, and then draw parallels with the study skill under consideration. Offer concrete examples where possible. Draw out the relevance to the subjects the student is studying and variations in applicability. Exercises or activities can be found in:

- Allison, B. (1993), *Research Methods* (Leicester: De Montfort University).
- Bourner, T. and Race, P. (1990) *How to Win as a Part-Time Student* (London: Kogan Page).
- Rickards, T. (1992), *How to Win as a Mature Student* (London: Kogan Page).
- Williams, K. (1989), *Study Skills* (Basingstoke: Macmillan – now Palgrave).

Course-specific materials

Wherever possible, use materials which are relevant to the student's course. The writing skills required by a scientist are not the same as those required by a historian or a lawyer. As a rule of thumb:

- Offer three examples of each type of material.
- Annotate examples to draw out strong or weak aspects, preferably in relation to the requirements of subjects being studied.
- Offer an alternative example, as a point of ref-

erence. The contrast brings out more clearly what is required.

• Explore the rationale for the conventions.

Reading

There is no shortage of items to suggest to students for reading. Articles from the *Times Higher Educational Supplement*, the *Studies in Higher Education Journal*, and personal development texts are useful starting points. Each study skills section in Part II suggests a basic reading list for students. In addition, study skills teachers may find the materials at the end of this chapter useful for particular groups or topics.

Recording and monitoring development

Given that learning development is an ongoing process over the whole of a student's academic career, it is important that records are kept which enable individuals' particular issues to be followed up, and progress to be mapped. This might be through tutorial records, or a portfolio that the student keeps, or a mixture of both. A portfolio might contain initial stock-taking and reflection undertaken by the student at the beginning of the course, along with material used by the student to appraise their learning, and especially any position statements and action plans that were written. An example of a piece of early work and a representative recent piece of later work can provide useful benchmarks for comparing progress. Either all or representative feedback from tutors should also be included to assist monitoring and guidance.

The personal tutor, or a support tutor in some cases, might wish to arrange set times to check when and where the proposed action was followed up and to help the student to evaluate its effectiveness. It is important to highlight successes and to update records of skills development which might boost confidence or be applicable to career aspirations. Towards the end of their time at university, students may need guidance on removing some of the materials used for formative assessment or monitoring objectives and with reshaping the portfolio so that it presents them in a more professional light. Portfolios tend to be overladen with unnecessary examples. Summaries, a few key examples, CVs, details of references, certificates of qualifications and an updated position paper are usually sufficient. Very few employers are likely to want to wade through overstocked, poorly constructed portfolios.

Records of achievement

Higher education institutions are being required to provide students with records of achievement or progress files that contain more than simply a list of grades for modules or degree classification. Experience at Manchester University suggests that, like skills development, engaging students in the process of recording achievement works only if embedded within the teaching and learning process. The process of recording achievement at Manchester has gone hand in hand with 'making skills more explicit within degree programmes', and building personal and academic development into the personal tutorial system (O'Connell *et al.*, 2000).

The criteria-based marking sheets offered in Chapters 12 and 22 below offer an adaptable model for recording and assessing skills within the curriculum. On these sheets, the marking scheme is very transparent, and it is much clearer to students what they must do to accumulate marks to achieve a higher grade: Harrop and Douglas (1996) argue that increased transparency and 'explicitness' are the main routes to HE success. As well as an overall assignment grade (a 'vertical' score) students' achievement in particular skills could be tracked over time. For example, if key skills are indicated by a code at the side of the sheet (as on these marking sheets), they could be optically read, and students given ratings for skills at each level. Progress for individual skills could be tracked separately over time (a 'horizontal mark'). This would enable relatively accurate and meaningful ratings of skills at each level of study and allow progress in skills to be monitored so as to offer more appropriate input from personal tutors (Cottrell, 2000).

Assessment

Where skills are embedded in the curriculum, the purposes of assessment identified by Mehrens and Lehmann (1984) for assessing other aspects of the curriculum are just as pertinent for assessing skills. In other words, assessing skills serves to:

- identify successful learning of taught components for the student's benefit;
- check the effectiveness of the course in teaching skills;
- offer diagnostic or formative feedback, identifying areas of weakness for further development;
- measure improvement in skills over time.

Moreover, research suggests that assessment plays a key role in how students perceive their learning, identify priorities and orientate themselves to study (Snyder, 1971; Innes, 1996; Gibbs and Lucas, 1997; Gibbs, 1999). Moreover, as Kemp and Seagraves (1995) point out, key skills are used, anyway, by students in order to address the traditional curriculum. However, Kemp and Seagraves found that approaches taken by courses towards developing key skills were often very incoherent. This was especially manifest in the area of skills assessment, where they found 'wildly different assessment criteria and regimes being applied by lecturers to the same students', leading to 'confusion . . . demoralisation and consequent failure'.

  Students orientate their study strategically towards the mode of assessment. If study skills, learning skills or professional development are not part of the formal assessment process, these are likely to be given a low priority by students. For consistency and coherence of approach, courses that stress self-evaluation and self-reliance ought to include self-assessment as part of the process of assessment. Assessment criteria could usefully address factors such as:

- the student's evaluation of the effectiveness

of their initial action plan and the appropriateness of their revised action plan;
- how far their position paper reflects an advance on their preliminary attempt;
- how far they demonstrate that they have been able to apply to their studies the learning skills upon which they have chosen to focus, such as in the production of their position paper or other coursework;
- the student's evaluation of their own work and the accuracy of their self-assessments according to the marking criteria.

Formative assessment

Skills development requires feedback, preferably soon after a task has been accomplished. Students benefit from input at interim stages so as to ensure that they are on track. The larger the assignment, the more important it is to provide early formative assessment of some kind. For widening participation intakes, especially, formative assessment processes can be assisted by:

- early diagnostic work;
- rapid turn-around on initial assignments so that students receive feedback and suggestions for action whilst the piece of work is still fresh in their minds;
- clear and focused feedback on a limited number of priorities;
- deferral of summative (formally graded) assessment until the students have had at least two opportunities to receive and act upon feedback. Some universities defer examinations for first-year students until the second semester or the end of the academic year, building in practice attempts and trial runs during the rest of the year.

  It can be helpful, especially for early assignments and when a new type of assessment mode is used, to ask students to submit assignment plans and more descriptive self-evaluations to enable the marker to see where difficulties may have originated. In other words, the process and the overall task management, as well as the end product, may need to be addressed and assessed.

Assignments and sessional work may be constructed which give opportunities for the development of many skills, through exposure, practice and familiarity, without these skills being included in each piece of formal assessment they undertake. This is especially important where skills are difficult to assess. For example, students may be asked to engage in group work, team work, or oral presentation in informal ways for several modules each year, but be formally assessed on this only once or twice at each level. This allows skills assessment to be more focused.

There are a number of external influences, such as the Dearing Report (1997), which are encouraging institutions to offer students opportunities to develop portfolios of skills. Although it may be important that all students gain opportunities to develop relevant oral communication, written communication, numeracy, IT skills, and so forth, what is appropriate for one kind of degree might seem very advanced or very basic to another. The intrapersonal skills and self-management required of counsellors or social workers would need to be much more advanced than that of engineers, whereas their numeracy and IT requirements would probably be regarded as very basic by engineers. Gibbs (1995) has argued that standards for key skills may need to be defined locally rather than institutionally.

Summative assessment

Where possible, skills assessment should be included within the overall assessment structure or else students will tend to rate it as less important than their formally assessed curriculum. It is good practice, in any part of the curriculum, for students to discuss what they learnt from the assessment process itself, to evaluate their own responses and reactions to different parts of the process and identify ways they could improve their performance. Unfortunately, this very rarely takes place. For skills-based courses, there is an excellent opportunity to build post-assessment self-appraisal into a second stage of reflection, action planning and evaluation. For this

area of work, it is important that students reflect upon how they prepared for and approached the assignment or exam, and be assessed on this too, rather being graded solely on their performance with subject-specific material.

Assessment criteria

It is easy to generate too many criteria, in an effort to be precise and to cover all angles. An optimal point needs to be found between clarifying criteria for students and overloading them with so many details that the assessment becomes confusing. It is also important not to set criteria which are hard to assess in the circumstances given or which are not necessarily essential to the outcome. For example, lists of criteria for oral communication often include such features as dynamics of voice and gesture, variations of intonation, volume and suchlike which are difficult to assess objectively and at the necessary speed. This is especially true for group presentations, peer assessment, and when there are several criteria to assess simultaneously. Moreover, this also raises equal opportunities issues. It is important to be clear about the relevance of the criteria in relation to the purpose of the activity. Students may convey a message forcefully even though they have speech impediments, language difficulties or are not dramatic in their presentation style.

If the course wishes to promote such skills as independence, creativity, self-reliance, 'problematising', these need to be included within the marking criteria. Students need to recognise that these skills and attributes are being assessed. Examples of marking criteria sheets, which integrate marking for skills into mainstream assignments, are offered in Chapters 12 and 22 below. The exact criteria can be adapted and weighted to meet the aims of different curricula: what counts as 'excellent IT skills', for example, will vary depending on whether one is taking a course in engineering studies or fine art or social work. What is important is that it is clear to students what is expected of them, how they are to be assessed and that they gain credit for skills that they do manifest. If students are expected to work with others in a constructive way, or to generate innovative approaches, or to use IT, then evidence of this needs to be gathered and used in their overall marks. Not to do so, could mean that the student undervalues those skills and may also be disadvantaged later when seeking work.

Students do not necessarily need long lists of secondary criteria to make sense of the marking criteria. The meaning of the criteria can be offered in a short paragraph that contextualises each skill being assessed. For example, if students have undertaken explorations of group work and discussed what makes groups work, analysing their own and others' performance in a formative way, then the criteria should be serving as a summary and a reminder of what they have learnt. Students could be provided with an overview of what the assignment is looking for and how each of the marking criteria is regarded as relevant in terms of the learning outcomes, for example:

> The point of the oral communication assignment is to see how well you can persuade the client group of the benefits of the recommendations you have made, bearing in mind that the client group is likely to be resistant to change and uncertain of the benefits for themselves. Remember that the client group is mainly multilingual and, for some, English will be a recently acquired language

or:

> The target group consists of industrialists who will be familiar with model X but may be unacquainted with recent technical advances and terminology.

Such overviews contextualise the criteria, making them meaningful in a way that is hard to achieve with long lists of secondary criteria. Students will gain more elaborate understandings of criteria through teaching and learning methods that integrate skills development into their learning, via progressive activities, materials and assessment.

Using criteria sheets: assessing skills within the curriculum

The marking sheets offered in Chapters 12 and 22 below are one way of incorporating skills assessment into the academic tasks. They use a criterion-referenced approach, setting out in advance what will gain marks. This differs from the vaguer, norm-based assessment still prevalent in higher education. In norm-based assessment, grade levels are determined arbitrarily by looking for norms within submitted papers. When close, explicit criteria are given, students are able to see what is required of them in advance and are therefore better able to orientate their learning to achieve success. Clearer marking criteria, including for skills, makes it easier for staff, students and external bodies to see whether marking schemes are valid.

The marking sheets offered here attempt to balance a number of important aspects of assessment. They can make the marking process much more transparent for students: it becomes clear what gains or loses marks. Moreover, as skills are often marked implicitly in HE, these marking sheets make explicit those skills which are being marked for a given assignment. Each assignment might assess a different range of skills: the lists of skills given on the sheets in Chapter 12 are only illustrative of what *could* be included rather than prescriptive of which skills *should* be included.

This approach also offers a way of weighting those components which are considered the most relevant for the course. For example, 'knowledge and understanding' can be weighted differently from technical writing skills, both by a different scale (1–10 rather than 1–5) for example, and by breaking the category down into several components (breadth of reading, referencing, analysis, selection), each of which can also be marked on a different scale. The knowledge section could contain several subsections, each offering marks for addressing particular issues. A further advantage of this is that students can identify how far they gain marks simply for 'factual knowledge' (as many believe) and how much for managing, evaluating, critiquing and applying such knowledge.

On the marking sheets used in Chapter 12, a code is used to tag skills, using (primarily) the skills from the SEEC descriptors (p. 193). If sheets are optically read and computerised, marks can be allocated for a given skill over several assignments and progress checked over time. This offers a tool for tutors offering academic guidance, as they can see more accurately which skills have developed over several semesters. If a transcript is to be offered, students can be offered precise marks for skills taught through the curriculum, used in particular assignments, and marked at the level of those assignments.

It is important to link learning outcomes, marking criteria and the marking sheet. Where possible, these could be combined into a single tool, saving staff time and making the process all the clearer for students. Where this is not done, it is easy for staff to divorce marking criteria from learning outcomes. For example, it is not unusual to see examples of marking sheets where the marking criteria are set as 'introduction: 15%; conclusion: 15%' and so forth when 'writing a good introduction' is not set as a learning outcome. Where reflection, self-reliance and self-evaluation are required as skills, opportunities to develop these should be built into the assessment process. For example, students can be asked to use a replica of the marker's criteria sheet to assess their own work, and this, along with a reflective log or evaluation sheet, can be used by tutors assessing the student's abilities in self-evaluation and reflection. This method offers a structure which enables students to develop self-evaluation using given criteria against which they can compare their own evaluations. Reflection is encouraged because it is explicitly marked.

Specific study skills-related assignments

Preliminary, interim and final Position Papers form a useful set of assignments for formative and summative assessment. Other study skills-related assignments could include:

- *a review* of a book on learning;
- *a critical analysis* of a course text, learning theory or approach;
- *a presentation* on an aspect of coursework or on an area of learning skills;
- *an essay* on a subject such as 'Is learning all about intelligence?' or 'Do we all learn in the same way?'
- *a portfolio* which draws together reflection, self-evaluation, a written piece on how their learning has changed over their time on the course (referring to examples of work they have included), and a final Position Paper;
- *an individual or group project*: exploring one aspect of learning in depth, such as how the brain works, learning styles, or pedagogic theory;
- a *mini-research project:* such as on learning styles in the year group, or the effects of previous learning on current motivation or skills, or developments in training or teaching for their subject discipline;
- a *personal case study:* using personal or small-group experiences of study as the basis of a critical review of literature on learning.

Final comments

Although the formal aspects of study skills teaching are helpful to students, it is also important to look at what inspired you at times when you found study to be difficult – or even what inspires you now when you have to produce a piece of writing or prepare for a lesson when you simply do not feel like it. Be aware of how your experiences may be different from those of your students: what works for you may not work for them, but you can still offer your experience as an example. It can be helpful to students to realise that there isn't a great divide between them, when they are struggling, and teaching staff who may impress them as competent and incapable of experiencing – much less understanding – difficulty. Your enthusiasm and honesty may encourage them to be open about their own difficulties and to look for their own ways of doing things.

Introductory books

Beaver, D. (1994, 1998), *NLP for Lazy Learning* (Shaftesbury, Dorset and Boston, Mass.: Element).

Buzan, T. (1993), *The Mind Map Book* (London: BBC).

Buzan, T. and Keene, R. (1996), *The Age Heresy: You Can Achieve More, Not Less, as You Get Older* (London: Ebury Press).

Gibbs, G. (1994), *Learning in Teams: A Student Manual* (Oxford: Oxford Centre for Staff Development).

Lawrence, G. (1995), *People Types and Tiger Stripes*, 3rd edn (Gainesville, Fla: Centre for Applications of Psychological Type).

Mandel, S. (1987), *Effective Presentation Skills* (London: Kogan Page).

Miles T. R. and Gilroy, D. E. (1995), *Dyslexia at College*, 2nd edn (London: Routledge).

Follow-up texts

Douglas, T. (1995), *Survival in Groups: The Basics of Group Membership* (Milton Keynes: Open University Press).

Gardner, H. (1993), *Frames of Mind: The Theory of Multiple Intelligences*, 2nd edn (London: Fontana).

Gordon, W. J. J. and Poze, T. (1980), *The Art of the Possible* (Cambridge, Mass.: Porpoise).

McKim, R. H. (1972), *Experiences in Visual Thinking* (Monterey, Cal.: Brooks/Cole).

Saljo, R. (1979), 'Learning about Learning', *Higher Education*, **8**, 443–451.

Structured reflection to improve learning and performance

This is a four-stage process for improving learning and performance. The whole process is part of a reflective approach to learning and professional practice, through which students can improve performance in an upwards learning spiral.

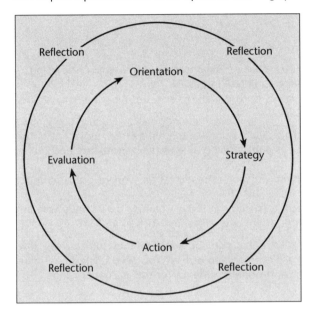

Orientation

(1) *Direction*: what do you want to achieve? Your goals and direction. Define the task.
(2) *Appraisal*: what are you bringing with you from your past? Your experience.
(3) *Review*: where you are now in relation to your goals? Your starting place.

Strategy

(1) *Establish opportunities*: educational; resources; advice, guidance and support; experience.
(2) *Consider alternatives*: how does this compare to similar things you have done? How good are the alternatives?
(3) *Action plan*: identify specific actions; identify priorities; set targets and timescales in order to achieve your goals.
(4) *Focus*: identify how you will manage motivators and inhibitors; identify 'triggers'.
(5) *Preparation*: organising resources (space, time, yourself, others, tools and materials).

Action

(1) *Follow through*: work through the action plan.
(2) *Monitoring*: how well are you progressing towards your goals?; monitoring progress.
(3) *Cyclical review*: review your orientation and planning.
(4) *Recording*: demonstrating reflective and effective learning; gathering evidence.

Evaluation

(1) *Evaluation*: what have you achieved?

(2) *Extrapolation*: what have you gained or learned, additionally, and perhaps unexpectedly, through the process?

(3) *Spiral appraisal*: identify how you have moved up through the learning spiral.

Orientation

(1) Direction

(a) What do you want to achieve? What is your overall goal or direction? At this stage you need to define your overall task in general terms.

(b) What specific objectives do you want to achieve. What are your desired outcomes? These might include:

- *personal objectives* (such as increased confidence; enjoyment of the course; the ability to speak in public; being able to receive criticism and use feedback from others, etc.);
- *professional objectives* (such as readiness for work or preparation for a specific vocation);
- *academic objectives* (such as improved grades; better understanding of a subject; progress towards a higher qualification such as an MA).

(c) What would be evidence that you had achieved these objectives? How would you demonstrate your achievements to others? You need to start considering this now in order to collect the appropriate evidence for the evaluation stage.

(2) Appraisal

What has brought you to study this course now? What are you bringing with you from your past that has influenced your decision and your current abilities to succeed?

- *Qualifications*: how have these prepared you for current study?
- *Experience*: what knowledge, skills, qualities and attributes do you have?
- *Inspiration*: what person, group, incident, music, lyrics, writing, art or other inspiration has had a positive influence you? How has this helped to motivate you towards becoming a student now?

(3) Review

Where you are now in relation to your goals?

(a) Skills

- *Study skills*: what are the academic or study skills expected of you as a student at this level?
- *Subject skills*: what are subject specific skills expected of you as a student at this level?
- *Professional skills*: what (if any) are the professional skills expected of you at this level?
- *Current performance*: how far do you meet the required skills at present?
- *Action needed*: what do you need to do in order to achieve what is expected of you at this level of study?

(b) Academic conventions

- *Conventions*: what are the conventions that apply to study in your subject discipline?
- *Expectations and responsibilities*: what else is expected of you as a student? What are your responsibilities?
- *Current understanding and performance*: how far do these make sense to you at the moment?
- *Action needed*: what do you need to do in order to achieve what is expected of you at this level of study?

(c) Personal orientation for learning

- *Motivation*: what is your own motivation for studying; why are you studying this module? This programme? At this university? What benefits will this bring you?
- *Inhibitors*: what obstacles might prevent you from succeeding in achieving your goals? How might you or others sabotage your study?
- *Learning history*: how do your past learning experiences impact upon your current learning and your confidence for study?
- *Attitudes and beliefs*: how far do your beliefs about learning and your attitudes to learning impact upon your current learning? How strongly do you believe that you can succeed?
- *Learning styles, preferences and habits*: how well do you understand your own learning processes? What helps you to learn best? What habits do you bring to your current study that might help or hinder you?

Strategy

(1) Establish opportunities

Identify means and opportunities for achieving your goals.

(a) *Educational opportunities*

- Which programme best meets your aims and personal needs?
- Which modules or study units would be best for you?
- Which modules would be of most use to you from a personal, academic or professional perspective?

(b) *Resources*

- What resources can you make use of in the Learning Resource Centre?
- What IT resources are available for you to make use of?
- What are the best journals for your subject?

(c) *Advice, guidance and support*

- Where can you gain the advice you need to help you make the right decisions (such as academic advice service; careers service; APEL adviser; work based learning unit? university web pages; the internet)?
- What support is available for you as a student at the university?
- What support can you create for yourself (such as study-support groups; baby-sitting circles; joint transport; book sharing opportunities)?

(d) *Opportunities for experience*

- ■ Are there opportunities for gaining credit for work you are undertaking or have undertaken in the past (such as through Accreditation of Prior (Experience and) Learning (APEL); workbased learning)?
- ■ Are there mentoring schemes at the university or in local schools that you could use to develop your experience and confidence?
- ■ What other opportunities are there for you to develop a range of skills and experience so that you develop a good curriculum vitae (CV)?

(2) Consider alternatives

(a) *Similarities*
How does this compare to similar things you have done? Are there aspects of previous learning or experience from work or everyday life that you can draw upon to help you with this aspect of learning?

(b) *Options*
Brainstorm alternative courses of action. How many ways can you think of for approaching this problem? What is your list of options? Do other people have ideas about how you could approach this task or improve your learning? What could inspire, guide or inform the situation? The more options you have at this stage, the more likely you are to be able to choose the best way forward.

(c) *Evaluate the options*
How good are the alternatives? What are the points in favour of each? Which is the most likely to work? What are the points against each?

(d) *Identify a course of action*
Decide on the best option to develop into a plan of action.

(3) Action plan

(a) *Identify a method to achieve your goals*

- ■ In general, what must you do to achieve your goals or succeed in this learning task? Identify an approach or method.

(b) *Actions*

- ■ Identify specific actions: what exactly must you do?
- ■ What are the main steps or stages?
- ■ What must be undertaken for each stage?

(c) *Priorities*

- ■ Identify priorities: what are all the things you need to do?
- ■ What is essential? What can be left?

(d) *Targets*

- ■ Set targets and time-scales for each stage.
- ■ Set SMART-F Targets (Specific, Measurable, Achievable, Realistic, Timely, Flexible)
- ■ How will you meet these targets?

(e) *Monitoring points*

- Set specific times for monitoring your progress as you go along.

(4) Focus

(a) *Motivation*

- What is your motivation (personal, academic, professional)?
- Identify how you will maintain your motivation.

(b) *Inhibitors*

- What are potential obstacles and hindrances? How might you or others 'sabotage' your success?
- How will you address potential obstacles and hindrances?

(c) *Personal 'triggers'*

- What are the 'triggers' that help settle you down to study?

(d) *Personal study strategy*

- How does your strategy suit your personal learning styles, habits and preferences?

(5) Preparation: organising resources

(a) *Space*: What is the best way of organising your space for study?

(b) *Time*: how will you manage your time to best effect? What are the best times for you to study?

(c) *Yourself*: What do you need to do to ensure you are prepared for study?

(d) *Others*: Who else needs to be involved, such as study partners or study support groups? Do you need to arrange for care of dependants? Who can offer support for study?

(e) *Tools and materials*: What equipment and materials do you need to purchase?

Action

(1) Follow through

Work through the action plan you identified under 'Strategy'.

(2) Monitoring

(a) in general, how well you are progressing towards your goals?

- What have you achieved?
- What remains to be done?

(b) How effectively are you managing your time? What could you do to improve your time-management?

(c) Are you using feedback from others to improve performance? How can you demonstrate this?

(3) Cyclical review

    (a) Does your overall strategy need to be changed?

    (b) Are you making the most of the opportunities you identified? if not, is there action you need to take?

    (c) Are you using the methods you identified as your strategy? If not, do these need to be revised?

    (d) Are you taking the actions you identified as your strategy? If not, do these need to be revised?

    (e) Are you meeting the agreed targets? If not, do these need to be revised?

    (f) Are you maintaining your motivation? If not, what can you do to improve this?

    (g) Are you managing obstacles to success? If not, what can you do to address these?

(4) Recording

    (a) *Demonstrating reflective and effective learning*

- Identify how you can demonstrate what you have learned to others.
- How can you demonstrate that you have worked to a strategy, reflected on your progress and revised your plan to increase your effectiveness?

    (b) *Gathering evidence*
Keep a record of what you do. You will need this for the evaluation stage. This may be a combination of several kinds of evidence, such as a written log; a video; artefacts; reports from others; certificates of qualifications, etc. Identify what evidence you need to meet:

- course requirements;
- professional requirements;
- to meet your personal goals.

The evidence should:

- Be brief: give precise examples.
- Demonstrate the skill: include only what is strictly relevant. One or two examples are all that are needed to demonstrate the skill or quality. Avoid including long documents.
- Be annotated: attach a few lines (on a separate piece of paper) to each example, to explain why it is included.
- Be regularly updated: gather, annotate and edit your evidence as you go along so that it is up to date. It is much easier to annotate evidence at the point where you first decide to include it, when it is fresh in your mind, rather than trying to put together all the evidence at the end of your course.

Evaluation

(1) Evaluation

    (a) Referring to your action plan, what worked well? What could have been improved? Would you have been more successful if:

- you had linked it to a similar problem or activity you had managed previously?
- you had more information?
- you spent longer playing with ideas?
- you spent longer working out what was required?
- you had considered more options and alternative solutions?

(b) What you have achieved? Refer this directly to your learning goals and objectives? These may be:

- personal;
- professional;
- academic.

(c) What evidence is there that you have achieved this? How useful is the material that you have been collecting?

(d) What is the best way of presenting this to other people? You may need to:

- *Document*: include transcripts or other documentation.
- *Select*: choose carefully so as to include representative examples.
- *Organise*: arrange and index evidence clearly so that it is easy for others to iden-tify your achievements easily.
- *Summarise*: prepare an overview such as a position paper to pull together the main points.

(2) Extrapolation

What have you gained or learned, additionally, and perhaps unexpectedly, through the process? This might include such things as:

- things you have found about yourself, your own personality, your beliefs, your habits, the way you work with others that you were not aware of;
- your attitudes to change;
- how well you manage uncertainty;
- skills you acquired that you had not expected;
- the relevance of your learning to other contexts;
- your understanding of what is meant by reflection.

(3) Spiral appraisal

(a) Identify how you have moved up through the learning spiral. For example, what have you learnt through this task that would enable you to approach it differently a second time?

(b) What have you learnt about your own learning or about the learning process that you can apply to new learning contexts?

8 Supporting individual students

Even when support is structured into teaching, there are always some students who require more focused individual attention. This is particularly true of students from 'widening participation' backgrounds. The overwhelming majority of students referred for additional support through the Learning Development Unit at the University of East London (UEL), for example, are mature students. Even within categories such as 'dyslexic', mature students and those from unusual study backgrounds require much more intensive input than students from 'A' level backgrounds.

Individual support may be offered through the usual course structures, such as through the personal tutor. Alternatively, it may the province of a learning development unit, study support team, or equivalent. In some institutions, Student Services cover all work related to study difficulties. This chapter is aimed at all those who may be called upon to support students with study difficulties on an individual basis.

Who needs additional or individual support?

All students benefit from some individual input. Ideally, this would be co-ordinated by a personal tutor, and might focus, for example, on priority setting and action plans for improved study, on guidance on choosing modules, and the development of 'progress files' or other 'records of achievement'. However, students with the following kinds of difficulties, conditions or life histories tend to require more intensive support for some or all of their course of study. In the case of students with disabilities, additional funding may be available for learning support. The following is a typical cross-section of students referred, or self-referring, for additional support during a single year – if facilities are provided. These students usually require more time and intensive support than could be reasonably expected of lecturers through on-course support.

Disability-related referrals

- Specific learning difficulties (dyslexia, dyspraxia, dysgraphia, dysphasia, Meares–Irlen syndrome) and other disabilities.
- Asperger's Syndrome and mild cases of autism.
- Ongoing hearing difficulties (apart from deaf students), including formerly deaf students who have regained hearing and who struggle in hearing contexts.
- Long-term effects of childhood coma.
- Current or recent brain tumour.
- Long-term effects of head injury or attack to the head.

Medically based referrals

- Long-term effects of previous alcoholism.
- Current medication for illness.

Social and financial difficulties

- Current racial abuse or suspected racial discrimination.
- Enforced or sudden homelessness.
- Anxiety about money, including worries about appearing in court for fines, non-payment of debt, etc.
- Recent trauma such as bereavement or attack.
- Dependants undergoing trauma or serious difficulties.
- Refugee students and military: post-war syndrome; loss of family.
- Inability to mix with people from the course.

Academic referrals

- Weaknesses in use of English or academic English.
- Prolonged truancy from very young age (from age 6–7 years, in some cases).
- Gaps in schooling.
- Pronounced negative experiences of formal education.
- Over-attachment to a particular learning style.
- Intransigent difficulties or difficulties beyond those of the rest of the cohort.

'Needs' in relation to continuing development

Bradshaw (1972) differentiated four types of need: *normative* (where an individual or group falls below the standard of the majority in some way), *felt* (where an individual defines their own needs), *expressed* (where services are explicitly asked for), and *comparative* (based on studies into parity or equal opportunities). Smith (1980) found that it is often administrative procedures which create categories of need into which individuals are slotted. 'Need is defined by demand but this is demand as defined by existing services and existing service interest' (Packwood and Whitaker, 1988). Bradshaw's taxonomy is useful in helping services to identify how far they are responding to or creating need. However, it does not give an indication of the intensity of need. Institutions will vary, according to their intakes, mission statements and pedagogy, in which type of need they respond to when providing individual support. However, from the perspectives of widening participation, adult education and continuing development, it is important that all four aspects are addressed somewhere within an institution.

Higher education institutions offer a range of methods by which 'needs' related to learning can be met on an individual basis. At one extreme, individual guidance about study needs is regarded as the preserve of student counselling. At the other extreme, teaching staff take on board a very wide range of counselling-related activities. In some institutions, individual support is offered by learning development units or their equivalent, either through appointments or drop-ins. The structures that are put in place and the way that individual support is presented make a difference to the way that 'needs' will be perceived by both students and providers. This will impact in turn upon the kind of demand that will be created.

The Learning Development Unit at the University of East London is in some ways unusual in that it offers a spectrum of support which includes support for English, academic English, study skills, specific learning difficulties and non-specific and temporary learning difficulties. Students may self-refer, especially if they wish to discuss their studies confidentially, or they may be referred by tutors after having received support within the department. Many students see advisers in the Learning Development Unit for study support as well as seeing counsellors in Student Services for emotional and general issues. This leaves the concept of 'need' quite open to interpretation by individuals and attracts a wide range of referrals. Departmental lecturers are strongly encouraged to present additional support in terms of continuing development, self-awareness, personal reflection on performance, and strategic use of resources to achieve goals, rather than as a remedial strategy.

This 'open' approach is combined with targeting support at groups identified to be most at risk of underachieving or failing. What becomes constituted as 'need' within this framework is usually framed by the desire to help students succeed. The main goals are to help students to complete their course of study and to prevent underachievement through known 'at risk' factors such as use of English, disability, and short-term crisis. The level of demand on a course basis is partly related to recruitment patterns but referral patterns tend to correspond more to the ways that additional support is presented, needs identified and support built into the thinking and ethos of a course. Courses with supportive frameworks tend to refer more students and to refer more from the target groups. Courses with weaker support mechanisms tend to refer fewer students and on a more haphazard basis.

In terms of Bradshaw's taxonomy, all four types of 'need' can, in principle, be addressed by this spectrum approach; in practice the involvement of departmental staff, as well as staffing resources, are key to this range of need being met. *Normative* and *comparative* factors tend to take priority in terms of funding, specialist staffing and identification for referral. However, the style of support for those referred tends to focus on *felt* need.

Students who self-refer may frame 'need' in terms of a desire for confidential advice. For example, students may not understand why they are doing well and wish to speak to someone to check what they are doing 'right', without drawing attention to themselves. Students may self-refer merely for reassurance that they are on the 'right track', in which case they can be assisted to identify their own criteria for answering this question. Students may also want simply to talk through, confidentially, the implications of taking up additional support. For example, they may fear that it will be recorded on their degree transcript.

Students must ultimately self-refer for additional support: the decision to take up support must be their own. Adult learners must set their own priorities and have the right to reject additional support if they wish. However, it is also incumbent on universities to represent such support in terms of its advantage to students. On courses where this approach has been taken, students come forward to ask why they have not been recommended additional support, rather than regarding it with a remedial taint. Where additional support is regarded in terms of benefits, such as when there are disability allowances, students come forward in large numbers for support and for assessment of needs. Additional support can be perceived as merely one end of a spectrum of learning development approaches and an opportunity to see experts for particular kinds of advice.

Needs evaluation

A needs analysis of some kind is likely to be the starting place for support. This may be a multilayered process, with initial stages being undertaken in departments, as outlined in Chapter 4. Once a student attends individual support, more in-depth analysis of needs is usually required. It is important to a developmental approach that students are active in the process of evaluating their own needs, with guidance on how to do this. If they are given an opportunity to do so, students may reveal, perhaps for the first time in their lives, the complex set of factors that they see as affecting their performance. For many students, their educational and language histories, familial histories and expectations, emotional factors and belief systems will impact upon their overall performance, although this may be most manifest in particular skills.

Early needs evaluation tends to works best for students when it is based on a discussion of their own work and their own perceptions of what is affecting their learning. These narratives are often as important as the specific interventions which are made to assist the student.

Sometimes students simply need to speak about their anxieties and use the opportunity, through talking, to map out their difficulties. In other cases, the work of the support tutor is in clarifying to students how far their perceptions of their needs are accurate. This may require cross-comparison of the student's account with their own analysis of the student's work, and by in-depth questioning. For example, students who think they study extraordinarily long hours but receive low marks may feel as though they are not bright enough for HE or that they have a learning disability. When their study time is mapped out hour by hour, it may become evident that they are studying only half the required hours, leading them to re-evaluate both their study practices and their perceptions of their own abilities. For particular areas, such as technical English or organisational skills, it helps to have more in-depth checklists of sub-skills than would be used for general skills work with whole groups.

The needs analysis is likely to be a mixture of student perceptions and objective criteria, based upon narrative, checklists, analysis of the student's work, use of tutor feedback and sometimes testing. The individual needs evaluation may be the basis for putting together a few support sessions, or alternatively, it might be the basis of an extensive support package requiring input from a range of professionals. In the case of students with disabilities, for example, there are national centres which can be used to draw up study aids and study strategies assessments (SASSA).

Objectives

Each support service will set its own objectives. However, in general, the aim of additional support is to assist the student to develop independence. Peer support mechanisms can be difficult for this reason: students are easier to pressurise into 'giving answers', despite training, and less skilled at not doing so. Students who lack confidence may not believe that they can be independent in their learning. This may

even have been reinforced by support they have received in the past. What some students want from support is often a quick solution to a short-term problem. It is more difficult to engage students longer term and motivate them in moving towards an understanding of the nature of their difficulties, even to see how the difficulties originated in some cases, and to develop the confidence to select appropriate strategies to solve them. It is also important to assist students in setting their own learning agendas, to discover what they really want to achieve from their learning apart from a qualification (if anything) and to enable them to recognise when they have achieved what they set out to achieve. Helping students to formulate criteria to evaluate their own performance can be a useful aspect of this.

Ground rules and responsibilities

Individual support can easily become a series of crisis management sessions if the ground rules are not clearly set. Those who need additional support often require greater guidance about the boundaries of the support being offered. It is very important to be clear with students about the function of additional support, emphasising independence as a goal. Students can find this frustrating, in the short term, if they want help in passing a particular assignment rather than longer-term self-management skills. A delicate balance needs to be established, so that students feel the sessions are worthwhile without succumbing to endless short-term goals.

Students who lack confidence or who have a history of additional support may see support as there merely to get them through each successive crisis, and confer the responsibility for their success onto the person offering support. Those offering support need to be very clear about when and where sessions will take place, how many sessions there will be, the start- and end-time of support sessions, what sessions can and cannot cover, and what the student is expected to do in preparation for each session. Without this, students may take quite eccentric exceptions to very reasonable requests on the part of the support tutor for such things as advance preparation or for plans for written work to be brought to sessions. It is useful to go over these boundaries and responsibilities at the beginning of the first session, and for this information to be provided in written form. Students can be asked to sign a 'contract' to say they have understood their responsibilities, especially in terms of punctuality, attendance, and preparation. It cannot be overemphasised how important this is, both for the student and for support tutors.

Establishing priorities

Students who need additional support often need this across a very wide range. This can be stressful for those offering them support, as it can seem an impossible task to address all the study requirements in time for the next assignment. It is useful for support tutors to have a checklist of the kinds of support that could be covered and to invite students to indicate all the areas upon which they feel they need to work. Once this has been done, the list needs to be narrowed down to a key number of essentials. The student may need guidance in selecting those areas which, if attended to first, will accrue the most short-term benefit. For example, the dividends of focusing on organisational strategies or writing a good conclusion are generally higher than those for spelling, as well as being easier to achieve in the short term. Students do not always realise the relative weighting given to different skills in the way that their assignments are marked.

Once two or three priorities have been established, in order of preference, these need to be recorded and both the tutor and the student should have a copy. It helps to return to this list at the beginning of each new session. At the end of a series of sessions, the student and tutor should return to the priorities list and both should assess how far these have been met. Again, one of the main roles of the support tutor is in assisting the student to establish objective criteria for evaluating how far their own objec-

tives have been met. This methodology trains the student in a range of ancillary skills, such as self-management, priority setting, criteria setting, self-evaluation and organisational skills, which are often at least as valuable as the main reason for referral. It is unusual for students needing additional support not to need support in these skills.

Forming a rapport

Good rapport is generally key to successful support. For those experiencing the most severe difficulties, there tend to be complex underlying patterns, habits and attitudes. If these students feel that it is not safe to reveal confidential and emotionally difficult background information, that is, if trust is not established, then the support offered may be inappropriate, aimed at surface and manifest difficulties rather than at the real 'knot' that has to be unravelled. It is advisable for people offering individual support to take at least a basic course in practical counselling skills; this is invaluable for fine-tuning listening skills and in developing techniques in feeding back, skilfully, to students what they have said so that they can hear the implications of what they have revealed.

One key factor in forming rapport is a willingness to elicit from the students what they perceive to be their difficulties and to identify their motivation for attending the first session. Another factor is the ability to listen with genuine interest to what the student has to say about their study difficulties. As Wheeler (1983), commented 'the student in difficulties urgently needs to be understood; to be known; to be met on his own ground'. It is not necessary for support tutors to talk about themself in order to form a good rapport: questions about the support tutor's experiences may be asked out of conventional politeness or may be a way of distracting from the task in hand. Inquisitive students can be reminded that this time is set aside for them to focus on their own learning. Good rapport is also fostered by being able to hold positive feelings towards the students, even when they are at their most frustrating, and being respectful and courteous to them as adults.

Offering study advice and guidance

It is not necessarily hard to identify possible solutions which could help struggling students to improve their work. What is more difficult is to hold back from giving the solutions, and to assist the student to arrive at a reasonable route towards a solution for themselves. Any solutions which are offered must sound reasonably easy, and provide a set of steps that can be easily managed. Students need to see clearly what the first step is, that this step is manageable, and how this step leads to the next. The skill for the tutor is in being able to judge when to step forward to scaffold the learning sufficiently to move the student along, but without taking over the learning from the students.

What works well for one student may not work well for another. Indeed, students referred for additional support are often those with more maverick ways of achieving success. Their problems often stem from their difficulties with traditional explanations or ways of teaching. Those offering support need to consider whether the routes suggested are likely to match the ways that the student works best. In order to find this out, some time needs to be spent with the student exploring what it is that makes aspects of study difficult and what they do in order to achieve success in the areas where they perform best. The expertise metaphor below is an example of such work.

Often, it is not what is said, but the way that something is said, which is critical in determining whether an intervention is likely to lead to success. Students who feel they are behind their peers, for example, often respond well to anything which is presented as a 'short-cut' or a good tip. Some like to feel they have gained hold of a 'magical solution' that has evaded them for years. If they have never had any academic guidance, the most basic of advice can often appear miraculous. It is important that

tutors make it clear to students what is an emergency tactic designed to get them through a tight deadline, and what is a more ideal long-term way of approaching the same task.

Working from strengths

Students referred for study skills support and for specific learning difficulties (dyslexia) at the University of East London are asked to begin by identifying their strengths. It is explained that, wherever possible, existing strengths and the students' own examples of good practice will be used as the basis for addressing areas they have identified as priorities. This is one of the most difficult aspects for some students, especially those with negative previous experiences of education. It takes time, patience, encouragement, careful prompting by the support tutor and sometimes extended dialogue in order to bring out these strengths. Students may genuinely feel that they have no strengths, or may have deeply ingrained fears of acknowledging their own strengths in case they will be regarded as 'arrogant' and rejected. For some, it is a case of it not being appropriate to 'blow your own trumpet'. Others have genuine fears that if they really do have strengths, then the criticisms that others have made of them in the past, of being lazy or not trying hard enough, were true. For still other students, long-held fears of trying and failing, or of being successful but not being able to maintain the pace, also play into anxieties about identifying strengths. Other students are delighted that, at last, somebody wants to hear about what they can do rather than what they cannot. This is especially important for dyslexic students.

Different approaches will be needed to bring students to identify their own strengths, depending on the student and the reason for the referral. One way is to provide a checklist of possible abilities across a wide range of areas, including non-academic areas. This can then be used as the basis of discussion about the sub-skills and attributes required for success. Sometimes this reveals strange fruits. One student, for example, who, as a dyslexic student, would usually be assumed to have difficulties in remembering numbers by rote, showed an outstanding talent for remembering very long lists of numbers of eight digits and more. He had worked in a warehouse where this skill was required of employees and so had developed his own ways of remembering. He was able to draw out from this achievement, originally presented as being of no consequence, his strengths in perseverance, application, task management, imaginative problem solving, memory strategies and others.

When working individually with students over several sessions, it helps to explore with them their preferred ways of studying, looking at learning styles, approaches and current strategies (see Chapter 11 below). This information can be used to structure support sessions and offers insights into which, out of many, strategies might be the best to suggest in the time available. The student may need guidance in applying their strengths and learning styles to particular aspects of study. The tutor may find, at first, that they need to remind the students that a strategy used elsewhere may also be transferable to a new area of study or to other difficulties. Peelo (1994) has argued that it is important for those supporting students with study problems to take a broad-based role, where the aim is to increase students' choices through an exploration of a range of strategies and approaches from which students can then opt for those most suited to their circumstances and learning style.

Case studies

The expertise metaphor: Victor, Roger and Luzia

The expertise metaphor is one way of assisting students to build from their strengths. It is also a useful method of developing transferable skills. Superficially, it may appear reasonable to assume that building from a skill in a related area is the best way of developing 'transferable'

skills such as academic writing. For example, the more obvious route for developing essay or report-writing skills might appear to be experience of any writing in a different context, such as letter writing or poetry. In other words, one might look to the task for aspects of apparent transferability. This is a task-centred approach to transferability. Where there is a high degree of skill and self-esteem in performance of the first task, this may be a reasonable approach to take in some instances.

However, this is not always a productive route to take with students who struggle with academic skills; here, the key to transferability can lie in a student-centred rather than a task-centred approach. This is not difficult to appreciate when one considers that struggling students may have a very poor perception of their performance in those skills which they are being asked to 'transfer' to an academic context. Moreover, in objective terms, the skills they are being asked to transfer may be very weak. In effect, students are being invited to 'transfer' a 'skill' which is weak when used in a relatively basic field of operation for use in a more sophisticated field of operation. One could describe this as asking them to draw on novice skills to develop expert skills. This tends to be counterproductive: if the students feel they are bad letter-writers, they feel, quite sensibly, they will be worse at academic writing.

A contrasting route is to help the student to identify any area where they feel themself to be, if not an expert, then at least competent. This is a student-centred approach to skills development and transfer. A basic introduction to this approach is laid out for students in *The Study Skills Handbook* (Cottrell, 1999), which encourages students to find academic skill correlates in everyday tasks. The example of 'The beautiful garden' leads students through the underlying skills and personal attributes that are required for a familiar task such as keeping a well-kept garden. Students are then invited to identify the skills that they use for a task they perform well.

Students whose self-esteem is particularly low can be resistant to identifying an area of expertise. It can require some exploration and delving with students, especially with those from 'non-traditional' backgrounds, who can feel that their life experiences are irrelevant to the academic context. Students may find it hard to employ the word 'expertise' for tasks that other people are also able to do. However, even the most severely disadvantaged and academically challenged student can, with guidance, identify something they do well. Ideally, this ought to be a task which incorporates several stages. It does not matter whether this is baking a cake, drawing a cartoon, making beer, running a club or whatever: the key is in how the student is guided in breaking the task into stages or approaches which can then be related to academic tasks they will need to perform. The results can be remarkable.

Victor: car engines

Victor was a very bright student, who had been partially deaf and used to lip-reading but had not yet adapted fully to listening rather than lip-reading. He had also been recently assessed as dyslexic and, as a mature student with disabilities, had some large gaps in his early education. Victor had previous education in further education which was relevant to his current course but this had not required him to produce written work unaided. He was very anxious about being at university and lacked self-confidence. He was extremely reluctant to write in continuous prose when he entered university, although he did have reasonable typing skills. He lacked a sense of himself as a writer, and had very little idea of how to approach academic writing.

Victor's resistance to writing was so pronounced when he first entered HE, that he would only produce information in the form of mind maps. He was terrified of failing and had little idea of where to begin. Assisting him was complicated by his strong identification with a 'global' learning style; he was resistant to the idea that he was capable of the logical, sequential skills needed for continuous prose, despite manifest ability. Instead of countering these beliefs head-on, Victor was encouraged to use the 'expertise metaphor'. He identified a strong

interest and practical experience in automobile engines. He was encouraged to create a mind map which addressed his skills and knowledge with engines and to take this as far as he could. As he worked, he was asked to consider all the times he used sequencing skills in automobile repair, to search out examples of planning, weighing up options, prioritising, re-evaluating, reflecting on performance, and to look at how he could draw out lessons from one experience to apply to another.

Once Victor had become enthusiastic about his own expertise, he was encouraged to draw parallels between this and the skills he needed for academic writing. This was an extremely exciting process for Victor: he realised that he had an expertise basis upon which to build – and that he could value his existing skills even in an academic context. Just as Donaldson (1978) has shown that children are capable of performing tasks above their supposed developmental level if the task is presented in a way that 'makes sense' to them, so Victor was able to use his knowledge of engines in order to make essay writing meaningful. Essays became something associated with the familiar and safe, rather than alien objects. Not only did he type out his own essays, but, despite his many difficulties, he performed at a high level and began to offer help to other students. This is Victor's account in his own words.

Victor: 'my engine'

When I first started university, I had not worked at the academic level required by university before. When I visited the learning development unit in order to undergo a dyslexia assessment, SC suggested that I treat an essay like a car engine. When I broke the metaphor (analogy) down, this is what I came up with:

(1) Fuel – this supplies the necessary stored kinetic energy to power the engine – research at the library, lectures, seminars.
(2) Battery – this stores the electrical energy – research notes, essay outline.

(3) Oil – this lets the engine run smoothly – spelling and grammar.

(4) The alternator – supplies electrical energy necessary for the engine to run – the essay question, unit guide, using aims, etc.

(5) Engine ignition system – supplies the spark to ignite the fuel, and the sequence in which the cylinders fire – paragraphs:
   - Introduction – where this essay is going
   - Main body – critical discussion of main points
   - Conclusion – insights gained and mileage from essay, i.e., 'What I have learned?'

(6) Tool box – this is where the necessary tools are bought, borrowed or acquired and stored – dyslexia workshops, English workshops, Accelerated learning seminars, etc.

This can be broken down even more. However, simplicity is as important as clarity. When all the elements of the essay are integrated successfully then it should flow like a smoothly running engine.

Roger: aircraft assembly

Roger was referred because he consistently failed to produce written work. He arrived with several pieces of writing, all well written but incomplete. When his time management skills were explored, it was found that these were generally good for other areas. As time management did not seem to be the root of the problem, we traced how Roger approached the writing task. His main difficulty was that he took a perfectionist approach to his early paragraphs, and continually rewrote these as his ideas changed. Each time, he wrote out the whole of his work 'in neat', assuming that each draft would be his final draft, but then finding he had to start again. It was a habit he found difficult to break.

Roger's area of expertise was assembling light aircraft that arrived from overseas as 'flat packs'.

We explored how he would go about assembling a plane and how this might be similar or different to assembling an essay. For example, Roger was asked what would happen if he treated the first section of the aircraft he assembled in the same way he treated his essay: if he tightened all the nuts and bolts, sanded it down, painted it and so forth before he went on to the next stage of assembly. He thought this was highly amusing: once bolts are tightened on one side, there is no possibility of assembling the rest of the plane as it would be impossible to manoeuvre the pieces into place. Instead, Roger worked towards the final point of assembly in several stages, only tightening all sections when the whole plane was in place. He could easily see the comparison with writing several drafts of an assignment before fine-tuning a final version of any one section, and see the advantages of leaving proof-reading to the final version.

Once he had drawn the initial parallel, Roger was able to see all kinds of comparisons between aircraft assembly and academic problems and called upon his previous expertise to address these. When introduced to new information, for example, he felt students should play around with it, like pieces of the flat pack, observing roughly all the places they might fit: 'As you bring them closer together, you are working quite globally – with an eye on how it all fits together, then you can home in and complete sections. Keep an eye on how the sections will link. Aircraft glue is like a linking sentence, or a logical sequence that dovetails into the next item.'

Luzia: Dressmaking

Luzia was also referred for problems with essay writing. She had extremely low self-esteem and was very reluctant to identify any area of expertise. She listened with interest to the experiences other students had had with comparing essay writing to an area with which they were more comfortable. Finally, she settled on dressmaking as her area of expertise, as she made most of her own and her family's clothes. Like Victor, she soon began to find many points of comparison.

First of all, she thought, both needed a vision of the final product: she couldn't set about choosing a pattern or buying materials until she had a sense of what she was trying to achieve: this she compared to interpreting the assignment title and having a strong argument: 'Your vision is your interest in it – without which you just wouldn't get it done.' Similarly, both newly made clothes and essays need structure: before she began to make a new item she would have a sense of whether it was to have arms, collar, legs, etc., and use this to guide her choice of pattern and material. For Luzia, laying out a pattern was like drawing up an essay plan: 'the pieces of a dressmaking pattern have to be laid out in a precise way so that the cloth falls properly'. Similarly, in a well-planned essay, all the pieces of the argument fall logically into place. Further comparisons were made between tacking a dress together before the final sewing and writing drafts before a final write-up, or trying a dress on to check for 'final flaws' and proof-reading. For Luzia, the most important element of dressmaking was having 'equal seams'. She compared this to treating different schools of thought equally when writing an essay: 'you must ask the same questions of each'.

What the experiences of these students suggest is that with guidance, similar problem structures can be found to address apparently very disparate kinds of problem. The 'expertise metaphor' utilises current experience creatively in order to find similar underlying structures to different kinds of problems. This enables students to look within themselves for answers, and to value their experience, whatever it might be, as holding potential clues to other kinds of problem. Sometimes, the connections the students made seemed rather tenuous to an outside observer. However, despite this, the associations made sense to the individual students and enabled them to approach a current task with much more confidence and applied skill. In each case, the students did break the mould of their former approaches to study.

Supporting students who miss deadlines: Michael, Suzy, Marsha and Joelle

As the case of Roger showed, the apparent reason for missing deadlines may not be the obvious one. Usually, difficulties in missing deadlines are due to poor time management, anxiety about beginning a task, overinflating the task, or are related to issues of self-esteem.

Michael: deadlines and time management

Michael missed deadlines because he underestimated how many stages there were to completing an assignment. He rarely left sufficient time for each stage and overestimated the amount of time he spent studying. This is very common. In Michael's case, we addressed it by:

- Mapping out his week so he was clear exactly where he spent time. It became clear that he needed to increase his overall study hours, as he was covering only half the required amount of independent study. He had not grasped what 'independent' study meant.
- Listing each stage necessary to complete a given assignment. For this, Michael's own concept of what constituted a 'stage' was used; with prompting, he added in some additional stages he had not considered, such as undertaking a literature search and writing new drafts.
- Mapping out how long each stage was likely to take him. Some of Michael's projections were clearly unrealistic. When his time expectations were explored, it revealed that he had underestimated how much reading was required. He also had not put time aside for such things as proofreading and writing out references which were likely to take him considerable time.
- Working backwards from deadlines, writing time slots for each stage into his diary so it was clear when he was going to complete each stage – and leaving time for mishaps.
- Exploring potential distractions and considering ways of avoiding these. For Michael, distractions were mainly chats with other students on his landing. His solution was to

work late at night and get up later, which seemed to work for him.

- Identifying study 'triggers' which could ease him into study. Michael created a ritual for himself of laying out his books and papers before he went to the bar, putting the computer on as soon as he came in, making a coffee whilst the computer booted up, and browsing his notes as he waited for the kettle to boil, highlighting items with a marker pen. All these elements were essential for him.

Suzy: anxiety about beginning a task

Students like Suzy often delay starting an assignment because they have feel they write badly, and fear settling down to a task which they feel will ultimately fail them. Suzy rarely left any time to redraft and proofread work adequately, which meant that her writing was full of unnecessary errors. A final draft would have increased her mark significantly. Dealing with 'starter' anxiety can have beneficial effects along the whole assignment process. The important breakthrough with Suzy was in reframing the idea of 'beginning'. A piece of 'writing' does not start with the writing itself but with a lecture or reading or thinking and talking. It can help to:

- Encourage the students to keep notebooks of ideas.
- Encourage them to use mind maps to brainstorm ideas, to talk onto tape and type it out, or to just put down words onto paper in any form.
- Encourage them to write ideas down in any order on the computer, and then to organise these into headings and points: then they are not starting from a blank screen.
- Encourage students to set limited targets for each session. This develops their awareness that they will not finish a piece of writing in one session. Their goal may be, for example, simply to put something down – to use as a starting place the next time. At a second sitting, they work from what is already there, rather than starting from scratch.
- Reassure students that early drafts do not need to be in sentences: they can come back

to such fine-tuning later, once they have got started.

Marsha: overinflating the task

Marsha's difficulty was that she built the task up into something much bigger than it was, and then convinced herself that she could never achieve anything so great. Again, this is not uncommon. In such cases, it can help to:

- Assist the student in breaking the assignment down into manageable bites.
- Explore, with the student, why they overinflate the task. This is sometimes a kind of perfectionism, related to previous experiences of punishment or humiliation.
- Rephrase the task in everyday terms: if you had five minutes to tell a friend your opinion about this subject, what you would you say? Is there anything you've read that says something similar and which would back you up? Does everybody think like that? Would everyone agree with you? What have you read that gives a different opinion? etc.

Joelle: time management

Joelle was an architecture student who, though gifted at architectural studies, found it extremely difficult to organise time: 'I don't have a sense of it . . . I can't grasp what time is', she argued. Rather than using logical-sequential approaches to time management, Joelle explored the relation between space (her area of expertise) and time (her area of perceived weakness). She had not considered them as part of a continuum, nor how the definition of one is dependent on the other. This helped to break down the barrier between 'safe' areas for her (spatial relations) and unsafe areas (time management).

Joelle was asked to describe her abilities in manipulating objects in space: she was able to orientate objects quite easily, mentally, in three-dimensional space. She could rearrange walls, floor plans or furniture for whole buildings, all in her head. She was then invited to explore the idea of tasks as mental objects on a space–time continuum. For example, each entry written in a diary could be viewed as an object within space. Tasks are organised spatially in a diary – on a two-dimensional page and across time (from page to page). Joelle suggested that she could view the diary as 'a block of flats', each 'week to view' in the diary represented one floor of a 52-floored block of flats. The slot for each day was a separate apartment on the same floor: there were seven apartments to each floor. Each 'line' in the diary represented a room. She gave each task she had to undertake dimensions: it took up a room in the diary. Once a room was full, she could not put any more furniture (tasks) into it. Activities became 'just blocks or furniture to arrange in space'.

It took some time to elaborate this method with Joelle. One reason for this was that she began to identify the emotional blocks which prevented her from addressing the problem. She was so ashamed of her difficulty that she could not 'look at it'. It was easier to pretend it didn't matter – except that then she failed assignments. She was encouraged to 'put a task into her hands' and draw her hands in towards her. As she did so, she reached an optimum place in time–space beyond which she began to get very distressed. This was, she said what happened as a deadline approached. When asked to identify the emotion, she said it was fear: 'I'm writing as a child and other people write as adults.' When this was explored further, she admitted that lecturers said her writing flowed well (she had writing ability) but was not analytical. This is not an uncommon weakness in student writing: what was interesting was that Joelle used an adult–child frame of reference to express her inability to do something. This was a useful breakthrough for her; she began to see a counsellor to explore the deeper emotional issues which were undermining her learning.

Understanding academic writing tasks: Ayeesha and Misha

Ayeesha: the exciting plot

Some students latch onto a particular idea about writing which they apply in an inappropriate way to academic writing. For example, Ayeesha based her writing around a model she had been given at school for creative writing and her assignments were structured like murder mysteries. She felt that she must make her writing interesting by 'not unravelling the plot until the end'. She began assignments with her weakest points so that the main points tended to get lost. Ayeesha needed to be told that, for academic writing, the aim is usually to draw the reader in quickly, and to orientate them to your line of thinking. However, this was not simply a question of clarity about requirements; Ayeesha was emotionally attached to her model of writing and needed reassurance from her tutors that she would not lose marks if she changed approach. She also was encouraged to write stories and to consider taking a module where she had a chance to write in the style that she enjoyed so that a place was created for her preferred writing style.

Misha: visualising spellings

Misha had great difficulties with spelling. Good spellers tend to be able to visualise words, but Misha said she was unable to do this. Using very basic methods from neuro-linguistic programming, Misha was asked to visualise a word that she identified as important to her. She looked down to visualise. When she was asked to visualise the word at different angles, she found that when she looked up to the right she could 'nearly' see the word. When she was asked for the colour of the letters and their background, Misha said that she had visualised the word as 'black on dark grey'. After experimentation, she said she found it easiest to see pale green letters on a blue background. Once she had altered the colours, Misha was able to visualise learnt spellings in her head in order to help recall.

This method does not work for all students – or at least, not so effectively, but in Misha's case the motivational effects were significant. For the first time she was able to 'see' words in her head. This gave her a great deal of confidence in trying new methods to assist her study. From here she went on to experiment with colour-coding notes, quotations, and sections of books according to themes, which she found greatly assisted categorisation skills, comprehension and memory.

The 'reasonable persona'

Students may have been told to 'fight their corner' when arguing a point, and be unfamiliar with academic conventions such as citing the arguments of others clearly and fairly. However, once this has been broached, the student may not feel like giving fair weight to the arguments of others, especially if they feel that the texts they are expected to cite are racist or prejudiced. To do so might make them feel extremely angry. Injunctions to write in a 'reasonable persona' may seem very unreasonable to the student. Such students need guidance in how to channel their anger effectively, including through their writing, so that they feel they can get their point across just as forcibly but within the required conventions.

Final comments

There are likely always to be students who need support on a more individual basis even when course design and teaching methods are supportive of aspects of learning that might traditionally have been addressed through 'additional' support. With widening participation intakes, the need and/or the demand for learning support is likely to be greater, and it is all the more important that a developmental approach to learning is adopted by institutions and departments so that all students are actively engaged in improving their approaches to study, their attitudes, strategies, task management and self-management. It helps if departments build a culture of learning development where asking for specialist assistance is not regarded as remedial but rather as evidence of critical self-awareness, and as a means of acquiring appropriate skills and advice to achieve an objective.

A range of staff may be involved in offering individual support, often without formal training. There are several key elements that such staff can use to guide their support of students, especially those with complex learning histories. These include forming a rapport with the student and setting clear boundaries and ground rules. The student should have chosen to attend support sessions and should be centrally involved in the process of identifying priorities. Students should be encouraged to work from their strengths and assisted in identifying learning styles, preferences and existing strategies that they can apply to new areas. Above all, it should be borne in mind that if a student is in need of individual support this is often because generic or blanket advice has been unhelpful. Individual sessions should be used in order to explore what is 'individual' about that student in their response or approach to their learning, in order to assist them to achieve their own learning objectives.

Teaching to support learning: the reflective practitioner

In higher education, students are being asked, increasingly, to extrapolate from their experiences, to evaluate and profile their skills, to reflect on performance and attitudes, and to work with peers. It is often helpful for those in authority to undergo the kinds of activities that are set for those over whom they have influence. This chapter is designed to offer teaching staff an opportunity to experience for themselves some of the approaches which are used with their students, focusing on learning development and study skills teaching. It also offers practitioners a chance to develop a greater appreciation of what they achieve as lecturers and tutors, and to pinpoint their own staff development needs.

Chapter 3 argued the case for more positive environments to foster learning and integrate support for learning development. Lindblom-Ylanne and Lonka (2000a) state that conceptual change is unlikely to occur in universities unless teachers become conscious of their own approaches to teaching. 'To achieve a qualitative change in their mental models of their own teaching, teachers must also become conscious of their teaching *in relation to their students' learning*' (their italics) and that this must include knowledge of their students' skills (Lindblom-Ylanne and Lonka (2000b). Most lecturers have not been trained to teach study skills; there are, indeed, few training opportunities to learn how to teach and support skills. Supporting the development of skills in others is likely to be an ongoing learning experience for teachers and Kolb has argued that reflection is an important part of the learning cycle for all learners, including teachers.

What stimulated your own learning?

When groups of people are asked what had the most positive impact upon their learning, or what they remember most about positive learning experiences at school, a similar list of points emerges. This can be demonstrated by the exercise on p. 174.

Positive learning experiences: common responses

Below is a list of common responses to the exercise above. Check your list against it. If your list is considerably different to that given here, what reasons might there be for that? The common responses list is typical of that put together by very different groups of people within educational contexts. You may not have completed the above exercise and have been tempted to look at the list below first. If so, is this 'cheating' or a learning strategy for you?

Positive learning experiences
- Think back to your own time at school. Call to mind lessons and occasions when your learning seemed to flow, when it was fun, when you enjoyed learning and felt a sense of accomplishment from learning. Make a list, now, of all the conditions that gave rise to positive learning experiences for you, before reading on. If you find yourself struggling, you may find it easier if you keep beginning the sentence: 'My best learning experiences were when . . . ' or 'I got most out of learning when . . . '.
- When you have completed your list, compare it to the list of common responses to this exercise printed below.

© Stella Cottrell (2001), *Teaching Study Skills and Supporting Learning* (Basingstoke: Palgrave).

'My best learning experiences were when...'

Nature of the task
- I felt the task set was interesting, worthwhile or of value to myself or others;
- the learning was relevant to the real world or had practical uses;
- the work was going to be seen and appreciated by somebody other than a teacher;
- it was clear what was expected;
- I could move around or there was movement built into the activities;
- there was a creative aspect to the task;
- there was personal choice over some aspect of the task;
- there was a 'teaser' or mystery or puzzle to be solved.

Materials
- the materials were visually interesting;
- materials were clear and easy to read;
- we got new books.

Feelings and emotions
- there was praise and appreciation which came across as genuine;
- I was treated as though I mattered or my opinions and ideas counted.

With whom
- I could work with my friends;
- we did small group work or worked in pairs;
- we taught each other.

The teacher
- the teacher was fair;
- the teacher thought of interesting ways of introducing new material;
- the teacher worked beside us and inspired rather than preaching at us.

Timing
- I had time to finish what I was doing without rushing;
- I had time to take it in;
- there were lots of breaks so I didn't feel overloaded.

Mastery
- I felt I understood one thing before moving onto another;
- the tasks set were manageable but challenging so that there was a sense of both competence and achievement.

Assessment
- I felt the way it was marked was fair;
- I felt I had a fair chance of handing in what was expected;
- my hard work was recognised;
- I knew I couldn't get away with not doing my best.

Special features
- we went on field trips or visits;
- we had guest speakers or celebrity visits;
- we performed or showed our work to parents or visitors.

© Stella Cottrell (2001), *Teaching Study Skills and Supporting Learning* (Basingstoke: Palgrave).

You might also find it helpful to use this list to consider positive aspects of learning for your own group of students. Are there features from the list that you could use in planning your own lectures and seminars or in course design? You could set this activity for your students and compare their answers with your own.

Anxieties, challenges and opportunities

Students in difficulty can arouse all kinds of fears. They can, in particular, remind us of our own limitations. It is natural for lecturers, especially those new to lecturing or to student support, to worry about being 'up to the job'. Lecturers may wonder whether students will bring problems which are too large or complicated for them to deal with, or show emotions and behaviours to which they will not know how to respond; they may worry about giving the wrong response or advice. They may fear their teaching or support will not help students or may even adversely affect course retention figures. It would be unusual for subject-based lecturers not to have some anxieties about supporting learning.

Anxieties and resources
Consider the following:
- What are the anxieties that you face with regard to supportive teaching?
- Is there anybody with whom you can discuss these anxieties?
- What resources are there at the university that you could make use of, such as an educational development unit, staff development officers, student counselling services, or mentors? Do you make as much use of these as you could?

Opportunities
Our weak points, areas of challenge, are also the points where we can learn most. Dealing with them can be frightening, but may also open up a new set of opportunities.

- How could you reframe your worries and fears into challenges that you go out to meet? What opportunities do they hold for you, either personally or for improved teaching?

Inspiration

Students who are inspired by either their own aspirations or the subject they are studying tend to have great perseverance in overcoming even very serious obstacles to their learning. It is worth considering what is the inspiration that you as a teacher bring to the classroom, as this is likely to have an effect upon how you teach and upon your students.

- What do you find inspiring about your students?
- What inspires you about the subject you teach?
- Whose teaching style or theories inspire you?
- What is 'inspired teaching' for you?
- What keeps you going on the 'bad days'?

Similarly, it may be helpful to consider what inspires your particular intake of students? What is the match between the source of their inspiration and what inspires you? Is the way that the content of the course is packaged and delivered likely to inspire the students?

Teaching style

Personal metaphor

As teachers, we are likely to use one or more internal models to frame the way we think about our teaching and our students, which influence our professional practice. Lecturers have described themselves variously as:

- architects structuring students' thinking;
- sales managers dealing with customers;

- subject specialists who deliver content to those prepared to study;
- social workers mopping up student problems;
- nannies looking after needy children;
- performers playing to an audience;
- management consultants, shaping students' lives and choices;
- artists attempting to inspire;
- trainers, assisting students to become self-reliant learners.

Reflection

You may feel you fill many such roles. Which ones dominate the approach you take with students?

- Experiment with using different metaphors. For example, if you regard yourself primarily as having to take a performing role, imagine yourself as a trainer or as a sculptor, shaping new students to fit an academic culture. Notice how the metaphor you select can influence how you conceptualise your relationship to the student and to different aspects of course delivery. For example, at open days or during Induction, are you primarily attempting to 'capture', motivate, perform damage limitation exercises, offer guidance, inform or something else?
- For each role you imagine, consider whether the role is likely to lead students primarily to listen quietly or to write, to talk to you, to talk to each other, to admire you, to feel their own worthlessness, to feel good about what they can do, to support each other or to compete with each other? Or something else?
- How does the role or metaphor you usually use influence the way your students orientate themselves to their learning?
- Which metaphors for the teaching and learning relationship would encourage active, motivated, self-reliant learners who leave university with a professional outlook and capabilities?

Visual, auditory or kinaesthetic approaches

- Do you tend to rely more on using overheads, imagery, demonstrations and visual input (visual approach), delivering information orally or with music (auditory approach), or involving the students in activities (kinaesthetic approach)?
- Which of the following phrases are you more likely to use when teaching: 'As you can see . . . ' or 'As you can hear . . . ' or 'I feel . . . '?
- Do you use a mix of visual, auditory and kinaesthetic approaches to appeal to a wider range of students?

Global holistic vs. analytic serialist approaches

- Do you give an illustrative example, tell a story that shows the main themes, draw a diagram that links all the session or give some other overview first (appealing to 'global' learners) or do you introduce examples and ideas one by one until students begin to draw these together (appealing to 'serialist' learners)?
- Do you give very general guidelines, leaving room for personal interpretation (global) or do you give specific step-by-step instructions (serialist or analytic)?
- Do you present information in broad categories (global) or do you work with lots of 'hard data' (analytic)?
- Do you use set formats for each session (analytic) or use plenty of variety (global)?
- Do you show how information links up (suits holistic learners) or do you present new information as discrete items (serialist)?
- Do you provide opportunities to integrate information (holistic) or focus each session on a discrete topic (suits serialist learners)?
- Do you use a mix of global and serialist approaches to appeal to a wider range of students?

'Charismatic' vs. 'facilitator' approaches

- Do you regard your role as a teacher to be primarily to 'transmit' knowledge to students or to 'facilitate' students in a learning process? (See Willcoxson, 1998.)
- Do you take a 'charismatic approach', using most of the teaching time for 'delivery', or a 'facilitator' approach where you hand over as much of the learning process as you can to your students (e.g., through activities, group-led sessions, discussion)?
- Do you undertake all the assessment of students' work yourself or do you build in student self-assessment and peer assessment?
- Does your teaching focus on delivering new information (charismatic) or working through material that the student has prepared prior to the session, whether through reading, group work or activities (facilitator)?

Student groupings

Do you prefer to set activities for:

- individual work?
- paired work?
- small groups?
- teams?
- a variety of the above?

What kinds of students respond to which of the above groupings?

Awareness of students' access to the curriculum

- Are you clear about your learning objectives and marking criteria?
- Do you provide a glossary of specialist terms in advance of lectures?
- Do you provide preparation work for lectures?
- Do students have access to hand-outs, notes or references to reading to ensure they have complete access to material covered in teaching time? Are these given prior to the teaching session to ensure familiarity? Are they available via web pages?
- Is there discussion or support work to clarify student difficulties with course material?

Teaching goals

How important are each of the following goals to your teaching objectives?

- covering the syllabus (concepts, theories, facts, course-specific methods and skills);
- encouraging and inspiring the student to continue with the subject;
- developing the students' thinking abilities;
- improving students' motivation and self-esteem;
- developing a range of learning and interpersonal skills;
- encouraging a love of learning;
- encouraging students to apply learning to new contexts;
- enabling students to become more independent learners;
- preparing students for employment;
- instilling values or ethical considerations.

You may find it useful to follow up this work using the *Teaching Goals Inventory* (Cross and Angelo, 1992) or the 'Approaches to Teaching Inventory' (Prosser and Trigwell, 1999).

Teaching strengths and weaknesses: self-evaluation

When we are engaged in the same job every day, we can build up skills without realising that we have done so. In the same way, things that we really ought to address can keep being put onto the back burner. It is worth taking stock, from time to time, of where we are in relation to our skills and weaknesses: this is something that students in HE are increasingly being asked to do.

Strong points
- Make a list of your strong points, successes, gifts, positive attitudes and attributes in your role as 'teacher'. List at least 21 things. If that sounds like too many, you are under-estimating yourself.
- What is it like to recognise these

strengths? How often do you stop to value them?

- Are they appreciated by your students and by your line management? If not, how do you account for this? What could you do to change the situation?

Areas for improvement

- Make a list of weak points and areas for improvement in your teaching. List at least seven.
- What is it like to recognise these weak areas?
- What do you do to cope with them or to work around them on a day-to-day basis? Do you hide them, blame others or seek support?
- Who or what can help you to manage better in these areas? Do you have sufficient support for your teaching? If not, what do you need? What can you do to help yourself?

Teaching strengths and weaknesses: peer evaluation

- Would you have the confidence to take the above lists to a colleague (peer) for consideration? If not, what stops you?
- What would make you comfortable about revealing these evaluations and reflections to your colleagues?
- Would you be comfortable for all the staff in your department to observe and comment upon your teaching? What would you find difficult and what useful?
- What would make it easier for you to be observed?
- What does your response tell you about difficulties your students might have about performing in front of others and with peer evaluation exercises?
- How could you make such tasks more manageable for them?

The 'added value' you bring to your teaching

Consider your students ten years down the road. When they think back upon their time spent with you, the assignments and exams you set, the feedback you offered, the passing comments or facial expressions in the corridors, the implicit messages inscribed between the lines of course materials and lecture prose, what will they have taken away from your course that made a difference in their lives? Responses from lecturers to this question about their experiences of their own lecturers include:

- small acts of kindness;
- caustic sarcasm that left them with dread of a subject forever;
- a telling word of praise at an unexpected moment;
- an anecdote that gave them hope;
- the way they were spoken to that gave them a sense of being a 'person';
- a lecturer who took an interest and showed that they mattered in some way;
- someone who bothered to show them how to succeed;
- lecturers who explained things without making them feel small.

ACTIVITY

(1) Think of three lecturers you had when you were at university. Apart from the subject knowledge they taught you, how else did they affect your life, if at all?

(2) How do you consider your own role as a lecturer or teacher? How much of the content of your course will students really remember or make use of in ten years' time? What else will your students take from you that will be of use to them in the world?

(3) What attitudes and beliefs do you hold that will affect your students' learning and self-esteem?

(4) Look back over your list of strengths and

weaknesses as a teacher. Add in any changes you might like to make in self-evaluation as a result of this activity.

Study skills requirements for your subject

One of the difficulties students face with study skills is that their lecturers are not aware that the requirements for their own subject are not identical to those for other subjects, or even that there are variations from one branch of their own discipline to another. For example, there is very wide variation in what is required for the conclusion of a psychology report – and opinion varies over whether these need conclusions at all. The following activity gives you an opportunity to consider more exactly what are the study skills particularities of your own field. It is easiest to gain a clearer idea of what is distinct about your subject if you exchange ideas and concrete examples of texts, vocabulary, instructions, guidelines and ideal examples of student writing with colleagues from other disciplines. Looking through the skills activities in tPart II of this book may also help.

ACTIVITY

Identify subject-specific study skills requirements
The following questions may help to clarify your awareness of the requirements for your own subject.

Reading and other source material
- What are the most useful *types* of source material for your subject?
- How can students identify *good* source material for your subject?
- What distinguishes poor sources for your area?
- Are there smart ways of finding information quickly in texts for your subject?
- How can a student decide what does not need to be read?

- Is personal experience a viable source for your subject?
- What are the most useful and least useful ways of using the internet for your subject?

Ideas, opinions and thinking skills
- Is the use of personal opinion encouraged or taboo for your subject?
- Are your students really meant to develop their own ideas, or do they gain credit primarily for the way they use the ideas of others?
- What are your subject's conventions for introducing or using other people's ideas?
- Is what constitutes plagiarism in your subject (maybe history or politics) the same as for others (such as fine art, medicine or maths?)
- What are the kinds of underlying thinking skills needed as a foundation for your subject?
- Where does your subject lie on the North–South Pole diagram on the use of 'scientific' conventions for research and writing? (See p. 299 below.)

Writing
- Are there particular ways you require students to mix personal experience with academic material?
- Are there particular ways you expect students to present their writing?
- Do you require students to write in the active or the passive voice?
- Are they expected to write in first, second or third person (I, you, we, one, it)?
- How do you require sources, including unusual sources, to be referenced?
- How many different types of writing style are required for your subject? Do you require students to use analytical, descriptive, critical, evaluative, personal, emotive and/or other writing styles? Is it clear when they should use which style?
- What is distinctive about the way each of these styles is used in your subject? How

do they differ from similarly labelled writing for other subjects?

- How important is it within your subject area that students are able to write persuasively?
- How far are you influenced, when marking student work, by the style?
- Are facts, understanding, argument or style the most important issue?

Numeracy and numbers

- What kinds of numerical operations must students be able to perform at entry?
- Are there specific ways that numbers or 'amount' should be written or presented for your subject?

Listening

- For how long do students need to sit, listen and note at a stretch? What kinds of listening skills does this demand?
- Will students be listening to lectures which involve heavy use of terminology to which they have only just been introduced? What are the implications of this for listening, teaching and learning?
- Do students need skills to listen to different client groups? How are these different from the kind of listening skills they use elsewhere?
- Are students assessed on listening skills?

Speaking

- What kinds of speaking skills are required for your subject area?
- Are students assessed on speaking skills?
- Are students expected to speak in front of peers in small groups only, in front of the whole group, or not at all?
- Will oral presentation work be performed singly or in groups?
- How much practice will students get at developing public speaking skills?

Interpersonal

- How much group work, teamwork, or joint project work is there?
- How far are students expected already to have skills in working together productively? Do they need training?

- Are students expected to offer mutual feedback and criticism?
- Are they trained to offer constructive criticism?
- Are students expected to work with the public?
- Are students likely to face aggression or emotion either from each other, the public or clients?

Exams and assessment

- Are students expected to be able to read accurately, at speed, under exam conditions (such as for multiple choice)?
- What is the average writing speed for students you take? At what point does writing speed begin to disadvantage students on your course?
- Are your exams 'open book' or must students remember data in their heads? What is the difference in the kinds of preparation required for each method?
- Are your exam questions weighted towards memory or understanding? For example, are students expected to *recall* large amounts of data and names, or to *demonstrate* an understanding of the issues, or show an ability to *apply* what they have learnt to new situations? Who is likely to be most disadvantaged by your style of questions?

Other skills required for your subject

- What other key skills are required for your subject which are not generally required for other subjects?
- What are the sub-skills of these key skills?

Skills profile for teaching study skills

Skills profiles are useful for catching a snapshot of current performance and self-perception. The questionnaire below offers a starting point for drawing up a personal profile of your strengths and weaknesses in relation to study skills teaching.

Study skills teaching: audit of training, experience, attributes and resources					
	True	Sort of	Not at all	Don't know	Comments
TRAINING					
I have a teaching qualification					
I am trained to teach study skills or 'learning to learn					
I have had counselling training					
I have been trained to teach English language/learning difficulties					
Other:					
Other:					
EXPERIENCE					
I have prior experience of teaching study skills					
I have experience of teaching adults					
I have been a student myself within the last five years					
I had difficulties myself so know what it feels like					
I developed strategies for overcoming my own difficulties					
I have listened to students talking about their difficulties					
I have advised students on their study difficulties in the past					

	True	Sort of	Not at all	Don't know	Comments
I have followed up on the advice given to see how effective it was					
I have experience of breaking down different types of assignment into criteria for marking					
I have experience of marking work according to marking criteria					
I have read around the subject of study skills and supporting students' learning					
I know how to break down the subject area I am supporting into its component study skills					
I know how to evaluate performance for each of those study skills' component areas					
I am aware of subject–specific study skills needed for the area I am supporting					
Other:					
ATTRIBUTES					
I am confident about this type of work					
I have patience in dealing with adults experiencing difficulties					

	True	Sort of	Not at all	Don't know	Comments
I am good at encouraging others to work out solutions to problems for themselves					
I am sensitive to the issues around adults asking for help or revealing weaknesses to others					
I am good at thinking up practical solutions to problems					
I am a good listener					
I am aware of my own strengths and weaknesses in teaching study skills					
I know my priorities for developing my skills in this area of work					
I take a reflective approach to my own work					
Other:					
RESOURCES					
I know of materials that I can use					
I know of staff development in this field that I can attend					

	True	Sort of	Not at all	Don't know	Comments
There are colleagues to whom I can go for support					
There are specialist staff at my institution I can consult					
Other relevant considerations (skills, attributes, etc.)					
Summary:					

Skills profile for integrating study skills into teaching

Integrating study skills into teaching					
TEACHING APPROACHES					
I feel confident about . . .	True	Sort of	Not at all	Don't know	See page
Orientating students to HE study					pp. 98–101 and Chs 4 and 10
Being precise about requirements					pp. 103–4, 131–3
Using repetition through concrete examples					pp. 104–5
Using multi-sensory approaches					pp. 105–6 and Ch. 11
Teaching to suit varied learning styles					pp. 101–3 and Chs 11 and 23
Using active learning methods					pp. 106–7
Giving constructive feedback and guidance					pp. 117–18
Building motivation and interest					pp. 23–8, 107 and Ch. 11
INTEGRATED PRACTICAL SUPPORT					
I feel confident about developing the following areas through my teaching . . .					
Presenting skills development to students in a way that makes sense and appeals to them					Ch. 12
Creating opportunities for students to focus on what they are learning *as* learners and as future professionals, rather than simply in terms of course content					pp. 225–6 and Chs 11 and 25

	True	Sort of	Not at all	Don't know	See page
Building in effective small-group work					pp. 112–14 and Chs 13 and 22
Creating a basis for mutual support groups					pp. 214, 283–4 and Ch. 10
Helping students to manage 'information overload'					pp. 109–16, 201 and Ch. 16
Creating opportunities to offer guidance on research techniques, writing and reading for my subject specialism					Chs 17–20
Developing my students' thinking skills					Chs 15 and 21
Training students in self- and peer assessment					pp. 213 and Ch. 22
Ensuring the needs of a variety of learners are met, including those with disabilities, dyslexia, English language needs or who lack confidence or experience					pp. 50–1 and Ch. 4

© Stella Cottrell (2001), *Teaching Study Skills and Supporting Learning* (Basingstoke: Palgrave).

Drawing on your area of expertise: transferable skills

Chapter 8 introduced the idea of the 'expertise metaphor'. This offers ways of using existing expertise to develop confidence in tackling new and even distantly related tasks. It was found that students can sometimes find a way of reconceptualising tasks they consider difficult through identifying points of contact with the underlying problem structure of a pre-existing area of expertise. Their area of expertise may be very distant, on the surface, to the one they are currently being asked to undertake. For some students, dressmaking, drawing, cooking or mechanics may offer more accessible transferable skills for academic writing, for example, than the more obvious route of referring to another kind of writing task.

Lecturers are often placed in analogous positions to students. They may see themselves primarily as subject or vocational specialists, and recognise that they do not have training in developing students' abilities to learn. Many academics feel very anxious about stepping outside of their role as subject specialist. If you feel that there are gaps in your own expertise, then seeking training or staff development is a good idea. However, you may also find that you can boost your confidence by looking for parallel skills in a distant area of expertise.

ACTIVITY

The expertise metaphor
- Read through the examples in Chapter 8 again.
- Reflect upon an area of your professional practice that you wish to improve.
- Break down your 'area of expertise' into component parts. Consider such things as your overall vision, the order in which you do things, what you do to prepare yourself or others, who you have to bring on board and how you do that, how you can tell that what you are doing is working, and what you do when you come up against unforeseen obstacles. Look for ways that the current area of expertise offers you insights or structures to develop your professional practice.
- Once you have found some links, push the metaphor as far as you can take it. Students are often surprised at how many different problems they can tackle using the same expertise metaphor.

Critical incident

Select one occasion when you were called upon to develop students' skills, either for an individual, group or cohort of students. Select an incident that you feel yields important information about yourself as a teacher and a learner.

- What did you learn about your own responses, skills and abilities from that experience?
- How is your experience of that learning deepened by drawing on pedagogical theories or the reading suggested at the end of this chapter?
- Does your experience confirm or refute the theories you read?
- What insights does the incident yield about the behaviours and learning of your own students?

Drawing reflections together

Based on the activities you have undertaken above, draw together your reflections on:

- the kinds of skills, values and experiences which are ideal for study skills teaching;
- the skills, experiences, values and training you bring to this area, which you can draw on to develop and support study skills and learning in others;
- your own areas of potential weakness in relation to effective study skills teaching;
- resources that are available to you;
- your staff development needs for this area.

Action Plan

Based on the profile activities above, and on your reflections, draw up a list of actions that you need to take to improve your work in relation to study skills and learning development.

Action to be taken	Order of priority	When I'll do this

Closing reflections

- How did you feel about undertaking the activities in this chapter before you started them?
- Have your attitudes towards yourself, your teaching or your students changed or developed in any way through this process of evaluation and reflection?
- What insights have you gained into study skills development from a student's perspective? How might the attitudes of your students differ from your own?
- What steps would you take to ensure that the process of reflection and self-evaluation was productive for your students?

Bibliography

In addition to the above activities, lecturers may wish to read more deeply into the subject in order to reflect in a more informed way on the notion of reflection. A useful starting place is Schon (1987) on reflective practice; this is a key text for those interested in becoming more reflective professionals. Other seminal texts are Boud *et al*. (1985) on writing reflective journals or diaries, and Boud (1995) on self-assessment. Brown and McCartney (1999) have produced interesting work on the transformative effects of reflection upon experience. Brockbank and McGill (1998) look at reflective practice from an HE teaching perspective, Prosser and Trigwell (1997, 1999) and Biggs (1996) have shown a relation between approaches taken to teaching and the quality of students' learning outcomes: awareness of oneself as a teacher can impact positively upon students' learning. This offers an interesting perspective on student success or failure. A critique of Schon's reflective model and an alternative approach to reflection can be found in Usher *et al*. (1997); this includes extracts of discussions undertaken with university lecturers, offering some different perspectives on reflective practice.

Part II

Menu: Outlines for Study Skills Sessions

Introduction to Part II

Using the menu to design skills sessions

Part II offers a selection or 'menu' of sessions from which those offering study skills support can choose depending on what best suits their students. Each menu item offers a range of strategies and activities from which those designing skills courses can draw. Each menu item contains more than could be covered in a single taught session.

The material offered here is set out so as to be as easy as possible for staff to use with minimum preparation. However, it is unlikely that any tutor would want to use the material exactly as it stands. It is important that a subject-specific angle is given as far as possible, and guidance is given in each chapter on how this might be achieved. It will also be necessary for lecturers to choose which activities best suit their students, and where to give weight at different times to suit their own curriculum. For some intakes, certain skills may already be in place. For others, more extensive work may be needed, and the activities in Chapter 8, 'Supporting Individual Students', might be usefully adapted for group work.

As far as is possible, the activities described are offered in a generic way, with guidance given about how subject specific content can be brought in by the lecturer. The sessions are likely to work best when they are related to a particular course, using supplementary course materials, and course-specific examples, rather than offered as generic sessions. Study skills guidance works best when it is contextualised, when the examples are seen as relevant to the student's subject area, and where it can be made explicit how the activities will pay off in terms of managing the course and gaining credit in assessment.

The Study Skills Handbook

Several sections refer the student to material in the *Study Skills Handbook* (Cottrell, 1999). This is the natural companion to this present text which has been designed partly to assist tutors to make use of that *Handbook* with their students. The *Handbook* contains useful back-up materials and activities which were devised to save tutors time in preparing study skills materials. Tutors will still, of course, need to provide subject-specific examples. However, sessions in this book are all designed so it is not essential that students use the *Handbook* if lecturing staff prefer to use alternative materials. Alternative texts are suggested in the resource materials for each session.

Features of the menu section

(1) Time allocations for activities

These are not given unless they are essential. Many activities would benefit from more time rather than less, but as courses vary so much in the time they allocate to skills work, lecturers can adapt the timing to suit their own conditions. Some departments offer three-hour skills sessions as part of the curriculum; others offer only hour-long sessions with personal tutors. The material given under each menu heading is likely to be more than could be covered even in a three-hour session. This enables those arranging sessions to choose activities which best suit their students and their current level of performance.

(2) Order of session

There is no strict order in which menu sessions should be offered, although some skills such as developing confidence in speaking, group work skills and reflective self-evaluation are developed progressively over several sessions. In general, the earlier items benefit from being addressed near the beginning of the student's time at the university.

(3) Group work

Group work is addressed throughout the menu, with a particular emphasis on students hearing their own voices and bonding as a group. It will vary from course to course how relevant it is to focus specifically on the mechanics of group work. In general, this works best if it is approached early on, either in induction or soon after. Good group work makes a great difference both for student retention and for mutual support work, especially if these are introduced as part of the culture of the course. The more students can assist each other, the more independent and self-reliant they are – and the less demand there is on lecturers for avoidable additional support. Early priorities should be on developing student confidence in speaking at all, building up to more challenging group and individual tasks over several sessions.

(4) Reflection and self-evaluation

Reflection and self-evaluation run throughout the menu items. Reflective journals are introduced in Chapter 11. It helps students if lecturers make references to these during sessions, giving time to jot brief notes, or asking for contributions of ideas written in them. It adds more depth to the sessions and allows students to develop, over time and with guidance, the art of reflection.

(5) Advance preparation by students

It is useful if students can be inducted to a culture of preparation for all taught sessions. However, it is preferable that they attend rather than absent themselves because they have not done the preparation. Resource Sheets follow each of the menu sessions. These could be used either in the sessions themselves or given as advance preparation. Session activities are set out so that they can be run even if students have not undertaken any preparation.

You may wish to use the Resource Sheets as a stimulus to devise your own. You may also like to collate them into a booklet and distribute them together at the beginning of the course to ensure any absentee students have access to them for the following session. It is advisable to go through them with the students at the end of the previous session so they are clear what needs to be completed for the following session.

Contents of menu sessions

This varies slightly depending on what is appropriate for each study skills area covered. In general, each menu item contains several of the following features:

- *Student difficulties*
  Background on common errors or difficulties faced by students with that particular aspect of study skills. This can be helpful for the lec-

turer taking the session or for teaching staff more generally. Sometimes it helps students to hear that these are common difficulties and to discuss them.

- *How lecturers can help*
  Ways that lecturers can help to alleviate difficulties in this area through their general teaching.

- *Aims of the session*
- *Learning outcomes for the session*
- *Tutor preparation*
  Brief guidance on preparing for the study skills session and useful approaches to take. Guidance on any subject-specific materials that lecturers need to prepare.

- *Activities*
  Suggested activities for a study skills session.

- *Resource Sheets*
  Handouts for students to help them prepare for the study skills session or to use as resource sheets during sessions.

Adapting the menu to suit you

You may feel that some of the suggestions for activities can be used just as they stand. However, it is more likely that once you have used them, you will find that the menu acts as a stimulus for even better ideas of your own. That is ideal. Activities which you devise yourself, or where you have developed course-specific examples, will probably feel more 'alive' to both you and the student. However, when you are in a hurry or if you are just starting out, activities and resources from the menu should prove a useful starting place.

SEEC/HECIW descriptors and the study skills menu

To facilitate the work of course staff who already use SEEC/HECIW descriptors (see Appendix 2), I have used HE Level 1 SEEC/HECIW descriptors

for each of the activities suggested in the sessions below to indicate the types of skills that students could be expected to develop through the learning outcomes for each session and for each activity. I use the following code, given below, to identify which SEEC/HECIW descriptor is used for each skill. This code is used in the Learning Outcome box for each session, and on the title line of each activity. Clearly, this merely indicates that particular skills are being addressed or rehearsed through the activity rather than that the activity is sufficient to equip the student with that skill.

Some skills have been separated out further from the SEEC/HECIW list. Investigative and research skills have been made into a separate category; creativity has been separated out from synthesis, and employability awareness has been added.

Where suggestions have been made for marking criteria (as in items 3, 11 and 13), these also refer back to the skills list below. If those criteria were used or adapted, students would need their own copy of the following Skills Code.

Skills code for marking criteria	
Code	**Skill (adapted from SEEC/HECIW descriptors)**
A	Analysis
C	Creativity and generative thought
E	Evaluation
Emp	Contextual awareness and employability skills
I	Information management, research and investigative skills
IGS	Interactive and group skills
KU	Knowledge and understanding
M	Planning and management of learning
OC	Oral communication
P	Problem-solving
R	Self-appraisal; reflection on practice
S	Synthesis and summary
WC	Written communication

10 Induction: orientation to learning

This chapter suggests activities to accompany the induction programme outlined in Chapter 4 above. Activities in the following chapters could also be included as part of induction depending on the length of induction and the priorities and approach of your course.

Aims of the session

- To settle students into university in a friendly and supportive way so as to ease their transition into Higher Education and develop a feeling of 'belonging';

- to give opportunities for students to socialise and form group bonds before term begins;

- to orientate students to the academic culture of higher education so that they know what is expected of them;

- to ensure students are provided with information to which they are entitled and which helps them to make sense of the new learning context.

> ## Learning outcomes
>
> At the end of these activities students should be able to:
>
> | Learning outcomes | Skills (see p. 193) |
> |---|---|
> | (1) Interact with others with increased confidence, showing respect for the views and feelings of others | IGS |
> | (2) Make contributions to groups of differing sizes | IGS, OC |
> | (3) Identify areas of difficulty for themselves and the group and take some responsibility for formulating solutions | IGS, M, P, R |
> | (4) Draw on a range of group-building strategies | IGS, KU |
> | (5) Clarify myths, expectations and responsibilities about study in Higher Education | KU, M, R |
> | (6) Identify some of the skills, attributes and knowledge they are bringing with them as individuals and as a group | Emp, IGS, KU, R |

Activities

Group bonding   **IGS**

Just after they arrive, in the first few weeks of the term, is the time when students can be at most risk of leaving. The transition to Higher Education is not necessarily easy. Students may feel lost in a large group, isolated, lonely, out of place, thinking they are the only ones who do not fit in, who have no friends or who are struggling to make sense of all the information coming at them. They may travel from one study module to another, each time meeting new sets of students and lecturers whose names they cannot remember. They may feel that nobody cares who they are or would notice if they were not there. However, universities do not have to be like this. Courses could structure 'bonding' activities into both induction events and taught sessions. Early exercises which require paired work, discussion groups and practical activities could help students to start making contributions in relatively painless ways and to make bonds with others on their courses.

Names

It makes a big difference to students if they know the names of the people in their groups.

> **ACTIVITY**
>
> **Learning names**
> - Ask each student to bring in a photo that they like of themselves and to attach their name to it. Arrange these on a board in alphabetical order.
> - Encourage students to say their name before they speak.
> - Ask people to say their names, and give one adjective that describes them that begins with the initial letter of their name, e.g. Sleepy Steven.
> - Standing in a circle, each person says the name of one person in the group, and throws a cushion or large ball at them. Continue until all names are known.
> - Round: everybody says their name and, after the first person, the name of everybody who has already given their name

Icebreakers   IGS

Icebreakers are most useful when groups do not know each other very well, especially if some members might be anxious or nervous. Two or three icebreakers in the first session and one for subsequent sessions are usually beneficial. There are all kinds and you can invent your own. The rule of thumb is that they do not lead to anyone feeling left out, that they are not threatening, and they can be contained so they don't take up the whole teaching session. When using icebreakers, start with the least threatening examples, where students do not have to speak alone in front of a large group; build up confidence gradually. A list of examples is given below.

- **Introductions**   Within a short period, everyone must introduce themselves to everybody in the room. It is each person's individual responsibility to make sure they have not missed anybody out. Alternatively, each person can also present one piece of information about themselves.

- **What's in common?**   As above, but each person must also find two things in common with each person they introduce themselves to (e.g. their names begin with A, same star-sign, football club, etc.).

- **Connections**   Call out, one by one, a list of things people might have in common, avoiding personal information which some might find threatening (e.g. everyone wearing a blue jumper, who arrived by bus, who has been to Brighton, etc.). Avoid things which can lead to exclusion (such as age, race, sexuality, politics, etc.). For each item called, those for whom it is relevant run into the centre (or to another allocated space).

- **Find someone who . . .**   Everybody is given a list of 'characteristics', perhaps presented in a 'bingo card' format, and they have to find and list at least one person in the room for each characteristic. For example:

Has a birthday on the last day of the month
Is a Gemini
Has been to China
Lives in Halls of Residence
Has travelled on a hovercraft
Has twins in the family
Has travelled furthest to study here
Speaks the most languages in the group
Owns a cat
Has been to the Caribbean
Has appeared on TV or stage
Reads science fiction
Hates spaghetti
Studies on more than one site or campus
Loves photography
Can sing
Can cook bread
Has built a wall
Can change a plug
Can juggle
Has visited Stonehenge
Has lived near the sea
Uses a particular route to campus
Plays a sport
Has children
Rides a motor bike
Is allergic to peanuts
Listens to Moby
Plays or played with Nintendo
Has worked on a farm

- **Trivial Pursuits 1**   Students collect three pieces of 'trivial' information from each person present.

- **Trivial Pursuits 2**   Alternatively, divide into pairs for the above exercise. Each person narrates their partner's 3 'trivialities' to the whole group (to become used to speaking in the full group).

- **Interviews**   In pairs: interview a partner for three minutes each. Form foursomes so that partners can be introduced to a second pair. In the full group, each person makes a one sentence introduction of one person from the other pair.

- **Tall tales**   In pairs: each person says 3 things about themselves, one of which is not true. In the full group, each person introduces their partner by name, relays the three pieces of information, and guesses which they believe is false. Their partner then reveals which information was false.

- **Achievements** Each person names one achievement in their life.

- **Changes** Each names one thing they want to change about their life within the year.

- **Fame** Each names a famous person from the past they would like to have been.

- **Objects** If they were an animal (or plant, colour, musical instrument, etc.), which one do they think they would be?

- **Mood.** Round: at the beginning or end of a session, each person says one word or phrase to express how they are feeling or how they found the session.

- **Rorsach blots** Teams compete to list as many ways as possible that an ambivalent image (presented on an overhead projector or handout) could be interpreted.

- **Jig-saw** Present a question or some information that the group needs, cut-up as a jig saw. Teams compete to complete the jigsaw and answer the closed question hidden within the jigsaw.

Acknowledging anxieties   `IGS, M, OC, R`

The following activity is almost always useful. Anxieties and worries are usually at the forefront of the mind, and if they are addressed and dealt with, then students can start to relax. As people can feel isolated by their anxieties, addressing them early on works very well as a bonding activity.

ACTIVITY

Sharing anxieties

- ■ *Individually* Ask students to make a quick list of any concerns they have about coming to university and studying at this level or on this course.

- ■ *Small group* Ask students to discuss items from their list in groups of about six people.

- ■ *Whole group* Ask a person from each group to contribute an anxiety that was raised, without mentioning who it was that had originally contributed this to the group. If you go round more than once, ask for a different person to respond each time. Write responses up into a mind map or long list which they can all see.

- ■ *Whole group* Once the list is complete, ask them to reflect upon the list of anxieties. Ask if they are surprised at how many other people had anxieties about starting the course and how this makes them feel about their own anxieties. Usually, students are surprised and comforted to know most other people are also feeling vulnerable.

- ■ *Small groups of three and then whole group* If there is time, ask students to suggest ways that they or others behave when they are feeling anxious or afraid in groups. Draw attention to the fact that irritating and difficult behaviour in groups often derives from fear or avoidance tactics. It is useful for students to be aware of this. Draw attention to how it can sabotage their learning and might affect their interactions with each other.

Turn anxieties into challenges or 'learning opportunities'

Suggest that students try to approach their anxieties in a positive or problem-solving state of mind. It is worth making explicit that it is natural to feel some concerns at the beginning of a new course, and that excitement and fear are closely linked. Remind them that they are not expected to know already the things that they are there to learn: a confusion made by many anxious students.

   When we were children most of us used to be delighted by puzzles books, mazes and word games: we found it exciting to address problems for which we did not already know the answer. Often, we have lost this fresh outlook and eagerness to take on challenges when we are older: we are too afraid of failure. It is useful if students can bring some aspects of adventure, playfulness and inquisitiveness to any difficulties they encounter. This will serve them well when they return to employment. Encourage students to turn their anxieties into challenges and to consider the range of resources, including each other, that may be open to them.

ACTIVITY

Spot the opportunity
Return to the list of difficulties and anxieties drawn up above.

- *Small groups*   Ask students to make suggestions, in groups, of how each could be viewed as an opportunity to learn something new.
- *Whole group*   Take suggestions from each group. If possible, offer to write these up for the group for the next session, or ask for a volunteer to do so.
- If you use a volunteer, ensure they are able to make free photocopies through the department.

ACTIVITY

Problem-solving
- *Small groups*   Break the list of anxieties down into types of difficulty. Ask each group to brainstorm some ways that each problem could be tackled. This is useful in encouraging students to regard each other as a resource rather than the tutor as the answer to all their problems. It is also a good basis for building support groups later. If there is a *university guide of services*, ask students to use this to assist in their problem-solving.
- *Full group*   Ask each person in the group to contribute one item from their list of possible solutions.
- *Individually*   Ask students to write down the solutions they feel apply to their own situation. It can help if they do this in the form of a basic Action Plan, saying what they will do and by when.

- *Threes*   Ask students to share their action plan with two others, who will undertake to check with them, at a mutually agreed time, whether they are sticking to it.

Expectations and responsibilities   `IGS, M, R`

Being very clear about what is expected of students both for Higher Education generally, and the course in particular, is key to students taking responsibility for their own learning. If this is not addressed during induction and the first few weeks, it is very difficult to change habits and practices later. If good practices are established early on, not only do students gain, but lecturers are put under less pressure in supporting students with bad study habits or a low sense of personal responsibility for their learning. It can help to link this theme to that of personal, professional and academic development or personal development planning (see p. 203 below).

ACTIVITY

Myths and expectations
- *Small groups*   Ask the students to move into small groups, with people they know least. Ask them to introduce themselves by name.
- Ask the groups to draw up a list of their assumptions and expectations about Higher Education, their lecturers, and other students. Suggest that they think, too, about how Higher Education may differ from school or college in what it expects of students.
- *Whole group*   Brainstorm ideas onto the board or chart so everyone can read them, taking one from each group in turn. Tell students not to identify who made which point. Encourage each person to contribute an item.

Use the brainstorm as a starting-point for discussion and for addressing any misconceptions.

Students like to know what happens if a tutor becomes ill. How do communications work within the department? Which teaching strategies are used? What are the students' responsibilities? Make explicit any of the assumptions underlying academic life. Students may be used to a very different set of academic conventions, especially if they have studied overseas – e.g. they may be used to being given credit for copying from texts, or they may be used to far more or far less contact with tutors. It may be helpful here to move onto a consideration of how students manage uncertainty and how far they expect lecturers to provide them with 'the right answer'.

Mutual responsibilities

Student responsibilities
Be explicit about students' responsibilities. Guidance may be needed, for example, on:

- total time commitment;
- how much self-directed learning is expected, especially reading around the subject and being responsible for monitoring their own progress and personal development;
- attendance for induction, lectures, seminars, practicals, tutorials, field-trips, exams;
- punctuality;
- meeting deadlines;
- their responsibilities in claiming disability assistance or extenuating or mitigating circumstances for exams;
- advising the university of changes in circumstance such as change of address.

Staff and university responsibilities
Students respond better to the idea of responsibilities when there is some aspect of mutuality. Courses and lecturers offer a great deal to students, although this is not always visible to the student or else it is taken for granted. This could be addressed by:

- giving undertakings about what students can expect from you and from the university;
- being clear about your expectations and how you will enforce these;
- spelling out what you will offer. Examples

might include: providing structured reading lists, advance notice of assignment titles, guidance notes on how to undertake an assignment, annotated examples of what is required, structured feedback on a pro-forma sheet as part of your marking, a set time limit for returning marked assignments, set times when staff will be available for questions;
- discussing what the university offers in terms of equal opportunities policies, grievance procedures, external examiners and academic standards, as well as for their personal and social needs.

Contracts
It is useful if responsibilities are formalised into a contract of some kind. This may be a simple list of responsibilities on each side, as outlined above. Students and staff would sign this and have copies. The contract might also include a general agreement to follow ground rules formed by group consensus, as outlined below. It is very useful for sorting out difficulties later if students have signed a commitment of this type.

Setting ground rules   `IGS, M`

ACTIVITY

Ground rules for the group

- *Individually*   Ask students to make a quick list of things that they feel they should be able to expect from each other in the group. This could be a wish list for how they would like sessions to run. For some groups, it may help to give examples such as 'mobile phones switched off before you come in' or 'no interrupting when someone else is speaking'.
- *Whole group*   Invite suggestions on what should go into the ground-rules. Discuss each, and if there is general consensus, write it down as a group list.
- Encourage consideration of essentials that may have been missed, such as confidentiality, respectful listening when others are speaking, punctuality, non-discrimi-

natory language and behaviours, and everybody taking responsibility for contributing.

■ *Tell the group* that you will write this up for the following session so everyone has a copy. Also make clear that ground-rules can be changed.

■ *Discuss* how these will be monitored by the group; for example, will you or they draw attention to infringements?

Managing induction information

Students are usually inundated with information at induction. Although universities like to feel they have covered all angles, both for the benefit of the student and to cover themselves legally, it would be foolish to expect that students take in most of what is said to them. On the other hand, if students are disorientated about the essentials for survival on-course, they will not pay sufficient attention to their study. It is important to ensure students are well orientated to the course and to the university more generally. Three ways of engaging students' interest in what can seem like a very great deal of information are:

(1) a checklist;
(2) question and answer: a student-constructed list of questions to be answered, with students playing a role in answering the questions;
(3) a quiz.

Combinations of these three are possible.

Checklist

Offer students a checklist of all the things they need to do during the initial induction period, arranged under different headings, such as:

- before induction week
- bring with me to induction (essential)
- essential procedures
- special induction events
- materials I should have been given
- course information I should have received

- things to enter in my diary
- key university services
- key people

Ask different presenters to draw students' attention to this during induction and encourage students to check off each item as it is covered. Leave spaces for 'questions that arise' and offer time to answer these later. The list should include items related to study, such as filling key dates into a diary, purchasing set texts or essential early reading, making themselves familiar with the library and with other learning resources such as IT training. Ensure they enter key dates and deadlines into diaries. Give guidance regarding essential books, equipment, software, computers, etc. for your subject area. Remember that many students will not have much money for these items. Make it clear which books and facilities are available in the department or faculty, and the procedures for using these (e.g. arranging a tutorial appointment, using photocopiers, booking rooms and resources).

Question and answer IGS, M

Students usually arrive laden with questions although they may feel it is not appropriate to ask these. From your perspective, the answers to many of these questions may already have been provided. It is not unusual for students to fail to make the link between being given a handbook of information and the idea that the information they need might be contained within it. It is easy for students to regard lecturers as the source of all information. To discourage this, and to promote the use of handbooks and other materials which have been provided, you could try the following activity.

ACTIVITY

Finding general information

■ *Small groups* Ask students to draw up a list on a large sheet of paper of all the questions to which they want answers about the course, the lecturers, and about study skills more generally. The questions must be clearly stated. Attach their lists at the front where everyone can see them.

■ *Whole group*   Once the lists are complete, run through them quickly together. Ask students to say whether each question is one to which they could probably find the answer for themselves (such as in the course handbook), or whether it is something only you could answer.

■ Alternatively, you can devise a list of questions which students tend to ask year after year.

■ *Organise students into teams of 4–5 people* Teams compete to find as many of the answers to the questions as possible in the literature provided, noting exactly where it came from. Have back-up materials from other services to which they can refer.

■ *Whole group*   Ask teams to report back the answers, saying where they found the information. Encourage all students to look immediately at that source, where possible, so they have seen it for themselves. Teams award themselves a point for each question answered correctly. (Offer three cheers to the winning team.)

■ At the end, draw attention to how many questions students were able to answer between themselves. Answer outstanding questions – or direct students to appropriate resources.

Quiz: essential information

• The above activity could be replaced by or followed up by a quiz in order to reinforce essential information. It is a good opportunity for you to ask students to search out answers to all the questions your students tend to raise over the course of the year.

• The quiz could be undertaken in pairs or small groups.

• This could be marked by the students and collected in for you to browse through. Emphasise that this is to help students, not to judge them.

• It is worth noting who left gaps or picked up information incorrectly as these are often the students who will get into difficulties later and it is one way in which students can be considered to be 'at risk'. Students, able in many others aspects of study, may not be adept at administrative practicalities and some may need extra guidance.

Campus exploration   IGS

Set up a treasure hunt to encourage students to explore the campus early on for all the key places they may need over their time at university.

ACTIVITY

Treasure hunt
Give students a list of items that they have to note from the walls or desks or information boards at various locations around the campus. This might be the colour of the door, the name of key personnel, the numbers of windows in the room, etc. – as long as it motivates them to wander round the campus and get a feel for where key offices and facilities are located. Include all the places that your students may need to visit at some point during the year, such as Student Administration, Student Services, Student Union, Learning Resources, photocopier facilities, IT labs, exam rooms, lecture rooms, studio space, cafes, etc. Finding awkwardly located rooms can help foster group bonding, and develops a sense of direction for the campus.

The 'treasure' might be, for example, a set of letters that students have to copy down as they visit each place on a list. One letter from the set would be attached to the wall beside the main door of each place to be visited. The letters may spell out the name of a concept or famous person from the area of study or the heading of a page in the *Handbook*. Once this is worked out, you might even reward the students by exchanging the answer for a prize: such as a drink of coffee and a biscuit.

Use a distinctive set of letters in case another course has the same idea. For example, your students may have to hunt down all the red-on-yellow letters, whereas another course would be trailing a different clue using another set of colours.

Introducing personal, professional and academic development to students `Emp, M, R`

Personal development planning should be introduced to students as early as possible (see pp. 72–3 above). Bring out the advantages to students of the approach being offered to them at university, both to future academic aspirations and to employment:

(1) It will train students to study more effectively so that they make best use of the time available and have a better chance of attaining a good grade.
(2) Learning should be more enjoyable and less stressful as it becomes more consciously skilled.
(3) Students will be more aware of how what they learn applies to wider contexts, such as to other academic courses and to the world of work, and will be better able to articulate their awareness to employers.
(4) It will give greater focus to their learning.
(5) Students will develop skills of self-evaluation and reflection which are useful in most life contexts.
(6) They will receive more than just a degree from their education.
(7) They will be better able to compete for jobs.

Clarify how personal, professional and academic development is delivered
Clarify whether this will be offered through:

• activities such as those undertaken in this session;
• professional or academic skills modules;
• integrated throughout their course;

• opportunities for work placement;
• opportunities to receive credit for current employment;
• careers education;
• other routes.

Be explicit about how students' learning will be drawn together. It is important that students are aware of what they learn and are able to articulate their skills and personal development to others in appropriate ways. This may be through personal tutors, portfolios, progress files, transcripts, dedicated units, etc.

Skills and experience: what are students bringing to the course?

This is a useful activity to introduce early on and to introduce personal development approaches to skills training. It encourages students to start examining the skills they are bringing to higher education, which is a good preparation for later skills sessions, especially for activities in Chapter 13. It indicates to students that a range of skills and perspectives is valued, including their ability to reflect upon and evaluate their own current performance. Moreover, it reveals the diversity of skills, qualities and perspectives available in the group as a resource. The lecturer can draw on this to encourage students to think about the advantages of working in groups.

The reflection and discussion from the following activity can contribute towards writing a Position Paper as a diagnostic exercise (see pp. 235–6 below).

ACTIVITY

Skills qualities and perspectives

■ *Individually* Students list the varied roles they play either now or in the past – such as mother, pupil, householder, cook, friend, partner, school governor, employee, etc.
■ *Whole group* Brainstorm the list of roles that exist in the whole group. Keep going

until the list or the time allowed is exhausted.

■ *Whole group*   Select one role and invite the group to brainstorm all the skills and qualities needed for that role. Encourage them to tease out skills such as managing other people, organisational skills, reading, writing, number work, speaking, keeping to deadlines, planning ahead, budgeting, etc., which go into many everyday activities.

■ *Individually*   Once you have established the idea, ask students to do this for just one of the roles on their own list.

■ *Small groups*   Ask students to list, on large sheets, all the skills they have as a group: such as word-processing, using a drill, sports, community work, etc. Hang these up around the room and ask students to walk round and read the list. Alternatively, ask one person from each group to present their list, excluding anything already mentioned by a previous group.

■ *Whole group*   Invite students to draw out the diverse knowledges, perspectives and talents within the room and the richness this offers when it is pooled into group work.

Group project   `I, IGS, M, S, WC`

One good way to break the ice, encourage group work and to integrate skills early in the semester is to set a group project in induction week or the first week or two of the semester. This should not be formally assessed but is useful for diagnostic purposes.

Useful characteristics of an induction group project

(1) It relates clearly to the material that will be studied and is a good mini-taster of what is to come on the course.

(2) It is easily manageable in the time but creates a sense of challenge.

(3) It requires students to work together in teams – or even to collaborate across teams.

(4) There are clear and explicit criteria for the final products.

(5) There are very clear instructions for the task with back-up materials on where to go for information and advice.

(6) It requires some work in the library and includes an induction to the library.

(7) It involves some use of IT – such as a literature search on CD-ROM or the internet.

(8) All students are required to speak about the project: two minutes each is sufficient. For example, one person could say why they selected that topic, another how they planned the task, a third how much information was available, etc. For very large groups, it may be necessary to break the group into smaller units for this feedback.

(9) Students are asked to assess each other's projects – as group work rather than as individual efforts, using the criteria that have been given.

(10) Each student is required to write the project up by hand and submit it. Explain that this will be used as diagnostic material to help staff to identify strengths and weaknesses.

(11) In the written work, students reflect upon their own performance, saying how well they contributed to the group, what they found most difficult, and which areas they need to work upon. This could be linked to other work on identifying skills and difficulties.

(12) Students are expected to submit references as part of the written work.

Orientation to HE thinking

No 'right answer'   `E, IGS, KU, R`
See p. 75 above.

ACTIVITY

The right answer

■ *Individually or pairs*   Give students three or four issues to consider. It may help to give them the issues to consider in advance of the session. Where possible, use examples that are relevant to the course of study. If the unit is a generic one, possible issues are:

- Children who consistently misbehave should be severely punished.
- All things can be categorised. For example, to be considered a chair, a piece of furniture must have legs, back support and a seat.
- If resources are limited, young people should be offered health-care before the very old.
- Everyone seeking a lasting life partner should let their friends or family make the choice for them.
- The most important thing we do in life is prepare for our death.
- If we witness a wrong-doing, we should always speak out.

◼ Ask students to write down their viewpoint for each issue. They can keep this confidential.
◼ *Whole group*   Offer students the Resource Sheet or a list of Perry's stages (see pp. 75 and 207). You may wish to adapt this to reduce the number of stages. At this point, do not present them as stages – merely as different approaches to the idea of there being a 'right answer'. Read the list through aloud whilst the students follow the text.
◼ *Individually*   Ask students to identify which of Perry's approaches best describes the final position they took when considering each issue. Ask them to state why they have suggested that stage.
◼ *Whole group*   Discuss the different answers that people came up with for each issue.
◼ Point out that Perry said these were developmental stages that students went through. Discuss their response to this. Discuss the implications of holding viewpoints in each stage for their chosen area of study:

- How open are they to learning new material and considering different viewpoints?
- How comfortable are they with the idea that there may not be a 'right answer'? If they are uncomfortable, reassure them that this is common at the start of an HE course.

◼ Use the opportunity to talk through what is meant by 'truth' or 'fact' in their own subject area.

Originality and individuality   KU

Discuss what is meant by originality and individuality, and make links with plagiarism (see below, pp. 277 and 279). It may help to cover the following points:

- Some students worry that if they are asked for an 'original' piece of work, they must produce something that bears no relation to what has gone before. That is not usually what tutors mean. Reassure students that they are not expected to invent whole new schools of thought.
- Explain what tutors mean by 'original'. They are usually looking to see how students make sense of the ideas that they encounter through the course. In other words, they want to see that students have done some research, given some thought to what they have read and heard, reflected upon it, evaluated different approaches, and come to their own conclusions. They want to see that students are capable of presenting this in their own words, with due reference to source materials. If students do this, their work will come across as 'individual'. Their own style will emerge through their writing.

Ethics and values

The following pair of related exercises are used at Birmingham University to introduce a consideration of values relevant to the course. Although devised for students on the Diploma in Social Work course, the exercise could be adapted for students on other courses.

Thinking about oppression

Rationale

We need to start students off thinking about oppression as soon as possible. Whilst later sessions are our main way of doing this, there is value in giving students an early opportunity to think about oppression in general, rather than breaking the topic down into forms of oppression. Part 1 and Part 2 are each allocated 2 hour.

Part 1:   labelling exercise

Each student is given a sticky label with a word or phrase on it (e.g. 'queer', 'HIV positive', 'paki', 'educationally sub-normal'). They are asked to wear this label and consider their initial responses. They are asked:

- What are your first feelings about the label you have been given?
- Are you happy about being labelled in this way or do you find it offensive?

Students are then asked to discuss, in pairs, their first thoughts on being given these labels. They are also asked how they feel about each other's labels.

This is fed back to the main group. Students are then asked to leave the room, go to the cafe or walk around the campus for 10 minutes with their labels on. They are asked to note:

- Any feelings they have about displaying the label in public?
- Whether they make any effort to hide their label or prevent other people from seeing it?
- Whether they stay close to any of the other students or stay alone?
- Whether anyone comments on the label? If so, what response do they make?

On their return, students are asked to feed back their experiences to the group.

Drawing on this, they are asked to discuss what the exercise tells them about:

- the experience of being a member of an oppressed group;
- the experience of being labelled;
- the experience of people given specific labels;
- how other people respond to people who have been identified as members of oppressed groups.

Students are also asked for their own attitudes towards these labels: were they offended by any of the terms or whether they found any of them funny?

Part 2:   social work values and anti-oppressive practice

The afternoon's session builds upon the morning's exercises, considering what is really meant by anti-oppressive practice. Students often come up with phrases such as 'showing respect' or 'being non-judgmental' without having a sense of what this might mean in practice. The session uses structured discussion to consider questions such as:

- How would someone know you were practising in an anti-oppressive manner?
- What behaviours do you see as indicative of anti-oppressive practice?
- How you demonstrate to someone that you respect them?

Other potential induction activities

It is useful to address the other aspects itemised below as part of induction activities, whether these occur within induction week proper, or within the first few weeks.

- Attitudes and approaches
  to learning   menu session 2
- Identifying skills and
  learning priorities   menu session 3
- Working with others   menu session 4

RESOURCE SHEET
Is there a right answer?

Issues discussed in higher education may not have 'right' answers. There may be several answers or it may depend on how particular evidence is assessed or there may be insufficient evidence to come to a firm conclusion.

You have been asked to consider your approach to certain issues. Below is a list of approaches that students take when considering issues (adapted from Perry, 1970). For each of the issues you are asked to consider, decide which of the following positions best describes where you stand on the issue.

(1) Absolute answer

I think this is a question of right and wrong or that the right answer to this issue is obvious. I know where I stand, I know my own opinion, and I don't think an alternative answer is acceptable. Recognised authorities such as my tutor, a book, the law or a professional body will be able to tell me what the right answer is on this

(2) Temporary unacceptable uncertainty

The right answer hasn't been found yet but needs to be. Professionals, academics or other authorities need to clarify what the right answer is in order to avoid confusion.

(3) Acceptable uncertainty

Everyone has a right to their own opinion. All answers are equally acceptable. My answer is as good as anyone else's.

(4) Relativism

It's all relative. The appropriate answer depends on the context. The 'right answer' would depend upon the circumstances. Another person may think differently to me and still be right. Really, there are no right answers. One answer is as good as another: there is no real way of deciding who is right. Lecturers and authorities don't know the answers.

(5) Commitment to a considered viewpoint, taking responsibility for the decision

I understand and can appreciate other viewpoints on this issue, but I believe some answers or perspectives are better than others and that I need to make a personal decision on where I stand amongst conflicting opinions. I realise that making this choice of an answer may carry responsibilities and have implications for how I think, speak, and the choices I make.

(6) On-going development

I am committed to this viewpoint, appreciate other viewpoints and realise that my decision carries personal responsibility However, I also feel that this is something that I need to keep returning to, even if it means some uncertainty. The answer I have committed to is of great importance to who I am, to my values, and the kind of person I want to be.

Managing learning: attitudes and approaches to learning

Students' difficulties: beliefs, attitudes and habits

From a tutor's perspective, the greatest difficulty in this area is the variety of unhelpful approaches students bring with them in their attitudes to learning, their attitudes to themselves as learners, and their attachment to unhelpful habits and beliefs.

Anxiety about 'not being good enough'

Anxiety about not being good enough for university, hopelessness about achieving high marks, or pressure to keep up the marks already attained is very prevalent in the student body, and a source of great stress. Anxiety about failure is not necessarily linked to actual failure. Many students' under-performance is related to self-belief, past experience, internal negative messages, worry and stress which make it difficult to focus and learn. When that thinking cycle is broken, performance can improve.

Assuming success is the result of chance

Lack of awareness of the range of conditions that affect learning is a cause of great worry in successful students and of defeatism in weak students. If learning is seen as a product of the genes or luck in which tutor you are allocated, then there is little incentive either to examine other conditions which affect performance or to take responsibility for them.

'If it doesn't hurt, it's not doing you any good'

Some students who are referred for learning support study very long hours, but take in little that they read, and are overwhelmed by the sense of burden or boredom. They can be resistant to the idea of changing their study habits as they believe study is meant to be hard.

Using virtuous rather than effective approaches

Students can be anxious about taking short-cuts, which they regard as cheating; they expect 'punishment' will inevitably follow in the form of lower marks. A typical example is the student who reads all recommended books from cover to cover, taking extensive notes on each chapter even though the relevance is unclear. Those too concerned about 'total coverage' may neglect essential skills such as critical reflection and selection. Extra work can be counter-productive: for example, students may spend time rewriting notes for neatness, or because the first set were too detailed to use. This introduces needless layers into the study process. Such students can be helped by tutors who model effective short-cuts.

Early enthusiasm cannot be maintained

It is not unusual for early enthusiasm to wane as

study (or life generally) becomes difficult. Students may need assistance and reminders to stay connected to their motivation.

The role of affect in learning

Emotional well-being is very important to study. Students need to feel that they can succeed and that the lecturers have some faith in them. This can be difficult for lecturers to manage, in an honest way, when a student is failing badly. It helps to focus on the student's relatively strong areas, so that the student need not feel they are doing badly in an undifferentiated way.

How lecturers can help

(1) Challenging beliefs about learning

Lecturers have an important role to play in challenging students' focus away from a belief in a pre-determined view of the self as 'inadequate'. In order to do this, it can be necessary first to acknowledge how far their beliefs about intelligence and themselves as learners are currently undermining their confidence, and to look at where those beliefs and ideas arose.

(2) Maintaining motivation

Lecturers can help to maintain motivation by making a space to discuss it, by setting manageable goals and realistic challenges, and by organising work into short, clear and manageable sections. It helps if course content is made relevant to the lived realities of the students' experiences: it is difficult to maintain interest in abstract ideas when motivation is low. Concrete and relevant examples, case studies, and relating information to personal life make abstract ideas meaningful. Time-tabling careers education may also be appropriate.

(3) Constructive feedback

Constructive feedback which gives clear guidance on how one or two aspects of study can be improved is very important in reminding students that there is action they can take to improve their performance. It is important for lecturers to be able to restrain their frustration at poor English, at students not following directions, and to maintain an attitude of constructive advice. Covering the student's work with exclamation marks, irritated comments and lists of things left undone does not help – however tempting it might be.

Avoid feedback that implies that students know what to do already and are wilfully not doing it, such as 'You have not written in proper sentences!' or 'Please use paragraphs!' or 'Not enough detail!' It is unlikely students know how to respond to such comments, which leaves them feeling helpless about how to improve. Often, they will feel they have already written the correct amount of detail or done their best to organise their ideas. Refer the students explicitly to what they could add, or where they can find the instructions or information required.

For example

- 'Your line of argument is interesting and would come across even better if you improved your sentence structure and punctuation. For guidance on this, see the Learning Development web page at . . . '
- 'I would love to see the good ideas you present here organised more clearly so that they really stand out. Guidance on structuring your writing can be found in the *Study Skills Handbook.*'
- 'A line or two about the exact numbers and ages of those involved in the experiment is needed here. See the example on p. ● of . . . '.

(4) Relating to the person

Low self-esteem increases anxiety which in itself makes it more difficult to study. Although this becomes increasingly difficult as student numbers rise, students who seem doomed to failure can make remarkable come-backs if a lecturer shows interest and some faith in them. They may then hear the message that they are worth caring about, and this can encourage them to do better.

Aims of the session

- To encourage students to develop a reflective approach to their own learning;
- to provide opportunities for students to develop interactive group skills so that they feel more confident working with each other, contributing in class, and using each other as mutual support.

Learning outcomes

At the end of these activities students should be able to:

Learning outcome	Skills (see p. 193)
(1) Reflect upon their learning through group work and by using a reflective learning journal	IGS, R
(2) Build upon supportive group work started in the previous session(s)	IGS
(3) Demonstrate greater awareness of themselves as learners through an exploration of their learning histories	A, IGS, M, R
(4) Evaluate how their ideas about intelligence and their previous learning experiences may influence their beliefs about themselves as learners	E, IGS, R
(5) Reflect upon varieties of learning and the conditions which facilitate learning	E, KU, R
(6) Discuss some aspects of the CREAM approach to the learning process – and ways they could apply these to their own study	E, IGS, KU, R
(7) Organise a plan to optimise their learning, and to use this as a basis for peer support	IGS, M
(8) Explore the importance of reflection to learning and to professional practice	Emp, IGS, M, R

Tutor preparation

Approaching the session

Be prepared for a mixed response. This session can come as a relief to students who feel they have been 'written off' by teachers in the past. It can give a great deal of insight and hope to many students. On the other hand, students who have done well in the past may be resistant. They may feel that their identity as 'the naturally clever one' may be under threat, and they may worry that they will have to work twice as hard if everybody else starts to improve. If they have been used to working very hard to exceed others' achievements, the idea of having to work even harder to stay ahead may be exhausting. In reality, all students have something to gain from a focus on attitudes and approaches. All students are likely to have strategies and tips which they could be encouraged to share with others and from which others can learn

Materials

Resource Sheets (see pp. 214–24) are included at the end of this menu item. You may wish to adapt these or offer alternative reading to suit your course.

Activities

(1) Icebreaker to warm up

'What I hope to achieve through having this qualification is . . . ' (or see p. 197 for other suggestions).

(2) Ground rules

If ground rules were set in a previous session, run through these quickly and modify or extend these if appropriate. (See also Chapter 13, 'Working with Others'.)

(3) Learning histories   `A, IGS, M, R`

Individually   Ask students to think of as many answers as they can to complete one of the following statements. They can draw on experiences from school, college, work, or life in general:

- 'My best learning experiences are when . . .'
- 'I get most out of learning when . . . '
- 'I learnt how to be good at what I do by . . . '

Small groups   Pool experiences and draw up, together, a list of things that apply to either all or most of the group

Whole group   Ask for contributions. As each contribution is made, ask whether everyone

generally agrees with it. Write up the contribution under 'similarities' and 'differences'.

Whole group   Ask the group to discuss what the lists indicate about: (1) what assists learning, and (2) individual learning differences.
Encourage students to draw out the significance for their current study. How can they adapt their approach to their current study in order to play to their strengths?

(4) Intelligence and learning   `E, IGS, R`

Individually   Ask students to reflect for three minutes upon how their attitudes to intelligence and learning may have affected their learning. The Resource Sheet (see p. 214) can help to guide this activity.

Small groups of three   For the following task, give close guidance on when to change activity, when to switch over, and who should be doing what at each change.

> *Guidance*
> - Ask students to form groups of three.
> - Each member of the three should number themselves 1, 2 or 3.
> - Each person will have three minutes to speak.
> - The other two will listen without interrupting, even if they feel they need some essential information. This will develop listening skills and respect for the person speaking. Try to listen and to remember the main points about what you heard.

Task   Person 1 tells the other two about their reflections on learning. If the speaker looks really stuck, person 3 can prompt with a general question about their learning. At the end, person 2 will have up to two minutes to repeat back the main points, whilst the other two listen and check that it is generally right.

Switch over 1   person 2 speaks; person 1 prompts, and person 3 sums up.

Switch over 2 person 3 speaks; person 2 prompts, and person 1 repeats back at the end.

Reflection on the group-work Whilst it is still fresh in their minds, give students a few minutes to discuss this process. Suggest that they make brief notes in their reflective journals about:

- What is was like to speak for three minutes without interruption?
- What it was like to listen without interrupting or asking questions?
- How good were their prompts (if needed)?
- How accurately did they feed back the information to which they had listened?

Full group Ask for contributions about people's own reflections and experiences on learning. Bring out the general points that are made from specific examples. What are the lessons to be learnt about how attitude, self-esteem and environment affect learning?

(5) Developing as a reflective learner/ practitioner   **Emp, IGS, M, R**

Pairs Identify at least one thing which each person gained from reflecting about intelligence or from their group discussion

Same pairs Identify any questions or difficulties they might have about reflective work.

Whole group Ask for contributions, based on what they have been discussing, for why reflective work is important. What is to be gained from it?

Whole group Ask for contributions of remaining questions or difficulties. For each one, as it arises, ask the group to provide suggestions or answers. This encourages students towards mutual support.

Suggest that students write in their journal two or three times a week. Their entries do not need to be lengthy. Ask for suggestions about the kinds of things that could be entered and check with the group whether each is appropriate.

Answers to encourage are:

- Changes in motivation and what helps them to maintain motivation;
- Practical tips that they pick up – and why these work for them;
- What it is they are finding difficult about study and why this might be;
- Suggestions about how they could change an aspect of study (and how useful they found this after they tried it).
- Ideas that come to them about leaning more generally.
- What their anxieties are and how they deal with these.

(6) Optimising your learning   **IGS, M, R**

In groups of 4–6 The Resource Sheet (p. 214) asks students to identify three things they could do now to enhance their own learning. Give students about two minutes each to state briefly how they think each of these three things might be useful. Each of the other people in the group should write down the suggestions of each person in the group and bring them to future sessions. In future sessions, they could help each other to monitor progress. This is useful groundwork towards developing support group activity later.

(7) Creative, Reflective, Effective, Active and Motivated approaches   **E, IGS, KU, M, R**

Full group:

- **CREAM** stands for Creative, Reflective, Effective, Active and Motivated. (Suggest that acronyms can be a useful way of condensing information for learning, such as for exam revision.)
- Ask for suggestions about how work undertaken already in study skills sessions, or elsewhere on their course, has been creative, reflective, effective, active and motivated. Check that students are aware of the differences between passive and active learning.

Students should identify 'reflection' fairly easily. Working with others and doing activities in the group are forms of active learning. They may also have examples of being motivated or effective from their own approaches.

- What other ideas do they have about introducing these approaches to their study?
- Point out that there will be more about effective learning in the session on organisation skills in particular, and all the sessions in a more general way.
- Work on motivation and creativity will also be looked at in future sessions.

(8) Learning styles   A, E, M, R

There are a number of ways that learning styles work can be approached depending on the time at your disposal. These include:

- *Standardised 'statement' tests*: such as those produced by Honey & Mumford, and Dunn & Dunn, or the Myers Briggs Type Indicator used in conjunction with Lawrence (1995) in *People Types and Tiger Stripes*. These require students to grade comments or statements, which can be analysed manually or by computer. A learning 'type' is identified, along with brief, and usually fairly standardised, guidance on what this means for the individual's study.
- *An exercise-based approach:* for example, the memory exercise on p. 202 of the *Study Skills Handbook* or the VAK exercise below (p. 215).
- *Reflection-based models*: the approach taken by the *Study Skills Handbook*, which uses stimulus materials to prompt thinking on a wide range of factors that affect learning.
- *A question-based approach*: an example is offered for use below (p. 223).
- A combination of the above.

Some source materials are provided at the end of this section.

(9) Self-appraisal of course work   A, E, M, R

Self-appraisal of course work is one way of encouraging the development of individual responsibility for the learning process. It is not necessarily easy but can reap very good rewards if students are nurtured through the process and if it is linked to other reflective and self-evaluation practices. Ideally, it needs to be introduced from the beginning of the course so that students have time to develop it as a skill and regard it as part of the course culture.

The advantages to staff are that it can greatly ease the marking and feedback process. It can also help identify 'at risk' students.

The advantages for students are that the self-appraisal document can gain them marks. Tutors can offer a percentage of the overall marks for the appraisal sheet. This also helps students to focus on marking criteria and to demystify the marking process.

- Ask students to consider the benefits of learning to appraise their own work.
- Link this to student exercises in marking examples of course work
- Give examples of what good self-appraisal might look like.
- Discuss what makes good self appraisal for the coursework in question.
- Give opportunities for group feedback and discussion on how they went about self-appraisal and how to improve their approach to it.

Examples of self-appraisal sheets are offered below, pp. 237–8, 300–1, 319–20.

(10) Summing up   R, S

- On the basis of what has been covered as either advance preparation or in the session, ask for contributions from the whole group about why it is important to consider approaches and attitudes to study.
- You might like to supplement their ideas with material from the start of this section, (*Students' difficulties*, p. 208).
- Encourage students to write down in their reflective journals ideas that inspire them.

RESOURCE SHEET
Attitudes and approaches to learning

Purchase a notebook to write down your reflections and ideas for each of the topics below – or you may prefer to use a file. Bring it with you to future sessions.

(1) Recommended reading

Aim to read at least one of the following:

- Cottrell, S. (1999) *The Study Skills Handbook* (Basingstoke: Macmillan – Palgrave), Chapters 3 and 4.
- Rose, C. and Goll, L. (1992) *Accelerate Your Learning: The Action Handbook* (Aylesbury: Accelerated Learning Systems)
- Gardener, H. (1993) *Frames of Mind: The Theory of Multiple Intelligences*, 2nd edn (London: Fontana), Chapter 4.
- Entwistle, N. (1997) *Styles of Learning and Teaching: An Integrated Outline of Educational Psychology for Students, Teachers and Lecturers* (London: David Fulton Publishers), Chapter 5.

(2) Intelligence

- What ideas do you hold about intelligence? Where did these ideas come from?
- In what ways were you affected by the attitudes that teachers or parents held about intelligence and their ideas about you as a person? Did it affect your ability to learn?
- Do these beliefs motivate you to learn or discourage your learning?
- How were other people you know affected by such ideas in their life or their learning?

(3) Strategies to improve learning

Based on your reading or reflection, write in the notebook three things you could do now to enhance your learning and how you think these would be useful.

(4) Working with others

- How is your confidence in being around other students developing as the course progresses? Are there particular students you admire? If so, what are the qualities that you admire in them? Where in your own life do you demonstrate similar qualities?
- Are there any ways that you are not contributing to your study groups or seminars? What is going on for you that prevents you from taking part fully? What could you do to begin to change this pattern?

Visual, auditory and kinaesthetic learning styles

Rate each of the following statements, depending on how true you think it is of you, by drawing a ring round the number.

4: 'Yes, this is *very* true of me'   3: Yes, it is true of me,   2: Sort of true/don't know
1: Hardly ever true   0: Not true of me at all

		Score
1.	When I'm reading, I picture the scene in my head	4 3 2 1 0
2.	I have a good memory for conversation	4 3 2 1 0
3.	I will remember something better if I have seen it written down	4 3 2 1 0
4.	I remember things best if I get up and move about	4 3 2 1 0
5.	I use my hands a lot when I'm speaking	4 3 2 1 0
6.	I like to picture what I'm learning	4 3 2 1 0
7.	I remember phone numbers by the movement I make to dial to them	4 3 2 1 0
8.	I repeat things out loud or over and over in my head to remember them	4 3 2 1 0
9.	I doodle whilst I am listening	4 3 2 1 0
10.	I add up numbers out loud	4 3 2 1 0
11.	I can't add up unless I can see the numbers written down	4 3 2 1 0
12.	I'm good at remembering the words to songs	4 3 2 1 0
13.	I prefer to watch something being done before I try it myself	4 3 2 1 0
14.	I like to ask a lot of questions in class	4 3 2 1 0
15.	I find it easy to remember where I last saw something	4 3 2 1 0
16.	I write out words to see if the spelling feels right	4 3 2 1 0
17.	I have a good eye for colour	4 3 2 1 0
18.	I'm good at sport	4 3 2 1 0
19.	I'm able to learn things off by heart quite easily	4 3 2 1 0
20.	I have a good ear for music	4 3 2 1 0
21.	I'm good at practical things	4 3 2 1 0
22.	If somebody gives me a set of instructions, I can remember them quite easily	4 3 2 1 0
23.	I tend to move around a lot on my chair when working	4 3 2 1 0
24.	I tend to fiddle and play about with my hands a lot	4 3 2 1 0
25.	I prefer to have instructions written down so I can see them	4 3 2 1 0
26.	I like to learn by doing	4 3 2 1 0
27.	I visualise a spelling to see if I have got it right	4 3 2 1 0
28.	I run a film in my head of what I have to learn	4 3 2 1 0
29.	I prefer to learn through discussion	4 3 2 1 0
30.	I like to hear exactly what I have to do	4 3 2 1 0
31.	I like to 'just try it out' rather than following instructions	4 3 2 1 0
32.	I like to learn by getting up and trying it out	4 3 2 1 0

33.	I remember a phone number by the way it sounds	4 3 2 1 0
34.	I like to learn from slides and pictures	4 3 2 1 0
35.	I sing and hum a lot	4 3 2 1 0
36.	I like the tutor to use overheads and write on the board	4 3 2 1 0

Scoring

Each statement that you rated above indicates a preference for either a **visual**, **auditory** or **kinaesthetic** way of learning.

- **Visual** learners find it easier to learn if information is presented so they can see it and where they use their eyes to learn.
- **Auditory** learners learn best by hearing and using their ears.
- **Kinaesthetic** learners tend to learn best where there is a physical sensation, such as movement, touch or a feeling.

Write down your scores for each item and then add up your totals

Visual scores	Auditory scores	Kinaesthetic scores
1.	2.	4.
3.	8.	5.
6.	10.	7.
11.	12.	9.
13.	14.	16.
15.	19.	18.
17.	20.	21.
25.	22.	23.
27.	29.	24.
28.	30.	26.
34.	33.	31.
36.	35.	32.

Total

Interpreting your score

No strong preference
If your scores for all three areas are similar, then you may not have a strong sensory preference for learning. If your scores are high (40–8 for each area), then you use all of your senses well to assist your learning. If scores are low (under 0–24), you may need to use your senses more consciously to assist your learning and to experiment more with how you learn best.

A strong preference
The more marked the preference for one sense, the more you may need to ensure that you find ways of making good use of it, in order to make learning easier. Consider how you could incorporate into your study all the items listed above for that sense. Be creative. You might also like to consider whether you would gain from using the other senses more.

Learning styles, habits and preferences

The following exercises are designed to help you explore the way you study at present. A high score in one area does not necessarily mean that you are a certain 'type' of learner; it suggests that you have habits, styles or preferences which may influence the way you study.

(1) Structure

The following exercise looks at how far you prefer to work in structured or unstructured ways. Rate each pair of statements only once, depending on which is more true of you. Rating: 3 for very true; 2 for true; 1 for 'sort of true '; 0 for no preference.

Less structure		More structure
(1) I enjoy creative chaos	3 2 1 0 1 2 3	I enjoy being very organised
(2) My desk/workspace is a mess	3 2 1 0 1 2 3	My desk is always neat
(3) I like to personalise my workspace	3 2 1 0 1 2 3	I keep study surfaces very clear
(4) I remember things in my head	3 2 1 0 1 2 3	I write lots of lists
(5) I never use bookmarks	3 2 1 0 1 2 3	I always use bookmarks
(6) I leave my papers out overnight	3 2 1 0 1 2 3	I tidy my papers away at night
(7) I work whenever I find the time	3 2 1 0 1 2 3	I work to a strict routine
(8) I study what interests me that day	3 2 1 0 1 2 3	I work to a strict timetable
(9) I have a relaxed approach to time	3 2 1 0 1 2 3	I always meet deadlines
(10) I write all over my own textbooks	3 2 1 0 1 2 3	I never write on books

Score for 'less structure':   Score for 'more structure':

Total score:

Score

0–10 suggests you have no strong preferences for structured or unstructured approaches. **20–30** suggests you have very strong preferences about the way you study.

A score of 20–30 for the 'less structure' column suggests you have a strong preference for studying in your own way in your own time. This can be a very creative and independent way of working. It is worth considering whether a more organised and structured approach would help. Danger points to watch for are missing deadlines and not fulfilling the requirements for an assignment.

A score of 20–30 for the 'more structure' column suggests you have a strong preference for studying in an organised and systematic way. This can be a very productive way of working, and you are likely to be someone who gets things done. It is worth considering whether more flexibility and openness to new ideas would benefit your study. Danger points to watch for are over-rigid ways of thinking and working.

Scores of 10–20 for either column suggest moderate over-dependence on your personal preferences for study. It may be useful to experiment with features of the opposite column.

(2) External direction

The following exercise looks at how far you prefer to work with or without external direction. Rate each pair of statements only once, depending on which is more true of you.
Rating: 3 for very true; 2 for true; 1 for 'sort of true'; 0 for no preference.

Less external direction		**More external direction**
'I prefer . . .'		

(1)	lectures to be unpredictable	3 2 1 0 1 2 3	to know what to expect in lectures
(2)	a lecture just to unfold	3 2 1 0 1 2 3	an agenda at the beginning of lectures
(3)	to develop my own projects	3 2 1 0 1 2 3	to be given set assignments
(4)	to invent my own assignment titles	3 2 1 0 1 2 3	tutors to set assignment titles
(5)	to explore topics for myself	3 2 1 0 1 2 3	tutors to give clear outlines
(6)	to develop my own reading list	3 2 1 0 1 2 3	tutors to give the reading list
(7)	to do things my own way	3 2 1 0 1 2 3	to be told exactly what I have to do
(8)	to pick up how to use computer software as I go along	3 2 1 0 1 2 3	to go on a course to learn new software
(9)	to just get on with study by myself	3 2 1 0 1 2 3	the lecturer to give an early overview of the subject
(10)	to work out how to solve new problems for myself	3 2 1 0 1 2 3	clear guidance on how to approach new problems

Score for 'less direction':   **Score for 'more direction':**

Total score:

Score

0–10 suggests you have no strong preferences about external guidance
20–30 suggests you have very strong preferences about the way you study.

A score of 20–30 for the 'less external direction' column suggests you have a strong preference for taking control over how you study. This can be very useful in developing as an independent, autonomous learner, capable of taking on new projects for yourself. It is worth considering whether you need to be more open to ideas from others. Danger points to watch for are possible weaknesses in team working and not fulfilling the requirements for an assignment.

A score of 20–30 for the 'more external direction' column suggests you are very open to direction and leadership from others. This can be very useful in assuring that you are going in the right direction, for using time economically and for team working. It is worth considering whether you need to start taking more control over your own learning and being more open to exploration and risk-taking. Danger points to watch for are reliance on others to do your thinking and planning, and under-developed personal independence and leadership.

Scores of 10–20 for either column suggest moderate over-dependence on your personal preferences for study. It may be useful to experiment with features of the opposite column.

(3) Working with others

The following exercise looks at how far you prefer to work with or without other people. Rate each pair of statements only once, depending on which is more true of you.

Rating: 3 for very true; 2 for true; 1 for 'sort of true'; 0 for no preference.

Preference for working with others		Preference for working alone
(1) I prefer assignments to include group work	3 2 1 0 1 2 3	I prefer individual assignments
(2) In the library, I prefer to sit near others	3 2 1 0 1 2 3	In the library, I prefer to sit on my own
(3) I like to go through lecture notes with a friend	3 2 1 0 1 2 3	I prefer to do my own notes
(4) I value hearing other people's ideas	3 2 1 0 1 2 3	I prefer to develop my own ideas
(5) I enjoy the interaction in group work	3 2 1 0 1 2 3	I enjoy thinking through an idea in quiet
(6) I learn more through discussion than reading	3 2 1 0 1 2 3	I learn more from reading than discussion
(7) Groups come up with more ideas	3 2 1 0 1 2 3	I come up with more ideas on my own
(8) For me, team working is really useful	3 2 1 0 1 2 3	For me, team work is a waste of time
(9) I like to discuss assignments with others	3 2 1 0 1 2 3	I prefer working alone on assignments

Score for 'working with others':   **Score for 'working alone':**

Total score:

Score

0–10 suggests you have no strong preferences about working with others.
20–30 suggests you have very strong preferences about the way you study.

A score of 20–30 for the 'working with others' column suggests a strong social preference when studying. This can be very useful for gaining a wide set of perspectives and ideas, for developing social skills, for team working and for developing mutual support. It is worth considering how far you would benefit from more time studying independently. Danger points are possible over-reliance on others and not developing your own ideas in an independent way.

A score of 20–30 for the 'working alone' column suggests a strong preference for solitary working. This can be useful in avoiding distractions, in achieving goals and developing independence. It is worth considering in more depth what can be gained from working with others, the benefits of collective thinking and the skills that emerge from reconciling different sets of opinions and personalities. You may lose out by not gaining access to a wide set of perspectives, especially in real life or 'applied' settings. Danger points may be failure to appreciate the work of others and underdeveloped interpersonal skills.

Scores of 10–20 for either column suggest moderate over-dependence on your personal preferences for study. It may be useful to experiment with features of the opposite column.

(4) Physical factors

The following exercise looks at how far physical factors may affect the way you work. Rate each pair of statements only once, depending on which is more true of you.
Rating: 3 for very true; 2 for true; 1 for 'sort of true'; 0 for no preference.

High stimulus		Low stimulus
(1) I need to work in a very bright room	3 2 1 0 1 2 3	I need to work in a very dim light
(2) I need music or TV in the background	3 2 1 0 1 2 3	I need absolute quiet to work
(3) I could work through an earthquake	3 2 1 0 1 2 3	My attention is very easily distracted
(4) I always eat when I am studying	3 2 1 0 1 2 3	I can't think about food when I am studying
(5) I need to drink a lot when studying	3 2 1 0 1 2 3	I never drink while studying
(6) I work best when it is either very hot or cold	3 2 1 0 1 2 3	I prefer a moderate room temperature
(7) I tend to move about or fiddle with things	3 2 1 0 1 2 3	I am quite still when I settle down to work
(8) It helps me to think if I walk about	3 2 1 0 1 2 3	I can't think if I am moving
(9) Doodling helps me to listen in lectures	3 2 1 0 1 2 3	I focus on listening and making notes in lectures
(10) I prefer to work on several things at once	3 2 1 0 1 2 3	I need to finish one thing before starting another

Score for 'high stimulus':   Score for 'low stimulus':

Total score:

Score

0–10 suggests you have a high tolerance for working in most conditions.
Scores of 0–1 for any item suggests that you have a reasonable tolerance for working without that stimulus being present.
Scores of 2 for any item suggest that your study might be affected if that stimulus is not present.
Scores of 3 for any item suggests your study might be seriously affected if that stimulus is not present. You may need to think creatively about how you can make it possible to provide that stimulus for most study contexts (for example, if you are light sensitive, by using bright lamps, or wearing hats or sunglasses to dim light).
A score of 20–30 for either column suggests a very strong overall preference for working with or without stimulus. If these stimuli were not present when you were learning as a child, it may have made it harder for you to learn then. High scores may also be indicative of a high level of stress. It may be helpful to speak to a counsellor or adviser about this.

Experiment

It is worth experimenting with different kinds of stimuli present or absent. Monitor how far these do affect your study. For example, many people have been surprised at how far they follow a pattern set down when at school as if it were the only 'right' way to study when alone. You may find that you learn more easily if you find the stimulus combination that suits you best.

(5) Global or serialist

The following exercise looks at how far your learning responds to 'global or 'serialist' approaches. Sometimes these are equated with 'right-brain' and 'left-brain' thinking. Rate each pair of statements only once, depending on which is more true of you.
Rating: 3 for very true; 2 for true; 1 for 'sort of true'; 0 for no preference.

Which of the statements in each pair is more true of you? How does this affect the way you study?

Global styles		Serialist styles
'When studying, I prefer to . . .'		
(1) start off by gaining a broad overview	3 2 1 0 1 2 3	start off from interesting details
(2) see the whole subject mapped out in a diagram	3 2 1 0 1 2 3	see the logical sequence
(3) see things explained through image	3 2 1 0 1 2 3	have things laid out in a list
(4) use mind maps or 'picture' notes	3 2 1 0 1 2 3	use headings and bullet points
(5). jump in at the deep end	3 2 1 0 1 2 3	plan things out carefully first
(6) use my intuition	3 2 1 0 1 2 3	adhere strictly to the facts
(7) use my imagination	3 2 1 0 1 2 3	reason things out
(8) look for connections between things	3 2 1 0 1 2 3	classify and categorise information
(9) look for similarities	3 2 1 0 1 2 3	look for differences
(10) draw things together	3 2 1 0 1 2 3	analyse the detail

Score for 'global styles':   **Score for 'serialist styles':**

Total score:

Score

0–10 suggests you have no strong preferences for global or serialist learning styles.
20–30 suggests you have very strong preferences about the way you study.

A score of 20-30 for the 'global style' column suggests you have a strong preference for taking a holistic approach to study. This can be very useful for synthesising information and making creative links. It is worth considering whether you need to bring more order and system to your study. Watch for possible weaknesses with clarity, detail, order and sequence.

A score of 20–30 for the 'serialist style' column suggests you take a logical, analytical approach to study. This can be very useful in ensuring clarity and structure in your work. It is worth considering whether you need to create opportunities for developing your imagination and intuition. It may help to experiment with searching out links and connections between ideas. Possible weaknesses may be in drawing together your ideas into a strong whole and in making connections between what you are studying and the bigger picture.

Scores of 10–20 for either column suggest moderate strengths for that style of working. It may be useful to experiment with features of the opposite column.

(6) Method

(1) When you have something completely new to learn, how do you set about learning it?

Tick all the boxes that are true of you.

☐ listening	☐ reading
☐ personalising the material	☐ asking questions
☐ watching others	☐ adapting the task to suit yourself
☐ picturing it in your head	☐ writing it out
☐ writing about it	☐ making a chart
☐ turning it into a picture	☐ colour-coding it
☐ turning it into headings	☐ talking it through with others
☐ categorising and labelling it	☐ linking it to what you know already
☐ day-dreaming about it	☐ describing or explaining it to others
☐ talking it onto tape	☐ thinking about it whilst you do housework

(2) Are there other methods you could use that you are not using currently?

(7) Honey and Mumford learning styles

Honey and Mumford (1982) developed a questionnaire which divided people into four main types. A broad outline of their learning types is given below. Which of the following are generally true of you (there may be more than one)? Which is the most true?

(1) **'Activist' learning style**: I prefer to work in intuitive, flexible and spontaneous ways, generating ideas and trying out new things. I usually have a lot to say and contribute. I like to learn from experience, such as through problem-solving, group work, workshops, discussion, or team work.

(2) **'Reflector' learning style**: I like to watch and reflect, gathering data and taking time to consider all options before making a decision. Lectures, project work and working alone suit me.

(3) **'Theorist' learning style**: I like to learn by going through things thoroughly and logically, step by step, with clear guidelines, and to feel I have learnt solidly before I have to apply what I know. I prefer to learn from books, problem-solving and discussion.

(4) **'Pragmatist' learning style**: I like to learn by 'trying things out' to see if they work, just getting on with it, getting to the point. I like to be practical and realistic. I prefer to learn on work-based projects and practical applications.

■ Do you think you might benefit from choosing certain types of study module or programme in order to ensure the teaching and assessment match your preferred learning type?
■ Could you organise your study to suit your learning type?
■ Do you think it is helpful to see yourself as a 'type of learner'?

Reflections on your learning SHAPE

SHAPE stands for: **S**tyle, **H**abits, **A**ttitudes, **P**references and **E**xperience.

There is no general agreement on what is a style, what a habit, what a preference. However, there is growing acceptance that we each learn in different ways and that awareness of one's own learning can make a significant difference to how one learns. By going through the learning styles questionnaires, you should have a much clearer picture of yourself as a learner.

(1) Style?

Some people believe that learning styles are like personality traits – that they are part of you and that you cannot really change them. If that is the case, you have to adapt your learning to fit your own style.

■ Which of the approaches that you identified on the 'Learning styles, habits and prefer-ences' questionnaire (see p. 217) and the 'Visual, auditory, kinaesthetic learning styles' questionnaire (see p. 215) do you feel are really unchangeable?
■ If you had ten words to describe your own learning style, how would you describe it?
■ How could you change the way you study in order to ensure that you make the best use of your own learning style and study preferences?

(2) Habit?

How much do you think the style or preferences you identified could be the result of past habits? Are you over-attached to habits and patterns of study behaviour that do not really help you as an adult learner? If so, what would happen if you changed those habits? What opportunities would open up for developing your learning? What risks might there be?

(3) Attitude?

How far do you think your learning is affected by the attitudes and beliefs that you bring to your own learning? For example:

■ What are your beliefs about why you do or do not learn?
■ What are your beliefs about what makes a good student?
■ Do you believe you can study very successfully?
■ Do you ever under-perform because you are worried about being successful?

(4) Preferences?

How far do you think that your study characteristics are the result of personal preferences? Would you be able to change these preferences if you wanted to?

(5) Experience?

Could your current learning preferences be the result of your previous learning experi-ences? For example, were there particular experiences at school which have influenced the approach you take to study now?

Summary

- ■ What have you discovered about yourself as a learner?
- ■ What are the key factors that assist your learning?
- ■ Does the way you study really work for you? Could you make more use of your own styles and preferences to make study easier?

Further reading
Introductory reading

- ■ Beaver, D. (1994/1998), *NLP for Lazy Learning* (Shaftesbury, Dorset and Boston, Mass.: Element).
- ■ Cottrell, Stella (1999), *The Study Skills Handbook* (Basingstoke: Macmillan – now Palgrave).

More advanced reading

- ■ Dunn, R., Griggs, S., Olson, J., Beasley, M. and Gorman, B. (1995), 'A Meta-analytic Validation of the Dunn and Dunn Model of Learning Style Preference', *Journal of Educational Research*, **88** (6), 353–62.
- ■ Honey, P. and Mumford, A. (1982/1992), *The Manual of Learning Styles Questionnaire* (Maidenhead, Berks.: Peter Honey Publications).
- ■ Lawrence, G. (1995), *People Types and Tiger Stripes*, 3rd edn (Gainesville, Fla: Center for Applications of Psychological Type).

12 Managing learning: identifying skills and learning priorities

Students' difficulties in evaluating skills

Students may not be able to see the relevance of reflection and monitoring to their overall progress

Students may argue that they 'can't see the point' of self-evaluation or study skills. In some cases, this may be because students are used to content-based courses, where rote learning and regurgitation led to success. Although these students may have good grades, they do not necessarily have a good grasp of how to learn more generally. Such students can be very threatened by methods which seem to disrupt a routine that has worked for them. Entrenched habits are hard to break. Others may be worried that they do not have enough skills. Tutors should emphasise that reflection on skills and drawing up profiles are strategies for moving forwards, rather than an exercise in past recrimination.

Students may not be aware that skills can be broken into sub-skills

For such students, it can be a great relief to realise that skills have component parts, and that these can sometimes be addressed separately. Similarly, students may not realise that

an apparent weakness in a skill may be the result of a missed step or an over-looked aspect which has a knock-on effect on overall performance. It can be useful to point out that weaknesses in one skill may actually originate in a weakness in a completely different skill. Weak essay writing, for example, may be the result of under-developed organisational, thinking or research skills, rather than a writing difficulty per se.

Students are not used to thinking positively about themselves

Students may feel they are being arrogant or bigheaded if they say that they are good at something. It can help to set the exercises and reflection in the context of self-improvement and priority setting. By gaining a better picture of relative strengths and weaknesses, time can be spent more appropriately on areas that really need attention

Students don't know what criteria to use to make self-evaluations

Self-evaluation exercises are only a rough rule of thumb. Students often have no idea of their strengths and weaknesses, because they have never been taught to develop criteria to evaluate them.

Students over-evaluate or under-evaluate themselves, depending on what they think the purpose of the exercise is and who they think will see it

It is important to be clear to students what the exercise is for, and who will get to see it. This is particularly important with respect to reflective journals. If these are to be collected in, students should be told from the beginning of the course, so that personal information which they wish to keep private is not entered by mistake.

They may not 'see the point'

Self-evaluation work is one step in moving towards better management of learning. This is especially true when skills 'profiling' is set in isolation from skills development. For students to gain real value from skills profiling and diagnosis of needs, such work must be linked to constructive support. If the support cannot be offered, the student may feel they have wasted their time. Students who have succeeded at 'A' level may not see the point in study skills at a new level. The benefits may need to be clarified.

How lecturers can help

(1) Higher purpose

Make links between study skills, professional development and employer requirements, (or the requirements of advance degrees). Make it clear that skills development is integral to their time at university. Encourage them to keep a record of their skills development and a 'portfolio' of their achievements.

(2) Course design

Where possible, build a wide range of study experiences and learning styles into the course design. For example, vary the styles and audiences for student writing; include opportunities for project work, group work, peer evaluation, peer support, oral presentations, and work in business or the community. This enables students to acquire a breadth of skills 'painlessly'.

(3) Work to the students' strengths

Use students' prior experiences to draw out a range of skills. Mature students offer a deep pool of resources in this respect, as do other 'non-traditional' students.

(4) Give guidance on criteria and sub-skills

Analyse key skills in terms of their component parts. This enables students to identify sub-skills which they possess and those they still need to develop. Encourage those who believe they have 'no skills' to identify sub-skills, in order to build their confidence. It is also worth investigating whether students are comparing themselves unrealistically to an image of a 'super-skilled' person. Remind them that they are not expected to be outstanding or at a professional standard yet. For those who feel that they do not need study skills, some prompting may be needed to find areas for improvement: it is unlikely that they will be perfect already in every area.

(5) Support structure

Ensure there is adequate support for those who identify areas of need. In particular, avoid skills 'contracts' unless support is in place.

Aims of the session

- ■ To further develop students' confidence and skill in working with others;
- ■ to build skills of self-evaluation and reflection;
- ■ to enable students to recognise that learning is something over which they can exercise control: it can be managed;
- ■ to help students to identify skills they already possess and those they still need to develop, in order to advance their learning.

Learning outcomes

By the end of these activities students should be able to:

Learning outcomes	Skills (see p. 193)
(1) Participate with confidence and skill in a range of group sizes	IGS, OC
(2) Reflect in more depth upon their learning	IGS, M, OC, R
(3) Describe what is meant by a transferable skill and identify qualities they bring with them to university	A, E, Emp, IGS, KU, M, R
(4) Identify areas of strength in their current study skills as well as areas to be improved	A, E, M, R
(5) Identify subject specific skills	KU
(6) Write a Position Paper on their learning	Emp, S, WC
(7) Set priorities and draw up an Action Plan for developing their study skills and improving their learning	Emp, IGS, M, P, R

Tutor preparation

Approaching the session

(1) Emphasise a developmental approach

Encourage students to think in terms of *priorities* for improvement, drawing attention to professional and academic development over time. Ensure that you gain a sense of group priorities so you have an idea of where more time may need to be spent in later sessions.

(2) Encourage students to use skills materials

If students have been given skills materials, encourage them to make frequent use of these –

and refer to them yourself as you go through sessions.

(3) Identify 'at risk' students

Set a diagnostic assignment as early as possible. Some departments do this prior to term beginning; others in induction week or within the first few weeks.

Materials

- Resource Sheets are provided below (see pp. 231–9).
- Create a checklist of subject-specific skills (for **Activity 6**).

Activities

(1) Icebreaker

'What most inspires me is . . .' or 'The thing I am best at is . . .'.

(2) What is a skill?   `IGS, KU`

- *Individually*   Ask students to jot down what they think a 'skill' is.

- *Threes*   Ask students to form groups of three to share their ideas on what they think is a skill. What are the differences, if any, between knowledge, experience, good performance, and skill?

- *Whole group*   Open up the floor to discussion, making sure they grasp that a skill requires the ability to perform well at will and on more than one occasion.

(3) Developing skills of reflection   `IGS, M, OC`

Check that everybody has started their reflective journal. If not, emphasise that this is an important part of self evaluation and will be referred to in many sessions.

- *Individually*   Ask students to check through their reflective journal entries and jot down a few ideas about how they are using it, what kinds of entries they are making and anything they could do to improve their use of it.

- *Threes*   Give each person 2 or 3 minutes to speak. Each takes a turn at time-keeping for the person speaking. Each speaker mentions briefly how they are using the journal currently and ideas about they could their improve use of it.

- *Appreciations*   After each person has spoken, the others say one positive thing either about what was said or about some aspect of behaviour of that person in that group (such as their openness about their difficulties, or their honesty about not having started the journal, or their enthusiasm for the task, or how well

they listened). Each person should note down the feedback they received into their journal.

- *Whole group*   Brainstorm ideas about how people have made use of the journal. Encourage students to note down ideas for their own use.

(4) Transferable skills   `A, E, Emp, IGS, KU, R`

- *Individually*   Ask students to jot down how one area of expertise provides them with skills which can be applied to study. If they completed this reflection activity for advance preparation, ask them to draw on their notes.

- *Whole group*   Ask each person to make one contribution of how skills acquired in non-academic settings may be helpful to their study.

- *Individually*   Ask students now to note down in their journal, briefly, any further skills they appreciate about themselves having heard other people's contributions.

- Draw attention to the way that academic skills are also transferable to employment and that this is something they might like to keep a record of for later sessions.

- *Whole group*   You might like to take this opportunity to introduce the idea of keeping a portfolio of their achievements, skills, CV, etc. Ask what they consider to be the advantages of keeping and developing a portfolio as they go through the course.

These reflections can also be used as background for writing a Position Paper as a diagnostic exercise (see activity 7 below).

(5) Study skills priorities   `E, IGS, M, P`

If students have been asked to undertake a skills profile as advance preparation, ask them to refer to this now. Otherwise, give time for students to complete these now.

In groups of three   Using the Priority Organisers, take turns to identify:

- two areas of relative strength at present in your study skills
- two priorities for study skills development in the immediate future.

(6) Subject-specific skills checklist KU

- Discuss your list of subject-specific skills with the students.
- Identify how the areas on your list will be taught.
- Indicate the dates by which students will be expected to have covered or assimilated these areas;
- Indicate stages in development. What differences will be expected of them for the first assignment, the rest of the year, future years?
- Indicate how these skills will be assessed if they are to be assessed directly, or else how they will affect other assessments. If there is no perceived link to assessment, students are less likely to take them seriously.
- What should students do if they have difficulties in acquiring these skills? Who should they approach for support in the department, and when?

This discussion can be used as background work for writing a Position Paper as a diagnostic exercise (see below, pp. 235–6).

(7) SWOT analysis on subject readiness   R, P, M

Explain that a SWOT analysis is a tool that can be applied to many situations. In effect it is a ready-made, easy-to-remember outline for considering a new plan of action or exploring one's own reactions to a new situation. **SWOT** stands for Strengths, Weaknesses, Opportunities, Threats. Draw up a SWOT chart for students to copy or give copies of the Resource Sheet on p. 234 below. Ask students to:

- Give a page in their learning journals the title: 'My readiness to be a student in: [your subject]'.
- Draw a large cross that divides the page into

four equal sections. The box at the top of the page is for 'Strengths', the second is for 'Weaknesses'. The lower boxes are for 'Opportunities' and 'Threats'.

- Ask students to brainstorm as many examples of strengths and weaknesses as they can under each heading. Suggest that they include a consideration of their general readiness to be a university student as well as their awareness of the needs of the subject area.
- Consider what opportunities they feel may arise from studying the degree subject(s) they have chosen?
- Consider what they find threatening about their new course of study? What are their worries?

- *Whole group*   Take answers for each section and write them up.
- Use this as the basis for discussing both the students' attitudes to the subject area and to check whether they have a good grasp of what is expected from them.

If the students are going to be asked to produce an Action Plan or a piece of diagnostic writing, this exercise can be used to build towards these.

(8) Action Plan and Position Paper   E, IGS, M, P, R, S, WC

It is useful to ask students to draw together an interim Position Paper on what they have learnt through their early experiences at university and on the course. Encourage them to make use of their past life experiences and to think forward beyond the course, in order to give context to their current skills work. Chapters 2–4 of the *Study Skills Handbook* (Cottrell, 1999) have been designed to help students to develop their thinking about the past influences on their learning and to analyse their current skills. It may help with these activities.

Diagnostic or formative assessment
The following activities can also be usefully incorporated into diagnostic assessment. One method of identifying needs is to include students in the process so that it feels less of a test

and more of a developmental process. The use of self-evaluation questionnaires, self-reflection exercises as well as reading and discussion help to bring students to a point where they can begin to write about themselves as learners.

Both the Action Plan and the Position Paper should be collected in. These give tutors a perspective on priorities for the group, enable them to see whether individuals have realistic plans for developing their skills, and help to identify who might be in need of additional support. See Chapter 4 for further details on identifying needs.

(a) Action Plan

Ask students to draw up a brief Action Plan under the following headings (no more than 150 words for each).

- Self-assessment: summary of my current strength, skills and qualities. What do I need to develop further?
- Formulating desired outcomes: where do I want to be? What do I want to achieve?
- Prioritising: what I am going to do, when and how? What is the first step?
- Evaluation: how I will know that I have improved? What changes would I expect to

see in myself, my work, or in the attitudes of others.

(b) Writing: personal statement or position paper

My learning: past, present and future
Ask students to use the material they have covered in sessions so far, and especially the Action Plan, to produce a piece of writing of about 1000 words or about 2–3 pages. Encourage them to regard this as a constructive step towards clarifying their ideas and making a commitment to working positively on their learning and skills development. This can be the basis of a more formal assessment at the end of the course (session 16) or used in later career planning activities. An outline for the assignment is given as a Resource Sheet below (see pp. 235–6).

If this is used for assessment purposes, a marking criteria sheet will need to be given to the student. A suggested list is given below (see p. 239). A student self-appraisal sheet is also included adapted from a version developed by staff and students in the Fashion, Design and Marketing Department at the University of East London.

RESOURCE SHEET
Identifying skills and learning priorities

It will help you in the next session if you put some time aside for advance preparation. Aim to do at least one of the following activities. If you do them all, you will get the most out of the next session.

(1) Recommended reading

Aim to read at least one of the following:

■ Cottrell, Stella (1999), *The Study Skills Handbook* (Basingstoke: Macmillan – now Palgrave), Chapter 2.

■ Boud, D., Keogh, R. and Walker, D. (1985) *Reflection: Turning Experience into Learning* (London: Kogan Page).

(2) Self-evaluation

■ Complete the priority organisers.

(3) Appreciating your current skills

■ Make a list of the skills you have developed in the different roles you occupy in life. Consider how 5 of these skills could be helpful in some way to academic study. For example, keeping minutes for a meeting might help with note-making skills, or taking children to school with keeping to deadlines. Use five examples of your own.

■ How do you go about assessing how good you are at doing something? Do you think you are too easy or too hard on yourself?

(4) Reflection

In your reflective journal, note down:

■ What has inspired you in life? This could be a person, a book, music, or other things. What was it about this that inspired you?

■ What, if anything, inspired you to come on this course or to return to study?

■ Your ideas about what we mean by a 'skill' and how skills could be developed.

■ How your self-knowledge about your own skills has changed since being at university and from your reading.

Study Skills Priority Organiser: Stage 1

Column A   tick if the statement is generally true of you.
Column B   rate how important it is to acquire this skill (*6 = unimportant; 10 = essential*)
Column C   rate how good you are at this skill now (*1 = very weak; 5 = excellent*)
Column D   subtract the score in column C from column B (B – C). The highest scores in column D are the most likely to be priorities. Then turn to the next page.

Later in the term do this exercise again and compare your ratings.

Study skills statements	A This is true *(tick)*	B Skill needed? *scale 6–10*	C Current ability *scale 1–5*	D (B – C) **Priority**
I am aware of what I need to do to learn best, and how to reflect upon and evaluate my own work				
I am well-motivated and know how to set myself manageable goals				
I have good time and space management skills and am able to organise my workload				
I have strategies for getting started with a new task or assignment				
I am confident of my research skills				
I am aware of which strategies suit me best for reading under different conditions				
Note-making: I am able to make, organise, store, find and use my notes effectively				
I am able to use lecture time effectively and get the best out of lectures				
I know how to prepare for, and deliver, oral presentations				
I know how to make the most of group-work and seminars				
I am able to manage a range of writing tasks appropriately				
I know how to use IT to help academic study				
I am able to think critically and analytically and evaluate my own and other people's arguments				
I have good memory strategies				
I have good revision strategies and exam techniques				
Other priorities				

From: Stella Cottrell (1999), *The Study Skills Handbook* (Basingstoke: Macmillan – now Palgrave).

Study Skills Priority Organiser: Stage 2

Column A   Using the scoring from Stage 1 as a guide, decide whether each item *really* is a priority, or whether it could wait, or who else could do it or any other options you have.

Column B   Number the order in which you are going to tackle each priority. Highlight in yellow the one you are going to do next. Highlight it in red once you have worked on it.

Study skills statements	A **Priority for action?** (*tick*) **Or: Can wait? Other options?**	B
I am going to find out how I learn best, and how to reflect upon/evaluate my work		
I am going to be better motivated and learn to set myself manageable goals		
I am going to improve my organisational and time-management skills		
I going to develop strategies for getting started on a new task or assignment		
I am going to improve my research skills		
I am going to develop my reading skills		
I going to improve my note-making and organise and use my notes effectively		
I am going to use lecture time effectively to get the best out of lectures		
I am going to improve my oral presentations		
I am going to make the most of working with others (group-work, seminars, etc.)		
I am going to develop my writing skills		
I am going to make more use of IT to help my academic study		
I am going to develop my critical and analytical thinking skills		
I am going to improve my memory strategies		
I am going to develop good revision strategies and exam techniques		
Other priorities		

From: Stella Cottrell (1999), *The Study Skills Handbook* (Basingstoke: Macmillan – now Palgrave).

SWOT analysis

My readiness to be a student in this subject at university

Strengths	Weaknesses
Opportunities	Threats

Writing a Position Paper

A Position Paper is simply a 'snap-shot' of where you are now. Writing this Position Paper offers you an opportunity to draw together work undertaken during the induction period, such as your self-evaluations, reflections, priority setting and action plan. A summary of what to include and how to organise information is offered below. Use these to guide you but do not feel you have to include every point. Do not use headings in your final version. Ideally, you should include references to texts you have read in order to support your reasoning.

My learning: past, present and future

(1) Orientation

Aspirations and motivation: where am I going in the future?

- What are your aims and aspirations for your future? Where would you like to see your-self in five years time? (Be imaginative and bold.)
- In what ways do you think this course of study will help you to achieve those aims?
- What are the skills and attributes you wish to develop whilst at university?

(2) Review

What do I bring to the course from my past?

- What has led you to the present stage in your study or career?
- What has inspired you? (Give references where possible.)
- How has your past learning and life experience equipped you for this course and for being a student now? Evaluate the knowledge, qualifications, skills, attitudes and experiences that you bring with you and which are relevant to your study.

(3) Appraisal

Evaluation of knowledge and skills: where am I now?

- What skills and abilities will be required of you as a student on this course?
- What are your main strengths and weaknesses as a student on this course?
- What will you need to improve in order to succeed?

(4) Planning

Achieving success: how will I achieve my aims?

- How do you plan to achieve your ambitions and study aims? What are you going to do, when and how?
- What difficulties do you feel you may face?
- In what ways might you sabotage your own success? What steps will you take to prevent yourself or others from sabotaging your success?
- How will you keep yourself motivated?
- What other preparation do you need to undertake?

(5) Evaluating progress

- What changes do you expect to see in yourself, your work, and in the attitudes of others when you have achieved your aims?
- How will you be able to demonstrate to others what you have achieved?

(6) Extrapolation

- What have you learned about yourself or your learning already, that was unexpected?
- How might this help you with your studies or more generally in life or at work?

(7) References

Include references to books, films, music, or other sources that have inspired you on your journey to where you are today. Include references to all materials you have used in writing this paper.

Sample introduction

In this Position Paper, I demonstrate how my past experiences and future objectives are influencing my current study on a degree course in media technology. The paper is based on an in-depth consideration of my previous life and learning experiences, and shows the ways in which prior learning has provided me with skills, knowledge and personal qualities which are relevant to my present studies. In particular, I draw attention to the range of skills and insights I acquired through working as a volunteer last summer and how these, unexpectedly, have provided me with starting points for my design work on the degree. My main aim is to use this qualification to advance my professional career. This statement of my present position outlines both the areas where I feel I need to investigate more in order to improve my career prospects, my considerations about the module choices I think I should take, and the skills I need to focus on in the next year in order to improve my marks. I also demonstrate how I think the programme I am on and the decisions I am making will help me to achieve my goals.

Student self-evaluation of assignment

Name: Date

Course/Unit:

Assignment title:

Work completed on time?   Yes/No

Sections missing?   Yes/No

If Yes, please state what is missing:

Do you feel you understood what was required of you for this assignment?   Yes/No
What do you think you were expected to do to get good marks for this assignment?

Did you have any difficulties completing the research or preparing and planning for this
assignment?   Yes/No
If so, please give details. What could you have done differently that might have helped?

Did you attend all taught sessions and make full use of the resources you were given?   Yes/No
If not, what could you have done to improve your performance?

How much private study (i.e. study outside of taught sessions) did you do for this assignment? Was this sufficient? Comment on how useful your private study was.

Would you have liked more help or input in order to help you with this assignment? If so, please give details.

Do you have any difficulties in writing assignments for which you need help? Give details.

If you wish, please make any other comments about how you feel you could improve your performance for this or other written assignments.

Please complete the marking criteria sheet. The tutor will use the same criteria to mark your work. You will receive a mark (out of 5) for this evaluation sheet.

Student signature: Date:

Tutor: Date:

Tutor comment and mark for this evaluation

Marking criteria

		Marks given	
		weak ◄————► excellent	
KU	Shows evidence of wide background reading or research relevant to the assignment title	0 1 2 3	4 5 6 7 8 9 10
KU	Shows understanding of the concepts of the course relevant to this assignment title	0 1 2 3	4 5 6 7 8 9 10
A	Employs good critical analysis of material covered in taught sessions and through reading	0 1 2 3	4 5 6 7 8 9 10
I	There is an appropriate selection of material, relevant to the assignment title	0 1 2	3 4 5
I	It is accurately referenced throughout and includes a full list of references	0 1 2	3 4 5
IGS	Shows evidence of having made use of peer support and discussion	0 1 2	3 4 5
R	Shows evidence of constructive personal reflection	0 1 2	3 4 5
E	Constructive use is made of the Self-Evaluation sheet	0 1 2	3 4 5
C	Shows imagination and creativity in combining examples, personal experience, taught material and research	0 1 2 3	4 5 6 7 8 9 10
M	Evidence of good planning and management of learning	0 1 2	3 4 5
M	Ideas and concepts are well organised and structured	0 1 2	3 4 5
WC	There is a strong and identifiable line of reasoning	0 1 2	3 4 5
WC	Writing is well presented, with accurate spelling, grammar, punctuation and paragraphing	0 1 2	3 4 5
WC	There is a clear, flowing, easy-to-read writing style	0 1 2	3 4 5
S	Draws materials together well, towards a good conclusion	0 1 2	3 4 5
Emp	Shows awareness of the relevance of skills development to future study and employment	0 1 2	3 4 5

Marks to the right of the line are of an acceptable level. Pass mark: 40.

Overall mark:

Comments:

13 Working with others

Students' difficulties in working with others

Group work is extremely rewarding when it works well, and can make the lecturer's life much easier. However, it can also be experienced as threatening and exposing and may leave students feeling very vulnerable if it is not managed well. In a student consultation exercise undertaken to examine the reasons for poor retention on a particular course at the University of East London, students attributed the high drop-out to 'whole groups' just leaving because they were so unhappy with the way the group work had been arranged. It is important to ensure that students are given adequate training and support so that they can experience the benefits of group work.

Fear of strangers
Students are understandably anxious about other group members at the beginning of the course, and uncertain about how difficulties and vulnerabilities will be received. They may fear being mocked, considered stupid, or generally excluded, and therefore build walls to protect themselves. Higher education does not usually feel like a safe place to admit to anything which may be perceived as a weakness. Large classes and lack of interactive study can add to

the difficulty: students may know very little about the people with whom they are expected to work.

Fear of being left out
Some students bring long histories of being the last to be chosen by peers for group work. Extremely vulnerable feelings can be aroused if students are left to form their own groups.

'Nothing to offer'
Some students are frightened that they will let the group down or have nothing to offer. Activities which look at skills involved in everyday roles help to break down this attitude, as does positive feedback about what each person contributes.

Assessment anxiety: 'Others will hold me back'
This is very common amongst those who have succeeded very well academically, especially through lone study, and who fear that group work will mean either that their work will suffer or else that they will be left to carry the group.

Lack of experience
The above attitudes tend to go hand in hand with little experience of structured group work and the skills and techniques involved.

How lecturers can help

(1) Build up a supportive group atmosphere

Bonding activities and discussion of the group dynamics can sometimes be viewed as a waste of 'real teaching' time. However, it is useful for settling in first-year students, and for any class which sets assessed group work for students who have not worked together before.

(2) Develop group skills before setting formally assessed group work

Through a mixture of paired work, threes, small groups and whole group activities, build up group work skills before requiring students to form longer term groups. When students cling to the same small group or move extremely reluctantly when asked to form a group, this ground work is essential.

(3) Break down the sense of being amongst strangers

Use ice-breaker activities so that students develop a broader sense of the people they are working with. In the early days, build in activities which require people to change between working with the people they know best and those they know least. If you indicate that the activity will be brief, it will be less threatening. It builds students' confidence in talking to and

Aims of the session

■ To train students in effective group work, which they can apply to different contexts;
■ to enable students to build up their confidence in speaking in front of others;
■ to build the foundations for effective mutual support groups.

Learning outcomes

By the end of these activities students should be able to:

Learning outcomes	Skills (see p. 193)
(1) Co-operate with others in order to generate ideas	C, Emp, IGS, OC
(2) Recognise the importance of clarity and accuracy when speaking to others	Emp, IGS, OC, R
(3) Recognise the importance of close listening skills and employ strategies to improve their own listening	Emp, IGS, OC, R
(4) Identify what makes groups work well together	Emp, IGS, OC, R, S
(5) Offer constructive criticism to others	Emp, IGS, OC, S
(6) Complete an audit of skills and tools they have acquired for working with others	A, E, Emp, IGS, R, S
(7) Reflect upon their own behaviours in group situations and take action to improve their performance	Emp, IGS, R

working with people they don't know very well, and reduces the chances of some people being left out when support or project groups form later.

(4) Pro-active group division

For early group work, use strategies which necessarily move students into new groups quite frequently. For example, allocate a letter, e.g. A, B, C, D, E, and group all those of the same letter together. Alternatively, group them by the month they were born, star-signs, learning style, etc. Once they are used to working with strangers, they may start to move into groups more naturally. This also serves to break up 'problem groups' and cliques. Giving opportunities for students to keep logs of how the group progressed can help in allocating marks for group work. Students can also be invited to contribute to the marking process. It is important that group process (how the group worked together) rather than merely the end-product (the assignment) is assessed.

(5) Assessment criteria

Draw out the skills which will be assessed for group work, such as critical analysis of how well the group worked together, evaluation of their own performance, or the ability to give constructive feedback. If the skills are assessed, they are taken more seriously. Avoid setting group projects where only the end product is assessed or where students can have undue influence over each others' degree grade.

Tutor preparation

Approaching the session

There are many ways of approaching group work, and much depends on the type of group you recruit. What works for one group will not necessarily work with another, although there are 8 basic steps that can be taken to ensure maximum success with students:

(1) name reinforcement;
(2) icebreaking;

(3) addressing anxieties;
(4) addressing how anxieties can be perceived as opportunities;
(5) setting ground-rules together;
(6) training in constructive criticism;
(7) being clear about the focus, purpose and advantages of the group work;
(8) providing time to discuss and address group dynamics within the ground-rules.

It is important to be aware of the level of anxiety that students may bring to group work, even though they may dislike the sense of isolation they have without it. Group work is not without its pains but much of the best learning arises from addressing the difficulties in a constructive way. Use the group as far as you can to develop a problem-solving attitude to difficulties, under your guidance at first. Bring out the learning involved in dealing with anxieties and difficulties, and give students a chance to appreciate how far they shift in breaking down their barriers when working with others.

It is a good idea to bring in some aspects of group work gradually, building up skills and then taking stock of what has been achieved. Where names, ice-breakers, games, and various types of group work and team building have already been introduced, this gives a good basis on which to begin to analyse the dynamics of group work.

Materials

- For each team: a pair of scissors, 2 pieces of A4 paper, sellotape and glue for **Activity 6**.
- If working with others is regarded as an essential skill for a vocational area associated with your subject, or a careers path taken by your graduates, then it is helpful to provide some material from that profession to focus appreciation of the skills involved. The Careers Service may be able to help with this. Professional guidelines or job specifications may be useful starting points for discussion, as many specify 'good inter-personal skills' or 'working in teams' as requirements.
- If students are encouraged to set up study-

support networks, you may like to offer them the list of icebreakers (p. 197) as a resource.

Activities

(1) Icebreaker   `OC`

Each person states briefly one idea for an ice-breaker that could be used on another occasion.

(2) Pooling ideas   `C, IGS`

* *Individually*   Ask students to jot down, in one minute, as many possible uses that they can think of for a flower pot (alternatively, you could suggest a piece of A4 paper, a cornflakes box, etc.).
* *Whole group*   Find out who has the most items and ask them to list these. Write them up.
* Ask for other contributions until all ideas are exhausted.
* Draw attention to how many more ideas are generated when you work collectively.

(3) Advantages of working in groups   `C, Emp, IGS`

* *Threes*   Ask students to brainstorm, rapidly, as many advantages as they can about working in groups.
* *Whole group* Take contributions. Ensure that as many people as possible get a chance to speak.
* Draw out the advantages of working together for mutual problem-solving for academic difficulties.

(4) Speaking and listening   `Emp, IGS, OC, R`

* *Whole group*   Draw attention to the importance of precise speech and close listening skills for all kinds of social interaction.
* *Pairs*   They will need a pen, paper, and something to lean on to write. They should sit back to back. Let them decide who is A and who B. A will speak first. Give all the 'A's a copy of

diagram A. Ensure that person B cannot see the diagram. Give the following directions.

Person A, the speaker, will give instructions on how to draw the diagram on their sheet. Person B will listen carefully and follow the instructions exactly. Only the speaker is allowed to speak: so no questions can be asked by person B at this stage.

After they have finished, or after 5 minutes have elapsed, swap over and give the new speaker diagram B. When A and B have played both parts, they can compare their diagrams and discuss what they found to be easy and difficult about the exercise and how they felt during it.

* *Whole group*   Ask for contributions about their experiences. Ask what lessons can be drawn about listening skills and speaking skills from the activity?
* *Whole group*   Draw out the other tools we use when listening and speaking, such as body language, eye contact, expression, checking for understanding, etc.
* *Whole group*   Ask for ideas for occasions when good listening skills are useful: (a) for their studies, (b) in employment?

Deaf and partially hearing students
Where there are students with hearing difficulties, pairs can be asked to sit facing each other so that lip reading is possible, but without the listener being able to see the diagram.

(5) Effective listening   `Emp, IGS, OC`

* *Whole group*   Ask students to consider all the things that might prevent them from listening during a teaching session or a meeting. Suggest such issues as tiredness, the subject being too difficult, the speaker being boring, etc. Write these up as a list or as pattern notes.
* *Small groups*   Allocate one or two of these 'preventive factors' to each group. Ask students to suggest strategies for improving listening in each case.
* *Whole group*   Take suggestions from each group. Check that they include such potential solutions as: orientating themselves to the

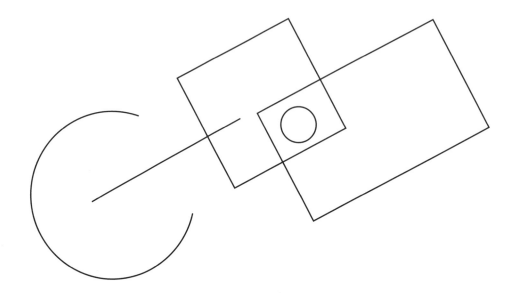

Diagram A (for person A only)

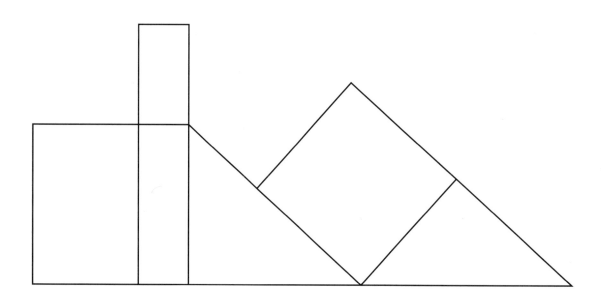

Diagram B (for person B only)

session before they go in and mentally 'switching off' to distractions, using active listening strategies such as devising questions that they wish answered and then listening out for the answers, looking for links with their assignment questions, looking for questions that they could ask, making notes of main points, mentally questioning the speaker's line of argument or examples, preparing in advance, etc.

- *Individually* Encourage students to write, in their reflective journals, at least one strategy they could employ to improve their listening skills and to identify when they will put this into practice.

(6) Team work C, Emp, IGS, OC, S

- Divide the group into teams of roughly 4–6 people.
- Give each team a pair of scissors, 2 pieces of A4 paper, sellotape and glue.
- Teams have 12 minutes to construct a bridge which is at least 6 inches high and can support a bag of sugar.
- Tell teams that they will be given marks for meeting the specifications and for how good the bridge looks, i.e. its aesthetics.
- At the end of the time, teams give the bridge a name and then place it where everyone can see it.
- Appreciations. Ask the whole group to find one positive thing to say about each bridge.
- Take a vote on which bridge looks the best – for artistic merit. (People cannot vote for their own.) Write up how many votes each bridge receives.
- Quickly measure that each bridge is roughly 6 inches high. If it is less, then the bridge loses a third of the marks it gained for artistic merit. Then place the bag of sugar on it. If the bridge collapses, it loses a third of the marks it gained for artistic merit.
- Add up the marks and congratulate the winning team.

- *Whole group* What did people find best about working in teams?

- What did they feel was most difficult?
- What different talents or contributions did individuals bring?

- *Small groups* (different to the above teams) List suggestions about what makes teams work effectively.
- *Whole group* Take contributions from groups. List and discuss these.
- Ask: why do they think employers value team working skills so much?

(7) Constructive criticism Emp, IGS, OC, S

- *Whole group* Discuss what is meant by constructive criticism (see pp. 117–18). Ensure that students grasp that constructive criticism offers a clear and practicable 'next step forward' for action and is expressed in a positive way. Ask for examples of what is and is not constructive criticism to ensure they are clear of the difference. Write these up.

  Ask what it feels like to receive constructive criticism. Bring out that people may not agree with the constructive criticism they receive or may not be able to accept it gladly. Ask them to consider whether they are good at accepting criticism and at giving positive feedback.

- *Individually* Give students time to complete the reflection activities on the Resource Sheet (see p. 247).

- *In threes with people they know* Give each person a few minutes to discuss the notes they made about their behaviour in groups. The other two listen silently. At the end of each person's turn, the other two each offer:

  – one piece of positive feedback: something they appreciate about what the person contributes;
  – one piece of constructive criticism about the person's contribution to the group (how they could participate even more skilfully).

The receivers say how they feel about the constructive criticism offered, and whether it is difficult or easy to hear. They should write this into their journal to reflect upon. After each has had a turn, give a few minutes for the groups to discuss how they felt about the exercise.

- *Whole group*   Discuss what came up doing the exercise. What lessons are there to be learnt from their experiences?

(8) Tools and Skills   `A, E, Emp, IGS, R, S`

- *Individually*   Give students time to brainstorm a list of the strategies they have learnt in previous sessions that are of use in working with others

- *Whole group*   Ask students to list all the methods they have covered so far to develop group skills. What tools have they acquired which they could use if they were to set up groups of their own? Look for answers such as

paired work, threes, small groups, speaking in the large group, icebreakers, setting groundrules, offering appreciation and positive feedback, giving constructive criticism, being time keeper, listening skills.

(9) Successful groups and sabotaged groups   `A, Emp, IGS, OC, S`

- *Small groups*   Ask groups to draw up, on two large sheets, a list of all the things that people can do to sabotage a group.
- Next, ask groups to draw up a list of what people can do to make groups work.
- *Whole groups*   Ask volunteers from each group to stand and give feedback from what is on their sheet.
- Either offer to write these up so students have their own copy, or ask for 2 volunteers to type them up for you to photocopy.

RESOURCE SHEET
Working with others

(1) Recommended reading

Aim to read at least part of one of the following:

- Cottrell, Stella (1999) *The Study Skills Handbook* (Basingstoke: Macmillan – now Palgrave), Chapter 5.
- McGill, Ian and Beaty, L. (1992), *Action Learning: A Practitioner's Guide* (London: Kogan Page), Chapters 2, 5 and 9.
- Benson, J. F. (1987) *Working More Creatively with Groups* (London: Tavistock); useful to dip into to. Contains many ideas about making groups work effectively.
- Luft, J. (1984) *Group Processes: An Introduction to Group Dynamics* (Mayfield, Calif.: Mountain View); for more advanced reading.

(2) Activities

Icebreaker
Think of one idea for a simple icebreaker that we haven't used so far.

Drawing together previous learning

- Draw up a list of all the things we have done so far that assist in developing skills in working with other people. You may find it helpful to consider 'roles' you have played, tools we have used, and techniques you have acquired.
- Which do you find most helpful, and why?

(3) Reflection

In your journal, write a few lines about your experiences of being around others in your first weeks at university or college. For example, you might include:

- What are your feelings? Are you feeling shy and trying to hide this? Or confident?
- Are you finding it easy or difficult to contribute?
- Are you listening to what others say or do you tend to dominate?
- What else have you noticed about how you are around other students?
- What thoughts and reflections do you have about why you are feeling or behaving this way?
- Remember – this is primarily reflection about *your* responses rather than a time to consider how other people might be to blame.

14 Organising and managing study

Students' difficulties with organising and managing study

Individual differences

Organisation covers a wide spectrum. For some students the main difficulty will be time management; for others it will be organising information or study space.

Too many demands

Now that many students work, have dependants and other responsibilities, study has become only one of many things they have to fit into their week. In addition, modular schemes require students to juggle many ways of working, and assignment deadlines for different modules may coincide. This can lead to students feeling overwhelmed by how much there is to do.

Transferable skills

Students do not always value the organisational skills they have developed in their wider life experience. Analysing current coping strategies can help to identify a range of skills which could be adapted to organise study.

Identity

A sense of identity can be built into the way people organise time and materials. For example, some students argue that they prefer to work in chaos, as they feel it is more creative. This may be true for them. It is difficult to shift habits when students hold a strong belief and preference of this kind. If they choose to work 'creatively' in a mess, they will need to find a creative way of meeting essential deadlines and course requirements.

Scale

At first, many students do not appreciate the amount of reading and writing they will need to do. For example, they may buy only one folder, thinking that all of their university work will fit into it. In particular, they underestimate how long should be spent on different aspects of assignments. They may expect that a few hours should suffice for an essay, and be surprised when they have spent the allocated time simply looking for materials.

Monolithic approach

Students often consider only the final product, the finished assignment they are expected to complete, or a set of exams, and take fright at the size of the task, rather than considering ways of breaking the task into manageable parts, each with its own mini-deadlines and strategies.

Not starting

A major cause of missed deadlines is students being frightened of the task and putting off

Aims of the session

- To develop students' organisational skills, using tools such as a SWOT analysis, to apply in both academic and employment contexts;
- to develop interactive group work skills for mutual support, introducing Action Sets.

Learning outcomes

By the end of these activities students should be able to:

Learning outcomes	Skills (see p. 193)
(1) Apply a SWOT analysis in relation to organisational skills	E, Emp, IGS, M, P, R
(2) Identify organisational skills in relation to time, space, information, and IT	Emp, IGS, K, R
(3) Identify how they could use current strengths to build skills in areas of weakness	Emp, IGS, K, P
(4) Identify priorities for improving their organisational skills	Emp, P, R
(5) Use an 'action set' approach to problem-solving and mutual study support	IGS, M, P, R
(6) Summarise organisational strategies they could use	S

starting. This is connected to difficulties with scale and a monolithic approach. An assignment of 'thousands' of words can sound much more than it is; 'research' or 'statistics' may sound too frightening even to consider. If they leave too little time to complete, students may miss deadlines, or perform badly, confirming their opinion that the work was too hard.

Lack of a sense of hierarchy or priority

Depending on their backgrounds, students may lack a sense of how to arrange information or tasks into a hierarchy of importance, and how to select according to priorities. Students report

difficulties such as seeing all information they read as equally important so they do not know what to select, and anxiety about leaving anything out in case that was the information that gained marks.

How lecturers can help

(1) Modelling time management

This includes strategies such as putting up the agenda for the teaching session at the beginning, indicating roughly how much time is given to each section – and then sticking to it. This is not necessary for every session, but it shows students, for example, that even lecturers sometimes cannot fit in everything they want to say, and have to cut their material to fit a pre-scribed limit.

(2) Modelling how to organise information

Briefly, talk students through the way you have broken the overall subject of a lecture into com-ponents – and how sub-sections themselves break down. This could be built into the agenda. Using section headings, sub-headings, and bullet points not only clarifies the material for the student, it demonstrates concept hierar-chies, and the way that information can be structured.

(3) Indicating priorities

There are a number of ways of doing this. For example, emphasise which are the main theories or schools of thought for the subject. Use a diagram to show, visually, how these relate to each other. Organise your own mater-ial so that main points stand out clearly. Offer an assignment booklet or handout which encourages reflection of the main questions raised by the lecture, and include a list of any articles, books or other sources referred to, drawing attention to the main sections to be read.

(4) Guidance on time for assignments

Although the amount of time students will take to complete an assignment will vary enormously, it is useful if lecturers go through all the probable stages required to complete the assignment, from beginning to end, suggesting a realistic time to allow for each stage. For example, students may need to write three drafts, which may take over a day each to write and edit. This reduces the chance of the student beginning the assignment on the last day. Encourage students to work back-wards from deadlines, entering into their diaries the day they will tackle each stage of the process.

Tutor preparation

Approach to the session

There are so many variables in students' diffi-culties with organisational skills that not all of these can be addressed directly in a whole-group setting. One potential difficulty with such a session is that students can launch into all their difficulties, expecting them to be solved imme-diately. However, even students with poor skills in this area tend to have more resources than they think. Emphasise that the session is about identifying one or two priority areas, and using the group to bring out each other's current strengths and skills. The suggested activities introduce the idea of Action Sets, building on group work undertaken in previous sessions, and building towards the development of support groups.

Materials

There is a handout (below) for distribution in the session, outlining the principles of Action Sets, and a more general Resource Sheet.

Activities

(1) Icebreaker   OC, M

Each person gives one organisational tip about any aspect of life or study (serious or amusing).

(2) SWOT analysis   E, IGS, M, P, R

- *Individually* If SWOT analyses were not given as advance preparation, ask students to complete these now, using the Resource Sheet below (see p. 253).
- *Pairs* Ask students to discuss what were the most important features on their SWOT analysis. Were they surprised at what came up for them when they made the lists?
- *Whole group*   Take examples of strengths and list these.
- Ask for examples of weaknesses. Check how common these are in the group.

- Take as many contributions as possible of 'opportunities' and draw the group's attention to these. Encourage them to write down opportunities they had not thought of, and invite discussion of some of these.
- Take as many contributions as possible of 'threats'. Invite discussion of these and possible ways of addressing these threats and turning them into opportunities. Encourage students to list some of these.

(3) Using existing skills in new areas   Emp, IGS, K, OC, P

- *Threes*   Using the Resource Sheet (p. 253), each person identifies, briefly, the situation where they are best organised (to start off on a positive note) and *one* area of weakness they would like to improve.

    The other two people in the group help the speaker to draw out skills in the area of strength which may be of use in the area of weakness. For example, if someone is always on time for football matches, what planning skills are involved which could be used to plan for an assignment deadline?

- *Whole group*   Take examples of how existing skills could be used to assist study.

(4) Group characteristics   IGS, R

- Using the Resource Sheet, ask students to identify themselves by their area of organisational strength (e.g. organising time, space, etc.) and to stand in the area of the room the tutor allocates to each strength. If groups are unequal in size, ask people who identified a skill as their second (or third best) to move into a smaller group, until groups are of equal size as far as possible. Name each group A, B, C, D (or give each group a set of stickers with one letter, A, B, C or D).
- Ask people to form smaller groups of 4-6 people, each of which has at least one A, B, C and D person in it. This ensures more of a spread of skills. Explain that these are their Action Sets for the next two sessions.

(5) Action Sets   IGS, M, OC, P, R

- *Whole group*   Leave as much time as possible for this activity (at least an hour for a group of 4 people). Use the handout to explain how Action Sets work.

- *Individually*   Tell students: *Think of an area of your studies or work experience that you feel would benefit from better organisational skill. Choose something that you feel comfortable raising in this group*

Action sets   (use the group division established in Activity 4).

- Invite students to use the time allotted to them individually (preferably 15 minutes each) to gain support from their group to improve their area of organisational difficulty. Remind them to stick to the one area they have identified and not to stray off into all the other things they might feel they need help with.
- Go round to check that the groups are working as they should.
- Give clear signals of when it is time to change stage and remind them what that stage is (even though it is written down.)

- *Whole group*   Take contributions on how people found the exercise. Ensure that as many people as possible get a chance to speak.

(6) Pulling it together   Emp, S

- *Individually*   Ask students to update the list of organisational tips and strategies they have discovered since beginning work on this session (including through any advance preparation).
- *Small groups*   Ask students to consider how the organisational skills discussed in the session could be applied to a range of contexts, including employment.
- *Whole group*   Ask for contributions about the applicability of organisational skills more generally. Use this as the basis for a discussion

on key transferable skills and employability skills.

Ask each person to contribute to the whole group the most important organisational tip they will take from the day.

(7) Organisational strategy

Structured reflection to improve learning and performance   `E, Emp, IGS, M, R`

Organisational skills can be impaired when students lack an overarching organisational strategy. The problem-solving structure and handouts offered on pp. 153–9 above provide a conceptual and methodological framework for students to organise their approaches to new tasks, including improving their learning and performance. The structure facilitates the development of potentially transferable skills into 'transferred' skills.

Introducing the SRILP model

* *Whole group*   Give students copies of the first page of the handouts. Go briefly through the diagram and the main stages.
* *Small groups*   Ask groups to identify a relatively complex task to map against the framework. You may prefer to give each group an example of a task related to the subject area (such as organising a conference, writing a leaflet for school children, changing a plug, working out why a machine – won't work, designing a web-page, etc.).
* *Small groups*   Map the task against the framework, noting any adaptations they needed to make in order to solve the problem and to write this up in poster form.
* *Whole group*   Ask students to present their findings as a group so that each person takes a turn to speak. Alternatively, they can be invited to look at each others' posters. Draw out what students found difficult.

Focusing on the detail

Select one section of the model, such as 'strategy', and ask students to brainstorm how each component breaks down into more detailed steps. Write this up and then give out the handout for that section. Discuss how their own ideas compare to the framework.

Orientation

Go through the orientation section with students, describing how you are using this to introduce them to HE study. Link this to work on position papers.

Identify weak points

* *Individually*   Ask students to look at the fifteen steps identified in the overall framework. Ask them to identify their best four areas and the four steps they are likely to find most difficult or are likely to neglect.
* *Action sets or small groups*   Students say what they feel is their area of strength which they would best be able to advise others about. Students identify a means for each of them to improve in one of their weakest aspects of the framework.
* *Whole groups*   Identify group strengths. Share ways of approaching weak areas.

Action plans

Encourage students to work through the early stages of the model to write their first action plan and to return to the model when they come to evaluate and update their action plan. Provide opportunities for students to discuss their progress in applying the model.

Deepening understanding of the framework

Ideally, students should be asked to apply the model to problem solving in at least one other area of their course so that they gain a more elaborate understanding of its potential. Where possible, students should be asked to draw out how the model works in different contexts and how they have adapted it.

RESOURCE SHEET
Organising and managing study

(1) Recommended reading

Aim to read at least part of one of the following:

- Cottrell, Stella (1999), *The Study Skills Handbook* (Basingstoke: Macmillan – now Palgrave), Chapter 4
- Bourner, T. and Race, P. (1990), *How to Win as a Part-Time Student* (London: Kogan Page).
- Lewis, R. (1994), *How to Manage your Study Time* (Cambridge: National Extension College).
- Rickards, T. (1992), *How to Win as a Mature Student* (London: Kogan Page).

(2) Activity

SWOT Analysis (**S**trengths, **W**eaknesses, **O**pportunities, **T**hreats)

- Give a page in your learning journal the title: 'Organisational skills: SWOT analysis'.
- Draw a large cross that divides the page into four equal sections. In the first box at the top of the page write 'Strengths', for the second, write 'Weaknesses'. In the lower boxes write 'Opportunities' and 'Threats'.
- Brainstorm as many examples of your organisational strengths and weaknesses as you can under each heading.
- Consider what opportunities your current situation holds for you to improve upon your organisational skills
- Consider what you find threatening about changing the ways you do things at present. What habits are you attached to? Do they really work for you? What are your worries about change?

(3) Reflection

Think of the situation where you are the best organised. What exactly do you do which helps you to be organised in that situation? Are there other things you could do to be even more organised? Write down your reflections.

Look over what you have written, and list the skills you have already in relation to the following:

(1) Organising time
(2) Organising space
(3) Organising information
(4) Being organised when using IT

- In which of these four areas of organisational ability are your strongest skills?
- Which is your second best area of strength. Note these down in your journal.

Action Sets

Action Sets are another tool that you can use to enhance group work and mutual support. They can be very effective ways of addressing problems and pooling resources within a short time. They are also very straightforward to use. They work best when the people in the group have different strengths and experiences to draw upon.

For each person

Stage 1
Each person has a set amount of time to discuss the area they wish to improve, such as meeting deadlines for handing in assignments. Whilst that person is speaking, the others in the group listen without interrupting. Once the time is up, the person must stop speaking.

Stage 2
The group has a few moments to clarify any uncertainties with the speaker.

Stage 3
The person whose issue is being discussed listens without speaking, whilst the rest of the group brainstorms ideas for possible solutions or ways of thinking about the problem. For example, they may suggest starting earlier, studying in a different place, writing essay plans, etc. Again, there is a set time for this.

Stage 4
The person and the group have a set time to clarify and discuss options together briefly. Everyone can speak in this stage.

Stage 5
The person whose issue is being discussed has a set time to say which of the ideas they can put into effect and, briefly, when or how they will start this. For example, they may decide to avoid making phone calls on weekdays before 9 p.m. so they can concentrate on study during the evening. They undertake to report back on this in the next session. All group members write down what has been agreed, as a basis for monitoring this in the next Action Set session.

Stage 6
In the following session, each person reports back to this group what they have done to act upon what was decided the previous time. The group encourages successes and improvements. If the person has not done what was undertaken, this may become the focus of the process for that session.

Based on a concept developed by I. McGill and L. Beatty (1992), *Action Learning: A Practitioner's Guide* (London: Kogan Page).

15 Developing thinking skills

Students' difficulties with thinking skills

Lack of a problem-solving foundation

As these skills are basic to problem-solving skills, if they are under-developed or under-utilised, students can find it difficult to find a starting place for approaching a wide range of academic tasks. In particular, they do not know how to identify common underlying structures to problems that confront them, nor how to evaluate the significance of similarities and differences when transferring approaches from one task to another (see pp. 153–9 above).

Difficulty in transferring skills

Students can fail to identify the nature of the problems with which they are presented especially with regards to manipulating information. Often, students use analogous skills, in everyday life, to those needed for study but are not able to see the similarity between the everyday situation and the skills required for academic work.

Scale of the task

As the size of the task increases, from writing a letter to producing an essay or a dissertation or thesis, greater demands are made on organisational skills. If students cannot envisage the end-product (e.g. essay, project paper) and cannot envisage how information should be arranged within it, then it is hard for them to conceive an organisational strategy in advance of the task.

Panic

Students tend to panic when confronted with new assignment titles and academic tasks, and forget to apply what they know.

How lecturers can help

(1) Draw parallels with everyday applications

Make explicit the links with concrete experience and everyday usage, drawing out the common structure to the thinking skill. Sorting information can be like sorting out cutlery.

(2) Provide concrete examples of end-products

Provide more than one example so students can build up a more elaborate mental model. Draw attention to the main features and talk through how information is arranged. Students benefit from guidance on where approaches used for smaller tasks both do and do not assist in a scaled-up assignment.

(3) Modelling in lectures

As these basic thinking skills are key to the development of so many other study skills and to problem-solving skills in general, further ideas on how these skills can be integrated into teaching are given in Chapter 5.

Tutor preparation

Approaching the session

- This follows on well from a session on organisational skills.
- For **Activity 4.1**, you will need to identify a topic about which students could generate a range of ideas from common sense, experience and popular knowledge (such as changes in public health over the last 200 years, the effects of industry on world climate, the effects of IT on communication, whether

humans should be cloned). Where possible, select a topic related to the subject area which has not yet been covered by the syllabus.

- There is more material in the session plan than can be covered within a single session. For some intakes, it may be necessary to go slowly through these activities over several sessions. For more advanced groups, it may be possible simply to run through key weaknesses noted in previous years. It is important to ensure that students are aware of these skills, as they underlie the skills required in other areas of learning. These are a useful preparation for work on writing skills.
- Give out any reading in advance so that dyslexic students and slow readers have a chance to become familiar with it.

Aims of the session

- To enable students to develop the underlying skills which are needed for more advanced critical thinking;
- to develop the basic thinking skills which impact upon organising information for written assignments;
- to develop problem-solving skills.

Learning outcomes

By the end of these activities students should be able to:

Learning outcomes	Skills (see p. 193)
(1) Identify similarities, differences and connections	A, C, I, IGS, OC, P, S
(2) Draw upon a conceptual model for organising information	A, I, KU, M
(3) Use a range of strategies for generating ideas and solving problems	C, IGS, P
(4) Recognise the importance of generalisation, categories and hierarchies and use these to sort, select and amplify upon information	A, E, I, KU, M, P
(5) Draw on a basic introduction to analytical thinking	A, KU
(6) Apply thinking skills to written assignments	A, KU, WC

Materials

- Pairs of items to compare, in sets of increasingly similar pairs (for **Activity 3.4**).
- An overhead transparency of the diagrams used for **Activity 4**.
- 2–3 short passages which each contain some additional information on the topic you choose for the session (as identified above). These should be fairly short, with clear print (so that they do not panic those whose sight-reading skills deteriorate under pressure).
- A visual, musical or other stimulus (**Activity 4.1**: *Stimulus*).
- For **Activity 4.2** (*Categorising*), for each small group you will need identical, or near identical, sets of objects to sort, such as a collection of brushes or sticks, or DIY paint-shade cards, with each tone cut into distinct shapes. Try to select objects that could be categorised and sorted in a number of different ways.
- For **Activity 4.2** (*Concept categories*), various coloured card for students to write on.
- For each small group, a set of headings and a range of points to be arranged under headings. These should form the basis of an answer to an assignment title for your subject.
- For **Activity 5**, two pictures on a common theme, either on an overhead or as posters.
- For **Activity 5**, two brief video clips on the same topic.
- For **Activity 6**, at least two assignment titles to work on.

Activities

(1) Icebreaker   `C, OC`

Each person contributes a different use for an egg (wild suggestions accepted).

(2) Introduction

Introduce the session by explaining that the skills covered today underlie good performance in a range of study skills and for problem-solving. Bring out that students usually do have these skills, but may not know how to apply

them. Refer to the kinds of difficulties students often have (see above).

(3) Similarities, connections, differences

(3.1) Look for similarities   `C, IGS, OC, S`

- *Whole group*   Ask the group to brainstorm a list of random objects (socks, baseball bats, etc.) until you have a list of about twenty items written up. Number the list (e.g. bats = 1, scissors = 6, etc.).
- *Threes*   Students form groups of three. Allocate two randomly selected numbers between one and twenty to each group – for example, by groups selecting two numbers out of a hat. Each group then matches their numbers to the numbered items on the board (e.g. the bat and the scissors if they received numbers 1 and 6). Groups brainstorm ideas for all the ways the 2 items have something in common. Wild ideas are acceptable. They then identify the one most significant similarity and the reason for their choice.
- *Whole group*   Each group reports back. The whole group can add in other similarities, and confirm or negotiate which is the most significant similarity and why.
- *Draw out*   that comparing items and seeing significant similarities is a fundamental skill in academic thinking – and for many professional areas too. Point out their successes in finding similarities in items chosen even in such a random way.

(3.2) Search out the connections   `C, IGS, OC, S`

- *Individually*   Give students a sentence to complete where they must connect two random items, for example:
  - Studying this subject is like landing on the moon because . . .
  - Hospitals are like machines because . . .
  - Birthdays are like sugar because . . .
- *Whole group*   Collate ideas.
- Suggest an alternative ending to the previous sentence, such as 'Birthdays are like paper (royalty, books, etc.) because . . .'. What are their ideas now?

- *Draw out* the value of using metaphors to explore a subject. They almost always throw out some idea which can lead to a useful or unusual perspective on the subject, and free up thinking. Even 'wild' answers may bear unexpected fruit.

(3.3) Metaphors: finding a personal metaphor   `C, IGS, S`

- *Individually* 'Studying on this course is, for me, like . . . because . . .'. Ask students to find a personal metaphor for their study on this course, and to expand the idea as they did for *Searching for connections*. Tell them to choose whatever idea comes to mind or whatever they see around them, rather than spending too long selecting the perfect option to begin with. Whatever they choose may help to lead them towards a metaphor they prefer.
- *Whole group* Take suggestions. What insight does the metaphor offer students about how they view study at present?

(3.4) Differences   `A, IGS`

- *Whole group* Offer two similar items for consideration (e.g. a mug and a cup, or two items from the subject area). Ask for the main similarities and then the differences. Offer two items that are more similar (such as two cups) and repeat the exercise. Offer two, even more. similar items (such as two green cups) and repeat. Continue with increasingly similar items, so that students are stretched to find the differences. Repeat with examples (theories, experiments, or projects) from the subject area.

(4) Generating ideas and organising material   `C, IGS, S`

- *Whole group* Present the diagram below on an overhead projector or board to give an overview of a generative information management cycle.

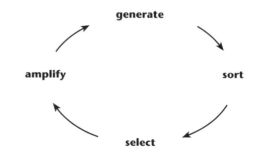

Diagram 1

For each of the sections 4.1–4.4 below, work your way around the cycle, identifying strategies appropriate to each stage. Confirm whether students already know how to use each strategy. If some do not, ask those who do know to help you to demonstrate, where appropriate. If all are happy, move onto the next.

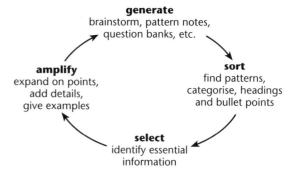

Diagram 2

(4.1) Generate   `C, I, IGS, P, WC`

Generating ideas is one of the most valuable skills that university lecturers can teach. From ideas come proposals and hypotheses, the starting points for more traditional critical thinking. Without these, there would be nothing concrete to analyse

To warm students up, ask for ideas about how ideas can be generated: what kinds of techniques can be used to generate ideas before even beginning a piece of work or approaching a new problem? Ensure they are familiar with each of the following:

Brainstorming

- This is throwing out all possible ideas and inspirations, including what is known, what needs to be done, where information may be found, resources, etc.
- Present students with a topic which has yet to be studied but where they could apply common sense and generally known information to generate a range of information. Write up what they say.
- Draw attention to this as a very quick way for getting started on almost any kind of assignment or task.

Pattern notes or mind map

- This is a useful strategy as one item can lead on to another by a process of association. The visual structure follows the way the brain structures information, which can make pattern notes more appealing.
- Organise the information that was generated in the brainstorm into pattern notes on the board, as a whole group activity. You may wish to organise the information generated for the brainstorming activity.

Question banks

- *Groups (of between 3–5)* Give a short period of time for groups to generate general key questions that could further any search for information: why, who, what, where, etc.
- Ask them to consider more specific questions that would push their search for information and generate ideas on the topic selected above.
- *Whole group* Take contributions of questions.
- Use these questions to structure thinking about the topic used earlier for the brainstorm or pattern notes. Do they help to generate additional information?

Stimulus

- Present an image, text, music, video clip or anecdote.
- Ask students to look for associations and connections between the stimulus item and the topic discussed for the brainstorm or pattern notes activity – or, alternatively, with a topic they are all studying.

- What other examples of stimuli can the group offer? Ask how could they use stimuli to work more creatively and generate ideas.

Research: reading

- *Individually* Ask students to read one of the brief passages you have given them on the topic under discussion.
- *Small groups* What additional ideas are generated by their reading?
- Add their additional ideas to the pattern notes
- Make reference to the importance of background research in generating and developing ideas.
- Ask for other examples of where they can get information to generate ideas.

Multiple-solutions: 'I've got one solution – now let me think of three more'

Those who feel they know the answer to a question rarely look for a better one. Bring out the importance of moving beyond the obvious answer or the first good solution that comes to mind. The more alternatives considered, the greater the likelihood of arriving at the best solution.

- Ask: 'What is the use of a house-brick?' and take responses. Draw attention to the effect of wording on the way we approach problems. 'What is the use of a house-brick?' suggests there is only one use, and you are more likely to search for only one answer. Compare the wording for the next activity.
- *Pairs* Ask: pairs: 'How many uses can you think of for a house brick?'
- *Whole group* Either yourself or a volunteer can make a list of contributions
- *Whole group* Present the question: 'There is a crowd of people outside a shop and a man with a bucket on his head. Give one obvious reason.' and then 'What alternative explanations might there be?'
- *Whole group* Ask a question, preferably related to the topic under discussion (above) that will generate several answers or possible solutions.

(4.2) Sort   `A, I, IGS, M, WC`

Once students have generated ideas on the topic, it is important that they appreciate different stages of organising the information they have accumulated. The following activities build up skills in re-organising information from a scatter-style pattern into categories, hierarchies and sequence. These skills are essential to most academic tasks.

Looking for patterns

India	Elephant	Yellow	Sea
White	Dog	Spain	Pet
Greenland	Sandy	Busy	Cat
Holiday	Tarantula	Sun	
Ice	Turkey	Cold	

- Ask students to divide the above word list into at least three groups and to note these down on a flipchart, with a brief label to say what the items in the group have in common. Assure them that they can group them in any way as long as they find something in common and that there are many possible patterns to look for. They must have at least three groups with at least two items in each. Give a short time (2 minutes) so they have to exert themselves.
- Ask them now to shuffle the words, find a different way of arranging them and write these out as before. Give a little longer this time.
- Ask groups to put the flipcharts up so everyone can see the patterns people found.
- Make a list of the different patterns that people made use of in order to group the objects (e.g. long words, words which refer to animals, words which contain the letter 't', etc.).
- Bring out the point that the mind can find many ways of observing patterns and that seeing patterns is useful for grouping things into categories. This enables us to think more quickly and, usually, more efficiently.

Categorising
- *Whole group*   Ask for suggestions of things we sort in everyday situations (e.g. cutlery, clothes, shopping).
- *Small groups*   Distribute the objects you have

brought to be sorted into groups. Ask groups to sort these into groups depending on some characteristic of the object that they choose to focus on. Set a time of about 3–5 minutes for the activity.
- *Whole group*   Ask groups to display their groups, and to state the principle they used to order them (e.g. by colour, length, etc.).
- Bring out that there are different criteria for sorting (colour, size, tone, shape, etc.). Similarly, there is not usually only one way to organise information. The more complex the objects and information, the more options there may be for ordering it. Reassure students that, in written assignments, they will not be able to cover every option for referring to information -- any more than they can simultaneously arrange sticks or objects in every permutation open to them.

Concept categories
- This can be a good point to introduce the idea of 'concepts' (or concept categories). Students are often thrown by the word 'concept' as if it were intrinsically difficult. Explain that a concept is simply a mental organisation of items which are similar in some way – such as 'cutlery' or 'sticks' or 'chairs'. They are generalisations. Draw out how important the ability to group things into categories is to learning: it allows us to generalise, to build on prior learning, to communicate much more easily, etc.
- *Small groups*   Ask students to place before them the information generated for the exercise 'generating ideas'. Ask them to divide this information into categories. If possible, ask them to write each category on a different coloured card. Ask groups to give each category a name that defines its content.
- *Whole group*   Compare the different ways that groups organised information.
- Draw out an awareness that categorising enables us to begin to predict characteristics – to infer. Ask, for example, if all we know about an item is that it belongs to the category of 'tree' or 'animal', what else can we predict about it?

Headings and bullet points
- These are useful ways of sorting information generated in scatter maps – and students have in effect produced the basis for headings and points on the cards they produced above.
- *Small groups* To reinforce the above exercise, give students the set of headings and cards with points which you prepared in relation to an essay title for your subject. Give them the title of the essay. Ask groups to arrange the main points under the three headings.
- *Whole group* Go through the exercise and discuss any variations from what you expected.

Hierarchies
Using either the cards generated in the *Concept category* activity or from the *Heading-and-bullets* exercise, bring out that information can be organised at several different levels. Introduce the idea of concept hierarchies, either by drawing up a simple hierarchy from your subject area or using examples from the pattern notes exercise. For example:

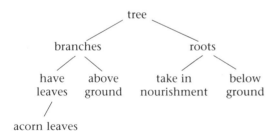

- Draw out differences in information at different levels of the hierarchy, such as that information at the lower levels of the hierarchy is more specific, and therefore of less general application.
- Point out that when tutors ask for more detail, they usually want information from the lower parts of the hierarchy. If the tutor feedback on an essay asks for more argument, the student may be including too much detail from the lower parts of the hierarchy.
- Point out that adding or removing information at the lower end of the hierarchy can help to meet word deadlines.

(4.3) Select   A, I, IGS, M, WC

Essential information
- *Small groups* Ask groups to come up with the shortest list of characteristics that would define a 'chair' (as in 'seat'). The full list must not be applicable to any other object (such as 'table') and must include all types of chair. If the group finds this task easy, substitute the word 'seat' for chair. Alternatively, select a word relevant to the subject discipline.

  This is useful in helping students to select the basic information needed in order to be precise. Bring out that it is often quite difficult to be clear exactly where the boundaries of categories are as there are often exceptions to the rule. It is important to do this, as students may feel that they are failing when they find it difficult to categorise course information.
- Returning to the headings-and-bullet points cards you used before, offer a change in the wording to the essay title you gave previously. Which information in the bullet points is now the most essential? What needs to be edited out?

(4.4) Amplify   C, WC
Once we have an idea of the main areas we want to focus on for a project or assignment, we may need to elaborate upon the information that we already have. In a way this closes the loop, as many of the methods used for 'generating' ideas become useful here. However, the process is rather different to simply generating ideas as it is specifically focused.

Take one aspect of the topic under discussion above. Ask students to imagine that they are writing about this for an assignment and are short of words. How can they amplify the point they are making? Make clear how this kind of brainstorming can be structured through use of the following techniques:

(1) expanding on points already made;
(2) increasing the level of detail;

(3) giving concrete examples;

(4) using information lower down a concept hierarchy;

(5) adding in an explanation of why something occurs;

(6) drawing out the significance of what has been said.

- *Small groups*   Ask groups to consider a second aspect of the topic being discussed and to amplify this from their general knowledge or the reading they have done.

    It may help if the lecturer models this process first, by taking one idea and building on it, systematically, through using specific techniques such as those listed above.

(5) Analysis   A, IGS, S, WC

'Analytical' is a word that can panic students. It is another term that they react to as if it were automatically difficult. Explain that analysis is either:

- a detailed break-down of something into its component parts;
- or a detailed explanation, looking at a subject from different angles.

Simple activities can again make this apparent.

Two pictures
- *Small groups*   Give each group two pictures on a similar theme – or present the images on an overhead transparency or as a poster. Ask students to draw up two lists, one of what the pictures have in common, and a second of what they find to be different.

    Explain that they have analysed the pictures in terms of similarities and differences. They will need this skill for 'Compare and contrast' essays and for part of almost every assignment.

Two points of view
Offer two brief video clips of speakers talking about an aspect of the course.

- *Small groups*   Ask students to draw up a list of the most interesting points that each speaker made.

- *Whole group*   What did the two speakers hold in common? Where did their views differ? It can help to replay the video in order to confirm or challenge these contributions.

(6) Simplifying   A, IGS, P, S, WC

Students often complicate their study, expecting it to be harder than it is. It is useful to build upon the skills developed above to extrapolate the patterns inherent in certain assignments.

- *Whole group*   Offer an assignment title that looks complicated. Model how to break it down into component parts – the number of parts to the question. What are the main activities that students are being asked to undertake. (Looking for similarities? Drawing out differences? Detailing the component parts? Saying what is good or bad about something? Working out which option is the best? Showing how one thing led to another? Explaining why something happened? Working out what will happen?).

    Make clear that more than one of these processes may be needed in the same assignment – such as working out what is different between two items and then what is good or bad about those differences.

- *Small groups*   Give students a different assignment title. Ask them to work out the simplest way of saying what is needed in their own words. What are the 'component parts' of the assignment? Tell them to use phrases or bullet points rather than writing out sentences.

(7) Elements of problem-solving   C, P, S

Draw out the different elements involved in solving the problem. That is:

(1) Clarity about what the problem is. This should be stated simply.

(2) Looking for a similar problem or area of activity which you can already do and which may offer strategies to help you solve a new problem. The key to problem-solving is finding a parallel problem, or area of

expertise, which is sufficiently analogous to offer up at least part of the solution.

(3) Being aware of differences between the two problems or situations.

(4) Being aware of the significance of these differences when trying to apply strategies from one situation to another.

(5) Knowing what else it is you need to know or where to go for help.

(6) Thinking of as many options as possible, as this increases the chance of coming up with the best options. Don't rest at the first option.

(7) Consider advantages and disadvantages of each solution.

(8) Weigh up the relative advantages and disadvantages carefully.

- *Individually* Undertake the problem-solving activity on the Resource Sheet (see p. 264).
- *Threes* Discuss their findings.
- *Whole group* Draw attention to the value of this basic problem-solving model in everyday life, for academic problems and also more generally.

(8) Problem-solving   `A, IGS, P, S`

- *Small groups* Set the entire group the same problem to solve in small groups. This can be anything from a puzzle to a problem issue in the subject area. It could be how everyone would fit into the room if numbers were doubled, or what to do with the problem of mobile phones going off or a case study relevant to the course. If setting a problem related to course work, it should be similar to something they have already covered on the course.

  Depending on the level of the group and the difficulty of the task, give a set time to complete the problem. Recommend that they use the same strategies as they did for the advance preparation.
- *Whole group* Take in suggestions from each group. If there is more than one possible answer, which one does the group prefer?
- Draw out the thinking skills they made use of in this activity which they used in previous activities (such as generating ideas, selecting, simplifying).

Follow-on

- Ideally, all activities here should be undertaken with three examples each and the links between the examples should be made explicit.
- Refer back to these skills when working on writing and critical thinking skills.
- The 'Structured Reflection for Improving Learning and Performance' model on pp. 153–9 offers a more developed structure for problem-solving approaches to different kinds of taste (see also p. 252).

RESOURCE SHEET
Developing thinking skills

(1) Recommended reading

Aim to read at least part of two of the following:

■ Cottrell, Stella (1999), *The Study Skills Handbook* (Basingstoke: Macmillan – now Palgrave), pp. 50–2, 128, 136–7, and 145–60; an introduction to 'concepts' and applying thinking skills to writing.
■ Bono, E. de (1994), *De Bono's Thinking Course*, revised and updated edition (London: BBC).
■ Bono, E. de (1996), *Teach Yourself to Think* (London: Penguin).
■ Inglis, J. and Lewis, R. (1980), *Clear Thinking: The Key to Success* (Cambridge: National Extension College); a short book with useful basic exercises.
■ Lovell, Bernard R. (1979, 1992), *Adult Learning* (London: Routledge) Chapter 3; more advanced reading, from a cognitive psychology perspective.

(2) Activity

Think of *one* thing that you have problems or difficulties with from time to time. This can be anything that you feel comfortable discussing with the group, and preferably some-thing quite limited in size. Some ideas are: being late; recording the wrong channel on the video; putting your foot in it when you speak to someone; losing your keys; misplacing your student card; forgetting something essential when shopping, etc.

Either in your journal or on a piece of paper, write answers to as many of the following questions as you can.

(1) What exactly is the problem?
(2) In what ways is this problem at all like any other activity that you do better?
(3) For the activity that you perform well, jot down a list of things you do which helps you to do it right.
(4) What makes the problem activity different to the one you do well? In other words, what makes you go wrong on one and succeed on the other?
(5) Could you use any of the things that you do right in the second activity to help you with the problem area? What else could you do?
(6) Do you need any additional information or help? Where would you get this?
(7) List as many possible suggestions and tips to yourself as you can about how you might overcome the problem you identified. For each possible solution, make a list of advan-tages and disadvantages. Which solution do you prefer?

16 Using lectures effectively

Students' difficulties with lectures

Students report two main types of problems with lectures. The first is a difficulty with sustaining attention. Course design or institutional planning can mean students are expected to sit, listen and take notes for several hours at a time, without a break. It is difficult for students to stay focused unless the time is broken into shorter slots with good use of activities and discussion. Unless this is addressed, improving skills may not help much.

The second difficulty is with making notes in lectures. The Supplemental Instruction Scheme of peer support developed in the USA was originally built around the idea that no student has a complete set of lecture notes. Dyslexic and overseas students are known to have particular difficulties in making notes, although when tutors are informed of these difficulties in simultaneous note-making and listening, they often comment, 'But all the students have that difficulty.' In other words, a great proportion of students are unlikely to gather the information they need from listening and note-making in lectures. This is an area where inadequate lecturer skills impact particularly hard upon the learning of the student.

Why students take inadequate notes

Ignorance of conventions
Some do not realise they are expected to take notes; as a result, they may not note anything. Some believe they are only meant to note down what is on an overhead transparency. Lecturers should make explicit what is expected of the students.

Over-dependence on the lecturers' words
Many students try to write everything down. This may be from fear of missing vital information. Usually it is associated with lack of confidence in their own research skills, and with not knowing where else to go to find the information used by the lecturer. Students using this method often lack the overall sense of the lecture. They focus on writing at speed rather than attending to what is said. Some catch only snippets, which do not make sense later when they read them back.

Poor skills in selectivity
Students who are unable to distinguish what is relevant tend to write too much, too little or the wrong information, especially if they are used to taking dictated notes. Students with extensive notes may never get to read them all through,

which can lead to panic and a sense of overload. Students with poor note-making skills miss key information, including proper names and where to go for further information.

Relevance

Often students cannot see the relevance of certain information to the rest of their course. Lecturers can help by making explicit the links between types of information and by offering concrete examples – such as how a statistics test would be applied in a real-life situation.

Lecturer style

A lecturer's approach may not be helpful. Students need to be able to identify the main points easily.

Lack of clear purpose

One lecturer wrote: 'I am becoming more and more convinced that students 'do' very little with notes made in lectures. . . . Taking notes can become a 'crutch' rather than a learning aid.' Students may use notes or tapes to quote back 'safe' material, rather than aiming to understand and engage with it.

How lecturers can help

(1) In general

- Ensure that students understand the purpose of the series of lectures and what you expect from them during the lectures.
- For first-year students, discuss methods of making notes and the purposes of notes.
- Ask the students what you could do differently to help them gain from your lectures.
- Break the lectures into shorter segments; build in activities to improve concentration.

(2) Clarity of purpose

In general, the main purposes of lectures are to offer an overview, to bring out current issues and discussion points, to offer opportunities for questions and for activities which offer experiential learning of the topic. Some lecturers use lectures simply to feed data which could be

better given in a handout or which is already contained in available textbooks – which is a wasted opportunity to develop their students' learning. It is optimistic to expect that students, through listening and noting, will extract, select and note accurately the information that they will need.

(3) Setting advance preparation for the next lecture

Setting a piece of reading, giving an advance handout, or suggesting a book to browse, helps students to orientate their minds for the next lecture. This orientation work should be brief, and give a general sense of what is coming in the lecture. Browsing for content, headings and topics helps students to orientate for the lecture so they gain more from it. It also enables them to prepare abbreviations in advance. If students have a general overview, they can attend better to detail during the lecture. Students often do not realise the advantages of advance preparation unless their attention is drawn to it. This also helps to encourage students to see themselves as having a role in the learning process rather than being a mere transcriber of lecture talk.

(4) Clarity of delivery

Basic good delivery techniques are invaluable and yet many lecturers neglect them.

- Summarise your key points and learning objectives at the beginning of a lecture. This provides models of good 'introductions' for students.
- Give one key sentence which sums up the lecture. Not only does this make it clear what the lecture is about, it also models the skill for students, who often find it difficult to sum up their main idea.
- Sum up each section of the lecture before going onto the next one, and again at the end of the lecture itself. Some repetition is useful as students may have missed the point the first time round. It also models structure and 'conclusions' for the student.
- Detail how many points you are going to make in each section, what these are (give

'keywords'), and make it clear when you start a new point. This helps students to structure incoming information and models techniques they can use in their writing or their own presentations. It also helps those with poor attention spans.

(5) Pacing and organisation

'The lecturer presented us with six ways of approaching this – one, two, three! I was completely lost by the fourth one. They all started to jumble.'

When information is new, especially when several different approaches are being compared, the pace needs to slow down and the same point may need to be emphasised by being worded in more than one way. When more than two or three models or examples are being compared, students may need to anchor the first three clearly before going on to others. Cover different models in different sessions, or use a break, or work in depth on some models before adding new examples.

A diagram or flow chart which draws attention to similarities and differences between models can be very helpful. In this case, the lecturer needs to follow, exactly, the order which information is presented in the model, or students become lost. An alternative is to provide a list of criteria against which models can be compared or to use one model as a base against which others can be compared. In other words, a sound foundation needs to be established in terms of overview, criteria or base model, before lots of detail is given about variations. Without such methods, students begin to jumble information and become frustrated: many people do not have the capacity to take in and manipulate large amounts of new information at speed.

(6) Vocabulary awareness

- Write up new or specialised vocabulary on the board, and provide it as a glossary in the student handbook. This is especially helpful if there are students from overseas, dyslexic students, students with poor vocabulary, etc. Students may not be able to identify the sounds of new words when spoken quickly

and therefore have no way of writing them down. It also distracts their listening while they try to recapture the sounds they have missed to gain the sense of a sentence where some words are alien to them.

- For those with poor academic English, it helps if lecturers contextualise words used incorrectly by students in their writing.

(7) Handouts

- Provide any detailed information, such as statistical data, references, proper names, names of reports, dates of key events or publications, etc.: in the form of a handout. This enables students to concentrate on the overall direction of the lecture while feeling confident that they have all 'essential information'.

- Give handouts which outline the structure of the lecture, with numbered blanks for students to complete the main points of each section. Again, this enables students to focus their listening.

- Provide this material in advance of the lecture, to orientate students to the lecture.

(8) Follow up

- Indicate to students where they can find information they may have missed during the lecture – either in books, on video, internet notes or some other media.

- Indicate interesting questions they may wish to follow up in their support groups or through particular texts you recommend.

Tutor preparation

Approaching the session

Draw out variations in the approaches that lecturers might take. Emphasize that good note-making on the part of the student is usually the result of both skilled listening and selectivity on the part of students and structured delivery on the part of the lecturer. Some flexibility will be needed on the part of the student in order to adapt to different lecturer styles. Emphasise that students are not expected to write information verbatim: difficulties with note-making often

Aims of the session

■ To help students to focus in lectures and make meaningful notes so that they make the most effective use of lecture time;
■ to draw students, attention to the importance of listening for meaning;
■ to offer students a strategy for working together to make sense of a lecture.

Learning outcomes

By the end of these activities students should be able to:

Learning outcomes	Skills (see p. 193)
(1) Identify ways of using lectures effectively	M
(2) Listen for meaning	IGS, M, OC, P
(3) Recognise the importance of selective note-making while listening	M
(4) Collaborate with others to address difficulties arising from lecture work	IGS, M, P
(5) Identify and apply strategies for good note-making	M, WC

arise because of a lack of selectivity. Advance preparation helps to identify what information is available elsewhere, so that less note-making is needed in the lecture itself.

Materials

Use the Resource Sheet below (see p. 271). Ask students to bring a set of lecture notes with them (about one hour's worth of lecture time) or to undertake the activities on the Resource Sheet in advance of the session.

Activities

(1) Icebreaker   `C, OC`

Each student suggests the name of a lecture they will give in ten years time on a specialist area

they will have developed by then. Creative suggestions welcome.

(2) Using lecture time effectively   `C, IGS, M`

• *Threes* Ask students to reflect upon their own attitudes and behaviours in relation to lectures – such as punctuality, preparation, taking a questioning approach, etc.
• *Individually* Ask students to list two ways that they could use lectures more effectively in order to assist their study.
• *Whole group* Brainstorm: what ideas did students have about how they could use lectures most effectively? Add your own advice.
• Ask students to brainstorm and discuss advantages of preparing in advance for taught sessions such as lectures.

(3) What is the purpose of making notes? `M, P`

- *Whole group* Brainstorm: what is the purpose of making notes for this subject? Add in your reflections from your own subject or course perspective.

(4) Listening for meaning `IGS, M, P`

- Either present a 20-minute lecture to the students, or show a documentary. Ask students to put their pens down and listen without writing, i.e. taking no notes of any kind.
- At the end of the talk, students are given 3 minutes to jot down the main things they learnt from listening.
- Students can write up to 3 questions to which they need an answer, based on what they have just heard. Each question should be clearly written on a separate Post-it.
- Students put their Post-its on the wall.
- All students read the Post-its and remove one (not their own) that they feel they can answer.
- Each student reads out the question they took and provides an answer. The other students confirm or amend the answer, and amend their notes if necessary.
- Use the Post-its remaining on the wall as useful feedback on what students found difficult. Encourage the group to work out answers to these as far as possible.
- Use the exercise to discuss how much students were able to remember by focusing on listening alone. What have they learnt that might influence their future note-making?

(5) Variation on listening for meaning `IGS, M, P`

- After the 20 minutes of 'just listening', ask students to make some notes as previously.
- *Groups of about five people* Ask groups to go through the lecture together, pooling the different points each took, so that, together, they have a fuller set of notes.
- Draw out from students any differences in their notes before and after they collaborated

with others. Bring out how useful this might be as a support-group activity.

(6) Tips on note-making `IGS, M, P`

- *Small groups* Ask students to use the material they read on note-taking and their experience of the above exercises, in order to draw up a list of useful tips about making notes.
- *Whole group* In turn, ask each group to give one tip, until ideas are exhausted (or the allocated time is up). For younger or more distracted groups, it can help to turn this into a team game and allocate points for each item contributed. Continue until the groups have contributed all their ideas. Make sure students note down the tips offered by their peers.

(7) Improving notes `IGS, M`

Use the Resource Sheet below (see p. 271).

- *Individually* Ask students to look through the notes they made during a recent lecture. Give them some time to write these (or part of these) out in at least one other format – such as in headings and bullets points, mind maps, scatter notes, patterns, using colour or images, etc. Encourage creativity.
- *Groups of three* Each person talks through the advantages of the method they used first and the one they tried for this activity, taking feedback from the group. Which method do they think works best for them?

- *Individually* Ask students to jot down what they think are the strongest and weakest features of their current note-making. What can they do to improve their notes?
- *Pairs* Ask pairs to help each other to set 2 priorities each for making their note-making more effective. Ask them to note in their diaries a date for checking their progress on these priorities.

(8) Using videos `M`

For longer sessions or those with more needy intakes, students can be given a video to watch and asked to take notes on it. This could be a section of a lecture or a film documentary.

- Draw out from the group what the main points in the video were and the kinds of things that they would be expected to note.
- Give students a few minutes to assess how far they had gathered the main points.
- Play the video again, showing the students the clues they should be picking up on to spot important points. Draw out how they can recognise these, from the language used, body language, and other cues. Point out the kind of detailed information they could get from elsewhere and therefore may not need to note now. They may find it easier to note from books rather than by ear. This is especially true of overseas and mature students.

- Depending on group size and the level of need, another video could be used to embed this learning. This time ask students to call out 'pause' each time there is a cue they should be picking up on. Replay it and ask other students if they agree.

(9) Employability links   Emp, S

- *Whole group* Ask students to brainstorm ways that note-making skills, when combined with listening, might be useful in terms of different occupations. Draw out uses, for example, such as taking minutes for meetings, making case notes for clients, keeping personal records of what is said in meetings, etc. Many jobs require people to sit in long meetings where it pays to be able to keep one's attention focused.

RESOURCE SHEET
Making the most of lectures

The key to gaining most from lectures is in the advance preparation.

(1) Recommended reading

Aim to read at least part of one of the following:

- Cottrell, Stella (1999), *The Study Skills Handbook* (Basingstoke: Macmillan – now Palgrave), pp. 115–20 and pp. 126–7.
- Northedge, A. (1990), *The Good Study Guide* (Milton Keynes: Open University Press), pp. 64–72.

(2) Activities

- Look through the notes you have made for any one hour's worth of lectures this week. Write these out in at least one other format – such as heading and bullets points, mind maps, scatter notes, patterns, using colour or images, etc. Be creative.
- What are the advantages of the method you used first and the one you tried for this activity? Which method works best for you?
- What are your weak points, currently, in note-making from lectures?
- What are your strong points?
- Comment (in your reflective diary if you keep one), how you can best set out your notes so that they are most useful for you.

(3) Reflection

Reflect upon your attitudes and behaviours in relation to lectures – such as punctuality, preparation, taking a questioning approach, etc. List two ways that you could use lectures more effectively in order to assist your study.

17 Reading for research

Students' difficulties with reading

Students probably have far more difficulties with reading than most teaching staff are aware. There are many reasons why students struggle with reading. A few are listed below.

Physical difficulties

In a survey of complete cohorts of students at the University of East London on two courses, almost two thirds of students referred to difficulties with physical aspects of processing print: covering one eye to read, sore eyes after a short period of reading, text blurring, skipping lines, losing place. Students followed up by interview reported that recent eye tests had not found anything to account for these problems.

Phonic difficulties

Similarly, McGuiness (1999) wrote that her undergraduates were surprised to find they had poorer reading skills than they believed, many being unable to break longer words down phonetically. Instead, they searched for small words within a longer word, and put these together to form a composite which did not match the target word (e.g. paramagnetism: para–ram–magnet–ism, to give pararamagnetism).

Selecting

Students lack both confidence and skills in what

to select. This is not simply a feature of weak students. High-achieving students are often afraid not to note something which they feel they may be tested on later, and can spend excessive amounts of time both reading and noting from books. As they work quickly, this can appear to be less of a problem than for weaker students, who may also be slow at reading and noting.

Reading speed

Students entering higher education from non-traditional routes often have very weak reading histories. Some have not read a book since school. The reading they have done may be in very short sections and with captions, such as in popular newspapers and magazines. Reading speed can be slow for a number of reasons, including the physical difficulties mentioned earlier, unfamiliarity with specialist vocabulary, poor overall vocabularies, as well as lack of practice. Unfamiliarity with the knowledge base can also slow students down. Many of these contribute to poor comprehension, which means the student has to read over short pieces several times, perhaps stopping to look words up and breaking their rhythm.

Amount of reading

Given the problems enumerated above, reading can be a slow process for many undergraduates.

In addition, they may have much less time to read now than students had traditionally. Students can develop serious anxieties about covering the set reading, especially if they feel obliged to read and note from cover to cover.

Reading lists

Long lists of book titles without any guidance on how to differentiate between them can create problems for many students. It can lead to either high spending on books which students cannot afford, or long waits in libraries while books they do not really need to read are brought up from the stacks, or even longer time spent reading non-essential and duplicated information.

How lecturers can help

Reading speed, accuracy and comprehension does tend to improve through the additional practice afforded by a higher education course; however, it is difficult to make up for the lifetime of missed practice which some students bring. Whilst decoding skills may improve, it takes much longer to make up vocabulary, familiarity with a range of writing styles, ability to follow complex syntax, and confidence in approaching complex texts.

(1) Guidance on selecting alternatives

When students are under severe financial and time pressures, and must select what to read, it helps if they are given guidance on which texts cover similar ground, and which books are viable alternatives for those they might not be able to find in the library.

(2) Orientation towards key information

For first- and second-year students, indicate key chapters and paragraphs rather than whole books, if only part of a book is essential reading. This helps the student to take permission to read selectively.

- Group books on the reading list according to topic.
- Give a star rating for what is best to read – and indicate a reasonable alternative.
- Be specific about relevant and essential chapters or pages.
- Annotate lists to give some insight into what is expected from the reading.

(3) Structuring reading

Setting key questions to guide reading helps students to focus on what is essential. This also helps them to develop a sense of the questions they should be formulating themselves to direct their reading.

(4) Good photocopies

When distributing photocopies of material, be aware that many students may struggle to decode even good print, so faded or reduced copies will put additional strain on reading.

(5) Details in writing

Some lecturers fire off names and titles as if students were very familiar with who is working in the field, and what books are around. One university student reported a lecturer suggesting: *'There is John's book on the banking system, and Robert wrote something chic on the Hanseatic League.'* Students may not be able to take proper names down accurately by ear, so book references and details should always be given in writing.

Aims of the session

- ■ To develop students' confidence in their reading;
- ■ to develop students' strategies in reading and noting for specific purposes;
- ■ to build students' basic research skills;
- ■ to develop further the skills of brainstorming, note-making, reflection and working with others which were introduced in earlier sessions.

Learning outcomes

By the end of these activities students should be able to:

Learning outcomes	Skills (see p. 193)
(1) Identify strategies for finding information more quickly	IGS, M
(2) Use different reading styles for different tasks, including reading selectively	IGS, M
(3) Recognise the value of structured approaches to reading	IGS, M
(4) Evaluate what can make reading difficult for themselves and devise their own list of tips on making reading easier	M, P, R
(5) Use subject specific approaches to reading	M
(6) Employ strategies for note-making when reading	IGS, M, P
(7) Employ correct usage of references and bibliographies	IGS, KU, M, WC
(8) Evaluate key source materials	E, M
(9) Collaborate with others to investigate a subject	E, IGS, M

Tutor preparation

Approaching the session

Sensitivity is the key here. Lecturers need to be aware of the extreme embarrassment people can feel about any kind of reading difficulty – even if it results from poor eyesight. Bring out that reading anxieties or difficulties of one kind or another are not unusual even in higher education. There is research based on Harvard students which shows not only that unexpectedly high numbers of students took up an option to improve their reading skills but that when they were trained to read at speed, they neglected the more essential task of reading for meaning.

Materials

This is a session which works best if there has been advance preparation, based on the Resource Sheet below (see p. 279). Depending on which activities you select, you will need to provide:

- **For Activity 4**: Select a short passage (about one page of easy-to-read print) to read in class. You will need a copy for each person. Draw up a short list of questions to focus reading. For half the group, attach this to the reading passage so it is not clear that half of the class receive different information. Do not give the questions to the other half of the group until after the activity.
- **For Activity 10**: A passage for students to read and make notes on in preparation for the session – or to use in the session. This can be a section of a book they have already. Give a question to focus their reading and note-making.
- **For Activity 12**: A copy for each person of a list of ten book titles, articles, etc., with the reference material out of order and sequence. An overhead transparency of the corrected list. Guidelines on making refer-

ences (see pp. 123–5 of Cottrell (1999) for ideas).

- For the internet activity, prepare a list of 5 internet addresses for the information you wish students to find, and a list of the useful search tools and search engines for researching a course-related topic you set for them.
- The Resource Sheet asks students to bring materials for these activities.

Activities

(1) Icebreaker

Each person, in turn, states which character from fiction they would most like to be and why.

(2) 'Flick through' exercise (1) (prepared activity)   IGS, M

- See the Resource Sheet below (p. 279).
- *Threes*   Spend a few minutes feeding back on the activity. What did students find helpful about the activity?
- *Whole group*   Take contributions on what was useful.
- Draw out how they might use this activity to their benefit before each assignment.
- If people found it confusing, offer clarifications. If relevant, open up a discussion on confusion as a necessary part of the learning process, rather than something to shy away from. Confusion often means that old ideas are being challenged, as a way of opening up to a wider understanding.

(3) Reading for meaning   IGS, M

- *Individually or as advance preparation*   What is the point of reading? What do you consider to be the most important characteristic of a 'good reader'?
- *Whole group*   Brainstorm ideas on what makes a 'good reader'.
- *Open up a discussion on the purpose of reading*   Draw out that the main objective when reading is to understand, to look for meaning.

Speed and fluency can help, but are of secondary importance, and will develop through practice. Reassure students that a good reader is not necessarily one who reads quickly. Bring out that very slow reading can interrupt flow: very slow readers may find comprehension improves if they go more quickly.

(4) Structured reading   IGS, M

- Divide the group randomly into two.
- *Individually*   Give all students the same passage to read. Give half the class questions to orientate their reading. Give time to read the passage. Do not allow talking or questions (say you'll explain later why not).
- Give the whole group a quiz, answered individually, based around the questions you set for half the group.
- Give the answers, letting people mark their own or those of the person next to them.
- Compare the scores between the two halves of the room to see if having the questions made any difference. Usually there is. If not, ask for possible reasons why not.
- What were people's feelings about reading the passage both with and without set questions? Would the group without them have found it useful to have them?
- Draw out the importance of orientating yourself to reading.

(5) 'Flick through' exercise (2) IGS, M

- *Pairs*   Ask students to exchange the book they brought with them with that of another student: Ask students to flick through for 30 seconds, see what catches their eyes and jot down what strikes them – even if it is only one word that stands out. Then ask them to flick through for five minutes, this time focusing on the back cover, the contents, headings, and any item that contains lots of entries in the index. At the end of the five minutes, ask them to jot down what they think the book is about or would be useful for.
- *Pairs*   Discuss the book you were given and

compare responses. How accurate were you in what you picked up in those minutes?

- *Whole group* Draw out the value of skimming through books to pick up the general flavour of a new topic.

(6) Reading strategies for different purposes   `M, P`

- *Whole group* Discuss different approaches to reading. Ask what variations people notice in their own reading depending on their purpose.
- Draw out that people move between rapid scanning and skimming to slow and focused reading depending on a range of factors such as the subject, the writing style, how new the subject matter is to them, the amount of technical or unfamiliar vocabulary, and how relevant the passage is to their needs.
- Draw attention to different reading styles required for the subject area.

(7) Subject-specific reading demands   `M`

If the subject area requires particular types of reading, offer students a page of text for each style. Go through the different types of text with the student, offering suggestions on how these can be read more easily. For example:

(1) *Law* where to focus attention for key information in different kinds of legal documents. What are the telling phrases to search for, and where are these likely to be found?

(2) *History* where to look for short sections of key wording in long preambles to statutes.

(3) *Science reports* the value of the abstract; how to vary reading styles for different sections of a report. The discussion part may be browsed quite quickly, for example, whereas the hypothesis and results may take much slower perusal.

(4) *Physiotherapy* using relevant physical movement when reading may help to make sense of the information.

(8) What makes reading difficult?   `IGS, M, R`

- *Small groups* Draw up lists of suggestions on what can make reading slow or difficult. These can be individual reasons, or things about the book or the particular task, or the environment, or anything else they can think of.
- *Whole group* Collate suggestions. Draw attention to the range of problems people can face with reading at some time.

(9) Tips for reading   `IGS, M, P`

- *Small groups* Ask groups to copy the list of difficulties onto a flipchart and then to consider ways that each difficulty be addressed. Ask them to write up their suggestions opposite each difficulty they address. You may find it appropriate to divide the list of difficulties between groups. If possible, ensure that more than one group covers the same set of difficulties, to increase the chance of options. Encourage students to write clearly.
- Students put their flipchart 'posters' of ideas on the wall.
- *Individually* Read through the suggestions on the posters, noting down useful ideas.
- *Whole group* Ask which ideas most appealed to people.

(10) Making notes when reading   `IGS, M, P, R`

- *Individually* Ask students to read a handout of a short passage you have selected. Give them a question to focus their reading and note-making. Ask them to make notes in the way they usually take notes when reading for a set question. If possible, give this as advance preparation. If this is set in class, ensure there is sufficient time for slow readers and dyslexic students.
- *Whole group* Go through the passage section by section, asking for suggestions of what is important to note in order to answer the question you set.

- Write each suggestion up and ask for confirmation or discussion of its relevance. If it is agreed that the suggestion is not essential to the question, score a line through it.
- Erase anything not essential to the question.
- As you write, use abbreviations and short understandable phrases, laying the notes out so that the information is clear. In effect, you are modelling a note-making technique.
- Are the notes clear and understandable? What tips on good note-making when reading arise from the exercise?
- Give students time to reflect upon their own notes. Did they take too many or too few notes? Did they pick up on the important points?
- *Threes* Discuss how they could improve their note-making when reading. Each person should identify at least one strategy to try out.

Alternative

For more sophisticated groups, this could be done as a small group exercise.

- After students have read the passage and made notes, as in the activity above, ask each group to draw up a collective set of notes in poster form on flip chart paper to display and discuss with the whole group. Their notes should contain only what is essential to the question. Encourage them to use abbreviations and other note-making short-cuts.
- Display the posters.
- Ask the group to draw out comparisons and contrasts betwenn the sets of notes. Draw attention to any inessential information in the notes.
- Are the notes clear and understandable? What tips on good note-making when reading arise from the exercise?

(11) Difficulties with note-making when reading   `IGS, M, P`

- *Small groups* Use an Action Set approach (see p. 254) to explore strategies for note-making when reading.
- *Whole group* Draw together ideas from the Actions Sets on useful strategies.

(12) References, bibliographies and plagiarism   `IGS, KU, M, WC`

- *Whole group* Draw attention to the importance of these and to guidelines for making quotations, references, and bibliographies. Refer to any policies on plagiarism and take questions on any 'grey areas'.
- *Small group* Give out the list of randomised information on books titles, articles, etc., for your subject. Ask groups to arrange these into order.
- *Whole group* Use an overhead transparency to go through the correct referencing procedure, taking questions on anything that is unclear about sequencing or points of detail.
- Link this to the session on writing skills and to any feedback they may have received on written work.

(13) Book reviews   `A, IGS, KU, S`

Ask students to undertake a book review, on which they will report for other students in their group. Let them know how long they will have to talk about the book. The book they choose must be in an area related to the course, or you may prefer to give them a set list to select from. They should aim to include:

(1) what the book covers, in very general terms;
(2) one interesting thing they found out from reading it;
(3) anything they disagreed with and why;
(4) an indication of whether it is worth reading and which parts are especially useful;
(5) something about the book they feel could have been better (if anything);
(6) if they prefer a different book on this subject and why.

After the review

- At the end of the review, others who have read the book may like to comment on their own opinion and use of the book. You might like to add your own input on its value.
- Draw out what students found valuable about doing this exercise.
- Suggest that this is a useful activity to undertake in support groups, or amongst friends on

the same course, as it helps to focus reading.

- You may also want to set the book review as a written assignment for first-year groups.

(14) Searching for sources on the internet

Ensure that students have already had training on using the internet or networked information. If not, guide them on where to go for training. Give students a list of addresses which you know contain useful information about:

(1) the university in general;
(2) topics they will cover on the course.

- Ask them to find specific information for 5 different items at given addresses, to build up their practice.
- Ask them to find out what kinds of information are available about one particular topic. Let them know the search tools which are the most useful for that topic (e.g. Yahoo, Lycos, Google, Ask Jeeves, etc.). Encourage them to browse and to list what they find and to note down the electronic addresses so they can find the information again.
- Ask students to share what they found out about using the internet that could be useful to their studies.

(15) Identifying a good source

- Draw out the characteristics of a good source for your subject area. How can students identify an appropriate source?
- Discuss the uses of the internet as a source of material for the subject.
- Bring out the differences between the way sources are validated for books and for the internet – for example, information on the internet may not be refereed or updated.

(16) Employability links

Small groups   Ask groups to brainstorm ways that the skills covered in the session(s) on reading, research and note-making might be useful in the world of work. For example, preparing reports for employers, looking for information on behalf of clients, researching a business project, etc.

Whole group   Discuss suggestions from the group.

RESOURCE SHEET
Reading for research

(1) Recommended reading

Aim to read at least one of the following:

■ Cottrell, Stella (1999), *The Study Skills Handbook* (Basingstoke: Macmillan – now Palgrave), Chapter 6.
■ Williams, K. (1989), *Study Skills* (Basingstoke: Macmillan), Chapters 1–3.
■ Northedge, A. (1990), *The Good Study Guide* (Milton Keynes: Open University Press), Chapter 2.
■ Entwistle, N. (1997), *Styles of Learning and Teaching: An Integrated Outline of Educational Psychology for Students, Teachers and Lecturers* (London: David Fulton Publishers), pp. 65–86; more advanced reading, looking at research into student reading.

(2) 'Flick through' exercise

■ Visit the library or a book shop. Flick through 3 books, preferably on the same subject, spending only a few minutes on each.
■ What differences can you detect in how each writer approaches the subject?
■ Does looking at several books help you to build up a better sense of the subject, or does it simply confuse you?
■ What puts you off some of the books: the print size? the page colour? the style?

(3) Making notes from reading

Read the passage given for this activity. Make notes in the way you usually take notes when reading. Bring these to the session on reading.

(4) Reflection

■ What is the point of reading? What do you consider to be the most important characteristic of a 'good reader'?
■ How many reasons can you think of why reading in general or for a particular reading task might be difficult for some people? Draw on your own experiences of occasions when reading was less easy than others.

(5) Bring to the session on reading

Bring any book you know well or have read recently to the session on reading. You will be asked to swap this with someone else during the session in an exercise on familiarising yourself with books. It is important that you have a good sense of what the book is about.

18 Writing skills I

Students' difficulties with writing

Judging their writing according to school priorities

Students under-estimate the relative importance, in an higher education context, of macro-skills such as analysis, compared to technical English skills such as spelling. They often attribute low marks to technical English, rather than focusing on developing thinking skills and higher-order writing skills such as organising ideas and developing an argument.

Words in thousands

2000 words can sound like 'a million' to new students, who may lack a visual sense of what this means in terms of pages in their own handwriting, and who may lack skills for generating ideas and words.

They do not know how to correct mistakes

Students generally presume that they have written in correct English, so comments such as 'incorrect English' do not make sense or offer a way forward, unless the correction is written out clearly. It still may not make sense, but the student will at least have a correct model to work from.

Imagining that 'complex' sounds clever

Text books appear to be written in very compli-cated and inaccessible English, which some students associate with sounding clever. They then try to produce writing which sounds compli-cated, often with long, compound sentences and strings of long words, believing this is what is required.

They fear being judged too harshly by their work

Handing in a piece of work can be a very expos-ing activity, even for accomplished students.

They do not understand the instructions or the title

This can arise for a number of reasons, such as not being able to make sense of very long assignment titles, especially if these contain several items of specialised vocabulary or unusual words. It can also be because the student is trying to second-guess what is being asked, especially if they are used to complex titles and are given one which looks simple.

How lecturers can help

(1) Clarify writing skills priorities

Prioritise higher-order skills for comment, and be more sparing on comments about comments on technical English until the higher-order skills are in place. Be clear about assignment criteria – and especially the relative weight given to macro-skills (research, analysis, critical appraisal, clarity of exposition, argument, etc.) and to micro-skills (spelling, punctuation, grammar).

(2) Offer guidance and support on meeting word limits

- Ask students to guess how many words a particular piece of text contains and jot this down before they hear the answer. How close was their estimation?
- If they have been keeping a reflective journal or other notes, ask them to count up how much they have written already – to get a sense of what 'hundreds of words' looks like in their own writing. Tell them to stop counting when they get to 500.
- Introduce activities to help them become used to generating words and ideas.

(3) Marking strategies

Ensure that students are clear about the marking strategy. For example, that on early assignments you will focus on the more important skills from a higher education perspective (research, argument, etc.) or that you will not correct more than three technical errors on any one piece of writing even if they are there. This saves you time but also offers a manageable limit for students, without them thinking that their work is necessarily correct. Identify those students with serious difficulties and either offer additional support or refer them for additional support within the university if any is available.

(4) Encourage clarity

Emphasise that clarity (the reader being able to understand what is said) is more important than 'sounding clever' when the message is not clear. Suggest they read their work aloud to a friend not on the course or a relative, and to ask the friend to interrupt every time something is not clear. Each time, they should stop reading and say, in their own words, what they mean, without using slang. If the friend understands, they should jot down what they said before reading on.

(5) Assignment details

Encourage clarity in student writing by offering clear assignment titles. Go over the title and make sure students can understand it. Offer guidance on the main aspects that students are expected cover. Be very clear about marking criteria. If something is either deceptively simple or requires more than meets the eye, be clear about this and give guidance on how to approach it.

Tutor preparation

Approaching the session

Sessions on writing need to be finely attuned to the level of need within the group, to the types of writing required, and to how support for writing is incorporated into teaching more generally. This session focuses on developing confidence around writing and the general expectations for a higher education setting. More advanced work is offered in Chapter 19. Some of the activities recommended for Chapter 15 are also suitable for this session, and if these

---

Aims of the session

- ■ To develop students' confidence with writing tasks in general;
- ■ to give students strategies to develop a piece of writing in its early stages;
- ■ to introduce students to writing support groups.

Learning outcomes

By the end of these activities students should be able to:

Learning outcomes	Skills (see p. 193)
(1) Identify their strengths and weaknesses in writing and set priorities for improvement	IGS, M, OC, P, R, WC
(2) Employ strategies for beginning and developing a piece of writing	C, IGS, M, WC
(3) Offer and receive support for writing	IGS, R
(4) Recognise the importance of clarity to effective written communication	WC

have been covered before, it is useful to make the link between thinking and writing skills. If the 'support for writing' activity is used, this must be based on previous group-building work and practice with constructive criticism. If these have not been covered, then the activity may be too threatening. The early activities are set to build up confidence in writing in front of others and in receiving feedback on writing.

Materials

Resource Sheets are offered below (see pp. 285–6).

Activities

(1) Icebreaker: what is the caption?

Put an ambivalent cartoon image or photo-graphic image on the overhead projector. Ask each person to devise a short caption for it, to be read out in small groups or to the whole group.

(2) Writing anxieties   IGS, M, OC, P, R

- *Small groups*   Ask students to form groups of 4 with people with whom they feel reason-ably comfortable. Explain that they will stay

in these groups for future group work on writing.
- Ask students to draw up a list of all the writing anxieties, worries and difficulties experienced by all those in the group.
- Ask students to draw up a second list of what they feel they have to gain by developing their writing and focusing on it for the next session(s).
- *Whole group*   Collate answers from the group.
- *Individually*   Ask students to jot down what their personal gains would be from improving their writing; encourage them to come back to this if they are ever feeling discouraged.
- Draw out how much anxiety and concern people have about their writing, and that this is very common, even with professional writers.

(3) Getting into the flow   C, IGS, M, OC, WC

- *Individually*   Ask students to think of a word they really like. If they had a favourite word, what would it be?
- Ask them to write the word so that the letters run down the page.
- Ask them to write either a single word or a very short phrase (2–3 words) beginning with

each of these letters. Each of these new words should be connected somehow to the main word. A student offered the following example: **STAR**

> S – sparkling
> T – tiny light
> A – astral, cold, distant
> R – rotating in space

- It can help if you contribute a version of your own that a student could reasonably be expected to have produced.
- *Small groups*   Invite students to read out what they have written. Tell groups to encourage each other to read it out, but nobody is forced to do so. Usually, those who have struggled with writing find this very rewarding, as it is very structured.
- *Feedback*   Each listener contributes *one* thing (only) they liked about what they heard.
- Do *not* ask for contributions to the main group, unless most people agree to read theirs out. The idea is to create confidence with each other and not a hierarchy of good writers.
- Draw attention to how much can be expressed in a few words.

(4) Developing an idea into writing   `C, IGS, WC`

- Write on the board, flipchart or overhead projector a list of words such as snow, leaf, spider, cloud, dream, island, friend, football, paper, dog.
- *Individually*   Ask students to choose, quickly, one word from the list.
- Building on Activity 3, ask them to write five lines about the word they chose; these do not need to be in proper sentences. The lines can be as short as they like but no longer than seven words.
- *Small groups*   Again, invite students to read out what they have written. Tell groups to encourage each other to read it out, but nobody is forced to do so.
- *Feedback*   Each listener contributes *one* thing (only) they liked about what they heard.

- *Whole group*   Ask what it was like to write, read their work aloud and receive feedback? Was the experience as bad as they might have imagined?

(5) Support for writing   `IGS, OC, WC`

- *Small groups*   Ask students to take out the brief piece of writing they did as preparation. Alternatively, set this as a writing activity in class. Emphasise that, at this stage, they are not expected to produce a work of art – the aim is merely to get in the habit of putting words down on paper. Encourage them either to read their writing out themselves or to invite someone else in their group to read it for them.
- Each listener in the group must jot down in clear writing:
  - three things they like about the writing: whether it is the overall idea, the passion of the writer, particular words they liked, etc.
  - two ideas about how the writing could be developed: for example, more information about something, changing the order around.
- Each listener takes turns to say aloud what they liked about the feedback and their ideas about how the writing could be developed further.
- The writers state which *one* idea from each person they consider to be the most interesting for them to take away and think about.
- The writer then receives what each person had written down about their writing so that they can take it away and use it to develop the piece of writing for the next session.
- *Whole group*   Ask how people felt about this activity. Let them know that they will be doing a similar activity in the next session. Let them know that professional writers have often used support such as this to develop their writing and that it is a very valuable opportunity for developing a piece of writing for assessment.
- Ask for ideas about how the kinds of feedback they were given could be divided into categories. Keep this list for the next session.

(6) Clarity and ambiguity

- *Whole group*   Put up a list or visual examples of ambiguous messages from public notices, hoardings and adverts. What different interpretations could these have. Where does the ambiguity come from?
- Draw out the importance of clarity to good writing. Encourage students actively to search out ambiguous phrases in their own writing.

(7) Priorities   IGS, M, OC, P, R, WC

Ideally, this activity should be set as advance preparation to allow time for reflection.

- *Individually*   Ask students to complete the self-evaluation questionnaire: 'How good am I at managing writing tasks?'
- Ask them to identify their main priorities for improving their writing.
- Ask them to identify their one main priority. (Do not include spelling, grammar or punctuation.)

- *Small groups*   Use an Action Set format, i.e., each person takes a turn at being the focus. In turn, give each student two minutes to say what they identified as their main writing priority. Remind them that spelling, grammar and punctuation are not included: these are too wide-ranging for useful peer support of this kind.
- Give the groups a short period (3–5 minutes) to brainstorm ideas on ways of working with each person's area of priority. They can refer to activities suggested by their reading material if they wish.
- Each person identifies the most useful idea for them to work with, and writes this down.

(8) Close

Whole group   Each person says the most valuable thing they have gained from the session.

RESOURCE SHEET
Writing 1

(1) Recommended reading

Aim to read at least one of the following:

- Cottrell, Stella (1999) *The Study Skills Handbook* (Basingstoke: Macmillan – now Palgrave), Chapter 7.
- Northedge, A. (1990) *The Good Study Guide* (Milton Keynes: The Open University Press), Chapter 5.
- Williams, K. (1995) *Writing Essays: Developing Writing* (Oxford: The Oxford Centre for Staff Development).

(2) Self-evaluation

- Complete the self-evaluation: 'How good am I at managing writing tasks?'
- What are your main priorities for improving your writing?
- Which is your one top priority? (Do not include spelling, grammar or punctuation.)

(3) Where does your interest lie?

- Of all the topics you have covered for any of your subjects since starting the term, what ONE aspect interests you the most?
- Jot down quickly what it is that you find most interesting and why this subject has relevance for you. Do this either in note form or your usual writing.
- Jot down a further five interesting points or details about this subject.
- Rewrite what you have written so that it flows better. It does not need to be perfect - so long as you have something down on paper. You can write in any style you wish for this exercise.

(4) Reflection

- Based on your reading and the activities above, jot down in your journal your general feelings about academic writing. Do you feel confident or anxious?
- What do you consider to be your writing strengths? What do you need to improve?
- When you are given a writing assignment, do you worry about it or are you quite confident that you will accomplish a reasonable piece of work within the deadlines?

How good are you at managing writing tasks?

On the chart below, tick the appropriate box, and rate how well you perform the skill now.
Rating: 9 = *excellent,* 1 = weak or *needs a lot of work.*

'Do I know . . .'	Yes	I just need practice	Not sure	No	Rating	Order of priority
How to get into the habit of writing?						
How to get started on a piece of writing (or overcome 'writer's block')?						
What an essay is?						
A procedure for writing essays?						
How to analyse assignment questions?						
How to organise information?						
How to use and organise concepts?						
How to structure an essay?						
How to structure a report?						
How to write good paragraphs?						
How to write persuasive argument?						
About different academic writing styles?						
How to use personal experience in writing?						
How to draft, edit and proofread?						
How to present my writing?						
What gets good marks?						
How to use feedback to improve my marks?						

What are the two main priorities for improvement in your next piece of writing? Highlight these two in colour. Repeat this self-evaluation when your next piece of writing is returned, using the tutor's feedback.

19 Writing skills II

Students' difficulties with writing assignments

Working in the dark
Students may have little idea what an assignment is supposed to be like. Even if they have produced assignments before, these may have been to different sets of requirements than those set for the latest assignment (see above, pp. 128–9). Even with concrete examples they may be uncertain what it is that is good or bad about what they are reading, especially if their own work is weak.

Lack of constructive feedback
Students may never have received feedback which was positive or which made it clear what they needed to do to succeed in any realistic way.

Inability to develop writing
Students can be uncertain what to do to improve upon a first draft, and may not even consider redrafting their writing. For some, failure to get it right first time is seen as a personal weakness rather than a necessary part of good writing technique. For example, students may have difficulties either in generating enough ideas and words to meet word limits, or write in too wordy a manner to be able to cover

the subjects they want to address. They may not know how to structure their work or the best order to present ideas.

How lecturers can help

(1) Concrete examples
Offer concrete examples of what is required – preferably three annotated copies of each type of assignment, bringing out the strengths and weaknesses of each example.

(2) Clear marking criteria
Clarify what gains and what loses marks.

(3) Constructive feedback
Offer constructive feedback which students can realistically address. Where appropriate group work has been undertaken, offer opportunities for constructive peer feedback and mutual support on writing.

(4) Interventions
Create opportunities for interventions such as peer or tutor feedback early in the writing process. Discuss your own reworkings of text and the principles you use for redrafting articles. Ask students to discuss how they redraft work.

Aims of the session

- To develop habits and strategies for elaborating a piece of writing;
- to give students a clear sense of what is expected from written assignments;
- to develop students' ability to identify and write to set criteria.

Learning outcomes

By the end of these activities students should be able to:

Learning outcomes	Skills (see p. 193)
(1) Develop an on-going piece of writing using support from their writing group	IGS, WC
(2) Recognise what a writing assignment looks like	KU
(3) Identify what gains and what loses marks	IGS, KU
(4) Identify what is required for different assignment titles, and how these relate to the way a piece of writing is marked	A, E, IGS, KU, M. WC
(5) Employ strategies for working to word limits and demonstrate an awareness of how this affects marks	C, IGS, M, WC
(6) Recognise the importance of 'structures' to effective written communication	A, S, WC

Tutor preparation

Approaching the session

This session builds on skills learnt in Chapter 18 ('Writing Skills I') and Chapter 15 ('Developing Thinking Skills'), and constructive criticism skills developed in earlier sessions. Students receive the opportunity to develop a piece of writing with feedback in the drafting stages, and to explore what lecturers are looking for when marking assignments. If the course is accredited, the writing developed over these sessions could be used as a marked assignment. Encourage students to work on their writing between sessions.

Materials

- A Resource Sheet is offered below (see p. 293).
- For **Activity 2**: if students are using the *Study Skills Handbook*, notify them that the two pieces of writing referred to under 'Activities' are on pp. 183–7.
- If you are not using the *Handbook* with your students, prepare two essays or other assignments of roughly 1000 words, which simulate students' writing. One should be noticeably better than the other, but each should have good points and areas for improvement. On a separate sheet, provide written feedback which indicates the strengths and weaknesses of each.

- For **Activity 3**: examples of essay titles for your subject area.
- For **Activity 5**: offer 2 pieces of text on the same topic (about 100–150 words), one written in a condensed way, the other more 'wordy'.

Activities

(1) Icebreaker

Each person says one distracter they have to deal with before they can settle down to write.

(2) Marking assignments   `IGS, KU`

- Using the 'Evaluating writing' section of the Resource Sheet below: either in the session or for home preparation, give students some assignments to mark for themselves, following your marking criteria and with 'tutor feedback' (either that in the *Handbook* or that you distributed).
- *Small groups* Ask students to brainstorm what they think lecturers are looking for when they mark an assignment.
- Ask for any questions the students might have about the tutor feedback. Was anything about the tutor feedback 'unclear'?
- *Whole group* Take suggestions on what lecturers are looking for when they mark and open this up to discussion. Confirm or clarify their perceptions and add anything else you feel they need to know about how course work is marked for your subject.
- Clarify any points arising from the activity.

(3) Working with titles   `A, E, IGS, KU, M, WC`

- *Whole group* Ensure that students understand what the different words used in titles mean (see p. 143, the *Study Skills Handbook*).
- Give examples of the styles of assignment titles that are used in your subject.
- Use these titles to develop some brief outline plans, showing how many sections the title implies. How can students tell how many

marks are allocated for each section so that they know how to weight their own answer? Might another lecturer weight the marks differently?

- *Small groups* If there is time, give students 2 titles to break down quickly into their component parts and to state what the question is getting at. Go over the suggestions, making clear what are acceptable possibilities.

- *Whole group* If students are going to be assessed on the writing they are developing in these sessions, discuss with them what makes a strong title for a piece of work.
- Encourage them to include either a question or wording which requires them to contrast different points of view.
- Ask students to generate titles on a topic you give them, so that they get the feel for this.
- Note any titles that students are likely to find difficult to answer, and explain how these should be addressed.

(4) Metaphor   `C, IGS, WC`

- *Individually* Ask students to consider which metaphor best applies to the way they approach an assignment such as an essay. Give some examples of extended metaphors (see Chapter 6). Ask students to complete the phrase: 'Writing an essay (or report, case study, etc.) is like . . . because. . . . '.
- Ask students to think of all the ways that writing the type of assignment is, or is not, similar to their chosen metaphor.
- *Small groups* Ask students to discuss the metaphor they chose.
- *Whole group* Take contributions of metaphors that students have used.
- *Draw out* what the metaphors reveal about how the writing process can be conceived.
- *Individually* Ask students to note down any ideas raised by others that help them to conceptualise the writing task more clearly.

(5) Awareness of word limits   `M`

Students can imagine 1000 words is much more than it really is. Using the piece of writing students have been working on in the previous session and for home preparation, check if they know how many words they have written. If they do not know already, ask them to guess and then to count. Ask for reactions. Compare what they have written with the word limits for subject assignments.

(6) Working with words   IGS, M, WC

- *Whole group*   Brainstorm one topic onto the board or a flipchart using pattern notes – or use the writing theme volunteered by any student who finds it difficult to meet word limits. Take one strand from these pattern notes and elaborate it through directed questioning: What else do we know? How? When? Why? Examples? Applications? Good points in the model or theory? Flaws in it? Interesting aspects to it? etc.
- If necessary, introduce activities which generate ideas and material to meet word limits (see Chapter 15, and the *Study Skills Handbook*, pp. 152–5: 'concept pyramids').
- *Small groups*   Give students examples of two pieces of text (see Materials above) which describe the same topic. One should cover the ground in quite a descriptive or wordy way; the other should be much more condensed. Ask groups to:
  - draw up a list of all the information and knowledge they gain from each passage
  - compare the two pieces, looking at how one manages to convey more information than the other in the same amount of words.
- *Whole group*   Discuss their findings.
- Link this to the way marks are allocated. Bring out how 'waffle' can eat up the word limits often leading to essential material which gains marks being omitted.

(7) Generating words: additional activity   C, WC

- *Individually*   Each person takes the writing they did as advance preparation (or during

the previous session) and maps out, as pattern notes, what they have written.
- Give them five minutes to expand these pattern notes using the questions used in activity 5 above. Write the questions up where they can be seen.
- *Small groups*   Each person shows their pattern notes to the group, describes them briefly and then the group brainstorms further ideas to add to them.

(8) Structuring writing   A, S, WC

Whole group   Emphasise that a good piece of writing has a clear line of reasoning – or one strong message. This message should be the spine upon which all other writing hangs. You may like to illustrate this with a 'fish-bone' diagram as below. This could be described as a river with tributaries or as a tree trunk growing new branches which then grew smaller twigs.

All the water in the river system ultimately flows towards the sea – it is the flow of the river that gives it direction. Anything which does not is left behind in lakes or puddles: it is missed out. Similarly, when writing, information should be grouped and organised into paragraphs (refer to their advance reading on paragraphs if possible). Each paragraph feeds into the main argument as tributaries do a river. Smaller points and details are grouped into paragraphs and sections, as narrower channels of a river feed into streams and tributaries. The whole piece of writing, including consideration of alternative points of view, should flow towards a single point. All detail and argument should be relevant to the main message.

If structuring is a real difficulty, the activities on thinking skills (see Chapter 15) may be a necessary foundation before the following activities can be undertaken.

- *Individually*   Ask each person to go over their own piece of writing and jot down the main message or line of reasoning in a few words. This does not have to be written as a sentence. If they find it difficult, ask them to put the writing away for a moment and imagine they are summing up their writing to a friend.

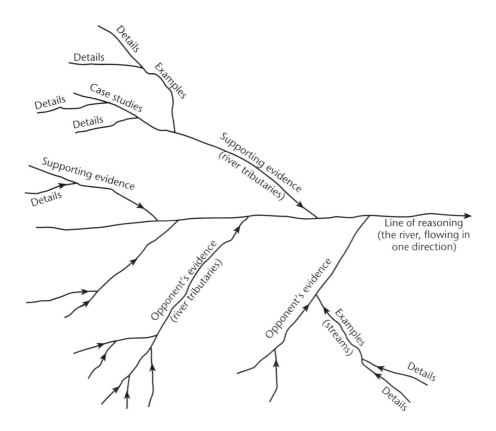

Details
Details
Examples
Case studies
Details
Details
Supporting evidence
(river tributaries)
Supporting evidence
Details
Line of reasoning
(the river, flowing in
one direction)
Opponent's evidence
(river tributaries)
Opponent's evidence
Examples
(streams)
Details
Details

If they still find it difficult, they can consult with their writing group.

(9) Developing writing further   IGS, WC

• *Whole group*   Using a brainstorm, remind the group of the list of categories used last time for group feedback, for example, 'writing flow', 'structure', 'imagery', etc. Write suggestions up where they can be seen. Ask if there are any other contributions.

• *Small groups*   Ask students to return to the writing groups they worked in the previous session. Ask students to take out the piece of writing they have been working on as preparation. Emphasise that at this stage they are still not expected to have produced a perfect piece of writing – just something on paper.

  Each person, when it is their turn, states:
  – what their writing is about briefly;

– why they chose it (its interest for them);
– how it has changed so far through re-writing;
– what feedback or help they would like from the group.

• The writer selects about a page or three paragraphs to read aloud, focusing on the area where they feel group feedback would be most helpful. They may ask a volunteer from their group to read if they prefer.

• As in the previous session, each of the listeners should jot down, in clear writing:
  – three things they like about the writing: whether it is the overall idea, the passion of the writer, particular words they liked, etc. These should be different, if possible to last time.
  – two ideas about how the writing could be developed: for example, more information about something, or changing the order around. Where possible, their feedback

should focus on structure and on the feed-back the writer requested;

- *and* each person should note down what they think is the line of reasoning.

• Each person takes turns to say aloud what they liked, their ideas about developing the writing, and states what they think is the line of reasoning or main argument.

• The writers say which *one* idea from each person they consider to be the most interesting for them to take away and think about.

• If the line of reasoning was not clear, the group can offer ideas about how to bring it out more clearly.

• The writer then receives the written feedback to take away and use.

(10) Advance preparation: writing

Encourage students to work on their piece of writing for the next session. Encourage them to read back over the set reading, and to focus especially on:

(1) writing a title which is suitable for their line of argument;

(2) focusing their argument carefully on the title;

(3) organising information and structuring their answer;

(4) meeting the word limit;

(5) if the assignment is going to be submitted for formal accredited assessment, be clear what the marking criteria are and ensure that students have these.

(11) Close

Each person states the most useful or valuable thing they are taking away from today's session.

RESOURCE SHEET
Writing II

(1) Recommended reading

Aim to read at least one of the following:

- Cottrell, Stella (1999), *The Study Skills Handbook* (Basingstoke: Macmillan – now Palgrave), Chapters 7–8.
- Northedge, A. (1990), *The Good Study Guide* (Milton Keynes: Open University Press), Chapters 5–6.
- Creme, P. and Lea, M. R. (1997), *Writing at University: A Guide for Students* (Buckingham and Bristol: Open University Press). Browse the early chapters.

(2) Evaluating writing

- Read through each of the two pieces of assignment writing and take careful note of the title and the marking criteria.
- Read through the first piece slowly and jot down anything that strikes you about it. Slowly read it through again. Using the notes you jotted down, as well as the marking criteria, offer the writer guidance on how the essay might be improved. You can write in the margin or number your points and write them out on a piece of paper.
- When you have finished, check your answers against the tutor feedback.
- Do the same for the second assignment.

(3) Developing your writing

- Redraft the piece of writing you were working on in the previous session.
- Make a note of what you did to develop the writing, such as brainstorming new ideas, researching new information, letting the ideas flow, using suggestions from the previous group feedback, following marking criteria to edit work, etc.
- Consider what kind of help you would like from your writers' group to advance this piece of writing.

(4) Reflection

- How similar was your feedback on the two assignments to the tutor's feedback?
- What questions arose for you in completing this activity?
- Did you identify anything you could change about your own writing?

20 Writing skills III

Students' difficulties and how lecturers can help

See Chapters 6, 18 and 19.

Tutor preparation

Approaching the session

This session builds on the work undertaken in previous sessions, and should enable students to bring a piece of writing nearly to completion, in line with the conventions of the subject area. Keep to the same writing groups as for previous weeks. It may be useful to leave this session until after the session on 'Critical and Analytical Thinking Skills' (Chapter 21).

Materials

- Resource Sheets are included below (see pp. 298–302). These include a suggested self-evaluation sheet and marking criteria sheet in case the piece of writing will be assessed.
- For **Activity 2**: offer students 3 examples of assignments, typed out, written by students from your subject area. The first should have received a high mark, the second a low mark, and one should be in the middle range. Make sure that student names and tutor comments are not on the work. Indicate the mark (roughly) that each received and give students a copy of the marking criteria used to assess them.
- For **Activity 3**: either three short texts of different academic styles or three examples of a subject being written about differently in

Aims of the session

- To give students strategies and time to develop a piece of writing, using support from others;
- to develop students' awareness of how marking criteria are used;
- to develop students' sense of what is required for academic writing, through concrete examples.

Learning outcomes

By the end of these activities students should be able to:

Learning outcomes	Skills (see p. 193)
(1) Demonstrate advanced understanding of what gains good marks for assignments	A, E, IGS, WC
(2) Evaluate student writing	A, IGS, WC
(3) Develop an on-going piece of writing with group support	A, IGS, R, S, WC
(4) Identify varieties within academic writing and the rationale for these	A, IGS, WC
(5) Reference their work	IGS, M, WC
(6) Recognise what is meant by plagiarism and identify strategies for avoiding it	IGS, KU, WC

varied sources including at least one academic text.
- For **Activity 4**: photocopy the Polar Opposites sheet (p. 299 below).
- For **Activity 6**: handouts of how to reference source materials particular to your subject (such as manuscripts, artwork, etc.).
- For **Activity 7**: overheads or handouts of examples of plagiarism.

Activities

(1) Icebreaker

Each person invents and shares the name of the title they will give to their first book.

(2) Evaluating student writing   `A, E, IGS, WC`

If possible, offer this as advance preparation. Otherwise, leave sufficient time for slow readers to read through each assignment.

- *Individually* Offer students 3 examples of assignments, typed out, written by students from your subject area, as described in

'Materials' above. Refer them to the Resource Sheet for instructions.
- *Small groups* Using the work on student writing, ask groups to compare their lists of good and weak points for the worst assignment.
- *Whole group* Collate the lists of points and check for agreement. Make clear what loses marks. Keep bringing the students back to the marking criteria, and how tutors use these to assess work.
- *Small groups* Ask students to compare their lists of good and weak points for the best assignment.
- *Whole group* Collate the lists of points and check for agreement. Make clear what gains marks.
- *Small groups* Ask students to compare their lists of good and weak points for the middling assignment. What advice would they give to the writer to bring the mark up?
- *Whole group* Take the list of suggestions about the advice they would have offered. Ask for any additional ideas. Add in any suggestions of your own. Make sure students write down this list.
- Repeat for the third assignment.

(3) Varieties of writing   A, E, IGS, WC

- *Whole group*   Ask for volunteers to give, in turn, the following message to another student (a listener) but as if the student were one of the following:

  (1) a close friend;
  (2) a child;
  (3) their boss at work or the Vice-Chancellor of the university;
  (4) a stranger;
  (5) someone they know is very anxious;
  (6) someone they know never pays attention;
  (7) A policeman who is expecting something suspicious to happen.

  Message: Tell the listener, who is [from the list above], that there is a person at the door who wants to speak to them in person. Say they have been waiting there for some time, waiting for the listener to arrive.

Draw out what they noticed about the way the message changed depending on the speaker's perception of the listener. Bring out that writing style also differs depending on the context and audience.

- *Individually*   Offer students 3 short passages of text related to the subject area. These could either illustrate different writing styles used for different purposes within the discipline, or the way that writing about a topic in the discipline is different to the way it would be treated in other subject disciplines or in the media.
- Ask students to read these slowly. Emphasise that they will not be asked questions about the content, but instead should look for differences in the way each is written.
- *Small groups*   Each group should list the differences they found and try to come up with some explanation of why the writing may have varied from one piece to another.
- *Whole group*   Take contributions about how writing varied from one passage to another and confirm or clarify the reasons for differences.
- If appropriate: what are the characteristics that are required for writing for your subject area?

(4) Polar opposites   A, E, IGS, WC

- Give students a copy of the Polar Opposites sheet (see p. 299 below).
- *Small groups*   Ask students to plot, in pencil, where they think their subject area, or one strand of writing within the subject area, lies for each aspect shown on the 'polar divide'.
- *Whole group*   Discuss their answers. Bring out what is meant by each of the aspects on the Polar Opposites sheet, and why the writing for the subject takes the approach it does.
- How do they think this might differ from other subjects they study or which are studied at the university?

(5) Developing a piece of writing   A, IGS, R, S, WC

- *Small groups*   Each person takes turn to update the group about their writing by stating briefly:

  (1) the title of the piece and the line of argument;
  (2) who the target audience is;
  (3) how the writing has developed since the last session;
  (4) what they think has improved;
  (5) what they feel needs work and the feedback they would like from the group, and then reads aloud one section (preferably not more than a page) for which they would like feedback. They may ask for a volunteer to read if they prefer.

- The group listens to the piece that is read, noting in particular:

  (1) whether the line of argument is clear;
  (2) whether the writing is likely to suit the target audience;
  (3) anything that relates to the feedback that was requested.

- Each person offers *one* suggestion in line with the feedback requested while one person draws up a list. Each person should offer a different suggestion. This can include things that the writer should definitely keep the same. The group discusses each of these briefly, saying whether they agree or not, and gives reasons why. The writer listens quietly and takes any notes they wish about what is said.

- The writer then says how he or she feels they can make use of the suggestions.

(6) **Referencing your work** IGS, M, WC

Link this to activities in Chapter 17 ('Reading for Research').

Ensure that students have a text which outlines how to reference their work, such as pp. 123–5 in the *Study Skills Handbook*. Go through this with students, checking whether they understand what is needed.

- *Individually* Write up a quotation taken from a textbook, and ask students to write down a sentence to introduce the quotation.
- *Whole group* Take suggestions and write these up. When you have several, go over them, making it clear which are correct, or how to alter these to correct them. Encourage students to write down correct versions.
- *Reinforce* Continue with several examples including the variety of sources that students could reasonably be asked to include for your subject. Ensure that students are given a handout with examples of how to cite and introduce any unusual sources for your subject (such as prints, videos, artefacts, manuscripts, oral testimony, etc.).

(7) **Plagiarism** IGS, KU, WC

- Discuss what is meant by plagiarism and cheating.
- Using an overhead transparency or handout, give examples of plagiarism from your subject area (not from the current intake).
- Be clear what action will be taken in cases of suspected plagiarism.
- *Small groups* Ask groups to brainstorm ideas on how to approach study so as to avoid plagiarism and to list any questions they have about possible grey areas.

- *Whole group* Take suggestions on strategies (such as not making notes with the book open; writing direct quotes in a different colour ink in their notes; not lending assignments to a friend until after they have been marked, etc.).
- Clarify grey areas.

(8) **Assignment types** KU, WC

- Clarify which types of writing will be required for the subject: essays, case-studies, reports, observations, etc.
- For each type, clarify the required structure, explaining why each section is required and giving examples: abstracts, outlines of methodology, extracts of discussion, results, etc.
- Set a marking activity for each type of writing (based on the advance preparation for this session).

(9) **Writing for different audiences** Emp, W

- Offer students several pieces of writing on the same topic, pitched at different levels and in different styles, depending on their purpose and target audience.
- *Small groups* Ask students to discuss the different pieces of writing, identifying the differences. How do they account for these differences? Do they think that each piece is suited to its purpose and audience?
- Ask students to redraft a piece of writing they have undertaken to suit a different purpose and audience.

(10) **Employability links** Emp

Ask students to consider what kinds of writing they are likely to need in the world of work? In what ways have they developed an awareness of writing and writing skills that they could apply in different contexts?

RESOURCE SHEET
Writing skills III

(1) Recommended reading

Aim to read at least one of the following:

- Cottrell, Stella (1999), *The Study Skills Handbook* (Basingstoke: Macmillan – now Palgrave), Chapters 7–8.
- Northedge, A. (1990), *The Good Study Guide* (Milton Keynes: Open University Press) Chapters 5 and 6).
- Creme, P. and Lea, M. R. (1997), *Writing at University: A Guide for Students* (Buckingham and Bristol: Open University Press).

(2) Evaluating student assignments

- Read through the three pieces of student writing that you have been given and the marking criteria.
- For each of the 3 assignments, draw up a list of good points, weak points and interesting points, using the tutor's marking criteria as a guide.
- Jot down why you think one assignment received the best mark.
- Jot down why you think one assignment received the worst mark.

(3) Developing your writing

- Redraft the piece of writing you have been working on for the previous sessions by:

  (1) using the Marking Criteria sheet you have been given;
  (2) writing a title which is suitable for your line of argument;
  (3) focusing your argument carefully on the title and for a target audience;
  (4) organising information and structuring your answer;
  (5) meeting the word limit.

- Bring the writing as near to completion as you can – although it does not need to be the final draft. Bear in mind that you may receive more ideas from your writing group during the next session.

(4) Reflection

- Make a note of what you did to develop your piece of writing this week.
- What did you find difficult about the above activities? What did you find easy?
- How does your own writing compare with the assignments you marked?
- What steps, if any, do you need to take to improve your own writing further?

Polar opposites in academic approach

For each of the aspects numbered below, find out whether it is the convention in your subject area to be nearer the North or the South Pole. This may vary depending on the type of assignment.

Consider how far each dimension is important for your assignment. You could indicate this by making a tick on the dotted line.

North Pole

(1) Every attempt is made to control the conditions under which the research takes place so that the researcher can decide which variables to manipulate and measure.

(2) Results can be generalised – that is, they would hold true if the rrsearchwas repeated.

(3) Numbers and standardised measurements make it easier to generalise results.

(4) Objective – based on evidence and facts rather than personal opinion.

(5) The role of the scientist in the research is minimised and rarely discussed

(6) Individual differences are not important – generalised findings are valued.

(7) Personal experience is regarded as individual and is not relevant. It is not referred to.

(8) The language sounds clinical, neutral, impersonal and dispassionate even if the researcher is passionate about the subject.

South Pole

(1) Every attempt is made to keep the research true to real life – that is, to give it *ecological validity*.

(2) The unique is considered worthy of study – results may be impossible to repeat exactly.

(3) Creative interpretation is highly valued.

(4) Subjective responses, feelings, intuition and creativity are regarded as valuable resources.

(5) The role of the researcher is made explicit – it is considered useful to discuss how the researcher's presence influenced the results.

(6) Individual instances and opportunities for detailed interpretation are valued.

(7) Personal experience is highly valued as giving insight and a deeper understanding.

(8) The language used allows the personality and feelings of the writer to shine through.

From: Stella Cottrell (1999), *The Study Skills Handbook* (Basingstoke: Macmillan – now Palgrave).

Self-evaluation: writing assignment

How this piece of writing has evolved
(What was your interest in the subject when you began. How did this change as you found out more about the subject? Did any text or other source inspire you? What use did you make of peer feedback?)

I consider that the strong points about my writing assignment are:

Ways this assignment could be improved if I were to continue to work on it are:
(For example, what would you have researched that you did not have time to look at for this assignment? How might you have approached it differently?)

Action Plan:
Things I need to do to improve my writing further:

I feel I need further help with writing: Yes/No (erase one)
Give details of the kind of help you feel you need:

Please complete the marking criteria sheet

Name: Date:

Title of course or option:

Marking criteria

		Marks given		
		weak ◄————► excellent		
C	Shows imagination and creativity in combining examples, personal experience, taught material and research	0 1 2 3	4 5 6 7 8 9 10	
M	Evidence of good planning and management of learning	0 1 2	3 4 5	
M	Ideas and concepts are well organised and structured	0 1 2	3 4 5	
WC	There is a strong and identifiable line of reasoning	0 1 2	3 4 5	
WC	Writing is well presented, with accurate spelling, grammar, punctuation and paragraphing	0 1 2	3 4 5	
WC	Writing style is clear, flowing and easy to read	0 1 2	3 4 5	
WC	There is a good sense of the target audience	0 1 2	3 4 5	
S	Draws materials together towards a good conclusion	0 1 2	3 4 5	
KU	Shows evidence of background reading or research relevant to the chosen title	0 1 2 3	4 5 6 7 8 9 10	
KU	Shows understanding of the concepts suggested by the chosen title	0 1 2 3	4 5 6 7 8 9 10	
A	Employs good critical analysis	0 1 2 3	4 5 6 7 8 9 10	
I	There is an appropriate selection of material, relevant to the chosen title and audience	0 1 2	3 4 5	
I	It is accurately referenced throughout and includes a list of references	0 1 2	3 4 5	
IGS	Shows evidence of having made use of peer support and discussion	0 1 2	3 4 5	
R	Shows evidence of constructive personal reflection	0 1 2	3 4 5	
E	Constructive use is made of the Self-evaluation Sheet	0 1 2	3 4 5	

Marks to the right of the line are of an acceptable standard (pass mark = 40).

Overall mark:

Comments:

21 Critical and analytical thinking skills

Students' difficulties with critical and analytical thinking

Tutor feedback on assignments often suggests that students could improve their marks by writing more analytically or critically. Students referred for support frequently admit that they do not know what this means. From feedback from such students, it is evident that some of the following reasons underlie their difficulties with critical and analytical thinking.

They are unaware of what is expected
Students may think they have been critical or analytical, and therefore they do not know what to do as a next step.

It sounds unpleasant
The words themselves can be off-putting. Students may 'feel bad' about being critical, which they have interpreted as 'being negative' and unkind.

Lack of confidence
'Analysis' can be perceived as a threatening word, denoting 'difficulty'. Anxiety about the word freezes the student. Looking at definitions of it and demystifying the word can defuse the anxiety.

Poor reading skills
Students may be unaware of how to read or listen analytically and this carries over into their writing and speaking. Their reading is insufficient and/or superficial. This is an area where the interlinked nature of study skills becomes very evident.

Over-reliance on one source
Students are not always aware that Higher Education requires them to read more than one source for an essay. If they rely primarily on one source, it is difficult to get a critical perspective on the subject matter. Reading and research strategies need to be linked to thinking skills. Comparing two texts is a useful way of developing critical skills, as well as emphasising the importance of extending their reading.

Lack of a model
Students may be unfamiliar with examples of critical and analytical writing on which to model their own.

Journalistic writing styles
One of the main weaknesses in student writing is using journalistic style, including too much unsubstantiated personal opinion. Students can interpret exhortations to 'put themselves into their writing' as an invitation to talk in general

terms about themselves and their ideas. Once launched into this style, it is difficult to enter into more analytical styles.

How lecturers can help

(1) Emphasise the constructive role of criticism
Build on earlier work on constructive criticism (see pp. 117–18, 245). Emphasise that criticism means drawing out the positive as well as areas that can be improved. Emphasise the practical or ethical values of critical thinking. Suggest that students make suggestions or recommendations for improvements rather than seeing criticism as a form of attack.

(2) Provide models of writing
Courses can help by offering 2–3 brief examples of analytical writing relevant to that subject. It

helps if tutors point out the features that make the texts good examples.

(3) Model techniques in lectures
Build analytical appraisals and constructive criticism of theories or ideas into lectures. Draw attention to what you did.

(4) Provide opportunities for students to develop the skills
Set activities in lectures where students' skills are gradually developed through discussion and feedback.

(5) Clear feedback on assignments
If students' work is not analytical enough, offer concrete suggestions on what they could do to make it more analytical – for example, some of the questions they could have raised about evidence.

Aims of the session

- To give students a clear understanding of what is meant by critical thinking and 'analysis';
- to develop students' abilities to employ critical and analytical skills.

Learning outcomes

By the end of these activities students should be able to:

Learning outcomes	Skills (see p. 193)
(1) Apply a critical, analytical thinking approach when reading and writing	A, E, IGS, KU
(2) Employ strategies for reading in an analytical way	A, I, IGS
(3) Develop criteria for evaluating evidence in a piece of writing	E, IGS, WC
(4) Draw valid conclusions	E, I, S
(5) Work together to address areas of difficulty	IGS, P
(6) Critically evaluate subject area source material	E, IGS

Tutor preparation

Approaching the session

Students are often daunted by this area of work, so it is important to:

- Demystify it. Acknowledge that students may find it challenging but treat it as a manageable area that will make it easier to address almost any area of study.
- Go slowly. It may take more than one session. Emphasise that it is important for students to do the preparation exercises.
- Critical analysis of texts or televised debates are good places to begin teaching critical analysis.

Materials

- Resource materials are offered below (see pp. 308–10).
- For **Activity 3**: select three texts for students to analyse (one such text is provided in the *Study Skills Handbook*, Chapter 9). Unless the group is already quite sophisticated, these texts should be short (approximately 200–300 words each) and prepared as indicated below.

Text A: Model analysis

Select a brief complete piece of writing that relates to your subject area. Number the lines. If possible, use wide margins to ease your annotation. Annotate the whole text, making a critical analytical evaluation of its weaknesses and strong points (using the categories used on the student preparation sheet,, pp. 309–10).

Texts B and C

Select a further two texts which exemplify different aspects of critical writing or which exemplify issues in critical analysis relevant to your subject area and student group. Ideally, each should show some weaknesses and strengths, with at least one showing some bias, subjectivity, or hidden agenda. Number the lines of each text.

Activities

(1) Icebreaker: visual messages   `A, E, OC`

Using a controversial poster or photograph, ask students to jot down what the picture means to them – for example, what they like or dislike about it; what message they think it is communicating. Ask each person for their response, and note down differences. Discuss why different people had different responses.

(2) 'Falsely accused'   `A, I, IGS`

Use an everyday example to help students to see the value of close critical thinking. For example, if somebody were to make an unjust accusation against your students, saying that they cheated in their exams or last assignments, the students would probably want to know such things as: *Who says so? Why did they say that? On the basis of what evidence? Was there an ulterior motive? Are they quoting somebody else? If so, how well placed is that person to make such an accusation?* This could be developed as a mini-drama, with you or one group of students challenging a second group of students who have to defend themselves. If you do this, choose a group who are likely to enter into the spirit of the challenge.

Alternatively

Use an extract of a television courtroom drama to introduce the idea of examining evidence from different angles. After showing the extract, draw out some of the ways in which the extract illustrates different types of critical thinking or analysis. Play back the extract in stages, so that students can take in each aspect separately.

(3) Critical and analytical reading   `A, I, IGS, OC`

- *Small groups* Ask groups to work through their answers to the set texts they analysed in preparation (see the Resource Sheet, p. 308). If students are not given advance preparation work, give time now to work through the texts in class first, using the Critical Analysis Sheet below (pp. 309–10). Ask groups to try to reach a consensus in their answers, and to notice any differences of opinion.

- *Whole group*   Go through at least one of the texts, taking answers on each of the seven sections of the Critical Analysis sheets.
- Discuss differences in opinion that arose in thew group.
- Draw attention to the level of detail at which they are reading.

(4) Analytical writing   `E, I, IGS, WC`

- *Threes*   Ask students to discuss the relevance of critical reading to their own writing. Ask them to draw up a list of points.
- *Whole group*   Collate ideas and discuss any issues arising.

(5) Brainstorm difficulties   `IGS, M, P`

- *Small groups*   Ask groups to brainstorm a list of any outstanding questions about this area of work and draw them up as a poster.
- *Whole group*   Students offer suggestions to clarify the difficulties or answer the questions.
- *Alternatively*   Break the group into smaller groups, and allocate a poster to each group. See how far the students can solve the difficulties between them. Invite small groups to feed back their suggestions to the main group.
- Clarify any outstanding points, referring to the texts used for preparation.

Alternative activities for less confident groups

Work through activities in class   `A, I, M`

For some student groups, it is worth spending more than one session on critical and analytical thinking, and taking the subject slowly. Rather than giving out the preparation materials before the session, begin by going through Chapter 9

of the *Study Skills Handbook* in an initial session, bringing out the main points. Read a very small section, or ask a student to do so, and then paraphrase it if necessary. Do each exercise in class and look up the answers together. Check they have understood each point before moving on to the next exercise.

Once the class has established the line of reasoning, ask them to:

- invent further information about the topic:
  - which would be irrelevant,
  - which would be relevant and which would support the line of reasoning,
  - which could undermine the line of reasoning;
- invent examples of false premises;
- invent examples of flawed reasoning;
- invent examples of distorted evidence.

Alternative activities for more confident groups

(1) Link to oral presentation work   `A, OC`

- Ask pairs or small groups each to prepare two short debate speeches on the same subject, one of which relies on emotive factors, the other on evidence. After each pair has presented an emotive speech, take a show of hands to see if the motion was carried.
- The same speakers then present their factual speech, avoiding emotive pleading, and the votes are taken again.
- Use this to discuss devices used to persuade listeners and readers.

(2) Course specific examples   `A, E, I, IGS, M, S`

Discussion   Ask students to suggest the kinds of hidden agendas, distortions, concealments and bias that could underlie the source materials encountered in your subject area – whether in experiments, case materials, client statements or accountancy returns. What makes these difficult to detect? Give classic examples, if possible.

(3) Using critical analysis to evaluate their work   `A, E, M`

Discuss how critical analytical skills can be used to analyse marking criteria for assignments. Encourage students to read their own work critically in line with marking criteria.

(4) More advanced texts   `A, E, I, IGS`

- Once students have grasped the essentials, move them onto texts where the evidence may be more difficult to analyse. This will develop their 'detective-like' approaches further.

- Select a range of short extracts to exemplify problems that occur in analysing materials in your subject area. Discuss these to bring out different issues in critical analysis.
- Offer a set of texts, some of which are examples of flawed reasoning and others not. Ask small groups to identify the examples of flawed reasoning (giving reasons).

(5) Employability links   `Emp`

Ask students to consider the uses of critical analytical skills in the world of work.

RESOURCE SHEET
Critical and analytical thinking skills

(1) Recommended reading

Aim to read at least part of one of the following:

- Cottrell, Stella (1999), *The Study Skills Handbook* (Basingstoke: Macmillan – now Palgrave), Chapter 9.
- Warburton, N. (1996), *Thinking from A–Z* (London: Routledge); useful basic text.
- Thompson, A. (1996), *Critical Reasoning: A Practical Introduction* (London: Routledge); an advanced text with logical exercises.
- Brookfield, S. D. (1987), *Developing Critical Thinkers: Challenging Adults to Explore Alternative Ways of Thinking and Acting* (Milton Keynes: Open University Press), for example, Chapter 8: 'Using the Workplace as a Resource for Thinking and Learning'.
- Garnham, A. and Oakhill, J. (1994), *Thinking and Reasoning* (Oxford: Blackwell); an introduction to the psychology of thinking – advanced reading. The early chapters are interesting background.

(2) Activities

- Read slowly through the model text which you have been given, examining the annotations. The annotations draw your attention to strengths and weaknesses in the writing from a critical and analytical thinking perspective.
- Use this model to help you to analyse the two short passages you have been given.
- Use the critical analysis sheet (pp. 309–10) to help you to work through your analysis of each passage. You may like to photocopy it so you can write your answers directly onto it. You can refer to the line number in the text rather than writing out your examples in detail, as long as you can find them easily during the class discussion.
- You may also like to use the sheet to evaluate your own writing.

(3) Reflection

- What are your feelings about critical and analytical work?
- Is this an aspect of study which you find interesting, easy or difficult?
- Make a note of anything you feel uncertain about in relation to critical and analytical thinking, both from your reading and from completing the activities above.

Critical analysis sheet

(1) Identify the main line of reasoning

(a) The main line of reasoning is: (write this out in your own words)

(b) Is the line of reasoning clear from the text? Give reasons for your answer.

(2) Critically evaluate the line of reasoning

(a) Give some propositions (or statements) from the text which add to its line of reasoning.

(b) Give any examples of points not following in the best logical order.

(c) Give any examples of flawed reasoning.

(3) Identify hidden agendas

(a) What hidden agendas might the writer have that might make you question the contents or conclusions of the passage?

(b) What information might be missing that could paint a different picture?

(4) Identify evidence in the text. What kinds of evidence does the writer use?

(5) Evaluate the evidence given in the text according to valid criteria

(a) Does the text use up-to-date data?

(b) Does the text use reliable sources? What are these? What makes you think they are or are not reliable?

(c) Do you think there may be any bias in the text? Give reasons and examples.

(d) Comment on any statistics used. Are these likely to give a true and full picture?

(6) Identify the writer's conclusions

(7) Does the evidence support the writer's conclusions?

22 Seminars and oral presentations

Students' difficulties in seminars and oral presentations

Trying to do too much

Students often panic because they hold unreal expectations of the task, which they feel they cannot live up to. Some feel they must emulate the lecturer, forgetting that lecturers' skills are built up through experience and (in some cases) training. Typical problems associated with this areas are of students spending too much time on research and too little on preparing the talk; building up too much information to use, and reluctance to edit material down to what can be delivered in the time available. As a result, students arrive with too much information and they are confronted with the difficult task of editing on the spot.

Deference to the lecturer

It is not always clear to students how they are expected to behave when someone other than the lecturer is leading a session. Presenters may address the whole seminar to the lecturer, which can leave the group in the role of observers. The whole group may feel it should defer to the lecturer to make comment and ask questions, which can make it difficult to stimulate group discussion and peer appraisal.

Fear of speaking in front of others

Public speaking is one of the most stressful activities people undertake. Fears range widely, and include anxiety about the voice, forgetting what to say, becoming tongue-tied, clamming up, inability to answer questions 'on the spot', sounding too nervous, stammering, knocking things over, the throat going dry, and many more. In general, people fear that they will look foolish or incompetent in front of everybody else.

Lack of practice

Many of the above anxieties arise when people have had little practice in public speaking. Even polished performers can be very nervous before they begin; students are no different – except that they lack positive experiences to use to bolster their confidence, have little sense of how well or badly they may perform, and usually lack practice in helpful techniques.

Anxiety about peers

It is especially daunting if students are asked to perform in front of groups where little has been done to build a supportive group environment.

Lack of awareness in giving and receiving constructive criticism

Seminars are a useful environment for building critical awareness and group skills. However, those new to criticism can think it means picking out the 'bad points'. In order to avoid being harshly criticised by peers, students may also take the opposite route and offer only praise – which does not help the speaker to move forward.

How lecturers can help

(1) Build up a sense of the group before beginning formal seminar presentations
Ensure that some group bonding has occurred and group ground-rules are set.

(2) Develop constructive criticism skills
- Include early work on constructive feedback, appreciations, and being a supportive listener before encouraging challenging group feedback.
- Spend part of at least some sessions looking at how the process of criticism is working.

(3) Build up slowly
- Provide opportunities, such as ice-breakers and whole-group discussion, for students simply to hear their own voice in the whole group.
- Build in activities of paired work, threes and small groups so students become used to speaking in class.
- Build in short feedback from small groups to the whole group so students become used to speaking to larger audiences.
- For early seminars, use short small-group presentations and build up towards longer small-group or paired presentations. Move on to short individual presentations.

(4) Early experience
Build in an early exercise where small groups offer feedback from their group, together, from the front of the room. The content spoken by each should be collectively written, so that anxiety about content is reduced. Be clear that each person need only speak for a moment or two, and can choose whether they read what they say. Once they have survived this challenge, further seminar work is less daunting.

(5) Constructive questions and responses
Help students to formulate constructive questions, especially by modelling this in lectures:
- 'I'm interested in how you chose this or went about researching this.'
- 'What is your source of information for this?'
- 'Have you had any ideas where we could apply this?'
- 'I wonder if there might be an alternative way of approaching this?'
- 'Where would you take these ideas next?'
- 'Let's see if we can work this out together?'
- 'I was interested in what sources you used for this?'

(6) Clear guidelines for presenters
Give a handout offering a format for presentations, the criteria by which the seminar will be assessed and generally what is expected. Be clear whether seminar presenters can include group work and activities or whether they are expected only to 'present'.

(7) Clear guidelines for group members
Be clear what is expected from group members, and whether their group skills will also be assessed. This should be the subject of discussion before any seminar takes place.

(8) Be clear about your role
To avoid the presenter deferring to you, sit far away from the front. Alert seminars leaders in advance that they should speak to the group rather than to you. Ask another student to introduce the seminar leader.

Tutor preparation

Approaching the session

Ideally, work on seminar and oral presentations should build upon skills acquired in previous sessions. Prerequisites are that all students have already had opportunities to work in a variety of settings which will have required them to speak; that everyone has heard their own voice in the full group, even if only in icebreaker activities;

Aims of the session

■ To develop students' skills in presenting work and speaking in front of others;
■ to build skills of constructive criticism and supportive group work.

Learning outcomes

By the end of these activities students should be able to:

Learning outcomes	Skills (see p. 193)
(1) Identify and apply methods for successful group work	A, E, IGS, KU, OC, P, R
(2) Appraise and address their own difficulties with speaking in groups	A, E, IGS, OC, P, R
(3) Contribute more effectively to groups	A, IGS, OC
(4) Make a joint presentation and reflect on the performance	IGS, OC, R
(5) Make a brief individual presentation	OC, R
(6) Offer constructive feedback on oral presentations	A, E, IGS, KU
(7) Develop criteria for evaluating performance	A, E, IGS, R, S

that some work has been undertaken on constructive criticism and on working with others in a supportive way.

It is worth spending time reflecting on your own experience of groups. How do you feel when you first join a group? What things do you dread being asked to do? How do you respond if asked to work with people you don't like the look of? What kinds of difficulties arise? Could these be avoided – or dealt with more skilfully? What made the best groups that you have been in work so well? What was your wish-list about how the group leader or the group could have been different? Would other members of those groups have wanted something different from what you needed?

Further guidance on group work is offered in Chapter 5.

Materials

For **Activity 6**: you will need a selection of short passages (about one page each) for students to read in advance of the session on some topic relevant to their course options. Devise a question for each passage that could be used as the basis of a very short group seminar presentation. This needs to be something which stimulates thinking, and where students should be able to come up with some opinions of their own. Avoid very complex passages. See the Resource Sheet on p. 318.

Activities

(1) Icebreaker

Each person names someone who they admire as a public speaker or performer.

(2) Seriminar difficulties   `IGS, OC, P, R`

- *In threes*   Ask students to make a quick list of the kinds of worries, anxieties and difficulties that they (or other students) may experience when preparing and delivering a seminar presentation. Emphasise that even small worries are worth writing down.
- *Whole group*   Draw up a group list, leaving space opposite each contribution so that you can write up suggestions on how to address it.
- Take each difficulty or anxiety in turn, and ask the group for practical suggestions of strategies to address it. Write these up and encourage students to write them up too.
- Ensure students have covered obvious points such as having water to drink; using audio-visual aids; arriving in the room before the group; using prompt cards with headings and bullet-points or overhead transparencies to help keep them focused; practising in advance and ensuring they have edited the material down to the time permitted; breathing out slowly to develop calm, etc.).

(3) SWOT for seminar work: an alternative first exercise   `IGS, OC, P, R`

- *Individually*   Ask students to do a brainstorm on their responses to leading a seminar. Suggest they use the headings: Strengths, Weaknesses, Opportunities and Threats (a SWOT analysis).
- *Groups of 4–6*   Compile a group list under each of the four headings. Ask groups to add in strengths and opportunities which come from being part of a group.
- *Whole group*   Collate responses under the four headings.
- How can the strengths be used to address weaknesses?
- Ask for suggestions about how can weaknesses be turned into strengths? Could any of the weaknesses be regarded as strengths?
- Ask for ideas on ways of addressing threats. How might threats be turned into opportunities?

(4) Sabotage and success   `IGS, M, OC`

- *Whole group*   Ask for ideas about how group members could sabotage the group? What could people do to ensure that the group failed and that everyone else was frustrated or miserable?
- Turn this on its head, and explore ways that everyone could make the group effective, fun and interesting.
- *Threes*   Ask students to consider their own fears about groups and to set themselves an objective for working better as a group member.
  Alternatively   If students have been introduced to Action Sets (see p. 254), set an Action Set activity around individual difficulties or anxieties about leading or contributing to seminars.
- *Whole group*   Discuss what kinds of ground-rules would be ideal for seminar groups.

(5) Seminar questions which advance discussion   `A, IGS, M, OC`

- *Whole group*   Ask what kinds of questions and comments would help to stimulate, clarify or advance seminar discussion? Write down the questions that are suggested. Give examples, perhaps drawing on the introduction to this chapter. Classify the kinds of suggestions that were made (to help to build categorisation skills). In doing so, work towards a group consensus over what questions are helpful – and those that are not.

  To clarify: 'Could you say a bit more about that?' 'Could you give an example?' 'Could you put it another way?'

  To focus: 'How does that relate to the subject?' 'How does that link to . . . ?' 'How is that different from/the same as . . . ?'

  To encourage: 'I liked what you said about this. Do you think . . . ?'

  To move forward: 'Are we ready to move on to the next point?'

(6) Practice joint presentation `IGS, OC`

Explain that the purpose of the exercise is to offer an opportunity of seeing what it feels like to deliver a seminar paper, in a safer context and where students are not being assessed. The best shows are said to have the worst dress rehearsals, so they should not worry too much about making a mess of it – as long as they learn from the experience. Offer flip-charts, pens and acetates as resources. Have water and beakers available. If possible give students a passage to prepare in advance, using the Resource Sheet below (p. 318). Otherwise give time for preparation in the session.

- *Groups of 4–6* Form groups depending on the passage received for preparation. Give groups a restricted amount of time to work out between them:
  (1) the most important points of the passage;
  (2) a brief answer to the question you set;
  (3) where they agree with the writer;
  (4) where they disagree with the writer or other arguments that could be raised;
  (5) interesting ideas raised by the passage;
  (6) or similar questions, so that each group member will have a chance to speak to one question.

Indicate that each person will be expected to speak for about a minute, so they need only to develop the bare bones of a talk. The emphasis is on gaining practice in speaking rather than on the content or on perfect presentation. Encourage groups to make a rough and ready audio-visual aid if they wish. Having little time to prepare means they cannot build too much anxiety about being 'perfect'.

- *Alternatively*: Groups pick a subject out of a hat and brainstorm ideas for a few minutes about what they wish to say about the subject. The whole group should be roughly agreed on what each person will say.

- Depending on the time available, ask groups to present either to the whole class, or to one other small group. Insist on silence before each person speaks. Tell the group to encourage the speakers through positive, silent listening and by applauding profusely at the end. Find something positive to say yourself – no matter how it went. Students can be very vulnerable to criticism at this stage and simply speaking at all may be a huge advance.

(7) Debriefing on presentations `IGS, M, OC, P, R`

- *Small groups* Ask students to debrief.
  (1) How did it feel to speak formally in front of others?
  (2) What went well?
  (3) What could have been improved through strategy or technique?

- *Whole group* Give some time for feedback on how it went, generally, as an activity. What tips do students have on how to make presentations easier? Check they mention such points as using prompt cards, speaking slowly, using large enough images and text on visual aids, etc. Refer to their ideas given in Activity 2 (above.)

(8) What have we learnt? `E, R, M, OC`

Ask for each person to contribute one thing they have learnt that they consider important and that they are taking away from the session.

Follow-up work on seminars and presentations

In an initial study skills session, only the basics of seminar skills can be touched upon. However these skills can become more sophisticated if a part of some seminar sessions is dedicated to analysing group and individual performance. Some ideas for follow up work are listed below.

(1) Two-minute individual presentations `A, E, IGS, OC, R`

- Ask each student to prepare to speak for

exactly two minutes on a subject of their choice (or one drawn out of a hat). Avoid anything to do with the subject area. Instead, suggest they speak on an area of personal expertise or about performing an everyday activity (making spaghetti; using a video-recorder; scoring a penalty; making a birthday card; using a parachute; starting the car, etc.)
- Encourage students to use aids, prompts, artefacts and audience participation if they wish.
- Ask students to follow a set format such as the one below.

Format
orientation: state the title, and say very briefly what the talk is about.
benefit to listener: state what will the audience know or gain by the end.
body: the main part of the talk.
closing line: one line that sums up or finishes off the talk.

Organising peer feedback
There are a number of ways of organising this, depending upon the time.

- The tutor could take the speaker out to unwind and be debriefed, while the group decide on their feedback, following the guidance for peer feedback given below.
- Alternatively, take the first five answers anyone in the group offers for each item from 'Structure of peer feedback' below, and then ask for a show of hands on which one piece of feedback the whole group finds most suitable.
- Or, each person in the whole group or a small group could give individual feedback to the presenter.

Structure of peer feedback
One useful structure is:
    how far the student followed the prescribed format;
    whether the audience gained the benefit stated;
    two things they liked about the talk or the way it was presented;
    one thing that could be improved further.

Receiving feedback
The speaker can be asked to say:
    what they appreciated most about the feedback;
    what they found most difficult to hear (without going into details why);
    what they will focus on to improve their next presentation.

Feedback from the lecturer to the group
Spend some time giving feedback to the group about how they gave and received feedback, drawing out what was good, including commenting on good individual contributions. Give ideas on what the group *in general* could do to improve feedback so that speakers are helped forward in a supportive way.

(2) Drawing it together `E, IGS, OC, S`

Groups discuss the best ways of presenting a clear argument to an audience, drawing on strong points from several seminar presentations that have been made already or by analysing a video of a public speaker.

(3) Self-evaluation of constructive participation in seminars `E, IGS, R, S`

Students devise questionnaires based on the ground-rules or on Activity 4 above, identifying criteria by which to evaluate their performance as group members (or use the *Study Skills Handbook*, p. 98) or using the Resource Sheets below, see pp. 319–21).

(4) Self-evaluation of a seminar or other presentation `E, IGS, R, S`

Similar to the above, focusing on giving a presentation rather than on group participation.

(5) Joint evaluation by self and peers   `E, IGS, R, S`

Individuals complete a self-evaluation and a small group of peers complete a group evaluation of that person. They then compare their results and discuss why there might be differences. More advanced groups could see if they can arrive at a consensus, based upon evaluation criteria.

(6) Group-evaluation and auction   `E, IGS, OC, S`

- *Smaller groups within the seminar group* Identify three things the whole group does well already, and three things it could do to improve its performance.
- *Whole group* Each group shares their suggestions, which are written up.
- *Auction* Each person has 3 votes on what they would like the group to do to improve performance. They can allocate these for any of the suggestions (including all three for one suggestion if they feel strongly about it).
- The seminar group discusses how and when they will put the suggestions into practice and how they will evaluate their own progress with them.

RESOURCE SHEET
Seminars and oral presentations

(1) Recommended reading

Aim to read at least one of the following:

- Cottrell, Stella (1999), *The Study Skills Handbook* (Basingstoke: Macmillan – now Palgrave), Chapter 5.
- Benson, J. F. (1987), *Working More Creatively with Groups* (London: Tavistock); useful to dip into too. Contains many ideas about making groups work effectively.

(2) Activities

In preparation for a short group presentation, read the passage on the handout, considering the question that has been set. Jot down some very brief notes on the following:

- What is the main point of the passage?
- List other important points covered by the writer.
- Do you agree with what is written?
- What other points of view might there be?
- Does the passage provoke any interesting ideas?

(3) Reflection

- Consider your own attitudes towards group work and the kinds of contributions you make.
- Do you tend to dominate discussion or do you find it difficult to find an opening to speak?
- Do you help to keep things moving or would some people find you disruptive?
- How many things can you think of which you could do, yourself, to make your seminar groups work better? Of these, which one or two suggestions could you put into action in the next seminar group?
- In your learning journal, write down your thoughts and suggestions.

Student self-evaluation: group presentation

Name: Date:

Course/module:

Presentation title:

Group members:

Do you feel you understood what was required of you for this assignment   Yes/No?
What do you think you were expected to do to get good marks for this assignment?

What were the strengths of the way your small group worked together?

What difficulties, if any, arose in your small group? How were these addressed?

How well do you think you contributed as a group member? What was the main role you played in the group?

How well do you feel you performed in your part of the group's presentation? What, if anything, would you do differently if you were to do it again?

How constructive were you in feedback to people from other groups when they made their presentations? Do you feel there is anything you could do better?

What did you learn more generally about how to work effectively in groups?

Give yourself and each member of your group a mark out of 5 for the contribution they made towards the group presentation (5 would be the highest mark, and 0 the lowest).

1. Your name: Mark out of 5:

2. Name: Mark out of 5:

3. Name: Mark out of 5:

4. Name: Mark out of 5:

Student signature: Date:

Please complete the marking criteria sheet. The tutor will use the same criteria to mark your work. You will receive a mark (out of 5) for this evaluation sheet.

Marking criteria

		weak				excellent	
Marks given							
OC	Clear introduction and overview of the presentation	0	1	2	3		
OC	Main information presented in clear, meaningful way	0	1	2	3		
OC	Strong conclusion, summing up main points	0	1	2	3		
IGS	Worked well as an overall group presentation	0 1 2		3 4	5 6		

Group presentation skills (individual marks)

OC	The message was clear, strong and interesting	0 1 2		3 4 5			
OC	Good sense of audience; held the audience	0 1 2		3 4 5			
IT	Use of audio-visual aids/Powerpoint/handouts	0 1 2		3 4 5			
OC	Handled questions well	0 1 2		3 4 5			
IGS	Contribution to the group's work (peer mark)	0 1 2		3 4 5			

Individual written assignment on the topic of the presentation

R	Constructive use is made of the self-evaluation sheet	0 1 2		3 4 5			
KU	Evidence of relevant background research for the topic	0 1 2 3		4 5 6 7 8 9 10			
KU	Shows understanding of the concepts of the course	0 1 2 3		4 5 6 7 8 9 10			
A	Shows good critical analysis of subject material	0 1 2 3		4 5 6 7 8 9 10			
I	Appropriate selection of relevant material	0 1 2		3 4 5			
M	Ideas and concepts are well organised and structured	0 1 2		3 4 5			
WC	There is a strong and identifiable line of reasoning	0 1 2		3 4 5			
S	Draws materials together well, towards a good conclusion	0 1 2		3 4 5			
WC	Writing is well presented, with accurate spelling, grammar, punctuation and paragraphing	0 1 2		3 4 5			

Marks to the right of the line are of an acceptable standard (pass mark = 40).

Overall mark:

Comments:

23 Memory

Students' difficulties with memory

Bad-memory 'identity'

A desire to improve their memory is one of the most common requests from students referred for support. Students may begin to adopt an identity of a person with 'no memory', which can become a self-fulfilling prophecy. Students may have little idea of what memory is, of how good our memories already have to be in order for us to carry out various everyday tasks and the sorts of things which can lead to improved memory performance.

Stress

Stress from such factors as exam anxiety, working while studying, looking after dependants, previous gaps in education, low self-esteem, high parental expectations, etc., can put strain on memory performance. Stress can create symptoms which appear as if memory is failing. An advertisement for 999 calls a few years ago suggested that everybody write down their address, the names of the next road junction and their phone number in case they had to report an accident: so many emergency callers forget even such basic information when they are under stress. The impression of a failing or a poor memory can be very demotivating for students.

Exam experiences

Students may feel that they revise hard for exams, only to find that they cannot recall the information they want in the exam room. This can undermine their confidence in their memory and their faith in the exam process.

Life-style

Students may be unaware of the ways that life-style can also have an effect upon memory: late nights, poor nutrition, excess alcohol, drugs, working while studying, and dehydration can all affect memory.

Memory vs. rote learning

Students may have strong beliefs that rote learning is the main way to remember information, or, alternatively, that rote learning is always wrong. Students often under-estimate the role of understanding in memory. As a result, they do not appreciate the memory for the subject that they are building up simply through covering the subject-matter at a steady pace throughout the year.

Personal meaning

Linked to the above is the importance of personal engagement with the subject-matter. Students who have difficulties learning the material sometimes report that they are 'not that interested in the course', or that the unit was a compulsory

Aims of the session

- To develop students' strategies for improving memory;
- to give students a better understanding of memory in general and to build their confidence in their ability to train their memory.

Learning outcomes

By the end of these activities students should be able to:

Learning outcomes	Skills (see p. 193)
(1) Appreciate how the memory functions and apply strategies to maximise their own memory	IGS, KU, P, R
(2) Identify personal strengths and strategies for optimising memory	C, KU, P, R
(3) Apply memory strategies to improve personal performance in formal timed assessment and other contexts	M, P, S

one, or that they did not get their first choice of unit, or that they cannot 'see the point' of material in the unit to their vocational path. Unless the student has unusually good memory skills, it is difficult to remember information with which there is no personal connection.

Individual memory styles

Some students find rote learning very difficult. For these, exploration of learning styles and memory styles is important. For example, some students who cannot rote-learn through reciting information, can remember the same information well when they sing it. Others need to see a visual sequence, and work best if they can attach what is for them a visually logical sequence to the verbal information they need to learn. Students may need to experiment using different sense modalities and sequences of modalities for specific kinds of information.

How lecturers can help

(1) Stress

Avoid putting students under unnecessary stress. For example, set exam titles that require students to show understanding of the subject, such as by applying it to a new area, rather than memory for detail. Be sympathetic to students who struggle, rather than questioning their intelligence or their right to be on the course. This will only exacerbate the problem.

(2) Different strategies for different occasions

Both over-learning and activity-learning have their place. Discuss which types of information lend themselves best to over-learning, such as tables, formulae, names and dates, and sequences of key-words for exam essays. For understanding theories, applications and how the subject links together, active learning strategies are best.

(3) Link course information to concrete examples

Tutors will automatically help their students' memory for the subject if they use, when teaching, concrete ways of making information relevant, linking it into people's personal experience.

(4) Build activities into lectures

Active learning assists the memory.

(5) Memory triggers

During lectures and seminars, draw attention to useful mnemonics or anecdotes that make the subject more memorable.

(6) Make links between topics

This helps the students to build up an interconnected web of information, which again assists memory. It also reminds the student of what has been covered previously.

(7) Bridges and summaries

Begin lectures with a summary of the previous lecture, or offer a bridge between the previous topic and the current one. It also helps to give a clear exposition of points and how they link in charts, hierarchies or schools of thought.

Tutor preparation

Approaching the session

Sessions on memory can be amongst the most enjoyable for students as there are many interesting exercises that give insight into personal memory. Students are often surprised to find that memory works in multiple and highly individual ways. They can be relieved to discover that memory can be developed. Self-beliefs about memory can be very entrenched and the best way around this can be through exercises where participants gain a different experience of their own memory. This work can be linked in with earlier sessions on learning style and on self-reflection.

Materials

For **Activity 3**: two sets of slips of paper, with enough of each for half the group.

slip A: Happy Birthday to you and to everyone whose birthday it is today.

slip B: PTYLRQNGYBKFHZJDQPFXWDMR.

For **Activity 4**: a chart of 49 words, arranged in rows of six by eight, with one word in a row on its own. Choose words randomly, except include a number of words referring to colours, some to place, some which sound distinctive or onomatopaeic, and a few which are linked by function or meaning. Use colour and shape to highlight some of the words. Alternatively, adapt the list on p. 202 of Cottrell (1999).

For **Activity 5**: a list of names and dates (5–10 examples) relevant to the subject.

For **Activity 8**: put together a work sheet which includes different kinds of materials students will need to learn for the subject. These should be subject specific if possible. Include, for example:

(1) formulae (3–5 examples);
(2) details of one or two case studies or experiments (up to 10 lines each);
(3) 1–3 examples of outlines of theories (headings and points) to be learnt for an exam.

Activities

(1) Icebreaker: first memory

Each person identifies, briefly, their earliest memory.

(2) The breadth of our memories `IGS, KU, R`

- Draw out the contrast between conscious memory and what we do without thinking.
- *Individuals* Ask students to draw up two lists, quickly, of the kind of things they tend to forget and those they remember well.
- *Small groups* Brainstorm as many ideas as possible of uses we make of conscious and

unconscious memory in everyday life. Ideas can be as big or as small as they like.
- *Whole group* On the board, make a list of suggestions for the ways we use memory.
- Draw out the comparison of all the things we *do* remember compared with what we forget, emphasising how capable our memories really are.

(3) Linking information   `IGS, KU, P`

- Give each person in the front half of the group slip A, and the rest slip B, face down (see 'Materials', above), and ask them to memorise as much of the contents as they can for one minute, in silence.
- Ask them to turn over the slip and recite a rhyme aloud – to prevent rehearsal.
- Ask them to write down what they remember of the contents of their slip.
- Ask them to count up how many letters they have in the correct order. Start by asking how many people got more than 3 letters right. After about 6, jump to 10, then 15, etc.
- Then show them, on an overhead, the differences in the two kinds of information and draw attention to how successfully 'meaningful chunking' can work.
- Ask: how is this relevant to the kind of information they need to learn for the course?

(4) Individual memory strengths   `P, R`

- Put up the 49-word chart. Give students three minutes to look at it.
- Cover the chart and ask students to write down what they remember.
- Put the chart back up and let students count how many they found correctly.
- Take some examples of specific strategies students used and write these up.
- Go through the chart, drawing out clusters of words linked either by colour, subject, place, type of word, whether they appeared first or last, etc. Ask students to note which of these sets of associations they used to remember the words. For example, if they

noticed all the words linked by colour or because they were bizarre, then colour coding information or using bizarre images may be particularly useful for their memory style.
- Ask students to consider how they could use this insight into their own memory style to improve their studies.

(5) Stories   `KU, P`

- *Small groups* Give groups the list of names and dates (see 'materials' above) and ask them to formulate a short story that links the words together by sound, association, or whatever way they choose. The story does not have to make sense.
- Ask students to put away or cover up the information and their stories.
- *Individually* Students write out, from memory, the list of names and dates, then check their answers.
- *Whole group* Ask for some examples of successful stories. How well did individuals feel that the story helped them to recall information.
- Ask for examples of when this would be a relevant technique for their studies.

(6) Encoding information   `K, IGS, P`

- *Whole group* Draw out that the more ways that information is encoded, such as visually or by association with place, the more routes the brain has for accessing it again. In classical societies (such as ancient Rome), a very common strategy was to link each type of information to a place. This was known as the Locus method. It is only one way of encoding information. Putting information into a story form is another way.
- *Threes* Using their experiences in the exercises above, brainstorm how many ways the group can think of for encoding information (such as by personal association, linking it to people they know, to numbers, to buttons on their clothes, to patterns, etc.).
- *Whole group* Collate ideas.

(7) Personal strategies   `IGS, P, R`

- *Individually*   Give time for students to undertake the Resource Sheet activity (see p. 327) or set this as advance preparation.
- *Small groups*   Ask students to share their personal strategies for remembering things. Give each a set time to speak.
- *Whole group*   Ask each group member to offer one thing they have heard from somebody else which they feel they could also use.
- Ask for any other ideas people have for improving memory which have not been voiced.

(8) Memory for subject discipline material   `IGS, M, P, R, S`

Give the students a work sheet of different kinds of course material they would need to learn (see p. 324):

- *Small groups*   Ask groups to devise a strategy or set of strategies for remembering each of the items on the list and as many items as possible in the time you give. Indicate how long they have to do this. Then tell them to put the information sheet away. Test how much they remembered. Give them sufficient time to write out what they remember about each type of information from the sheet. Give them time to compare their answers with what is on the sheet.
- *Whole group*   Take each type of information in turn, and ask the groups to share their ideas. How well did their ideas work in practice? What might have worked better?
- *Individually*   Having discussed the information, test the students again. Ask students to put away the sheets with the information they have just learnt. Again, give them sufficient time to write out what they remember about each type of information from the sheet. Give them time to compare their answers with what is on the sheet.
- *Whole group*   How did their performance vary between the two tests? What conclusions can they draw from this? How far did discussing the information help memory?
- What else, if anything, would they need to do to remember such information?

(9) My best tip   `E, R`

Each person says which is the best memory tip that they have picked up either from the reading or the session.

RESOURCE SHEET
Memory

(1) Recommended reading

Aim to read at least one of the following:

- Cottrell, Stella (1999), *The Study Skills Handbook* (Basingstoke: Macmillan – now Palgrave), Chapter 10.
- Baddeley, A. (1993), *Your Memory: A User's Guide* (London: Prion); very readable for general background about memory.
- Rose, C. and Goll, L. (1992), *Accelerate Your Learning: The Action Handbook* (Aylesbury: Accelerated Learning Systems).

(2) Activities

- Draw up a list of areas where you wish to improve your memory.
- Identify one area as a priority. What makes this your priority at the moment?

(3) Reflection

- Reflect upon what you do, exactly, to remember each of the following:

  (1) an unusual or difficult word you usually know how to spell;
  (2) whether you need to buy something;
  (3) the way to your best friend's room or house;
  (4) someone's birthday.

- Notice any body movements, things you think as you try to remember, where your eyes look, any tricks you use, whatever prompts the memory back.
- In your journal, write down what you noticed. Where do you think your memory strengths lie? Are you better at remembering things when you use visual methods, by talking to yourself, by moving, through associating one thing with another, or some other strategy?

24 Revision and exams

Students' difficulties with revision and exams

Mystifying the exam process
Students can project mystical ideas onto exams as if lecturers were expecting something unimaginable which they are incapable of delivering, or as if lecturers deliberately applied magical arts and mind-reading to see and mark only what the student doesn't know. This can arise from past experience of low marks, based on an assumption that exams are for demonstrating 'facts' when examiners simply wanted to see a broader understanding of the subject demonstrated through argument, application or appropriate selection.

Failure to distinguish between exam answers and course-work answers
Students may not know how to adapt from writing assignments of 2000 or more words to the shorter answers required under examination conditions. The tendency of weaker students is to sacrifice introductions, conclusions and even a line of argument, in order to add in extra facts to prove their knowledge base. There is an additional difficulty if the exam answers require a different style of writing than that for course-work – for example, if they have to write short prose answers for exams, but are more used to report writing for course-work.

Ignorance of the marking procedures
Students often imagine that exam markers go through their work with a fine-tooth comb and can tell where all the gaps are in the answer. If this is combined with a sense that there is only one 'right answer', this can create very high levels of anxiety during the exam.

Unstructured revision
Students can revise in an amorphous, unfocused way, so that too much time in the exam room is spent selecting and organising information. This can contribute to students running out of time because it takes too long to prepare an answer, or because they write in too much detail on early answers.

Poor exam-time strategy
Partly because they do not consider the way that marks are allocated, students give uneven amounts of time to questions that bear the same mark. Some have a fantasy that the lecturer will be impressed by two good answers and somehow let them have a higher grade even though they have not attempted a requisite third answer. They also tend to assume that full marks are possible for answers, whereas many universities use marking schemes where marks over 70 per cent are rare.

Lack of practice and exam habits

There are many entrants who will have taken primarily course-work options for previous qual-ifications. Some students may not sit an exam until they arrive at university or even until their second or third year at university. Other stu-dents have only a history of very poor exam per-formance. It is often difficult for such students to conceptualise what it will be like to sit an exam, much less what a good exam answer is. They may have very little idea of how to prepare for the exam, and no idea of how to approach the exam paper. It takes quite a lot of practice at exams to feel comfortable enough to perform well. There are also sub-skills which need to be developed, such as working at speed.

Speed

Students used to word-processing may simply not have the muscle strength to write at speed for any length of time.

How lecturers can help

(1) Demystify the exam process

Emphasise that lecturers generally want stu-dents to succeed, that it is in everyone's interest to help students to make the grade, that most will pass, and that the object is not to fail people unless it is unavoidable. Be clear about the purpose of exams, such as that it is merely a way of ensuring that it is the student's own work, or that it has a useful function on drawing under-standing together. Go through the kinds of things that you look for in exam answers, and offer examples of exam answers which received different kinds of grade. Offer students a chance to mark papers, or to brainstorm exam answers in class so they get a feel for the overall exam process. Ask them to design exam answers. Use these as revision tools.

(2) Clarify how exam answers differ from course-work requirements

Be clear about the differences you expect between course-work answers and examination answers. What kind of marking criteria do you use for exam answers? Demonstrate, using pieces of course-work, how such answers could be streamlined to make an appropriate exam answer. To help build confidence, bring out the advantages of exam answers over course-work (shorter, no detailed referencing, fewer concrete examples required, more leeway on presenta-tion, etc.).

(3) Guidance with revision

Brainstorm answers to past exam questions after topics have been completed in lectures. Offer revision sessions. Demonstrate the level of detail that is required for different kinds of exam answers. Emphasise the importance of cutting notes down to key points and examples to reduce revision and to save time during the exam. Reassure them that you know they cannot include every example and detail in an exam essay. If the exam is factually based, such as for multiple-choice exams, spend time devel-oping mnemonics to link related information, so that the process of learning seems more man-ageable and enjoyable.

(4) Guidance on how to approach the exam paper

Be clear about how marks are allocated and emphasise the importance of attempting the required number of questions in order to max-imise chances of a higher mark. Demonstrate how the marks add up. Link marks clearly to the way a paper or the degree is graded. Clarity on how to formulate a good exam answer, and especially where corners can be cut when com-pared with course-work, helps. Be clear how marks are allocated or lost for structure, argu-ment, facts, and use of English.

(5) Create opportunities for practice

Ensure that there are several examples of exam papers for students to practise on. This is espe-cially important for new courses or modules, where there may not be past papers to use. The follow-up activities below suggest ideas on offer-ing exam practice using peer support and pre-pared materials, in order to reduce the need for high levels of lecturer marking and feedback.

Aims of the session

■ To build students' confidence in taking examinations;
■ to demystify the assessment process;
■ to give students strategies, techniques and insight in how to maximise their marks.

Learning outcomes

By the end of these activities students should be able to:

Learning outcomes	Skills (see p. 193)
(1) Recognise how previous skills work contributes towards successful exam taking	IGS, P, R, S
(2) Apply strategies for approaching revision	IGS, M, P
(3) Apply strategies for approaching the exam paper	IGS, M, P, WC
(4) Address exam questions with increased understanding and confidence	IGS, KU, M
(5) Identify what gains and loses marks in exams	KU, M, P
(6) Adopt a more positive approach towards exams	M, R
(7) Identify how exam answers differ to course-work answers	A, E, IGS, KU, M

(6) Debriefing after exams

Students rarely know why they have performed badly in exams. This is an important issue in terms of retention and enhancing performance. Where possible, offer group feedback, clarifying what you were looking for, where the group did well or what could have been improved. Give individual feedback to those who need it most.

Tutor preparation

Approaching the session

The work needs to meet students at the level of their previous experience. Additional support may be needed for those with very little exam

practice or success. This is also a good time to revise what has been done in previous sessions, drawing out that skills developed in previous sessions are also key to good exam performance as well as to other aspects of study.

Materials

• Several examples of question papers or past exam papers (or give good advice as to where students can get these). Give these out as advance reading material.
• For **Activity 4**: examples of typical exam errors (for the subject) as an overhead transparency or handout.
• For **Activity 5**: one example of a typed-out

course essay, and the same answer adapted to meet a similar exam question.

- For follow-up work and additional support: Give a list of exam qustions for students to attempt on their own. Give them an accompanying set of outline plans for those questions along with marking guidelines, so students can evaluate their own answers.
- As for any new type of writing, offer students three examples of exam answers, annotated, to show strong and weak points, and indicating what lost or gained marks.

Activities

(1) Icebreaker

Each person says one thing that they would love to do in exams that is usually not allowed.

(2) Audit: skills, knowledge and experience   IGS, P, R, S

- *Individually* You may wish to use the Resource Sheet (see p. 334) for advance preparation or ask students to do an individual brainstorm of skills they have developed so far which can help with exams.
- *Groups of 4–5* Ask groups to draw up posters, as lists or pattern notes, of ways that previous work from these sessions has already prepared them for undertaking revision and exams.
- Ask students to put posters up.
- *Individually* Give some time for them to look at the posters and to make notes on ideas from other groups which they feel may be of use to them.
- *Whole group* Ask for some brief feedback on how they found this exercise? Were they surprised at how much they had already gained towards helping with exams?

(3) Purpose and advantage of exams   IGS, KU, R

- *Pairs* Brainstorm ideas about why exams might be set. Focusing on the positive, what advantages are there to exams over course-work?

- *Whole group* Take contributions from the small groups. Clarify any misconceptions.

(4) How do lecturers mark exam answers?   KU, M

- *Whole group* Go over the main things that lecturers look for in exam answers. Give an example of the kind of marking criteria that are used and how these might vary from those used for course-work.
- Demystify the process. It can reassure students if you talk through what it is like from the perspective of the lecture: thinking of questions to set, why the questions are worded the way they are, and what it is like going through a pile of scripts in a short period of time.
- Give some examples, perhaps as overhead transparencies, of mistakes that students have made in the past, such as obvious misreadings of the essay title or obviously incorrect answers. Avoid examples which would make students anxious about their own performance, such as dyslexic-type errors which are usually unavoidable in exam conditions.

(5) Characteristics of exam answers   A, E, IGS, KU, M

- *Small groups* Give students the example of the course-work answer and its adapted exam answer (see 'Materials', above). Ask them to draw up a list of ways that the two answers differ, and how one has been adapted to the other. Ensure there is time for slow readers to read the answers, or give students these to read before the session.
- *Whole group* Discuss the differences between the two kinds of assignment answer. Address or clarify any misconceptions.

(6) 'How could we completely mess up the exam?'   IGS, M, P, S

- *Individually* Give two or three minutes for students to jot down as many ideas as they

can about things they could do to make sure they failed their exams.
- *Threes*   Join lists and add in any other ideas,
- *Whole group*   Draw up a class list.
- *Whole group*   Ask students to devise an alternative list which offered a maximum chance of exam success.
- Broaden out the discussion to look at what is a sensible revision timetable, how many topics students need to revise to be safe, how to be in a positive state of mind for the exam, good use of time in exams, reading the exam paper, and giving equal time to questions of the same weight.
- Ask students to note the two lists down, or offer to type them up and circulate them.

(7) Writing groups   IGS, R, WC

Either: Ask students to make a quick list of their main worries or difficulties with exams.
Or: Refer to the advance preparation on the Resource Sheet (see p. 334).

- *In the writing groups they were in for earlier sessions or in Action Sets*   Give students 3 minutes each to describe the kinds of difficulties they envisage might arise for them in exams.
- The group has 5 minutes, following each presentation, to brainstorm and discuss ideas on strategies that might help that individual. The speaker simply listens or notes down ideas. If they wish, they can ask for someone to scribe what is said so they can focus on listening.
- The original speaker has 3 minutes to say how they will use or adapt the advice offered to suit them. They are *only* permitted to comment on how they will make use of ideas, or to offer any new ideas that have come up for them (i.e., they can't say 'that won't work because . . . ').

(8) Memory strategies   M, P, S

- *Small groups*   Ask groups to devise memory joggers for aspects of their course work.

- *Whole group*   Take ideas people have for useful mnemonics or strategies to make the course-material more manageable or memorable for revision.

(9) Exam questions   C, IGS, M

- *Whole group*   Ask for examples of potential exam questions that might come up. Give feedback on whether the proffered question is likely to come up in that form. Write the questions up in the way they are likely to be worded.
- *Small group*   Each group chooses a question from the board and together brainstorms the issues to be covered, the main line or lines of reasoning (as appropriate) and the kind of material they would bring in from the course. They should arrange these in the best order, as bullet-points under headings. Be available to offer guidance as they work on these.
- *Whole group*   Ask for an example, and write up what is said. Alternatively, you may wish students to present their answers as posters and to talk through these.
- Ask the group for any ideas about how each answer might be improved. Take any questions they might have about what would lose or gain marks. Give your own advice where relevant.
- Encourage students to write down the example questions to use for revision practice.

(10) Positive state of mind   M, P, R

- *Whole group*   Explain that a positive outlook on exams makes the whole exam process easier and success more likely. Indicate that some anxiety is inevitable and can be regarded as useful in giving focus and the necessary adrenalin.
- *Threes*   Ask groups to discuss what a student could do to approach exams with a positive mind-set.
- *Individuals*   Identify ways they could approach an exam differently.

(11) Practice answers   KU, M, WC

- Encourage students to make as many outline plans for exam essays as they can and to make these at speed following a revision session.
- Give out a list of exam questions and a set of outline plans for these. Encourage students not to look at the suggested plans until they have made an attempt at answering the question for themselves.
- Offer marking guidelines as well as the plans. Encourage students to meet in support groups to discuss each other's answers, using the suggested plans and guidelines.

(12) Mark and discuss example answers   E, IGS, KU, R

- Use annotated answers (see 'Materials', above) as the basis for small and whole group discussion of what is required.
- Offer students examples of exam answers to mark and to discuss what they learnt from being the marker rather than the writer.

- How would this affect the way they approached written answers in the future?

(13) Practice sessions

- Set a mock single question exam. Discuss the process with the group. Indicate what you were looking for and ask them to mark their own papers (unless you can mark them), using the marking guidelines you give them.
- Set a whole exam for students to have some practice at getting used to the set exam time.
- Offer feedback as far as is possible at group or individual level.
- *Groups*   Provide an opportunity for students to discuss what happened during practice sessions, offer support, and to identify where they need to change their exam strategy or approach.

(14) Summary

Ask each person to contribute the one most useful thing they are taking away from the session which will help them with their revision or exams.

RESOURCE SHEET
Revision and exams

(1) Recommended reading

Aim to read at least one of the following:

■ Cottrell, Stella (1999), *The Study Skills Handbook* (Basingstoke: Macmillan – now Palgrave), Chapters 10 and 11.
■ Flanagan, K. (1997), *Maximum Points, Minimum Panic: The Essential Guide to Surviving Exams*, 2nd edn (Dublin: Marino).
■ Northedge, A. (1990), *The Good Study Guide* (Milton Keynes: Open University Press) Chapter 7.

(2) Activities

■ Take one topic from your subject area and look up all the exam questions that have been set on this in the past.
■ What other exam questions could you invent which might also be set? What questions might be set which link this topic to another course topic?
■ Take *one* exam question, and write out a line or phrase that sums up your main line of reasoning in answering this question.
■ Work out a rough plan of what you would include, using headings and sub-points or pattern notes which indicate the order you would introduce each piece of information.
■ Write out a conclusion.
■ Organise or rework the material you have for this topic to make it easier to use and remember under exam conditions. Make use of ideas from the session on 'Memory', and build on your preferred memory styles.
■ Bring all of the above work and your ideas to the session on revision and exams.

(3) Reflection

■ What are the weak areas which you need to revise?
■ What are your ideas for your personal revision strategy?
■ Many of the skills you have worked on so far are also key to exam success. List a few examples of the ways that your skills work has already helped to prepare you for exams.

25 Drawing it together

Students' difficulties

Interconnectedness

Study skills sessions of necessity divide skills into different sections in order to develop an agenda for teaching and learning. However, there is a great deal of overlap between the different skills. Weaknesses in one area may arise from underdeveloped skills in a related area. Poor organisational skills, for example, impact upon many areas of study but may appear, on the surface, to be a weakness in reading or writing. Poor organisational skills can be related to underdeveloped skills in categorisation or time-management skills or to weak motivation.

Transferability

Students may not be able to see how to extrapolate from what they have learnt to other contexts or articulate their skills to other people.

Continued development

Students may feel that once they have finished a set of sessions on skills development they have 'come to an end'. It can be difficult to maintain the motivation to keep returning to personal reflection, self-evaluation and setting new priorities, especially when there are so many other demands upon their time.

How lecturers can help

(1) Draw out the links

Lecturers can help by asking students to make links between the different skills. It helps if lecturers are aware of these interconnections and can assist students in identifying the basis of their difficulties. Exploring sub-skills of different skills is one way of seeing where a weakness may be impacting upon different areas of study. In taught sessions, lecturers can point out ways that a particular strategy can be useful to more than one context.

(2) Contextual awareness

It can be helpful if students are offered at least one session to draw together what they have learnt, and to consider how their skills may be applicable to other courses and for employment. This would include drawing together the range of skills they have acquired across their selection of study modules.

(3) Progression

The skills covered through activities in this book take students to HE level 1, or the early stages of HE level 2, in terms of skills development. Some of the higher-level skills in managing information and critical thinking are traditionally well taught by universities. However, students need on-going opportunities, provided through teaching contexts and curriculum design, to practise and fine-tune their skills.

Tutor preparation

Approaching the session

Generally, create opportunities for students to appreciate how far they have come since they began to study. Encourage them to apply strategies they have applied for one session to different sessions. You may wish to give this an 'employability' focus, or you may prefer to encourage students to draw out how skills may need to be adapted for different modules or areas of a joint degree. It is also a good idea to link this session with Careers Education or Careers Planning work being undertaken by the University's Careers' Advisory Services.

Materials

Resource materials are included below (see pp. 339–42). You may wish to adapt these to suit known skill requirements for your own vocational area.

Aims of the session

- To enable students to identify skills they have developed through the year or the course and appreciate what they have achieved;
- to encourage an on-going developmental approach, building on achievements;
- to encourage students to consider issues of 'employability' and how they might articulate their knowledge, abilities, skills, and personal attributes to employers.

Learning outcomes

By the end of these activities students should be able to:

Learning outcomes	Skills (see p. 193)
(1) Demonstrate an understanding of what is meant by a transferable skill and identify how their skills and qualities can be applicable to other contexts such as work	E, Emp, P, R, S
(2) Identify their areas of strength	Emp, IGS, R
(3) Identify skills areas to be improved and recognise the importance of continual developmental work	E, Emp, IGS, P, R
(4) Recognise how apparently different skills are interconnected and identify how this may affect their own performance	A, Emp, IGS, P, R, S
(5) Recognise the importance of reflection to academic and professional practice	IGS, R, S
(6) Update their Action Plan and Position Paper, in relation to learning and employment	Emp, P, R, WC

Activities

(1) Icebreaker

Each student has to complete the sentence: 'In ten years I will be. . . '

(2) 'Where am I now?' and 'What's my next step?' `E, M, R`

- *Individually* Give students an opportunity to complete the Evaluation Sheets (below) or Priority Organiser Sheets (see pp. 232–3). Ask them to compare their current responses with those made earlier in the year. Are there many differences? Ask them to note their responses in their reflective journals.
- *Individually* Ask students to identify:

  (1) two areas of relative strength in their current skills profile;
  (2) two priorities for skills development in the immediate future.

- *Pairs* Give each person 5 minutes to discuss how their confidence about academic skills has improved since they began study in HE, and to identify two or three areas where they wish to focus attention for continued improvement. Ask them to note the areas for improvement in their reflective journals.
- *Whole group* Ask for contributions from the floor about how people have changed over the year. Ask each contributor what they feel is their next step. Bring out the importance of skills development over the whole course of study and professional practice. 'Is there is always a next step?'

(3) 'Take one strength . . . ' `C, E, Emp, IGS, P, R, S`

- *Individually* Ask students to identify and jot down *one* skill or area of expertise which they feel is their strongest. This could be a sub-skill such as organising space or drawing up timetables or planning a piece of writing. Give 2 minutes for them to brainstorm all the ways this area of expertise might be helpful to future study or employment or life more gen-

erally. Encourage them to think broadly, calling upon any context where that skill could be put to good use, or where it could be built upon to develop a similar skill.

- *Threes* Give 2 minutes for groups to brainstorm any other ways which the area of strength could be applicable to a wide range of contexts or provides the basis for developing a similar skill.
- *Whole group* Take several contributions, drawing up three lists which everyone can see, of 'academic applications, 'employment applications' and 'other applications'.
- Draw out the way that a skill can be transferred from one context to another.
- Draw out the 'employability' skills. Give students a few minutes to jot down what they think are their employability strengths from this list.
- Discussion: how might the skills need to be adapted from one context to suit another?

(4) 'Take one weakness . . . ' `C, E, Emp, IGS, P, R`

- *Individually* Ask students to identify *one* area of weakness. Again this could be sub-skill such as time-management, drawing conclusions, etc. Ask students to brainstorm all the obvious and the unexpected or less obvious ways this one weakness might impact upon their study, life and employment.
- *Whole group* Ask students to suggest one area of difficulty for the whole group to look at collectively: it does not have to be the one they have written down. Brainstorm as a whole group the way this weakness might impact upon study, life and employment, using three lists. Repeat, referring to other areas of difficulty.

  Draw out how skills are inter-linked; a weakness in one area can lead to difficulties in another area. Solving one difficulty may lead to beneficial knock-on effects for a range of other apparent difficulties. Give and ask for examples of this.

- *Small groups* Problem-solving. Allocate one area of study difficulty for each group to address. Ask students to brainstorm possible ways of addressing the difficulty, drawing upon the strategies and approaches they have looked at over the course. Ask students to draw up their suggestions clearly on 'posters' and display these around the room.

• *Individuals*   Give some time for students to write down strategies relevant to them from the posters.

(5) Top strategies   `E, Emp, IGS, S`

• *Small groups*   Ask groups to brainstorm all the tools they have acquired over the year, such as brainstorming, SWOT analyses, etc.
• *Whole group*   Draw up a composite list.
• *Small groups*   From the composite list, ask groups to identify their top three tools for use in a broad range of contexts and say, briefly, why they selected the ones they chose. Feed these back to the whole group.

(6) The importance of reflective practice   `IGS, M, OC`

• *Pairs*   Ask students:
  – to identify what they feel they have gained from taking a reflective and self-evaluating approach to their study;
  – how could they have improved their own performance in terms of reflective activity?
  – how could they maintain a reflective and developmental approach to their study for the rest of their time at university?
• *Whole group*   Discuss people's responses,

drawing out good ideas for continued practice.

(7) Transferable skills and employability

Ask students to read the sheet "What are employers looking for?' on 'Soft Skills' (see p. 340) and to complete the resource sheets offered below on 'transferable skills'.

• *Threes*   Ask students to encourage one another to find ways of filling in any gaps in the sheets they completed.
• *Whole group*   Brainstorm ways that students have been developing 'soft skills' already through their academic studies. Identify other skills that they may need to develop.
• This can be a good time to draw on input from Careers Advisory Services.

(8) Updated Position Paper   `IGS, M, P, R, S, WC`

In Chapter 3, students were asked to draw up an 'interim' Action Plan and Position Paper. You could now ask them to return to this, and write an updated Action Plan and Position Paper based on:

(1) the feedback they received for the interim Position Paper (see Chapter 12);
(1) their self-evaluation of the interim Position Paper;
(1) the skills, knowledge and attributes they have developed in the sessions since they completed the interim position paper.

RESOURCE SHEET
Identifying skills and learning priorities

(1) Recommended reading

Aim to read part of one of the following:

- Mezirow, J. (ed.) (1990), *Fostering Critical Reflection in Adulthood: A Guide to Transformative and Emancipatory Learning* (San Francisco, Cal.: Jossey-Bass); try the Introduction, pp. 1–7.
- Schon, D. A. (1989), *The Reflective Practitioner: How Professionals Think in Action* (London: Temple Smith).
- Schon, D. A. (1987), *Educating the Reflective Practitioner* (San Francisco, Cal.: Jossey-Bass).

(2) Self-evaluation

- Complete the 'Priority Organisers' sheets again and then compare these with the versions you completed earlier in the year.
- How has your confidence about academic skills improved since you began study in HE?
- What areas do you still wish to improve?
- How do you intend to achieve these improvements?

(3) Reflection: transferable skills

- How could the skills you have developed so far as a student be of use to you on other study units or courses? How might you need to adapt them to fit new contexts?
- How could the skills you have developed so far as a student be of use to you in your future career. How might you need to adapt these skills to fit a work context?

What are employers looking for?

As you can see from the diagram below, employers want graduates to have 'soft skills'. The white boxes indicate how desirable each skill is to employers, and the grey boxes indicate how few students demonstrate those skills. There is a noticeable gap between what employers say they want from graduates and the availability of these skills in job applicants and employees. If you develop these skills as a student you are likely to be more competitive as a job candidate.

Many HE courses do give students opportunities to develop these skills. Often students do not realise the skills they have because they do not 'translate' academic skills into employability skills. If students are not aware of the relevance of their skills to the workplace, it is difficult for them to articulate these clearly to employers. It can also affect their ability to do well in the workplace because they feel less skilled than they actually are.

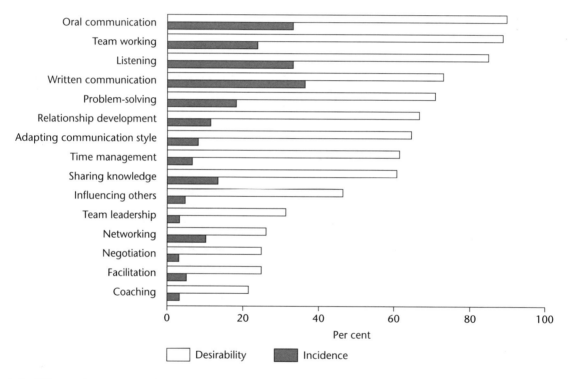

Soft Skills: As desired by employers and actual incidence

Adapted from: TMP Worldwide Research (1998), *Soft Skills, Hard Facts* (London: TMP Worldwide Research).

Translate academic skills into employment skills

On the chart below are some of the skills employers say they wish to see in graduates, which you could develop as a student. You will be able to think of others. On the next page is a resource sheet which can help you to map out the skills you actually develop as a student. This exercise is especially useful in your final year, but can be undertaken at any time you apply for a job.

Area of academic activity	Potential transferable and soft skills which could be developed
Attending lectures, seminars, tutorials, etc.	Time-management; working flexibly
Lectures	Listening skills; identifying and selecting relevant points; written communication; information management
Seminars, group work, team projects	Teamwork; negotiating; oral communication; learning to take directions from others and to give directions; taking responsibility; problem solving; listening; working with people from a variety of backgrounds; dealing with differences in opinion; relationship development
Oral presentation	Speaking in public; persuading and influencing others; making a case; time-management; presentation skills; using audio-visual aids; planning; sharing knowledge; adapting communication style
Writing essays and other forms of academic writing	Written communication skills; developing an argument and putting a strong case; working to word limits; working to deadlines; task analysis; sharing knowledge; breaking tasks into component parts
Maths and statistics	Problem-solving; presenting information; interpreting data; sharing knowledge
Observation	Listening skills; working with people from a variety of backgrounds; information management
Research	Time management; managing large amounts of information; working to deadlines,
Exams	Working to deadlines; managing stress and crisis; planning revision

From: Stella Cottrell (1999), *The Study Skills Handbook* (Basingstoke: Macmillan – now Palgrave).

Transferable key skills

The first four items from the employer's list are already written in. Add in others at which you are particularly good, whether developed at university or elsewhere. Give particular examples of where you developed, or currently use, each skill.

Skills, qualities attributes and achievements	Specific examples
Oral communication	
Team working	
Listening	
Written communication	

Other transferable skills I can offer

☐ Current driver's licence   ☐ Computer literacy   ☐ Languages:

Adapted from: Stella Cottrell (1999), *The Study Skills Handbook* (Basingstoke: Macmillan – now Palgrave).

Appendix 1

Graduate skills and qualities

It is now expected that students at university will have developed a range of skills, experiences and personal qualities as well as developing their knowledge and understanding of their subject specialism. The following list is adapted from several out of many similar lists of graduate requirements. These skills and attributes are useful for improving academic performance, but are also essential for professional and personal life.

(1) Traditional intellectual skills
Ability to organise, summarise, analyse and synthesise information
Ability to find meaning in, and 'make sense' of, complex concepts and information
Ability to make critical evaluation, selection and presentation of evidence
Ability to extrapolate general concepts, principles and procedures
Ability to argue logically and apply theory to practice
Ability to challenge taken-for granted assumptions and existing practice
Ability to study a subject both in depth and with breadth
Subject specific skills, including technical skills

(2) Key skills
Communication
Application of number
Information and communications technology
Improving one's own performance, including personal development planning, study skills, self-reflection, self-direction, self-monitoring and self-evaluation
Working with others
Problem solving: to model problems qualitatively and quantitatively

(3) Personal qualities
Self reliance and independence including being able to 'self-start' with new tasks.
Adaptability, flexibility and openness to change
Ability to take responsibility
Creativity and imagination
Ethical awareness

(4) Preparedness for work
The skills identified above
Careers planning
Knowledge and understanding of how organisations work
Ability to operate effectively within the workplace
Skills related to a vocational area

© Stella Cottrell (2001), *Teaching Study Skills and Supporting Learning* (Basingstoke: Palgrave).

Appendix 2

SEEC/HECIW level descriptors for HE levels

(1) Operational contexts

Characteristics of contexts

Level 1   Defined contexts demanding use of a specified range of standard techniques.
Level 2   Simple but unpredictable *or* complex but predictable contexts demanding application of a wide range of techniques.
Level 3   Complex and unpredictable contexts demanding selection and application from a wide range of innovative or standard techniques.

Responsibility

Level 1   Work is directed with limited autonomy within defined guidelines.
Level 2   Management of processes within broad guidelines for defined activities.
Level 3   Autonomy in planning and managing resources and processes within broad guidelines.

Ethical understanding

Level 1   Awareness of ethical issues in current area(s) of study. Ability to discuss these in relation to personal beliefs and values.
Level 2   Awareness of the wider social and environmental implications of area(s) of study. Ability to debate issues in relation to more general ethical perspectives.
Level 3   Awareness of personal responsibility and professional codes of conduct. Ability to incorporate a critical ethical dimension into a major piece of work.

(2) Cognitive descriptors

Knowledge and understanding of the subject discipline

Level 1   Has a given factual and/or conceptual knowledge base with emphasis on the nature of the field study and appropriate terminology.
Level 2   Has a detailed knowledge of major disciplines and an awareness of a variety of ideas/contexts/frameworks which may be applied to.
Level 3   Has a comprehensive/detailed knowledge of these major disciplines with areas of specialisation in depth and an awareness of the provisional nature of the state of knowledge.

Analysis

Level 1   Can analyse with guidance using given classifications/principles.

Level 2   Can analyse a range of information with minimum guidance, can apply major theories of discipline and can compare alternative methods/techniques for obtaining data.
Level 3   Can analyse new and/or abstract data and situations without guidance, using a wide range of techniques appropriate to the subject.

Synthesis/creativity

Level 1   Can collect and categorise ideas and information in a predictable and standard format.
Level 2   Can reformat a range of ideas/information towards a given purpose.
Level 3   Can transform abstract data and concepts with minimum guidance towards a given purpose and can design novel solutions.

Evaluation

Level 1   Can evaluate the reliability of data using defined techniques and/or tutor guidance.
Level 2   Can select appropriate techniques of evaluation and can evaluate the relevance and significance of data collected.
Level 3   Can critically review evidence supporting conclusions/recommendations, including its reliability, validity and significance, and can investigate contradictory information/identify reasons for contradictions.

(3) Other transferable skills descriptors

Psycho-motor

Level 1   Able to perform basic skills with awareness of the necessary tools and materials and their potential uses and hazards. Needs external evaluation.
Level 2   When given a complex task, can choose and perform an appropriate set of actions in sequence to complete it adequately. Can evaluate own performance.
Level 3   Can perform complex skills consistently, with confidence and a degree of co-ordination and fluidity. Able to choose an appropriate response from a repertoire of actions, and can evaluate own and others' performance.

Self-appraisal, reflection on practice

Level 1   Is largely dependent on criteria set by others but begins to recognise own strengths and weaknesses.
Level 2   Is able to evaluate own strengths and weaknesses; can challenge received opinion and begins to develop own criteria and judgement.
Level 3   Is confident in application of own criteria of judgement and in challenge of received opinion in action and can reflect on action.

Planning and management of learning

Level 1   Can work within a relevant ethos and can access and use a range of learning resources.
Level 2   Adopts a broad ranging and flexible approach to study; identifies strengths of learning needs and follows activities to improve performance; is autonomous in straightforward study tasks.

Level 3   Can mange own learning with minimum guidance using full range of resources for discipline; can seek and make use of feedback.

Problem solving

Level 1   Can apply given tools/methods accurately and carefully to a well-defined problem and begins to appreciate the complexity of the issues.
Level 2   Can identify key elements of problems and choose appropriate methods for their resolution in a considered manner.
Level 3   Is confident and flexible in identifying and defining complex problems and the application of appropriate knowledge and skills to their solution.

Communication and presentation

Level 1   Can communicate effectively in a format appropriate to the discipline and report practical procedures in a clear and concise manner with all relevant information.
Level 2   Can communicate effectively in a format appropriate to the discipline and report practical procedures in a clear and concise manner with all relevant information in a variety of formats.
Level 3   Can engage effectively in debate in a professional manner and produce detailed and coherent project reports.

Interactive and group-skills

Level 1   Meets obligations to others (tutors and/or peers); can offer and/or support initiatives; can recognise and assess alternative options.
Level 2   Can interact effectively within a learning group, giving and receiving information and ideas and modifying response where appropriate. Is ready to develop professional working relationships within discipline.
Level 3   Can interact effectively within a learning or professional group. Can recognise or support leadership or be pro-active in leadership. Can negotiate in a learning/professional context and manage conflict.

References

Allison, B. (1993), *Research Methods* (Leicester: De Montfort University).

Allison, C. W. and Hayes, J. (1988), 'The Learning Syles Questionnaire: An Alternative to Kolb's Inventory', *Journal of Management Studies*, **25**, 3.

Argyris, C. and Schon, D. A. (1974), *Theory in Practice: Increasing Professional Effectiveness* (San Francisco, Cal.: Jossey-Bass).

Ashby, E. (1984), 'Foreword', Brewer, I. M., *Learning More and Teaching Less* (Guildford: SRHE).

Baddeley, A. (1993), *Your Memory: A User's Guide* (London: Prion).

Ball, C. (1986), *Transferable Personal Skills in Employment: The Contribution of Higher Education* (London: National Advisory Board for Public Sector Higher Education/University Grants Council).

Bartlett, F. C. (1932), *Remembering* (London: Cambridge University Press).

Beaver, D. (1994/1998), *NLP for Lazy Learning* (Shaftesbury, Dorset, and Boston, Mass.: Element).

Benson, J. F. (1987), *Working More Creatively with Groups* (London: Tavistock).

Biggs, J. (1996), 'Enhancing Teaching through Constructive Alignment', *Higher Education*, **32**, 347–504.

Birnbaum, R. (1989), 'The Cybernetic Institution: Toward an Integration of Governance Theories', *Higher Education*, **18**, 239–53.

Bono, E. de (1994), *de Bono's Thinking Course,* revised and updated edn (London: BBC).

Bono, E. de (1996), *Teach Yourself to Think* (Harmondsworth: Penguin).

Boud, D. (1989), 'Some Competing Traditions in Experiential Learning', in Weil, S. W. and McGill, I. (eds), *Making Sense of Experiential Learning* (Milton Keynes: SRHE/Open University Press).

Boud, D. (1995), *Enhancing Learning through Self-Assessment* (London: Kogan Page).

Boud, D., Keogh, R. and Walker, D. (1985), *Reflection: Turning Experience into Learning* (London: Kogan Page).

Bourner, T. and Race, P. (1990), *How to Win as a Part-Time Student* (London: Kogan Page).

Bower, G. H., Clark, M., Lesgold, A. and Winzenz, D. (1969), 'Hierarchical Retrieval Schemes in Recall of Categorised Word Lists', *Journal of Verbal Learning and Verbal Behaviour,* **8**, 323–43.

Bradshaw, J. (1972), 'The Concept of Social Need', *New Society*, 30 March 1972.

Brah, A. and Hoy, J. (1989), 'Experiential Learning: A New Orthodoxy', in Weil, S. W. and McGill, I. (eds), *Making Sense of Experiential Learning* (Milton Keynes: SRHE/Open University Press).

Bridges, D. (1993), 'Transferable Skills: A Philosophical Perspective', *Studies in Higher Education*, **18**(1), 43–51.

Brockbank, A. and McGill, I. (1998), *Facilitating Reflective Learning in Higher Education* (Milton Keynes: SRHE and Open University Press).

Brookfield, S. D. (1987), *Developing Critical Thinkers: Challenging Adults to Explore Alternative Ways of Thinking and Acting* (Milton Keynes: Open University Press).

Brookfield, S. (1993), 'Breaking the Code: Engaging Practitioners in Critical Analysis of Adult Educational Literature', *Studies in the Education of Adults,* **5** (1), 64–91.

Brown, E. B. and Clements, J. (1989), 'Overcoming Misconceptions via Analogical Reasoning: Abstract Transfer versus Explanatory Model Construction', *Instructional Science*, **18**, 237–61.

Brown, R. and McCartney, S. (1999), 'Multiple Mirrors: Reflecting on *Reflections*', in O'Reilly, D., Cunningham, L. and Lester, S. (eds), *Developing the Capable Practitioner* (London: Kogan Page).

Bruner, J. (1966), *Toward a Theory of Instruction* (New York: W. W. Norton).

Bruner, J. (1975), 'The Ontogenesis of Speech Acts', *Journal of Child Language*, **2**, 1–19.

Butterworth, G. (1992), 'Context and Cognition in Models of Cognitive Growth', in Light, P. and Butterworth, G. (eds), *Context and Cognition* (London: Harvester).

Butterworth, G. and Harris, M. (1994), *Principles of Developmental Psychology* (Hove: LEA).

Buzan, T. (1993), *The Mind Map Book* (London: BBC).

Buzan, T. and Keene, R. (1996), *The Age Heresy: You Can Achieve More, not Less, as You Get Older* (London: Ebury Press).

Collop, J. *et al.* (1998), *Final Report: Graduate Higher Level Key Skills Programme* (Luton: University of Luton).

Cottrell, S. M. (1999), *The Study Skills Handbook* (Basingstoke: Macmillan – now Palgrave).

Cottrell, S. M. (2000), 'Assessing Skills within the Curriculum', Paper presented to the SEEC conference, *Crediting Key Skills*, University of East London, Autumn 2000 (London: SEEC).

Creme, P. and Lea, M. R. (1997), *Writing at University: A Guide for Students* (Buckingham and Bristol: Open University Press).

Cross, K. P. and Angelo, T. A. (1992), *Teaching Goals*

Inventory (Berkeley, Cal.: Berkeley School of Education).

CVCP (1991), Committee of Vice-Chancellors and Principals Occasional Green Paper, No. 1, *Teaching Standards and Excellence in Higher Education: Developing a Culture for Quality* (Sheffield: CVCP).

CVCP, DfEE (1996), *Helping Students Towards Success at Work: An Intent being Fulfilled* (London: Committee of Vice-Chancellors and Principals).

CVCP, DfEE (1998), *Skills Development in Higher Education*, Short Report (London: Committee of Vice-Chancellors and Principals).

Dahlgren, L. O. (1984), 'Outcomes of Learning', in Marton, F., Hounsell, D. and Entwistle, N. J. (eds), *The Experience of Learning: Implications for Teaching and Studying in Higher Education,* 2nd edn (Edinburgh: Scottish Academic Press).

Dearing, R. (1997), *The Summary Report of the National Committee of Inquiry into Higher Education* (London: HMSO).

Dilts, R., Hallbom, T. and Smith, S. (1990), *Beliefs: Pathways to Health and Well-being* (Portland, Oregon: Metamorphous Press).

Donaldson, M. (1978), *Children's Minds* (London: Fontana).

Donaldson, M. (1987), 'The Origins of Inference', in Bruner, J. and Haste, H (eds), *Making Sense: The Child's Construction of the World* (London: Methuen).

Douglas, T. (1995), *Survival in Groups: The Basics of Group Membership* (Milton Keynes: Open University Press).

Dunn, R. and Dunn, K. (1992), *Teaching Elementary Students through their Individual Learning Styles: Practical Approaches for Grades 3–6* (Boston, Mass.: Allyn and Bacon).

Dunn, R. and Dunn, K. (1993), *Teaching Secondary Students through their Individual Learning Styles: Practical Approaches for Grades 7–12* (Boston, Mass.: Allyn and Bacon).

Dunn, R., Griggs, S., Olson, J., Beasley, M. and Gorman, B. (1995), 'A Meta-analytic Validation of the Dunn and Dunn Model of Learning Style Preferences', *Journal of Educational Research*, **88** (6), 353–62.

Edwards, D. and Mercer, N. (1987*), Common Knowledge: The Development of Understanding in the Classroom* (London: Methuen).

Elton, L. (1995), 'Motivating Students: Relation to the World of Work', in Gibbs, G. (ed.), *ISL Through Assessment and Evaluation* (Oxford: Oxford Centre for Staff Development).

Elton, L. (1999), *New Ways of Learning in Higher Education: Managing the Change, Tertiary Education and Management,* **5**, 207–25 (Netherlands: Kluwer Academic Publishers).

Entwistle, N., Thompson, S. and Tait, H. (1992), *Guidelines to Promoting Effective Learning in HE* (Edinburgh: Centre for Research on Learning and Instruction).

Entwistle, N. (1997), *Styles of Learning and Teaching: An Integrated Outline of Educational Psychology for Students, Teachers and Lecturers* (London: David Fulton Publishers).

Fairburn, G. J. and Winch, C. (1996), *Reading, Writing and Reasoning: A Guide for Students*, 2nd edn (Milton Keynes: Open University Press).

Fazey, D. (1996), 'Guidance for Learner Autonomy', in McNair, S. (ed.), *Putting Learners at the Centre: Reflections from the Guidance and Learner Autonomy in Higher Education Programmes* (Sheffield: Gala and DfEE).

Fenwick, A., Assiter, A. and Nixon, N. (1992), *Profiling in Higher Education* (Sheffield: Department of Employment Group).

Flanagan, K. (1997), *Maximum Points, Minimum Panic: The Essential Guide to Surviving Exams,* 2nd edn (Dublin: Marino).

Flax, J. (1993), *Disputed Subjects* (London: Routledge and Kegan Paul).

Freire, P. (1974), *Education for Critical Consciousness* (New York: Continuum).

Fry, H., Ketteridge, S. and Marshall, S. (eds) (1999), *A Handbook for Teaching and Learning in Higher Education: Enhancing Academic Practice* (London: Kogan Page).

Gardner, H. (1993), *Frames of Mind: The Theory of Multiple Intelligences,* 2nd edn (London: Fontana).

Garnham, A. and Oakhill, J. (1994), *Thinking and Reasoning* (Oxford: Blackwell).

George, J. and Glasgow, J. (1988), 'Street Science and Conventional Science in the West Indies', *Studies in Science Education*, **15**, 109–18.

Gibbs, G. (1992), *Improving the Quality of Student Learning* (Bristol: Technical and Educational Services).

Gibbs, G. (1994), *Learning in Teams: A Student Manual* (Oxford: Oxford Centre for Staff Development).

Gibbs, G. (1995), *Assessing Student Centred Courses* (Oxford: Oxford Centre for Staff Development).

Gibbs, G. and Lucas, L. (1997), 'Coursework Assessment, Class-size and Student Performance, 1984–94', *Journal of Further and Higher Education*, **21** (2), 183.

Gibbs, G. (1999), 'Using Assessment Strategically to Change the Way Students Learn', in Brown, S. and Glasner, A. (eds), *Assessment Matters in Higher Education: Choosing and Using Diverse Approaches* (Buckingham: The Society for Research into Higher Education and Open University Press).

Gick, M. L. and Holyoak, K. J. (1980), 'Analogical Problem Solving', *Cognitive Psychology*, **12**, 306–55.

Gick, M. L. and Holyoak, K. J. (1983), 'Scheme Induction and Analogical Transfer', *Cognitive Psychology*, **15**, 1–38.

Given, B. K. (1996), 'The Potential of Learning Styles', in Reid, G. (ed.), *Dimensions of Dyslexia* (Edinburgh: Moray House Publications).

Given, B. K. (1998), 'Psychological and Neurobiological

Support for Learning Style Instruction: Why it Works', *National Forum of Educational Research Journal*, **11** (1).

Glasner, A. (2000), 'Is Employability the Only Graduate Key Skill?', Paper presented to the SEEC conference, *Crediting Key Skills*, University of East London, Autumn 2000 (London: SEEC).

Goertzel, V. and Goertzel, M. G. (1962), *Cradles of Eminence* (Boston, Mass.: Little, Brown).

Goodworth, V. (1999), *Exploring the Use of Learning Styles and Approaches to Learning to Develop the Teaching and Learning Environment within Fashion Design: Towards a Tutor Inspired and Learning Centred Approach*, MA dissertation (unpublished), University of East London.

Gordon, W. J. J. and Poze, T. (1980) *The Art of the Possible* (Cambridge, Mass.: Porpoise).

Hammond, M. and Collins, P. (1991), *Self-Directed Learning* (London: Kogan Page).

Hand, L., Knowles, V., Pybus, L., Seivier, J. and Simpson, S. (2000), 'What are we Learning about "Developing Learning" Modules', *International Journal of Management Education*, 1(1).

Harrop, A. and Douglas, A. (1996), 'Do Staff and Students See Eye to Eye?', *New Academic*, **5** (3), 8–9.

Hatano, G. and Inagaki, K. (1992), 'Desituating Cognition through the Construction of Conceptual Knowledge', in Light, P. and Butterworth, G. (eds), *Context and Cognition* (London: Harvester).

HEFCE (2000), *Foundation Degree Prospectus* (London: HEFCE).

HMI (1989), *The English Polytechnics* (London: HMSO).

Honey, P. and Mumford, A. (1982/1992), *The Manual of Learning Styles Questionnaire* (Maidenhead, Berks: Peter Honey Publications).

Honey, P. and Mumford, A. (1994), *Learning Log* (Maidenhead, Berks: Peter Honey Publications).

Hounsell, D., McCulloch, M. and Scott, M. (1996), *The ASSHE Inventory: Changing Assessment Practices in Scottish Higher Education* (Edinburgh: Centre for Teaching, Learning and Assessment, University of Edinburgh and Napier University, Edinburgh).

Hurd, S. (1999), 'Developing Skills for the Twenty-first Century: Lessons from Autonomy in Language Learning', *New Academic* Spring.

Hurley, J. (1994), *Supporting Learning* (Bristol: The Staff College and Learning Partners).

Inglis, J. and Lewis, R. (1980), *Clear Thinking: The Key to Success* (Cambridge: National Extension College).

Innes, K. (1996), *Diary Survey: How Undergraduate Full-time Students Spend their Time* (Leeds: Leeds Metropolitan University).

Jennings, C. and Kennedy, E. (eds) (1996), *The Reflective Professional in Education: Psychological Perspectives on Changing Contexts* (London and Bristol, Pa.: Jessica Kingsley Publishers).

Johnson-Laird, P. N. (1985), 'Deductive Reasoning Ability', in Sternberg, R. J. (ed.), *Human Abilities* (New York: Freeman).

Kemp, I. J. and Seagraves, L. (1995), 'Transferable Skills – Can Higher Education Deliver?', *Studies in Higher Education*, **20** (3), 315–28.

King, A. (1990), 'Enhancing Peer Interaction and Learning in the Classroom through Reciprocal Questioning', *American Educational Research Journal*, **27** (4), 664–87.

King, P. M. (1985), 'Formal Reasoning in Adults: A Review and Critique', in Mines, R. A. and Kitchener, K. S. (eds), *Adult Cognitive Development* (New York: Praeger).

Kolb, D. (1984), *Experiential Learning* (Englewood Cliffs, NJ.: Prentice Hall).

Knowles, M. (1978), *The Adult Learner – A Neglected Species*, 3rd edn (London: Gulf Publishing Group).

Lawrence, G. (1995), *People Types and Tiger Stripes*, 3rd edn (Gainesville, Fla.: Center for Applications of Psychological Type).

Lewin, K. (1952), *Field Theory in Social Science* (London: Routledge and Kegan Paul).

Lewis, R. (1994), *How to Manage your Study Time* (Cambridge: National Extension College).

Lindblom-Ylanne, S. and Lonka, K. (2000a), 'Dissonant Study Orchestrations of High-achieving University Students', *European Journal of Psychology of Education*, xv, 19–32.

Lindblom-Ylanne, S. and Lonka, K. (2000b), 'Interaction Between Learning Environment and Expert Learning', in *LLinE: Lifelong Learning in Europe*, 2/2000.

Little, D. (1991), *Learner Autonomy 1: Definitions, Issues and Problems* (Dublin: Authentik).

Luft, J. (1984), *Group Processes: An Introduction to Group Dynamics* (Palo Alto, Cal.: Mountain View).

Macdonald, R. (1997), *Teaching and Learning in Small Groups*, SEDA Special Report, no. 2 (Birmingham: SEDA).

Mandel, S. (1987), *Effective Presentation Skills* (London: Kogan Page).

Marton, F. and Saljo, R. (1984), 'Approaches to Learning', in Marton, F., Hounsell, D. J. and Entwistle, N. J. (eds), *The Experience of Learning* (Edinburgh: Scottish Academic Press).

McCombs, B. L and Marzano, R. J. (1990), 'Putting the Self Back in Self-regulated Learning: the Self as Agent in Integrating Will and Skill', *Educational Psychologist*, **25**, (19), 51–69.

McGill, I. and Beatty, L. (1992), *Action Learning: A Practitioner's Guide* (London: Kogan Page).

McGuiness, D. (1999), *Why Our Children Can't Read and What We Can Do About It: A Scientific Revolution in Reading* (London: Simon & Schuster).

McKim, R. H. (1972), *Experiences in Visual Thinking* (Monterey, Cal.: Brooks/Cole).

McNair, S. (1996), 'Introduction: Living with Diversity',

in McNair, S., *Putting Learners at the Centre: Reflections from the Guidance and Learner Autonomy in Higher Education Programme* (Sheffield: Gala and DfEE).

Mehrens, W. A. and Lehmann, I. J. (1984), *Measurement and Evaluation in Education and Psychology*, 3rd edn (New York: Holt, Rinehart and Winston).

Mezirow, J. (ed.) (1990), *Fostering Critical Reflection in Adulthood: A Guide to Transformative and Emancipatory Learning* (San Francisco, Cal.: Jossey-Bass).

Miles, T. R. and Gilroy, D. E. (1995), *Dyslexia at College*, 2nd edn (London: Routledge and Kegan Paul).

Miller, A. (1991), 'Applied Psychologists as Problem-solvers: Devising a Personal Model', *Educational Psychology in Practice*, 7, 227–36.

Miller, K. (1998), 'Tell me how to get a first . . . ', *New Academic*, 7 (2), 12–16.

Miller, P. H. (1989), *Theories of Developmental Psychology*, 2nd edn (New York: Freeman).

Murphy, G. L. and Wright, J. C. (1984), 'Changes in Conceptual Structure wth Expertise: Differences between Real-world Experts and Novices', *Journal of Experimental Psychology: Learning, Memory and Cognition*, 10 (1), 144–55.

NCIHE (1997), *Higher Education in the Learning Society* (Dearing Report), National Committee of Inquiry into Higher Education (London: HMSO).

Northedge, A (1990), *The Good Study Guide* (Milton Keynes: Open University Press).

O'Connell, C., Coe, E. and Anderson, J. (2000), 'Embedding Recording of Achievement in Teaching and Learning Processes: A Strategy Underpinned by Staff Development', *Recording of Achievement in HE: Network News* (Sheffield: DfEE).

Packwood, T. and Whitaker, T. (1988), *Needs Assessment in Post-16 Education* (Lewes and Philadelphia: Falmer Press).

Patterson, K. (1999), 'One Advisor's Perspective on VSI: An Interview with Andrea Drew', in *Supplemental Instruction Update*, Winter 1999 (Kansas City: University of Missouri).

Peelo, M. (1994), *Helping Students with Study Problems* (Buckingham: SRHE and Open University Press).

Perry, W. (1959), 'Students' Use and Misuse of Reading Skills', *Harvard Educational Review*, 19, 3, 193–2000.

Perry, W. G. (1970), *Forms of Intellectual and Ethical Development in the College Years: A Scheme* (New York: Holt, Rinehart and Winston).

Piaget, J. (1952), *The Origins of Intelligence in Children* (New York: International Universities Press).

Piaget, J. (1975), *The Development of Thought: Equilibration of Cognitive Structures* (Oxford: Blackwell).

Press, M. C. (1996), 'Ethnicity and the Autonomous Language Learner: Different Beliefs and Learning Strategies', in Broady, E. and Kenning, M. M. (eds), *Promoting Learner Autonomy in University Language Teaching* (London: AFLS in Association with CILT).

Prosser, M. and Millar, R. (1989), 'The "How" and "What" of Learning Physics', *European Journal of Psychology of Education*, 4, 513–28.

Prosser, M. and Trigwell, K. (1997), 'Using Phenomenography in the Design of Programs for Teachers in Higher Education', *Higher Education Research and Development*, 16, 41–54.

Prosser, M. and Trigwell, K. (1999), *Understanding Learning and Teaching: The Experience of Higher Education* (Buckingham: SRHE and Open Univeristy Press).

Quality Assurance Agency for Higher Education (1999), *Code of Practice for the Assurance of Academic Quality and Standards in Higher Education, Section 3: Students with Disabilities* (Gloucester: QAAHE).

Quality Assurance Agency for Higher Education (2000), http://www.qaa.ac.uk/HEprogressfile; 30/5/2000.

Qualifications and Curriculum Authority (2000), *Key Skills* (http://www.qca.org.uk/keyskills/what_are_ks.htm).

Qualifications and Curriculum Authority (2000), *Key Skills Units (Levels 4 and 5)* (London: QCA).

Ramsden, P. (1992), *Learning to Teach in Higher Education* (London and New York: Routledge and Kegan Paul).

Reed, S. K., Dempster, A. and Ettinger, M. (1985), 'Usefulness of Analogous Solutions for Solving Algebra Word Problems', *Journal of Experimental Psychology; Learning, Memory and Cognition*, 11 (1), 106–25.

Renery, I. (2000), 'WebCT: A US Perspective', *Association for Learning Technology Newsletter*, 29, 5–6 May (Oxford: Alt-N).

Richardson, K. (1991), 'Reasoning with Raven – In and Out of Context', *British Journal of Educational Psychology*, 61, 129–38.

Rickards, T. (1992), *How to Win as a Mature Student* (London: Kogan Page).

Rogers, C. R. (1967), *On Becoming a Person* (London: Constable).

Rogers, C. R. (1983), *Freedom to Learn in the 1980s* (Columbus, Oh.: Charles E. Merrill).

Rosch, E. (1975), 'Cognitive Representations of Semantic Categories', *Journal of Experimental Psychology: General*, 104 (3), 192–233.

Rose, C. and Goll, L. (1992), *Accelerate Your Learning: The Action Handbook* (Aylesbury: Accelerated Learning Systems Ltd).

Saljo, R. (1979), 'Learning about Learning', *Higher Education*, 8, 443–51.

Saven-Baden, M. (2000), *Problem-based Learning in Higher Education: Untold Stories* (Buckingham: SRHE and Open Univeristy Press).

Schon, D. A. (1987), *Educating the Reflective Practitioner* (San Francisco, Cal.: Jossey-Bass).

Schon, D. A. (1989), *The Reflective Practitioner: How Professionals Think in Action* (London: Temple Smith).

Shotter, J. (1989), 'Social Accountability and the Social Construction of "You"', in Shotter, J. and Gergen, K. J. (eds), *Texts of Identity* (London: Sage).

Shotter, J. (1993), *Conversational Realities* (London: Sage).

Siegler, R. S. (1991), *Children's Thinking* (Englewood Cliffs, NJ: Prentice Hall).

Silver, P., Bourke, A. and Strehorn, K. (1998), 'Universal Instructional Design in HE: An Approach for Inclusion', *Equity and Excellence in Education*, **31**, 47–51.

Simpson, R. and Wailey, T. (1999), 'Staff Development: AP(E)L as a Guidance and Support Model', in *Beyond Graduateness* (London: SEEC).

Simpson, R. and Wailey, T. (2000a), 'AP(E)L as a Guidance and Support Mechanism in the Diploma of Social Work (DipSW)', *Social Work Education Journal*, **19**, (4), 312–21.

Simpson, R. and Wailey, T. (2000b), *The Guidana Toolkit*, http://www.uel.ac.uk/caace/guidance/phase_1.htm.

Smith, A. (1996), *Accelerated Learning in the Classroom* (Stafford: Network Educational Press).

Smith, G. (1980), *Social Need: Policy, Practice and Research* (London: Routledge and Kogan Page).

Snyder, B. R. (1971), *The Hidden Curriculum* (Cambridge, Mass.: MIT Press).

Starkes, J. L. and Allard, F. (eds) (1993), *Cognitive Issues in Motor Expertise* (Amsterdam: North Holland).

Stevens, R. (1996), *Course Review, D317 Social Psychology* (Milton Keynes: Open University Press).

Thompson, A. (1996), *Critical Reasoning: A Practical Introduction* (London: Routledge and Kegan Paul).

Times Higher Educational Supplement, 21 January 2000, p. 17.

TMP Worldwide Research (1998), *Soft Skills: Employers' Desirability and Actual Incidence* (32 Aybrook St, London, W1M 3JL).

Trimmer, J. F. (1999), 'Real World Writing Assignment', *Journal of Advanced Composition, **19** (1), 35–49.

Usher, R., Bryant, I. and Johnston, R. (1997), *Adult Education and the Postmodern Challenge: Learning Beyond the Limits* (London: Routledge and Kegan Paul).

Utley, A. (2000), 'Students Misread Tutors' Comments', *Times Higher Educational Supplement*, 8 September 2000, p. 6. Richard Higgins' research was presented at the British Educational Research Association Conference, Cardiff, September 2000.

Vygotsky, L. S. (1962), *Thought and Language*, 2nd edn (Cambridge, Mass.: MIT Press). (First published in 1934.)

Vygotsky, L. S. (1988), 'The Genesis of Higher Mental Functions', in Richardson, K. and Sheldon, S. (eds), *Cognitive Development to Adolescence* (Hove: Erlbaum).

Wailey, A. (1996), 'Developing the Reflective Learner', in Wolfendale, S. and Corbett, J. (eds), *Opening Doors: Learning Support in Higher Education* (London: Cassell).

Warburton, N. (1996), *Thinking from A–Z* (London: Routledge and Kegan Paul).

West, T. G. (1991), *The Mind's Eye* (Buffalo, NY: Prometheus).

Wheeler, M. (1983), *Counselling in Study Methods* (Exeter: University of Exeter Teaching Services Centre).

Willcoxson, L. (1998), 'The Impact of Academics' Learning and Teaching Preferences on their Teaching Practice: a Pilot study', *Studies in Higher Education*, **23**, (1).

Williams, K. (1989), *Study Skills* (Basingstoke: Macmillan – now Palgrave).

Williams, K. (1995), *Writing Essays: Developing Writing* (Oxford: The Oxford Centre for Staff Development).

Williams, L. V. (1983), *Teaching for the Two-sided Mind: A Guide to Right Brain/Left Brain Education* (New York: Simon and Schuster).

Wolfendale, S. (1996), 'Learning Support in HE: Principles, Values, Continuities', in Wolfendale, S. and Corbett, J. (eds) (1996), *Opening Doors: Learning Support in Higher Education* (London: Cassell).

Worsham L. and Olson G. A. (1991), 'Hegemony and the Future of Democracy: Ernesto Lacau's Political Philosophy', *Journal of Advanced Composition*, **19**.1, 1–34.

Yorke, M. (1999), *Leaving Early: Undergraduate Non-Completion in Higher Education* (London: Routledge).

Index